Economics, Law, and Institutions in Asia Pacific

Series Editor

Makoto Yano, Research Institute of Economy, Trade and Industry (RIETI), Tokyo, Japan

The Asia Pacific region is expected to steadily enhance its economic and political presence in the world during the twenty-first century. At the same time, many serious economic and political issues remain unresolved in the region. To further academic enquiry and enhance readers' understanding about this vibrant region, the present series, Economics, Law, and Institutions in Asia Pacific, aims to present cutting-edge research on the Asia Pacific region and its relationship with the rest of the world. For countries in this region to achieve robust economic growth, it is of foremost importance that they improve the quality of their markets, as history shows that healthy economic growth cannot be achieved without high-quality markets. High-quality markets can be established and maintained only under a well-designed set of rules and laws, without which competition will not flourish. Based on these principles, this series places a special focus on economic, business, legal, and institutional issues geared towards the healthy development of Asia Pacific markets. The series considers book proposals for scientific research, either theoretical or empirical, that is related to the theme of improving market quality and has policy implications for the Asia Pacific region. The types of books that will be considered for publication include research monographs as well as relevant proceedings. The series show-cases work by Asia-Pacific based researchers but also encourages the work of social scientists not limited to the Asia Pacific region. Each proposal and final manuscript is subject to evaluation by the editorial board and experts in the field.

More information about this series at http://www.springer.com/series/13451

Committee on the History of Japan's Trade and
Industry Policy RIETI

Dynamics of Japan's Trade and Industrial Policy in the Post Rapid Growth Era (1980–2000)

Springer Open

Committee on the History of Japan's Trade and Industry Policy RIETI
Chiyoda-ku, Tokyo, Japan

ISSN 2199-8620 ISSN 2199-8639 (electronic)
Economics, Law, and Institutions in Asia Pacific
ISBN 978-981-15-1989-5 ISBN 978-981-15-1987-1 (eBook)
https://doi.org/10.1007/978-981-15-1987-1

This Springer imprint is published by the registered company Springer Nature Singapore Pte Ltd.
The registered company address is: 152 Beach Road, #21-01/04 Gateway East, Singapore 189721, Singapore

Preface

This volume is the product of research on the history of Japan's trade and industry policy in the late twentieth century. At the direction of the Ministry of Economy, Trade and Industry (METI, formerly the Ministry of International Trade and Industry [MITI]), the Research Institute of Economy, Trade and Industry (RIETI) established a Committee on the History of Japan's Trade and Industry Policy, which undertook comprehensive, systematic research under the leadership of Committee Chair Professor Konosuke Odaka. The research began in 2006 and was completed in 2013. The results of the project were presented in Japanese as *Tsūsho Sangyō Seisakushi: dai 2 ki, 1980–2000* (History of Japan's Trade and Industry Policy, The Second Era) in 12 volumes.

This exhaustive history, totaling almost 8,000 pages, was subsequently distilled and synthesized by Prof. Haruhito Takeda, Deputy Chief Editor of the Committee, and translated into English by Dr. Louisa Rubinfien. The result is this volume.

We deeply appreciate the contributions of Prof. Odaka, Prof. Takeda, the authors, and all others involved in this project.

Tsūsho Sangyō Seisakushi, dai 2 ki, 1980–2000 [2011–2013 published]

Vol. 1 General Overview
Odaka Konosuke

Vol. 2 International Trade Policy
Abe Takeshi (ed.), Takeda Haruhito, Ishii Susumu, Kuno Arata, Nishigaki Atsuko, Kobayashi Kenichi, Tojo Yoshizumi, Kunimatsu Maki, Kawase Tsuyoshi, Kawashima Fujio, Sekizawa Yoichi, Maeda Mitsuhiro

Vol. 3 Industrial Policy
Okazaki Tetsuji (ed.), Korenaga Takafumi, Uchiyama Yu, Sato Hitoshi, Oki Hiromi

Vol. 4 Commerce and Distribution Policy
Ishihara Takemasa (ed.), Fujioka Rika, Matsushima Shigeru, Osaki Yasuhiro, Takeda Ippei, Miyamoto Takeshi

Vol. 5 Location, Environment and Safety Policy
Takeda Haruhito

Vol. 6 Basic Industries
Yamazaki Shiro (ed.), Hashimoto Noriyuki, Kim Yongdo

Vol. 7 Machinery and Information Industries
Hasegawa Shin (ed.), Takeda Haruhito, Nakajima Yuki, Nishino Hajime

Vol. 8 Consumer Goods Industries
Matsushima Shigeru

Vol. 9 Industrial Science and Technology Policy
Sawai Minoru

Vol. 10 Natural Resources and Energy Policy
Kikkawa Takeo

Vol. 11 Intellectual Property Policy
Nakayama Nobuhiro (ed.), Kumagai Kenichi, Takakura Shigeo, Yamamoto Masafumi

Vol. 12 Small- and Medium-Sized Enterprise Policy
Nakata Tetsuo (ed.), Kaibori Shohei, Yasuda Takehiko, Kawakami Takahiro

Atsushi Nakajima
Chairman
The Research Institute of Economy
Trade and Industry (RIETI), Tokyo, Japan

Contents

1 Introduction: Overview 1
1 The Mission of the Ministry of International Trade and Industry (MITI) 1
2 The Keynotes of Industrial Policy 3
2.1 The Organizational Reform of 1973 3
2.2 Toward a Shift in Industrial Policy 5
2.3 Emphasis on Free Trade and Deregulation 10
2.4 Seeking Another Conceptual Shift at the End of the Century 12
Appendix to the Introduction 14
The "New Policy" Formulation Process 14

2 Japan's Industrial Structure: Forced to Change (1973–1982) 17
1 The Evolution of Japan's Trade and Industrial Policy in the 1970s 17
1.1 Pursuing the Shift to a "Knowledge-Intensive" Industrial Structure 17
1.2 The Turbulent 1970s: The Nixon Shock and the Oil Crisis 19
1.3 Policies on Industrial Structure in the 1970s 20
2 The Vision of the 1970s and the Machinery and Information Industries 22
2.1 Toward a Knowledge-Intensive Industrial Structure and Machinery and Information Industry Policy 22
2.2 The Machinery Industry as a "Strategic Industry" 28
3 Industrial Relocation and Pollution Regulation 35
3.1 Promoting Industrial Relocation Plans 35
3.2 Strengthening the Regulation of Pollution 39
3.3 Environmental Impact Assessment Legislation 44
3.4 Strengthening Policies on Industrial Safety 48

4 The Challenge of Stable Energy Supplies and the Development of Industrial Technology 52
4.1 The Two Basic Laws on Oil 52
4.2 Electrical-Power Development and the Move Away from Oil 60
4.3 The Energy Conservation Act 61
4.4 Coal and Resources Policy 62
4.5 Large-Scale Industrial Technology Development and the "Sunshine" and "Moonlight" Projects 65
5 Policies to Address Structural Depression in Basic and Consumer Industries: The Large-Scale Retail Stores Law and Small and Medium-Sized Enterprises 76
5.1 Policies on Industrial Structure Adjustment (The Industry Stabilization Law and the Law on the Structural Improvement of the Textile Industry) 76
5.2 Measures to Modernize Distribution 83
5.3 A New Emphasis on Quality of Life: Promotion of Consumer Protection and the Housing Industry 92
6 Friction with Foreign Countries 94
6.1 Trade Imbalances and Negotiations with Europe and America 94
6.2 Simplifying Import Procedures and Maintaining the Export Order 96

3 The Global Responsibilities of an Economic Superpower (1981–1992) 101
1 Keynotes of the Japanese Economy and Trade Policy in the 1980s 101
1.1 Fiscal Restructuring and Stable Growth 101
1.2 Publication of the *1980s Vision* 102
1.3 Yen Appreciation and International Contributions 104
1.4 "The Basic Design of 21st-Century Industrial Society" 105
1.5 Progress in Deregulation 106
2 Economic Superpower Status and International Contributions: Responses to Economic Friction 107
2.1 Export Adjustments—From Market-Oriented Sector-Specific (MOSS) Talks to the Structural Impediments Initiative (SII) 107
2.2 Negotiations on Specific Issue Areas Across Many Sectors . . . 111
2.3 Liberalization of the Domestic Market and Deregulation 121
2.4 Progress on the Uruguay Round Negotiations 126
2.5 International Harmonization of Intellectual Property Rights . . . 133

3 Coordination of Industrial Policy and the Antimonopoly Act 138
3.1 Coordination of Industrial Policy and the Antimonopoly Act 138
3.2 Industrial Adjustment and Structural Improvement 151
3.3 Basic Industries, Consumer Goods Industries, Coal Industry, and Others 159
4 Promotion of Domestic Demand and the Vitality of the Private Sector 169
4.1 Towards an Advanced Information Society 169
4.2 The Challenge of Next-Generation Technology Development 177
4.3 New Regional Development Policy 185
5 Making Progress on Extrication from Dependence on Oil 194
5.1 Policies Prioritizing the Stable Supply of Energy 194
5.2 Pursuing Non-petroleum Power Supplies 198

4 Long-Term Depression and Economic Structural Reform (1991–2000) 203
1 Keynotes of Japan's Economy and Trade and Industry Policy in the 1990s 203
1.1 The 1990 Trade and Industrial Policy Vision of the 1990s 203
2 Changes in Economic Structure and Regulatory Reform 208
2.1 The Revised Antimonopoly Act and the System of Business Laws 208
2.2 Respect for Corporate Autonomy and the Role of Government 213
2.3 Promoting Deregulation 217
2.4 Abolition of the Large-Scale Retail Stores Law 223
2.5 The End of the Textile Policy 231
2.6 Revision of the Small and Medium-Sized Enterprise Basic Law 235
3 Pursuing Rules-Based Multilateral Coordination 238
3.1 The Conclusion of the Uruguay Round and Launching of the WTO 238
3.2 Regionalism and Japan 244
3.3 Trade Friction and Multilateral Coordination 247
3.4 Import Expansion and Market Opening 253
3.5 Security Trade Controls and the Transformation of Policies on Exports 256
4 Measures for an Affluent Society 260
4.1 Promoting an Advanced Information and Telecommunications Society, IMS Programs, and the Home Health Care and Rehabilitation Equipment Industry 260

4.2 Establishment of the Environment Law and Promotion of Recycling ... 268
4.3 Industrial Location Policy and Promotion of Regions ... 278
4.4 Harmonizing Energy Development and the Environment ... 285
4.5 Technology Policy: A Shift in Emphasis from Basic Technology to Practical Applications ... 293
4.6 New Trends in Pro-Patent Policy ... 305

5 Conclusion: The Emergence of a Twenty-First-Century Policy on the Economy and Industry ... 309
1 Establishment of the Ministry on Economy, Trade and Industry (METI) ... 309
1.1 The Administrative Reform Council's "Final Report" ... 309
1.2 METI's "Organization Plan" ... 311
2 Trade and Industrial Policy at the Turn of the Century ... 313
2.1 Policy Development in Anticipation of Organizational Reform ... 313
2.2 Changing Policy Targets ... 315
2.3 Policy Areas Focusing on New Issues ... 318
3 Conclusion ... 319

References ... 321

Chapter 1
Introduction: Overview

1 The Mission of the Ministry of International Trade and Industry (MITI)

This book provides an in-depth examination of Japan's policy responses to the economic challenges of the 1980s and '90s. While MITI's earlier role in promoting rapid growth has been addressed in other studies, this volume, based on official records and exhaustive interviews, is the first to examine the aftermath of rapid growth and the evolution of MITI's interpretation of the economy's changing needs. Covering such topics as the oil shocks, trade conflict with the United States, and the rise and collapse of the so-called bubble economy, it presents a detailed analysis and evaluation of how these challenges were interpreted by government officials, the kinds of policies that were enacted, the extent to which policy aims were realized, and lessons for the longer term. The legal basis for MITI policies covered in this volume is found in the following sections of the 1952 Ministry of International Trade and Industry Establishment Law, Article 3 (Odaka 2013, p. 3–4):

- 1.1 Promotion and coordination of trade, and coordination of foreign exchange in commerce
- 1.2 Promotion of international trade and economic cooperation
- 2 Advancement, improvement, coordination, and inspection of the production, distribution and consumption of mining and manufactured goods
- 3 Administration pertaining to the rationalization and optimization of commercial enterprises
- 4 Administration pertaining to weights and measures, and to measurement
- 5 Operational coordination of electric, gas, and heat utilities (supply businesses)
- 6 Securing the supply of energy: development of mineral resources, promotion of the utilization of these resources, coordination of hydraulic power generation
- 7 Clerical oversight of mine security
- 8 Affairs concerning industrial property rights

Committee on the History of Japan's Trade and Industry Policy. RIETI,
Dynamics of Japan's Trade and Industrial Policy in the Post Rapid Growth Era (1980–2000),
Economics, Law, and Institutions in Asia Pacific, https://doi.org/10.1007/978-981-15-1987-1_1

9 Promotion and guidance of small and medium enterprises
10 Experimental research on the science and technology of the mining industry and dissemination of its results
11 Elucidation and dissemination of industrial standards
12 Oversight of surveys, statistics, and other duties related to commercial mining and manufacturing
13 State-owned trade businesses
14 Alcohol monopoly

Although responsible for industrial policy overall, MITI did not have exclusive jurisdiction over it: coordination and cooperation with the Ministry of Foreign Affairs were required on trade-related issues, and with the Ministry of Finance on the administration of foreign exchange and the introduction of foreign capital; shipbuilding, because of its relationship to the maritime industry, fell under Ministry of Transportation jurisdiction, and boundary questions also arose with the Ministry of Posts and Telecommunications with regard to the information and communications sectors.

The need for or pertinence of policy involvement in these areas was dictated in any given era by the then-prevailing understanding of Japan's economic issues (Nakamura 1995). In hindsight, using an economics framework, it is evident that policy involvement arose in cases in which: "(1) the market was under- or undeveloped; (2) information was biased or incomplete (in other words, cases of information 'asymmetry'); (3) an economic entity's behavior raised costs for third-party economic entities (in other words, cases of 'external diseconomies'); (4) market participant behavior was excessively selfish and therefore generating confusion in the market; and, finally, (5) government actions that were deemed necessary for political reasons (such as the resolution of international trade friction) were justified in order to correct, supplement, or revise market movements that did not fully meet their desired role, for the sake of upgrading and improving economic welfare" (Odaka 2013, p. 5). Based on the above, it is now widely accepted that the aims of trade and industrial policy were to (1) encourage market development, (2) correct information asymmetries, (3) remove external diseconomies, (4) maintain market order, and also (5) to respond when necessary for political–economic reasons.

However, a policy's legitimacy was not in its own day explained with words like "information asymmetries" or "external diseconomies," but rather in terms of Japan's economic backwardness, its structural vulnerability, or its lack of international competitiveness. It is probably beyond dispute that this perspective was especially pronounced in the years from postwar recovery to high economic growth, as is made evident in the first edition of the *History of Industrial Policy*, which focuses on the period up until the 1970s. Thereafter as well, however, the Ministry of International Trade and Industry continued to interpret policy issues along the lines of the earlier era and to formulate and promote prescriptions for their resolution. Because these prescriptions were justified in terms of the challenges facing the Japanese economy at any given time, they were not driven by a consistent set of principles. Rather, characteristic of industrial policy was its flexible response to changing times and its attempts through trial and error to develop prescriptive policies to resolve problems (Hashimoto 2001).

2 The Keynotes of Industrial Policy

2.1 The Organizational Reform of 1973

Although MITI's approach was characterized by this flexibility, it does not necessarily follow that its policies were ad hoc responses to circumstance. Each era was characterized by major economic trends, such as declining growth rates or the severity of international economic friction, and the attendant changes in the underlying policy philosophy are clearly discernible in the industrial policies addressing these trends.

To summarize in the broadest terms:

Two successive stages are evident in the basic "philosophy" of industrial policy during the period from the 1970s until the end of the century.

Even after the controls of the postwar recovery era had been lifted, MITI continued to adhere to the 1950s model, developing corrective market policy interventions as needed to promote the modernization and rationalization of the Japanese economy. Industrial policy aimed to rationalize key industries, nurture infant industries, and make adjustments for declining industries, and so on, while trade policy was designed to facilitate the orderly expansion of exports and controls on imports suitable for economic development under foreign currency constraints.[1]

These policies engendered moves by domestic business for greater independence from the government, as reflected in the Draft Law on Temporary Measures for the Promotion of Specified Industries, as well as international criticism of the close ties between government and business, encapsulated in the term "Japan Inc." It was against this backdrop that MITI undertook a broad reconsideration of its policy aims and measures and shifted its sights to the establishment of an internationally open economic system. Its means were the liberalization of trade and foreign exchange, which began in the 1960s, and the capital liberalization that followed.

The need for policy change was expressed explicitly in the call for a "shift to a knowledge-intensive industrial structure" in the *1970s Vision for Trade and Industry Policy*. This position was based on the recognition that as its heavy and chemical industrialization progressed, Japan was becoming a mature industrial society like the other advanced economies, and that it therefore needed to seek out new directions for industrial development. The limitations of the traditional policy framework were becoming evident as core industries became fully competitive internationally and as independent corporate entities no longer needed government support, meaning that policy questions needed to be addressed from a broader perspective than before.

This policy shift also reflected the need to ascertain what policy measures could be used by way of support, given that liberalization was proceeding more smoothly than expected and that the means of policy intervention were gradually being lost (the

[1]Sumiya Mikio, in his general discussion of the history of industrial policy in the first era, pointed out the multifaceted character of policy development, as seen in the terms "birth and nurturing," and "terminal care" for policy corresponding to the life cycle of industries (Sumiya 1994, p. 112).

biggest among these being foreign currency allocation). In the 1970s, when Japan's status as an economic power became fully apparent, it was no longer sufficient in international eyes for Japan to prioritize its domestic interests as if it were still a "small country." Rather, Japan was called on to take responsibility for its influence on the world economy and to make changes to reflect its changing international status.

However, that same growth gave rise to domestic challenges where economic development intersected with people's lives: environmental conservation issues, overcrowding and depopulation, consumer issues, and price problems, among others. The limitations of policies directed at export expansion and at upgrading an industrial structure centered on heavy and large-scale industries became increasingly apparent, generating calls for a more "knowledge-intensive" industrial structure (greater knowledge intensity). At the same time, new and mounting problems in external affairs, including trade friction, the international balance of payments problem, and currency exchange issues, required policy responses.

It was in this context that the Ministry of International Trade and Industry launched a large-scale organizational reform, which marked the starting point of the period under examination in this volume. The basic policy governing the organizational reform—"To achieve a comprehensive internal reorganization of this Ministry by utilizing the particular strengths of the bodies charged with design, planning, and implementation and coordinating among them for a well-balanced result"—was summarized by MITI as follows:

(1) Unification of the trade policy bureaus. This meant reconfiguring the existing International Trade Bureau and Trade Promotion Bureau as the International Trade Policy Bureau and International Trade Administration Bureau.

(2) Conversion of the existing Enterprise Bureau into the newly named Industrial Policy Bureau, in order to strengthen efforts toward cross-sector (horizontal) policy principles.

(3) Establishment of the Industrial Location and Environmental Protection Bureau to engage actively in their namesake issues.

(4) Reconfiguration of sector-specific organizations (vertical divisions). For this purpose, the various industries were reassigned according to shared organizational principles into the Basic Industries Bureau, the Machinery and Information Industries Bureau, and the Consumer Goods and Services Industries Bureau.

(5) Last but not least, the establishment of the Agency of Natural Resources and Energy, charged with promoting a strong and comprehensive energy administration (Odaka 2013, p. 262).[2]

The trade policy bureaus (item 1) were reconfigured so that international economic policy planning would be undertaken in one, and trade policy—a unified administration of exports and imports, insurance matters, etc.—in another. The Industrial Policy Bureau (item 2) was charged with the central task of coordinating shared policy areas, while its divisions focused on specific areas: the Price Policy Division concentrated

[2]Original materials are found in Ministry of International Trade and Industry, *Overview of the organizational reform of the Ministry of International Trade and Industry*. June, 1973.

on price problems, the Business Behavior Division "promoted appropriate corporate action," the Industrial Structure Division "forwarded the knowledge intensification of the industrial structure," and the International Business Affairs Division "promoted industrial structure policies from an international perspective." With the establishment of the Industrial Location and Environmental Protection Bureau (item 3), the departments related to industrial sites (previously in the Enterprise Bureau) and pollution protection were integrated into a single bureau. Similarly the Agency for Natural Resources and Energy, was established as an affiliated agency that combined the former Mining and Coal Bureau and Public Utilities Business Bureau. The merger was based on the reasoning that a comprehensive and powerful resource and energy administration is needed in order to advance policies in such areas as: the securing of stable supplies of resources and energy, energy efficiency, the increasingly serious pollution problem, resource conservation, and energy conservation (Fig. 1)."

2.2 *Toward a Shift in Industrial Policy*

In order to trace how policy trends changed based on the awareness described above, let us focus on the major issues as seen in the "New Policy" prepared each year by the Ministry of International Trade and Industry (Table 1). The document's subtitle, "Industrial Policy Priorities " corresponds to the basic policy stance of the government. In the 1970s, this meant responding to the ruling Liberal Democratic Party's reconsideration of the high-growth path and its shift to pledging to build a welfare society. The emphasis in domestic policy became the "improvement and enhancement of national welfare," and in foreign policy, the importance of international cooperation in areas such as foreign currency problems.

Under this framework, industrial policy from the mid-1970s on was from the most basic level addressing different policy problems than before, including: (1) how to locate new industries and bring their development to fruition, and (2) how to fulfill Japan's responsibilities in the international community. The principal areas of focus (the so-called *itchoume ichibanchi* or "priorities"), listed in the policy menus published from 1976–1979 (see prologue appendix), are shown below.

1976 Promotion of industrial policy to achieve Japan's economic recovery and stable development
1977 Newly developing industrial policy under stable growth
1978 Developing pump-priming measures and new industrial policies
1979 Formulating the *1980s Industrial Policy Vision*

Industrial policy had reached a stage of seeking new directions and that contributing to the world economy had become a major priority, reflecting the international pledge made in 1979 by the Takeo Fukuda cabinet. This is an indication that shift in policy principles had occurred.

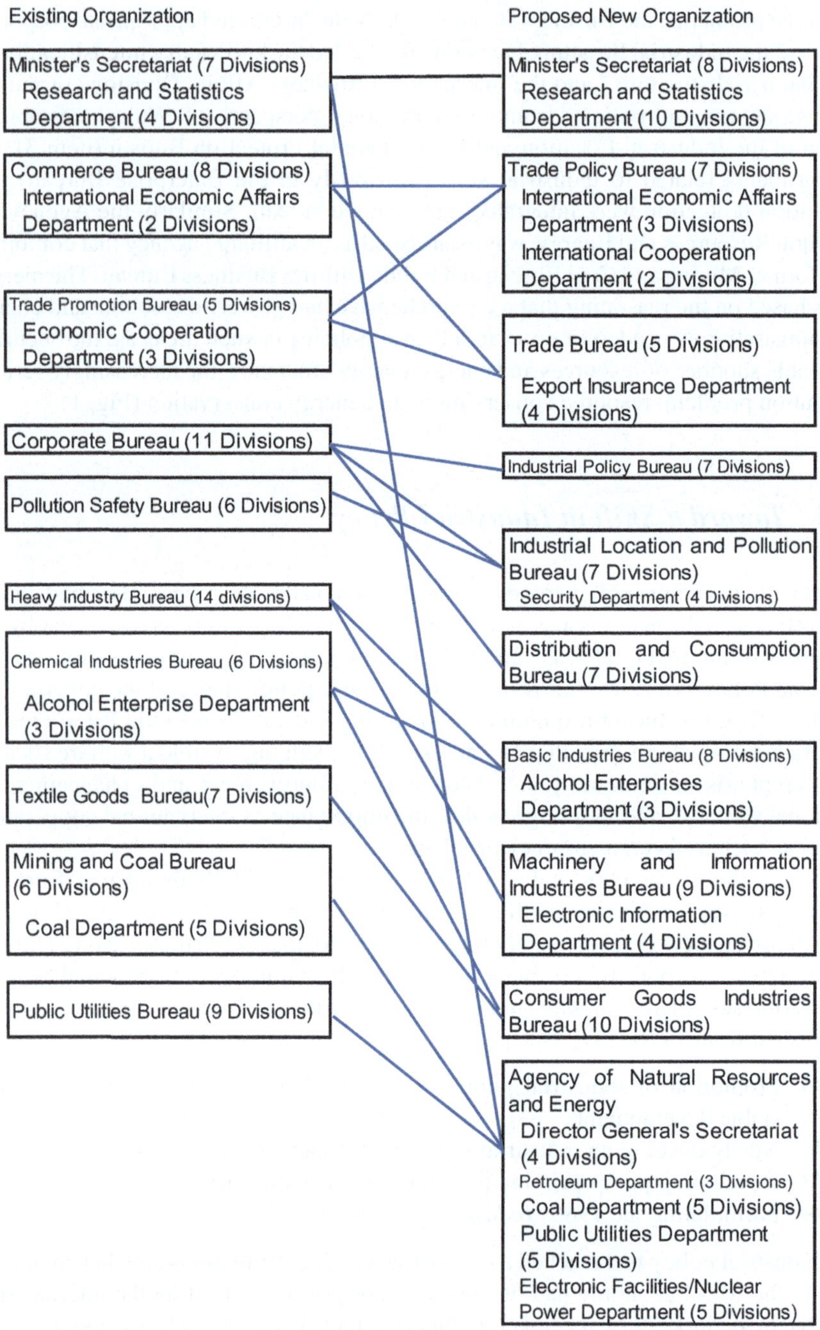

Fig. 1 Overview of the organizational reform (1973)

Table 1 Changes in the headings of the "New Policy Priorities" (FY1973–2000)

FY	"Industrial Policy Priorities" (Subheadings)	"Priorities" (Headings)
1973	The improvement of domestic welfare and promotion of international cooperation	To construct a non-polluted society
1974	The achievement of domestic welfare and promotion of international cooperation	Price stability and an enriched consumer life
1975	The further improvement of domestic welfare and cooperation with the international community	Price stability and an enriched consumer life, to establish the foundations for a comfortable life
1976	The improvement of domestic welfare; contributions to the development of the international economy and society	Promotion of industrial policy to achieve Japan's economic recovery and stable development
1977	The further enrichment of domestic welfare and active contribution to the stable development of the world economy	Newly developing industrial policy under stable growth conditions
1978	Opening of paths to a new prosperity; and development of Japan's economy and society	Developing pump-priming measures and new industrial policy
1979	Forming the foundation for achieving an enriched domestic life and a smooth transition to stable growth and securing the motive power for the prosperity and development of Japan's economy and society	Formulating the *1980s Industrial Policy Vision*
1980	None	Ensuring energy security
1981	Aiming for a society with vitality and economic security	Establishing energy security and preparing for extrication from petroleum dependency
1982	Aiming to establish the foundations for long-term development of the Japanese economy	Steadily developing a comprehensive energy policy
1983	Aiming for active contribution to the world economy and the establishment of the foundations for Japan's economic growth	Promoting industrial revitalization and technology development with a mid- and long-term perspective
1984	Contributing to the sustainable development of the world economy and establishing a creative society	Forming the foundation for creative development
1985	Establishing the foundations for long-term development and international contributions thereby	Building the foundation for technological development
1986	Achieving new dimensions of internationalization and establishing the foundations for long-term development	Aiming for new dimensions of internationalization

(continued)

Table 1 (continued)

FY	"Industrial Policy Priorities" (Subheadings)	"Priorities" (Headings)
1987	Toward constructing a new economy and industrial society aimed at creative development	Promoting policies on industrial structure based on an international perspective
1988	Aiming at international harmonization and bringing vitality to economic society	Bringing vitality to local areas
1989	Dedication to the world and new long-term development	Dedication to the international economic community
1990	Toward the realization of "Coexistence and coprosperity at a global scale" and "an economic society replete with leisure and vitality"	Correcting external imbalances and realizing internationally harmonized economic structures and industrial activities
1991	None	Realization of lifestyles of comfort and richness
1992	Seeking "links and coordination with international society" and "creating regional industrial culture"	Dedication to international society and promotion of self-reform
1993	Overcoming global issues and creating a "creative and comfortable society"	Comprehensive promotion of policies on energy and the environment
1994	Self-reform for further development and responsible responses to the international community	Structural adjustments and the maintenance of developmental foundations for creative innovation
1995	None	Promotion of reform to realize a rich economic society opened to the international community
1996	Aiming to create a new economic society	Accelerating structural economic reform
1997	Toward realization of a knowledge-creating country	Structural economic reform aimed at a knowledge-creation country—measures aimed at industrial hollowing out
1998	None	Strongly promoting structural economic reform
1999	Realization of economic regeneration through revitalization of industry	Breaking away from a sluggish macro-economy
2000	Foundations for the regeneration of 21st century economic development	Recovery to stable growth trajectory centering on private demand

Odaka (2013, pp. 30–32). Author's reconstruction based on Odaka's table

However, these new directions were not pursued in a clear and sustained way, because of exogenously generated "shocks." As is well known, price and energy problems came to the fore intermittently during these years because of the transition to a floating exchange rate regime and the turbulent rise in crude oil prices. In the two years immediately after the first oil crisis, MITI found it necessary to prioritize price stabilization and improvements to consumer life, as evident in the "priority" policies of 1974 and 1975:

1974 Price stability and an enriched consumer life
1975 Price stability and an enriched consumer life, to establish the foundations for a comfortable life.

Similarly, energy policies became the priority in 1981–1982 due to the worsening oil situation:

1981 Establishing energy security and preparing for extrication from petroleum dependency
1982 Steadily developing a comprehensive energy policy.

Among the policies on prices, MITI's Aggregate Demand Control Policy produced results in a relatively short period, even as compared with other advanced economies.[3] Energy conservation efforts began to penetrate, even as the issue rapidly lost its urgency with the stabilization of oil prices.

Moreover, the medium-range aim of decreasing Japan's dependence on fossil fuels was aided by the mid-1980s takeoff of nuclear power generation at light-water reactors. It became the dominant view that this tailwind would help enable Japan to achieve both economic growth and a stable energy supply.

In this way, the Basic Direction of Trade and Industrial Policies as defined in the early 1970s emerged once again as a top priority concern. Construction of a "long-term development base" frequently appears in the New Policy subtitles, as illustrated in the priority policies of 1983–1985:

1983 Promoting industrial revitalization and technology development with a mid- and long-term perspective
1984 Forming the foundations for creative development
1985 Building the foundations for technological development.

MITI's emphasis on technological development points to an expectation that the new technologies and systems would become the foundations for future industrial development. This was the case in new energy, developed against the backdrop of urgency in energy issues, in information processing and semiconductor technology, in factory automation (FA), the utilization of microelectronics technology (ME), and, related to these, the area of space development.

Fields such as these require large-scale investment in research and development, making it difficult to rely on voluntary action by private enterprises to assure sufficient investment. In other words, MITI sought policy involvement in areas that could not

[3] In general, due to small budgets (excluding bank loans based on the Fiscal Investment and Loan Program (FILP)), industrial policy was rarely affected by cyclical fluctuations such as economic stimulus measures. One feature of industrial policy, therefore, was that it was able to maintain its basic stance regardless of fluctuations in the economy. It is therefore not clear how much MITI contributed to the calming of prices under the policies of restraints on aggregate demand. Further investigation is needed on the contribution of MITI to cyclical conditions of this kind.

be left entirely to market forces, and began especially to take note of these as priority issues.[4]

Looking in aggregate at the measures aimed at new industrial development, however, it is clear that they could not be detached from policy authority over the information and communications industries that were at the core of that development.

Although communication means and information acquisition were expanded and diversified far beyond expectation in the data communications field (areas such as VAN, or value-added networks), MITI's involvement in the field, beginning with the liberalization of the principal communication networks, was restricted by its need to share that role with other agencies granted jurisdiction by the government.[5] This continued to act as a constraint on the effort to develop an integrated industrial policy.

2.3 *Emphasis on Free Trade and Deregulation*

The development of industrial technology was prioritized over international contributions in the early 1980s because Japan's trade surplus contracted temporarily with soaring resource prices, especially that of crude oil. When crude oil prices then fell, Japan's trade surplus recovered, arousing criticism from the United States and Europe and resulting in serious trade friction. For this reason, MITI's emphasis also shifted to trade policy in the latter 1980s. This is evident in the growing importance

[4]Nevertheless, with regard to pollution and environmental measures, which became policy priorities in this period, strict corporate emissions regulations were maintained based on environmental regulations. It is important to note that the stance of entrusting this to the voluntary action of businesses and expecting that markets would adjust accordingly was not equivalent to the pursuit of a hands-off policy. Of course, MITI's position on this matter served as a counterweight to the strong regulatory bent of the Environment Agency, aimed at preventing excessive burdens being placed on industrial enterprises. In the division of labor among ministries and agencies, MITI's position was in general to restrain interventions in the market. On the other hand, when it came to policy on industrial location, it could use financial and tax incentives to help ease the overconcentration of industrial sites in the Pacific belt. MITI pursued efforts to disperse industrial sites and achieved some results (although no greater a range of diffusion than was originally sought), and MITI therefore did not hesitate to adopt policy measures to correct external diseconomies. In policy on small and medium-sized enterprises as well, traditional interventionist policy measures were maintained in much their original form.

[5]It would not be correct, however, to see MITI's inability to fulfill its own claims as the result only of disputes over authority. Information and communications technology made more progress in development of software than in that of hardware (such as large-scale computers) that MITI had emphasized up to that point. As these became integrated in overall communications at production sites, greater significance was attached to a highly dispersed, guerilla-style development, accumulation, and transmission. This action resulted because MITI was not necessarily able to find policy issues and take appropriate measures to respond flexibly to change, because it had little experience with policy intervention regarding consumer goods. In that respect, the postal administration cannot be said to have been effective either. Regardless, given the continuing restrictions on MITI's involvement in the information and telecommunications field, it was difficult to develop ideas about Japan's future industrial structure and to establish adjustment policies to address them. It should be noted that those restrictions were not removed even in the organizational reform of 2000.

given to international harmonization, and illustrates the fact that in the later half of the decade, a greater priority was placed on international contributions.

1986 Aiming for new dimensions of internationalization
1987 Promoting policies on industrial structure based on an international perspective
1988 Bringing vitality to local areas
1989 Dedication to the international economic community
1990 Correcting external imbalances and realizing an internationally harmonized economic structure and industrial activities.

Where these policies concerned international relations, the following points are notable:

First, the demand that they be considered for diplomatic reasons—namely, Japan–US relations—placed strong constraints on the policy options; second, they bear the strong influence of the earlier temporary export restraints that had been promoted for the sake of "orderly exports." As a result, bilateral and bi-regional negotiations under these conditions were repeated endlessly, with only the item in question changing, and Japan was forced to make unilateral concessions.

Nevertheless, MITI continued to promote the development of the Japanese economy while at the same time reaching a clear understanding of the new direction Japan would have to pursue in order to fulfill its international responsibilities. That is, rather than promoting measures that limited free trade, such as voluntary export restraints based on bilateral agreements, Japan would adopt policy solutions based on international rules agreed upon multilaterally. This was the shift in principle that MITI had been seeking since the 1970s. In the negotiations that led to the World Trade Organization (WTO) agreement, Japan's response to international trade friction was to advocate "maintaining the free trade regime" and to limit the scope of issues handled either by single governments or by bilateral agreements between governments. In other words, it achieved better results in its negotiations with the outside world when it sought to avoid quantitative targets in trade and demands for preferential treatment for certain trading partners. This approach in turn exposed the need to overhaul the myriad regulations that shaped industry and the relationships among industries domestically.

Deregulation arose as a result not of foreign pressure but of internal pressures. To avoid raising corporate taxes, while at the same time overcoming the burden of government debt due to Japan's post-oil-crisis macroeconomic recovery measures, the Second Extraordinary Administrative Investigative Committee called for "small government," or administrative reform, in the early 1980s.

MITI, ahead of other ministries and agencies, aggressively promoted deregulation as a measure for easing trade friction. It is not clear that this approach contributed to an actual expansion of imports[6]; its significance was often only symbolic, but

[6]While it is true that Japan's import structure changed greatly by 1990 with an increase in imports of manufactured goods, the main reason for the change was the overseas relocation of enterprises due to the yen's appreciation and Asian industrialization; it was not that trade relations expanded with industrialized countries more analogous to Japan.

deregulation conveyed a clear message to the outside world that the government was doing its best within the limits of its jurisdiction. At the same time, given the marked confrontation that had always characterized the relationship between industrial policy and the Antimonopoly Law, this new emphasis on deregulation raised the question of how government could engage in a competitive order shaped by the Antimonopoly Law.

As I argue in detail in the main body of this work, it is apparent from the key industrial policy measures of this era that a major shift took place. The 1978 Law on Temporary Measures for Stabilization of Specified Depressed Industries and the Industry Stabilization Law, the 1983 Temporary Measures Law for the Structural Adjustment of Specific Industries and the Structural Improvement Law, the 1987 Law on Temporary Measures to Facilitate Industrial Structural Adjustment, the 1995 Law on Temporary Measures to Facilitate New Businesses, and the 1999 Law on Special Measures for Industrial Revitalization and the Industrial Revitalization Law all suggest that the thrust of industrial policy was no longer one of seeking exemptions from the Antimonopoly Law.

This approach did not change significantly even after the collapse of the bubble in the early 1990s. The subtitles of the Priority Measures were frequently omitted or the wording changed due to policy fluctuations in the short-lived government administrations of the first half of the 1990s, but as discussed below, there was no perceived need for a major change in the framework of priorities established in the 1980s: (1) to achieve balanced trade through multilateral coordination, (2) to promote regulatory reforms limiting government involvement, and (3) to achieve both a stable supply of energy and economic growth.

1991 Realizing a comfortable and affluent lifestyle
1992 Dedication to the international community and promotion of domestic reform
1993 Comprehensive promotion of policies on energy and the environment
1994 Structural adjustment and improvement of developmental foundations aimed at creative innovation.

2.4 *Seeking Another Conceptual Shift at the End of the Century*

As the recession dragged on, however, regulatory reform began to be deployed as part of the efforts to reform Japan's economic structure. It was also looked to for a comprehensive resolution to multiple policy issues, including the handling of non-performing loans, fiscal reconstruction, and economic recovery.

These efforts indicate that new principles were once again being sought for industrial policy. Because this process is still ongoing, caution is needed in making any definite assessments, but I will make a preliminary attempt to examine the prospects for a shift and the direction it might take.

The principle measures of the latter half of the 1990s are shown below. One of their key terms was the above-mentioned "economic structural reform," but in this case the explicit macroeconomic goal was economic recovery and a return to economic growth (see 1999 and 2000, below).

1995 Promoting reform for a rich economic society open to the international community
1996 Accelerating structural economic reform
1997 Structural economic reform aimed at knowledge creation, measures for addressing the hollowing out of industry
1998 Strongly promoting structural economic reform
1999 Pulling out of sluggish macro economy
2000 Recovering a stable growth trajectory centered on private demand.

To promote structural reform of the economy, MITI has shifted to a principle of promoting competition and undertaking comprehensive regulatory reform, for example attempting bold changes in its policies on small and medium-sized enterprises to make firms take on more responsibility. Trade policy has also changed somewhat due to Japan's long-term recession and to the advancing industrialization of South Korea, China, and others, but overall, MITI has adhered to its emphasis on multilateral coordination.

However, faced with the need to focus on macro growth, MITI's stance on policy has taken on a new dimension. Although industrial policy prior to the early 1990s indeed led ultimately to economic growth, that does not mean that the aim of the policies was economic growth itself. Rather, they were concerned with issues such as distribution and with the distortions to the economic structure that were caused by the market economy. For example, the reason MITI sought the modernization and rationalization of the tiny, small, and medium-sized enterprises that were hindering economic development in the first half of the high-growth period was that it concluded that policy intervention was the only way to resolve the problems posed by the dual economy. Its decision to address such issues as nurturing new industries or the tensions arising with declining industries was also due to its judgment that active intervention was needed for economic development to be realized in the medium term. In the latter half of the 1990s, however, when the long recession came to be viewed as a consequence of structural problems in the Japanese economy, MITI began to see not only structural reform but also economic growth itself as a policy concern.

Because macroeconomic policy was key to the market intervention regulations designed to address the vicious downward cumulative cycle inevitable in market economies, the logic that industrial policy could enable economic recovery simply by ensuring the broadest possible freedom for corporate behavior was insufficient as a foundation for policy thinking. Thus, while the macroeconomic perspective on business cycles remained a priority along with policies promoting the competitive order, it was also evident that companies were players in the market and therefore that their own reform and the reform of Japan's corporate and employment systems would also be necessary for achieving economic growth.

At the same time, it was becoming increasingly difficult to reach agreement with other countries on multilateral policies for resolving conflict, because of new moves to form regional and bilateral agreements. This in turn made it hard to pursue economic growth solely on the principle of "protecting the free-trade system."

These were the various elements leading to a second phase in the change in the underlying principles of industrial policy. The ultimate trajectory of these new moves is not yet clear, but the conclusion reached in the course of this study—that this represents a "transitional period"—is probably not far off the mark.

This volume proceeds as follows. This chapter explores the shift in industrial structure premised on the *Vision for the 1970s*, and it presents the prototypical policies formulated to respond to the crisis posed by the yen's appreciation and constraints on resources. It also discusses the policy-formation process. Chapter 2 traces the progress of the shift to a policy system based on rules and on a prioritization of external policies. Chapter 3 lays out the path by which "economic structural reform" became the clear focus in the course of Japan's long-term recession.

Appendix to the Introduction

The "New Policy" Formulation Process

Every year, MITI produced an explanatory document or "Approval Request Form" to accompany its new budget request for the next fiscal year (Odaka 2013, p. 88). This was included in the government budget plan after examination by the Ministry of Finance and the year-end Cabinet Decision, and its content was determined through debate in the Diet after the new year. To formulate its budget request, MITI thought through a variety of policy plans, or "New Policies," to serve as its constituent elements, and carried out broad-based preliminary discussions internally.

The New Policy was formulated as follows. From March to April each year, the Assistants to the General Affairs Division of each department gathered at the Minister's Secretariat General Coordination Division and created a draft. This draft became the springboard for discussion of the thinking that should underlie the New Policy and was forwarded to all the departments in the Ministry. These departments created "Materials for the New Policy" related to their own areas. At the same time, the General Coordination, Budget and Accounts, and Personnel Divisions examined the underlying laws pertaining to their particular areas, budgets, personnel, and so on. In April, two meetings (in-house hearings) to review the New Policy were conducted within each bureau. Based on the attendant reference materials, the Ministry conducted full-scale hearings focused on the bureau findings, with the aim of developing the pillars of the New Policy. In many cases, they met twice. At the first hearing, the Director of the Budget and Accounts Division carried out the examination of those proposals that had survived the process thus far (so-called *tama*). The proposals for the Fiscal Investment and Loan Program were decided on relatively early for accounting reasons. The last proposals to be deliberated were those whose funds would come from the General Accounting budget. The second hearing involved the entire Ministry, which carried on the discussions of the *tama*. The centerpiece or key points of the New Policy in the budget request for the following year were decided in mid-July. Then, from late July until early August, the "Industrial Policy Priorities for the Next Fiscal Year" were presented for deliberation by the governing party's Commerce and Industry Committee and the Industrial Structure Council. Once approved, an "estimated request (draft)" was created. This was submitted by the end of August to the Ministry of Finance Budget Bureau Budget Examiner in charge of trade and foreign affairs. Budget negotiations with the Ministry of Finance then began in advance of the Diet deliberations that started in November and the year-end Cabinet decision on the upcoming budget. That said, changes were rarely made to the content of the budget proposal and policy objectives.

This process changed in response to the needs of the times. In the early 1980s, the margin for political negotiation narrowed. In the early 1990s, the Prime Minister's Official Residence (*Kantei*) took center stage in the policy-formation process. Until the 1980s, Japanese administrative agencies had sufficient investigative and administrative capacity for policy planning, which enabled parliamentarians to redirect much of their time and energy to other tasks. Japanese politicians therefore did not necessarily have occasion to acquire policy-planning skills. Such skills could not be immediately upgraded, which led to a loss of credibility for the executive branch. It is fair to say that policy planning's becoming more politicized was not necessarily the best outcome for the national welfare.

MITI's internal policy-making process also changed. The Ministry continued to put younger bureaucrats to work seeking out new ideas but also reformed its approach in order to devise policies that would both align with and exert influence over the policy directions of the Advisory Council and the Cabinet. New Policy items accordingly became more extensive and exhaustive. Lastly, the turn of this century also saw changes in response to growing doubts within the Ministry about the New Policy planning process, which had become increasingly self-interested. Tentative plans (*tatakidai*) were proposed, serving as springboards for discussion; they were created and disseminated based on the assessments of current conditions heard by the Minister's Secretariat, and each bureau and division then revised and submitted their New Policy proposals accordingly.

Under what is known as the "1955 regime," preparation of the policy drafts—New Policy formation and the formulation of its associated budgets—was often delegated to central government offices by the ruling LDP. As politically neutral and competent actors, the government bureaucrats devised policy proposals based on Cabinet policies and also on what they themselves judged to be national needs; and while taking into account the views of private-sector members of the Industrial Structure Council and consulting with the relevant members of parliament, they submitted the approved draft (or revised draft) to discussion and negotiation within the Ministry. When it had been approved in these discussions, the responsible minister presented it to the Cabinet, along with the budget proposal and bills already assessed by the Finance Ministry. Once approved by the Cabinet, it was passed on for Diet deliberations.

The formation of the policy plan was thus based on mutual trust between the political and the bureaucratic parts of the government. Preparing an excellent policy plan required familiarity with the actual conditions and needs of the target of the policy. It is a task that requires significant time and effort on the part of those with specific expertise and skills, and it was therefore natural, even inevitable, that the process would be left in the hands of bureaucrats specializing in these areas.

This system began to change, however, with the end of the so-called 1955 regime. One of the factors spurring this change was the accumulation of budget deficits, which weakened the bonds that had enabled team play between the government and the bureaucracy. In addition, the eruption of scandals (such as the Recruit Incident) implicating politicians and bureaucrats triggered political reform and the introduction of a single-member electoral district system and so on. As the exploration of new political systems proceeded, greater emphasis was placed on political leadership in the policy-making process. This reform manifested itself in the instances of the top-down policy making mentioned above. The large-scale organizational reform of central government agencies at the turn of the century reflected the centralizing trend in policy making through demands for administrative reform.

Chapter 2
Japan's Industrial Structure: Forced to Change (1973–1982)

1 The Evolution of Japan's Trade and Industrial Policy in the 1970s

1.1 Pursuing the Shift to a "Knowledge-Intensive" Industrial Structure

The rapid growth of the previous decade had enabled the Japanese economy to catch up with the world's advanced economies and to overcome the constraints imposed by periodic balance-of-payments deficits, a limit that Japanese economists had come to call the "balance-of-payments ceiling." By 1970, Japan was making a structural shift to heavy and chemical industrialization, establishing a mass consumer society, and becoming a more open economy through trade and capital liberalization. Also becoming apparent, however, were the stresses of such economic growth on Japan, namely, rising prices, the twin problems of depopulation in the countryside and overcrowding in the cities, and pollution. These prompted mounting calls for a reconsideration of Japan's growth-oriented policies. The year 1970 was noteworthy for Japan internationally and domestically: the 1970 Japan World Exposition (Expo '70) in Osaka was the first World Expo to be held in Asia and showcased to the world the fruits of the country's economic growth; meanwhile, pollution issues dominated proceedings in the Diet, which established the Environment Agency and adopted regulatory measures to address escalating concerns about pollution.

In December 1969, MITI established a policy research group on industrial policies for the 1970s chaired by the Director of the Policy Planning Office in the Minister's Secretariat. The group was composed of four subcommittees, one tasked with considering the overall picture, and the other three focusing on international economic policy, domestic industrial policy, and policy regarding social overhead capital. After more than a half-year of deliberations, the group's summary report was released on August 4, 1970. The overview begins with the following enumeration of Japan's principal aims for the 1970s: "To secure for every citizen a life that is truly rich in human

Committee on the History of Japan's Trade and Industry Policy. RIETI,
Dynamics of Japan's Trade and Industrial Policy in the Post Rapid Growth Era (1980–2000),
Economics, Law, and Institutions in Asia Pacific, https://doi.org/10.1007/978-981-15-1987-1_2

spirit, to contribute actively to the peace and development of the international community, and, as the essential foundation for both of these, to maintain and enhance the creativity and vitality of citizens." Basic trade policy adhered to these aims and was intended to contribute to their achievement with policies for both domestic industrial activities and international undertakings. Domestic industrial policy was tasked with the following:

a. *Consumer life:* securing a sufficient quantity of consumer goods and improving their quality, ensuring stability in daily living, enriching leisure time, and other measures.
b. *Work environment:* raising income, increasing the number of rewarding jobs, assuring a safe and comfortable working environment, and shortening working hours.
c. *Social and natural environment:* preventing environmental destruction, improving social overhead capital, enriching education, and other measures.

Realizing these aims would also require the achievement of certain conditions in the international arena, including the formation of an international division of labor corresponding to advances in the domestic industrial structure and of an international economic environment favorable to the Japanese economy in other ways.

The report also addressed the ongoing problem of the relationship between the government and the private sector and proposed the establishment of a comprehensive system of trade and industrial administration that would respect the independence of the private sector, provide coordination in sectors that could not be expected to work together on their own, and develop the optimum mix of private sector and government leadership.

The 1970 report was an early presentation of the framework introduced more thoroughly in the May 1971 interim report of MITI's Industrial Structure Council titled *Vision of MITI Policy in the 1970s*. The interim report cited five major tasks for administration of the industrial economy: (1) cultivating industry's overall development capacity and the foundations for that development, (2) making qualitative improvements in the standard of living, (3) establishing a positive social and natural environment, (4) expanding the number of rewarding jobs and assuring a comfortable working environment, (5) developing the Japanese economy in cooperation with the international economic community.

The report further submitted that for Japan to achieve these aims, macroeconomic administration in the 1970s would have to shift its basic orientation from high-speed growth to "growth-utilization." The role and responsibility of industrial policy was to achieve this growth-utilization style of economic management. Because Japan had a market economy, that industrial policy had to be predicated on the maximum utilization of market mechanisms, an issue that required detailed examination. In other words, the industrial economy was facing changing conditions in the 1970s, which resulted in a growing number of sectors that could not achieve the anticipated results by relying on market mechanisms alone. Such sectors included both those in which non-economic social effects were coming under question, including rural depopulation and urban overcrowding, environmental degradation, safety, and job content; and those that might give rise to international issues, requiring policies to minimize trade friction and promote active international cooperation.

With the clarification of these parameters, the goal of trade and industrial policy for the 1970s became the promotion of "knowledge-intensive industries."[1] Major changes in policy focus were under way, which led in turn to the need to reconsider existing policies on industrial structure and organization. A novel and ambitious approach was accordingly needed even with regard to the promotion of technological development, not only to discover new industries but also to include the perspective of enhancing the welfare of the people. There was, moreover, recognition of the need for external cooperation as well as domestic policies, which required a review of the fundamental approach to foreign investment.

1.2 The Turbulent 1970s: The Nixon Shock and the Oil Crisis

Just three months after the release of the interim report, international currency problems, long a source of concern, erupted, marking the beginning of a decade of turbulence. The international environment was different from anything the Japanese economy had yet faced. US President Richard Nixon adopted a "dollar-defense policy," meaning the suspension of the gold standard for the US dollar, in response to the economic strains caused by the quagmire in Vietnam. Japan was therefore forced to raise the value of the yen, which had been fixed at 360 yen to the dollar for more than 20 years. Given Japan's persistent trade surplus, the yen appreciation should not have posed a problem, but both government and business overreacted to the change. Fearful that the yen's rise would bring about an export slump that would in turn cause a depression, the government sought to buoy the economy with an aggressive fiscal policy driven by deficit bond issues. As a result, the money supply increased rapidly, creating excess liquidity and spurring inflation. Wholesale prices, which had been stable until that time, soared in 1973. Consumer prices, until then growing steadily at somewhat over the 5% level, leapt as well, by 20%.

The first oil crisis, which followed the outbreak of the fourth Middle East war and the "petroleum strategy" adopted by Arab oil-producing countries, cemented

---

[1]The *1960's Vision,* released in 1963, regarded the following as the principle tasks of industrial policy: strengthening industry's international competitiveness, which in policy terms meant it was essential to "raise the level of the economic structure" and "promote the liberalization of trade"; and with regard to manufacturing industries, supporting those sectors with high "income elasticity value" and "rates of productivity increase." In industries with high-income elasticity values, the demand for goods increases more rapidly than income does. In industries with high productivity increase rates, production efficiency improves rapidly and markedly due to capital investment. In fact, the targets for policy support were presumed to be heavy and chemical industries and some other materials industries. Underlying the recommendations was the hidden premise that policies centered on these industries would ultimately nurture manufacturing industries as a whole and thereby lead to the successful modernization of the economy. Export promotion, too, was recognized as essential specifically so that Japan could acquire the foreign currency it needed to procure raw materials and other components overseas that were required by the country's basic industries.

the economic changes in Japan. In January 1973, the per-barrel price of oil was US$ 2.6. Based on predictions of a moratorium on supplies if the tensions persisted, it topped 3 dollars in October; after the war began on October 6, it rose to US$ 5.1, and then soared to US$ 11 by January 1974. The rise in prices internationally for agricultural products and raw materials had already been generating concern. Now it escalated all at once to what was dubbed "frenzied prices." Meanwhile, Japan was experiencing an upsurge in land prices due to the speculative investing sparked by the Kakuei Tanaka administration's "archipelago remodeling plan," and wages were up by 20–30% following on the increase in prices. The impact of the oil crisis reached every facet of daily life, setting off panic buying of necessities such as toilet paper and detergent.

1.3 Policies on Industrial Structure in the 1970s

Given this upheaval in the international arena, Japan needed to secure a stable supply of energy, in addition to addressing, as quickly as possible, the recession triggered by the appreciation of the yen. Although the oil crisis had not been anticipated, earlier organizational reforms had established an Agency for Natural Resources and Energy to promote a comprehensive energy policy, and this proved convenient for addressing the immediate disarray. But it was only after the second oil crisis, in the budgets of 1980 and 1981, that energy policy was given the highest priority. In the mid-1970s, the emphasis remained on stabilizing domestic prices and improving consumer life.

So abrupt a change in the economic environment made it difficult for policymakers to prioritize the *Vision of the 1970s*, but it is clear nevertheless that trade and industry policy was based on the *1970s Vision* throughout this time. Issues such as the promotion of industrial technology temporarily took a backseat, but the effort to establish a knowledge-intensive industrial structure continued without interruption.

Reference standards were established to serve as the basis for envisioning a future industrial structure built on knowledge-intensive industries. These reference standards included both those of the high-growth era—income elasticity and productivity growth—and new ones: "standards on overcrowding and the environment" and "standards on the content of labor." In other words, the Ministry anticipated the social demand for reduced reliance on scarce production factors and energy, and for the realization of safe, comfortable and fulfilling workplaces. The *1970s Vision* was notable for its consideration of how to meet the social needs arising in newly emerging sectors.

The following were cited as knowledge-intensive industries that could be expected to deliver particularly high growth in the 1970s:

(a) R&D-intensive industries (computers, aircraft, electric cars, industrial robots, nuclear power-related industries, integrated circuits, fine chemicals, new synthetic chemicals, new metals, special ceramics, marine development, and others.)

(b) Advanced assembly industries (telecommunications equipment, office machinery, computer-controlled machine tools, pollution control equipment, home heating and cooling equipment, educational equipment, factory-produced housing, automated warehouses, large construction machinery, high-grade plant engineering, and others.)
(c) Fashion-related industries (luxury clothing, high-end furniture, residential furniture, electro-acoustic instruments, electronic musical instruments, and others.)
(d) Information industries (information processing services, information provision services, education-related industries including video industries, software, system engineering, consulting, and others.)

The *Vision*'s conception of the structural transformation ahead highlighted the machine industries that would grow with heavy industrialization; it also envisioned a shift "from hard to soft," meaning a shift to industries that would contribute to consumer life and the development of the welfare society.

However, the changes already under way in the industrial structure only accelerated due to the yen's appreciation and soaring energy prices. In particular, smokestack industries such as petroleum refining, metal smelting, and production of vinyl chloride, other petrochemicals, and chemical fertilizers struggled with the sharp rise in costs, despite repeated efforts at energy conservation.

These basic materials industries faced an array of challenges: high energy costs, the difficulty of differentiating general-purpose products, substantial fixed costs and therefore a heavy burden of interest payments when operating rates decline. They were also at a disadvantage in price negotiations because so many of their consumers were large users, and they were extremely capital-intensive.

As a result, MITI had to adopt measures to address recession in these industries, while their declining position spurred changes in the industrial structure overall.

The shift to a knowledge-intensive industrial structure had originally been projected in the *1970s Vision* as the next step for a mature economic power, but the addition of energy conservation to the agenda made the country's turn away from smokestack industries that much more significant: machine industries began to receive greater emphasis within the industrial structure.

This policy perspective meant that the priority at this time was on adjustments to the domestic economy. International economic friction, although a concern, temporarily took a backseat even as great changes continued to rock the international environment.

This was because the balance-of-payments issue was temporarily obscured, first by the Nixon Shock and yen appreciation, and then because of the surge in crude oil prices, which was directly linked to import increases that masked the large trade surplus. Domestic measures to counter the ill effects of the higher yen were accordingly put in place, as were energy policies. After the first oil crisis, priority was given to policies addressing skyrocketing prices. For the time being, longer-term policies were shelved.

2 The Vision of the 1970s and the Machinery and Information Industries

2.1 *Toward a Knowledge-Intensive Industrial Structure and Machinery and Information Industry Policy*

2.1.1 The New Machinery and Information Industries Bureau

In the reorganization of July 1973, MITI established the Machinery and Information Industries Bureau. The new Bureau incorporated 10 Divisions previously in the Ministry's Heavy Industries Bureau: the Industrial Machinery Division, Cast and Wrought Products Division, Electronics Policy Division, Information Processing and Data-Processing Promotion Division, Electronics and Electrical Machinery Division, Automobile Division, Weights and Measures Division, Aircraft and Ordnance Division, Vehicle Division, and Machinery Insurance Division. To these were also added a General Affairs Division and an International Trade Division.

This reorganization was in line with the *1970s Vision*'s recommendation of a conversion to a "knowledge-intensive industrial structure." The Industrial Structure Council Machinery Industry Committee, to recommend concrete measures for the *1970s Vision*, released an interim report, *1975–1984 Vision for the Machinery Industry*, while the Information Industry Committee issued an interim report in September presenting the basic direction of policy for the machinery and information industry (Hasegawa 2013, p. 19).

The *Vision for the Machinery Industry* stressed the strategic importance of the industry as one "that is most suitable for our country and that is a frontier industry with the potential to constantly bring forth new industries and products as science and technology advance." The *Vision* accordingly called for an active response to the needs of the industry and active development internationally. The specific recommendations included: (1) strongly promoting the development of autonomous technologies through the development of cutting-edge products such as electronic calculators and aircraft, (2) promoting regularization and standardization, securing the supply of raw materials, strengthening the foundations of small and medium-sized machinery producers, promoting engineering and the modernization of distribution, and so on, to make the machine industry stronger and more efficient.

The Information Industry Committee's interim report showed an awareness that the expansion of information through the use of computer technology would in the long term enable Japan to overcome such constraints as the industrial pollution, environmental destruction, overcrowding, and depopulation that resulted from rapid growth, as well as the resources and energy shortages that emerged in the oil crisis. It pointed out that, in order to prepare the infrastructural foundation for the information-based economy, it would be necessary to establish a smooth system for information dissemination to enable the efficient advance of information processing and to train people for developments in the information field. These approaches would enable the development of the computer industry and of the information management industry, including areas such as software.

2.1.2 From the Electronics and Machinery Industries Law to the Machinery and Information Industries Law

The legal basis for machinery and information-industry policy was the Law on Temporary Measures for the Promotion of Designated Electronics Industries and Designated Machinery Industries enacted in March 1971 and based on the Industry Structure Council's July 1970 "Report on the future of machinery industry policy: The best path forward for the machinery industry in the 1970s." Ninety-five machinery models were covered by this law by September 1975, and plans for the advancement of each of these brought about joint ventures, research and development, and systematization.

The necessary capital was provided by the Japan Development Bank and the Smaller Business Finance Corporation within special frameworks and with favorable interest rates. For fiscal years 1971–1977, 48.86 billion yen of the loans went to the machinery industry and 16.555 billion yen to the electronics industry (Table 1). The automotive parts and semiconductor industries were particular priorities.

At a joint meeting of the Machinery Industry and Information Industry Committees in October 1977, as the Electronics and Machinery Industries Law approached termination, the Industrial Structure Council approved a report titled "The future direction of the machinery and information industries and the formation of machinery and information industry policy." This report defined the role of the machinery and information industries as follows: (1) to actively respond to new social needs; (2) to respond to employment problems, including providing comfortable employment opportunities; (3) to respond to social demands, such as consumer issues; and (4) to develop harmonious international economic relations (Hasegawa 2013, p. 32).

The first of these covered (1) planning for systems to supply social infrastructure, including medical care, urban development, education, transportation, and information needed in daily life, with the aim of achieving a higher level of social welfare; (2) supplying the new tools required to overcome resource and energy problems, environmental pollution, workplace accidents, and so on; (3) developing new products to advance resource and energy conservation, minimize pollution, and to improve safety in conventional as well as new machinery sectors. Because the machinery and information industries were seen as key to Japan's ability to respond to a wide range of needs, their development was consistently a central policy aim, leading to the July 1978 Law on Temporary Measures for the Promotion of Designated Machinery and Information Industries (Designated Machinery and Information Industries Law).

The new law, like its predecessor, was temporary legislation. It stipulated a seven-year period of assistance in the form of subsidies and policy-based funding, based on plans for upgrading hardware (equipment to promote testing and research, industrialization, and rationalization) as defined by Cabinet Order. Although the two laws took the same form, the new version established several new directions: first,

Table 1 Loan under the Electronics and Machinery Industries Law, FY 1971–1977 (*Unit* million yen)

Model	Machinery industry		Model	Electronics industry	
	No. of cases	Yen amount		No. of cases	Yen amount
(Production rationalization promotion model)			(Production rationalization promotion model)		
Metal machine tools	1	90	Measurement devices for electronics applications	2	300
Transport machinery	3	310	Electronic medical devices	2	170
Pollution control devices	2	300	Electronic calculators (for accounting)	6	785
Freezers, etc.	2	250	Calculators	4	455
Centralized air-conditioning systems	2	600	Multilayer printed circuit boards	9	525
Textile machinery	5	195	Connectors	11	1,270
Civil engineering construction machinery	5	740	Compound semiconductor elements	1	190
Agricultural machinery	8	2,160	Piezoelectric ceramic elements	3	600
Plastics machinery	1	200	Integrated circuits	22	8,415
Sawmill machinery	4	240	High-purity silicon	9	1,660
Automatic casting machinery	1	70	Ferrite products	2	200
Automatic packaging and packing machinery	1	30	(Industrialization promotion equipment)		
Industrial instruments	2	460	Semiconductor integrated circuits	4	1,350

(continued)

Table 1 (continued)

Model	Machinery industry		Model	Electronics industry	
	No. of cases	Yen amount		No. of cases	Yen amount
Pollution-related measuring devices	5	175	Compound semiconductor materials	7	635
Railway cars	3	680			
Nuclear equipment	2	1,010			
Cutting/grinding	5	580			
Bearings	17	2,400			
Precision molds	4	290			
Oil pneumatic equipment	21	2,720			
Auto parts	160	30,850			
Forged products	10	1,450			
Cast products	20	3,060			
Subtotal	284	48,860		82	16,555

Source Hasegawa (2013, p. 31)

within the machinery industry, it singled out for promotion those devices that integrated electronics (computers); second, its Cabinet Order designations eliminated the requirement that the target sector "contribute to labor-saving and other business improvement activities" and added instead that it "contribute to rationalization of resource use"; and third, it added the software industry as one of the areas targeted by the new law.

The new Cabinet Order therefore targeted 88 industries, seven fewer than before. The new law placed a greater emphasis on policies that treated the machinery and information industries as a single unit. The two had remained distinct even after the establishment of the Machinery and Information Industries Bureau, but from FY 1979 forward, they began to be conceived of as united. The increased emphasis on the electronics industry (especially semiconductors) is clear in the Designated Machinery and Information Industries Law financing shown in Table 2.

2.1.3 Electronics Industry Promotion Measures

One particular issue facing the 1970s information industry was how to respond to trade liberalization. Liberalization of the computer market began in July 1972 and was complete as of April 1976. The main focus of industrial promotion policy thereafter was the development of a 3.5-generation computer that could compete with the

Table 2 Loans under the Designated Machinery and Information Industries Law, FY 1978–1984 (*Unit* million yen)

Machine industry model	Amount	Electronics industry model	Amount
Automobile parts	7,500	Compound semiconductor elements	490
NCI machine tools	1,570	Semiconductor integrated circuits	46,600
Specialty steel screws	80	Connectors	50
Pneumatic/hydraulic instruments	900	Liquid crystal display cells	1,000
Valves	120	Electronic equipment materials	13,320
Specialty steel, carbide tools	270	Calculating computers	4,700
Forged products	1,000	Circuits/mechanical parts	9,180
Agricultural machinery	500	Integrated circuits	6,220
Metal/plastic processing goods	750	Devices with applications to medical electronics	100
Light-water nuclear reactors	100		
Railway cars	200		
Machine tools	400		
Subtotal	13,390		81,660

Source Hasegawa (2013, p. 71)

IBM (International Business Machines Corporation) 370 series. Based on the Electronics and Machinery Industries Law, a system for directing financial support to the computer industry had been established in 1972, enabling the provision of subsidies for the development of both computers and peripheral equipment (Hasegawa 2013, p. 608).

Three groups of domestic computer manufacturers (Fujitsu and Hitachi; NEC and Toshiba; Mitsubishi Electric Corporation and Oki Electric Industry) received the subsidies for computer development, which covered 50% of their costs. Manufacturers of peripherals also received subsidies for 50% of costs. The 1978 law also clarified that the software industry would be a target for support, and policies for nurturing the computer industry were strengthened through such measures as user taxes.

Even with these measures, however, IBM remained the computer industry leader in the late 1970s. MITI and industry stakeholders were shocked by the information they were getting about the new Future System (FS) model being developed by IBM in 1974. The core technology of FS was the Very Large-Scale Integrated Circuit (VLSI). VLSIs were expected to increase integrated circuit (IC) densities by 100 times or more, bringing computer prices down to one-twentieth their existing level and the unit price of computer processing down to one-third or even one-fifth its level. MITI recognized that it would be difficult for domestic manufacturers to independently develop IBM's FS and VLSI counterparts because of the enormous expenditure and risks involved, and determined that government subsidies were therefore especially necessary for VLSI development. It also concluded that the domestic development of

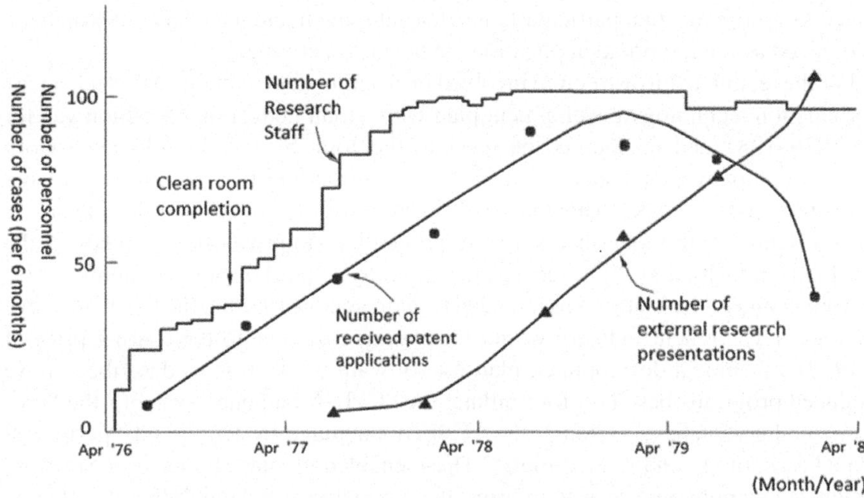

Fig. 1 VLSI research lab achievements and personnel. *Soruce* [II-7, p. 627]

computers equipped with VLSIs would lower prices and thereby contribute greatly to the advancement of small and medium-sized firms and economic society in general (Fig. 1).

MITI therefore began to explore ways of supporting the endeavor in 1975 and in March 1976 established the VSLI Technology Research Association to serve as the core mechanism in the development of concrete policy plans (Hasegawa 2013, p. 617). Subsidies covered 50% of the Association's development expenses, and from FY 1976 to FY 1979 MITI focused the necessary materials and talent as much as possible on the two groups under the Association's umbrella: Fujitsu–Hitachi–Mitsubishi and NEC–Toshiba.

The VLSI project bore fruit, improving the semiconductor industry's LSI manufacturing technology and contributing to Japanese firms' significant rise in the 64K DRAM and 1M DRAM industries. Factors in the success of this effort were the clarity of the goals, the focus on the development of manufacturing technology, the consistency of project organization and personnel with the targets set, and the role played by the external environment in promoting R&D. In a related effort, MITI introduced a five-year subsidy and other measures to promote the development of fourth-generation computer technology based on VLSIs.

2.1.4 Promoting Software Development

The Information-Technology Promotion Agency (IPA), launched in October 1970, played a central role in software promotion (Hasegawa 2013, p. 629). The IPA's concrete tasks were to outsource the development of particular programs and to create a credit guarantee business. The first involved planning and developing the spread of "programs that particularly need development and the results of which are recognized as having broad applications in business activities."

For the technical infrastructure involved in program development, MITI advanced a production technology development plan with a total budget of 7.5 billion yen for FY 1976–1981 and outsourced business to the Joint System Development Corp (JSD), a company established in April 1976 with funding from 17 major software companies and 13 banks. This plan had several aims: (1) to resolve the Japan–US software gap, (2) to modernize software production (improve the efficiency of the development task), and (3) to secure the autonomy of the Japanese economy.

The second of these aims was intended to address concerns that the labor-intensive software development industry would face rising costs due to the soaring price of labor. The technical development plan for software production as described above produced programs based on four pillars: the "CPL-A language system," the "program module/database system," the "CPL-B language system," and "peripheral related technology and related tools." These enabled greater efficiency in software design and manufacture so as to improve the productivity and reliability of software.

2.2 *The Machinery Industry as a "Strategic Industry"*

2.2.1 Measures on Automobile Pollution and Electric Vehicle Development

While these efforts to build a knowledge-intensive structure were under way, the industrial policy on the auto industry focused on (a) stronger exhaust-gas regulation and the pollution prevention and safety assurances that had suffered from the soaring gasoline prices, and (b) electric car R&D (Hasegawa 2013, p. 315). In a December 1974 report titled "The auto industry in 1985," the Automobile Industry Subcommittee of the Machinery Industry Committee suggested that measures should be taken to resolve the problem technologically and that plans should be made for expanding demand to a global scale through exports and overseas investment and for forwarding internationalization. While maintaining a strong export orientation, this report also stresses the need for efforts to resolve the pollution issue. These ideas were also presented in a March 1976 subcommittee report, marking a growing emphasis on the need for a prompt response to pollution, safety, and energy issues.

Pollution and safety policy were also important policy issues in promoting the automotive parts industry (Hasegawa 2013, p. 324). A major reason for the enactment of the Electronics and Machinery Industries Law had been the "mounting demand for greater harmony between industrial activities and people's lives in areas such as pollution and safety," and among the automotive sectors designated under the law were "automobile pollution-related measuring instruments, automobile testing and inspection equipment manufacturing industry" and "the automobile parts manufacturing industry." These received loans and other policy support based on the associated improvement plans. This area saw no change under the new law. When the Designated Machinery and Information Industries Law came into effect, support for the parts industry—chiefly for improvements in quality and performance and for cost reduction—narrowed its focus more specifically to pollution and safety. This is a good example of the flexibility with which industrial promotion policies could address changing policy objectives to respond to the demands of the times.

The development and diffusion of electric vehicles was promoted beginning in the 1970s as part of broader policies on next-generation automobiles. Since it was not easy to develop electric cars comparable in performance to gasoline-powered cars, policy support was offered through the "Large-Scale Project" framework (Hasegawa 2013, p. 373).[2] A six-year R&D period from FY 1971 to FY 1976 was set for the electric vehicle development project, with planned costs of 5.7 billion yen, delivery of the first prototype at the end of three years, and trial production of an experimental car in the fifth year. However, because the firms that were to have undertaken the research and development were not strongly convinced of the need to commit manpower and funding to the enterprise, it did not produce the desired results. In the process of identifying project goals, MITI established the Council on Electric Vehicle Diffusion Measures within the Machinery and Information Industries Bureau in October 1975 to consider measures for promoting the diffusion of electric vehicles. The Japan Electric Vehicle Association (EV Association), established in August 1976, was tasked with promoting electric vehicles, and 10 firms together established the Association for Research on Technology for the Standard Electric Automobile in February 1987 with the aim of advancing R&D enough to produce an electric car.

In 1976, MITI also established the Electric Vehicle Association as a private advisory body answering to the Director General of the Machinery and Information Industries Bureau, and put together the Basic Plan for Promotion of the Electric Vehicle (April 1977). Although this plan did produce an experimental electric vehicle comparable in performance to the cars with internal combustion engines, its market was expected to be limited until it could become more cost-effective. Proposed uses for the time being included vehicles for milk and newspaper delivery, which required low-noise emissions, commercial vehicles that traveled only short distances each day, short-route buses and government patrol cars, as well as vehicles used only within confined areas and requiring zero exhaust and low noise.

In addition, the plan set ownership targets for FY 1986 of 200,000 regular vehicles and 50,000 vehicles for use only in confined areas. To realize these targets, the plan urged (1) promoting technological development, (2) making the cars more economical (3) establishing the necessary service systems, (4) improving the social environment, and (5) education and PR activities through the EV Association mentioned above. Things did not proceed entirely smoothly, however, and even the new plan issued in December 1983 after review did not put ownership within range of the targets.

Subsequently, in its October 1991 Electric Vehicle Diffusion Plan, MITI began exploring new approaches to achieving these targets, saying that it "hope[d] to see further efforts by automobile, battery, and electrical manufacturers" and signaling

[2]See Sect. 4.5 for further information on "Large-Scale Projects."

that MITI would entrust the basic direction of development and diffusion to the private sector. An exception was made in the area of batteries, which required enormous outlays of capital. MITI recognized the need for government to bear the risks of development, and did so within the framework of the New Sunshine Project. This plan contributed, through the rapid diffusion of fuel cells, to the spread of a new generation of automobiles powered in part by electrical energy.[3]

2.2.2 Measures to Promote the Industrial Machinery and Engineering Industries

Promotion policies based on these legal frameworks were advanced in other areas as well, including machine tools, civil engineering and construction machinery, chemical machinery, textile machinery, and agricultural machinery (Hasegawa 2013, p. 197). Under the original law, specialized production systems and advances in systematization were developed to meet the plans for their specific industries, and inter-industry cooperation was promoted as an especially important goal. The revised law also recognized amortization of the "first quarter of the first year" as part of Measures for the Special Amortization of Important Complex Machinery such as high-performance computer-controlled metal-processing machinery, high-performance computer-controlled automatic design devices, and high-performance computer-controlled facsimile storage and exchange devices. This understanding dated back earlier than the 1978 revised law, having originated in the financing mechanism created in 1975 to promote machine systems.

These loans sought to create new high-value-added products (mechanical equipment systems) that could couple computers with other machinery based on mechanical engineering. Various measures for subsidizing the machinery and information systems were adopted with the goal of developing a more sophisticated machine industry.

Despite the emerging trade friction in the latter 1970s, the engineering industry showed little sign of it and was expected to become an important player in machinery exports (Hasegawa 2013, p. 277). In the midst of the first oil crisis, when domestic capital investment was sluggish, projects materializing in oil-producing countries boosted the export of machinery and contributed to the goals of securing resources and energy. MITI considered such exports, including soft services such as product management, as business sectors and made promoting them a pillar of its export promotion policies.

In November 1977, MITI established an engineering roundtable as a private advisory body of the Machinery and Information Industries Bureau Director General. Its interim report of April 1978 called for the development of financial systems and

[3]Having acted to introduce low-pollution vehicles, in July the Ministry of Economy, Trade and Industry, the Ministry of Land, Infrastructure, Transport and Tourism, and Ministry of the Environment worked together to formulate an "Action Plan for the Development and Diffusion of Low-emissions Vehicles."

the standardization of both hardware and software in terminology and other areas, to advance the engineering industry. MITI accordingly established the Engineering Advancement Association of Japan in August 1978, through which to develop measures for strengthening technology development and reinforcing the creditworthiness of the industry.

2.2.3 Nurturing and Advancing the Nuclear Power Industry

The nuclear power industry was another knowledge- and R&D-intensive- industry that was expected to grow. It is a high-value-added industry requiring extremely specific built-to-order plants and is also related to a broad array of industrial sectors (Hasegawa 2013, p. 451). The Machinery and Information Industries Bureau stressed the development of nuclear-plant equipment during this period because the exacting safety and reliability requirements in this field meant a need for policies ensuring that due effort was made from the initial stages of production and manufacturing.

The expectation was that after the import of the first nuclear power plants, the second-generation plants would rely on domestic manufacturing. The measures taken to promote domestic production proved effective: by the early 1980s, most of the machinery used in nuclear power plants was produced domestically (Table 3). Even so, the level of technology assimilation at this stage was not regarded as sufficient. As long as nuclear power plants relied on imported technology, there remained the danger that prompt and appropriate technical judgments would not be possible in the event of an atypical occurrence. Because Japan required strict oversight measures, especially of radiation exposure, technical improvements were an important responsibility of policy. This led to plans for improving and standardizing power plants and improving the reliability of nuclear power generation.

The basic design of nuclear power plants entails the immediate shutdown of the furnace whenever even small problems arise. Any suspension of operations increases the costs associated with temporarily switching to thermal power generation. One hundred fourteen such problems were recorded over the five-year period between FY 1974 and FY 1980. Of these, 40% were due to problems in design oversight, the most common being stress corrosion cracking (SCC) and thermal fatigue. These issues contributed to the recognition of a need for policy measures to address reliability and quality assurance.

In February 1975, MITI established the Committee on the Improvement and Standardization of Nuclear Power Plants and the Committee on Nuclear Power Plant Standardization Surveys within the Machine Information Bureau. Their task was to forward the improvement and standardization of light-water reactors, which were expected to play a central role in nuclear power generation. The results of the committees' investigations were issued in an interim report in April 1977, which presented the basic concepts that should govern standard specifications: "Plants must be safe, of course, but also improve reliability and capacity utilization, reduce employee exposure to radiation, and implement maintenance and inspection [systems to ensure that] human error would not be a factor." Standardization of earthquake-resistant

Table 3 Domestic production of nuclear power plants

Company name	Power plant	Ratio produced domestically	Primary contractor
Nihon Genshiryoku Hatsuden (Japan Nuclear Power Plant)	Tōkai	35	GEC
	Tōkai 2	51	GE/Hitachi
	Tsuruga	55	GE
Tokyo Electric	Fukushima Daiichi Genshiryoku 1	56	GE
	Fukushima Daiichi Genshiryoku 2	53	GE/Tōshiba
	Fukushima Daiichi Genshiryoku 3	91	Tōshiba
	Fukushima Daiichi Genshiryoku 4	91	Hitachi
	Fukushima Daiichi Genshiryoku 5	93	Tōshiba
	Fukushima Daiichi Genshiryoku 6	63	GE/Tōshiba
Chubu Electric	Genshiryoku 1	90	Tōshiba
	Genshiryoku 2	94	Tōshiba, Hitachi
Kansai Electric	Mihama 1	58	WH
	Mihama 2	72	Mitsubishi Heavy
	Mihama 3	93	Mitsubishi Shoji
	Takahama1	61	WH/Mitsubishi Shoji
	Takahama 2	90	Mitsubishi Shoji
	Ōi 1	67	WH/Mitsubishi Shoji
	Ōi 2	87	WH
Chugoku Electric	Shimane Genshiryoku	94	Hitachi
Shikoku Electric	Ikata1	94	Mitsubishi Heavy
Kyushu Electric	Genkai Genshiryoku1	87	Mitsubishi Heavy

Source Hasegawa (2013, p. 455). The original material comes from Yamaguchi (1980, p. 10)

design, although also on the agenda, was left for future consideration because of the great variety in local site conditions. On the assumption that steady progress would be made in the improvement and standardization of light-water reactors, the committees continued to build a series of time-based expectations to serve as standard specifications and eventually solidified their thinking on how to achieve a model for light-water reactors that would be suitable for Japan's specific circumstances.

The "Interim report on light-water reactor improvement and standardization surveys" issued by MITI in May 1978 reported that the first three-year stage of improvement and standardization had been completed in FY 1977, and that great strides had been made both in improving the efficiency of maintenance and inspection, and in reducing employee exposure to radiation. It also defined goals for the second stage, including standardization of earthquake-resistant design and improvement in load-following operating functions, and so on. While efforts continued to improve automation and remote control, therefore, the scope of the standardization efforts also expanded from nuclear-reactor steam-generation equipment to reactor building and other areas. The results of this second stage were compiled in April 1981, and the plan for the third stage was put into effect, to last until FY1985. Under this plan, Japan would rely on international technological cooperation until it could build its own reactors, including the core, as well as related equipment and systems. By the third stage, Japan had made considerable strides toward achieving this goal (Table 4).

2.2.4 Promotion of the Aircraft Industry

The challenge for policy on aircraft-industry development in the 1970s was how to develop a new commercial airliner to follow the YS-11, which was seen as "a technical success and a commercial failure." Among the issues was the question of how to determine the demand target. As presented in the Aircraft Industry Council's 1972 summary report, the decision was made to collaborate with Boeing Company to develop a 150–200-seat twinjet aircraft (Hasegawa 2013, p. 482).

The Civil Transport Development Corporation (CTDC) was established in March 1973 to pursue this goal based on a combination of private-sector energies and government subsidies. In April 1973, the CTDC entered into a Memorandum of Understanding (MOU) with Boeing, and negotiations between the two continued thereafter.

However, the spending cuts and changes in demand caused by the first oil crisis in the fall of 1973 led to a reconsideration of the YX development plan itself. The MOU contract was such that instead of following a joint development model, Japan would participate in the developmental stages of Boeing's process. Based on these new negotiations, CTDC and Boeing signed the YX/767 basic business agreement in September 1978, and full-scale development was under way. The US Federal Aviation Administration (FAA) gave its approval to the prototype in July 1982, and the development of the YX/767 concluded as planned.

Meanwhile, the Machinery and Information Industries Bureau began to define the next policy issues in aircraft-industry development. This was based on the thinking that next-generation development should always be in the works even before the completion of the current model in order to ensure the industry's sound development. According to MITI's explanation at the Aircraft Industrial Council meeting in April 1977, the 1980s forecast was for a market consisting of "Jumbo's, Airbus aircraft, new 200-seat aircraft, smaller new aircraft and to a certain extent the continued use of existing aircraft," which set the parameters for the central challenges of the next

Table 4 Improvement and standardization plan targets and results

		Reliability and Capacity Utilization		Regular inspection period (when repair work is not under way)	Employee exposure to radiation
		Time = use rate	Facility-use rate		
Existing plants	800,000–1,000,000 kW grade	Considerable variation among plants		90–100 days	Defined as 100%
1st plants improved and standardized	800,000–1,000,000 kW grade	About 75%	About 70%	About 85 days	About 75%
2nd plants improved and standardized	800,000–1,000,000 kW grade	About 80%	About 75%	About 70 days	About 50%
3rd plants improved and standardized		–	About 80%	About 55 days	About 40%
Examples of improvement policies	BWR	Adoption of anti-stress corrosion cracking material for improved core design		Adoption of control-rod kinetics with automatic switching mechanisms improvement of refueling machines	Introduction of pipes for automated in-service inspection; adoption of cobalt-free materials
	PWR	Fuel improvement (measures to counter fuel assembly bow); steam-generator improvement		Development of integrated structure for reactor vessel lid; improvement of fuel-inspection system	Development of steam-generator manipulation and mounting device; improvement of nozzle for steam generator water chamber
	BWR · PWR				Adoption of improved storage containers (1st-stage improvement measure)

Source Hasegawa (2013, p. 468). Original materials from Nihon Denki Kōgyōkai (1998, p. 128)
Note BWR Boiling water reactor; *PWR* Pressurized water reactor

phase of policy. In April 1979, MITI asked the Aircraft and Machinery Industry Council Committee on the Aircraft Industry for its opinion on the desired features of a next-generation civilian aircraft dubbed "YXX."

The Committee's August interim report proposed aiming for medium-sized aircraft of 100 to 150 seats. The Council continued to establish basic policies for this goal, but meanwhile the CTDC, too, launched preparations for the YXX in June 1981. In March 1984, the CTDC (renamed the Japan Aircraft Development Corporation or JADC in December 1982), together with Mitsubishi Heavy Industries, Ltd., Kawasaki Heavy Industries, Ltd., and Fuji Heavy Industries Ltd., announced the exchange of a first-stage MOU on the 7J7 development plan proposed by Boeing, which would be their official co-developer. In March 1986 they entered into a second MOU.

Policy support also went to the development of engines for use in commercial aircraft (Hasegawa 2013, p. 511). The new effort began with the FJR10 jet engine development project, which from 1971 to 1981 was counted among the Industrial Science and Technology Agency's Large-Scale Projects. The first period, ending in 1976, saw an investment of 6.8 billion yen in this area; an additional 1.3 billion yen was budgeted for the second period, ending in 1981. Development progressed accordingly.

Among the commercial aircraft engines slated to be put to practical use was the XJB project (RJ500 development) that was launched after the conclusion of a Japan–UK joint enterprise agreement based on consultation with British aircraft-engine maker Rolls-Royce Limited in December 1979. The "Outline of the commercial aircraft jet engine development subsidy" was settled on in November 1980, and the government offered support in the form of subsidies. This project was carried on by an international joint development enterprise comprising five countries and seven companies doing joint R&D on the basis of a March 1983 contract and led to the development of the V2500 engine.

3 Industrial Relocation and Pollution Regulation

3.1 Promoting Industrial Relocation Plans

3.1.1 Industrial Relocation Promotion Measures and Regional Recovery

With rapid economic growth came the twin problems of overpopulation in cities and depopulation in the provinces. In response to these challenges, MITI implemented the Industrial Relocation Promotion Law and the Law of Public Corporations for Industrial Location and Coal Mining Region Development (Takeda 2011, p. 11) in October 1972.

Records from 1972 show fully 72% of the country's industry concentrated in the Pacific Coastal belt, which constituted no more than 20% of Japan's total land area. The need for a reconfiguration of land use was obvious. Regions needing relocation—either inbound or outbound—were designated on the basis of this law in FY 1972, but formulation of a concrete plan proved difficult.

A draft proposal was compiled in December 1975, and in July 1977 the Inducements for Industrial Relocation were determined. The reason for the difficulty was that the Federation of Economic Organizations (Keidanren), along with key industries such as steel, oil refining and petrochemicals, opposed the relocation measures. Relocation ultimately was implemented through administrative guidance, which took their opinions into account.

The July 1977 plan set numerical targets for each of the outbound and inbound relocation areas. Beginning in FY 1978, areas that were regarded as especially in need of industry were designated "Special Induction Areas," including remote prefectures and those that had experienced structural decline (textile-producing regions, and coal and other mining regions). Aggressive efforts were made to disperse industry within these Special Induction Areas through higher subsidy levels and other measures.

Tax and financial incentives were offered to promote relocation. In addition, support was also offered to fund interest payments for local government bond issues and loans for creating local industrial complexes, subsidies to municipalities and companies for industrial relocation promotion, and for special corporate and third-sector policy financial institutions (Table 5).

Because of changes taking place in the industrial structure during the implementation period, this plan did not produce the target results. Although industry in the 1980s left the designated "outbound" areas, they did not necessarily relocate to the target "induction areas" but instead moved into undesignated areas. The industrial base in outlying areas therefore remained weak and did not show much improvement. The Industrial Relocation Promotion Law was abolished in 2006.

Other efforts were made to promote regional development, including the creation of regional *Visions* and the introduction of industry into agricultural regions. In contrast to the relocation plan's general focus on urban functions and the overconcentration of industry in Tokyo, these policies were principally concerned with correcting disparities among regions.

The first *Vision* for the agricultural regions was presented in The Long-term Vision on Industrial Structure, adopted in September 1974 by the Industrial Structure Council for implementation in FY 1976. It declared the need to envision the contours of a future industrial structure specific to each region. This approach sought to correct disparities not only in income, but also in the availability of appealing workplaces, of the types of services found in urban areas, and of connections with nature. In other words, it was concerned with enriching people's overall living circumstances.

Table 5 Long-term trends in industry site location (%)

		1955	1965	1975	1985	1995	2003
Number of firms	Metropolitan areas	58.2	58.9	49.2	48.1	45.2	45.6
	Coastal Kantō	24.7	26.2	20.8	20	17.6	16.7
	Tōkai	13.5	15.2	14.7	15.6	15.9	17.4
	Coastal Kinki	19.9	17.5	13.7	12.5	11.7	11.6
	Rural areas	42.9	41.9	51.5	52.6	55.4	55.1
Number of employees	Metropolitan areas	60.2	62.1	54.5	52.3	49.8	48.6
	Coastal Kantō	23.4	27.5	23.7	22.4	20	17.5
	Tōkai	16.9	16.6	16.5	17.3	18.3	20.5
	Coastal Kinki	19.8	18	14.4	12.5	11.5	10.6
	Rural areas	40.7	38.6	46.2	48.3	50.8	52
Shipment of manufactured goods (total amount)	Metropolitan areas	64.9	67.6	60.9	58.6	55.5	53.9
	Coastal Kantō	25.5	30.7	27.4	25.7	23.2	19.4
	Tōkai	16.2	16.2	16.9	19.5	20.8	24.2
	Coastal Kinki	22.9	20.7	16.6	13.4	11.5	10.3
	Rural areas	36.8	33.7	40.6	42.4	45.2	46.8
Tangible fixed-asset values	Metropolitan areas		63.9	54.1	53.7	52.3	50.2
	Coastal Kantō		28.6	23.4	23.4	21.2	18.7
	Tōkai		16.9	15.9	17	18.5	20.1
	Coastal Kinki		18.4	14.8	13.2	12.6	11.3
	Rural areas		36.1	45.9	46.3	47.7	49.8

Source Takeda (2011, p. 6)

3.1.2 Adjustments to Industrial Locations and the Establishment of Infrastructure for an Industrial Environment

The "Outline on industrial bills," compiled at the direction of MITI Minister Kakuei Tanaka in July 1972, proved an opportunity to create a legal framework for ensuring environmental preservation in cases of industrial relocation. The Law on Industrial Location Surveys and Related Matters was revised and a new Factory Location Act adopted in February 1974, leading to the establishment of regulations on location (Takeda 2011, p. 155). The regulations were made in response to a recognition that the worsening pollution in existing industrial districts and the progress of industrialization and urbanization overall were damaging the balance with nature. The rules on environmental preservation announced by the MITI Minister stipulated that (1) production facilities could occupy only up to a certain ratio of the site area, and that (2) notification reports had to be submitted for certain specified factories.

MITI also carried out the Comprehensive Survey of Large-Scale Industrial Sites and studies of the FY 1973–1981 expenses for coordinating all-round land development. These were intended to help determine the optimal siting of industrial facilities. It also developed measures to improve the factory environment, including notification reviews for specified plants, subsidies for the promotion of environmental improvements in industrial parks, and surveys on improving the factory environment.

3.1.3 Securing Industrial Water

Measures governing industrial water had been implemented under the 1956 Industrial Water Law to prevent the ground subsidence caused by excessive pumping of groundwater for industrial use. Regulations based on regional designations for the installation of industrial wells were implemented to address the expansion in target areas and the need for shifts in water sources.

These measures were consistent with the strengthening of the regulations required by the interim report of the Industrial Structure Council's Committee on Industrial Water Policy, summarized in "The basic direction of groundwater measures" of November 1975. The law was not revised, but the measures were pursued in the form of administrative guidance (Takeda 2011, p. 172).

In addition, the Industrial Structure Council once again took into consideration measures to secure industrial water in the mid- to long-term through the compilation of the June 1978 Plan for the Long-Term Supply and Demand of Industrial Water and the August 1985 Interim Report on the Industrial Water Basic Policy Committee. This led to efforts to promote the construction of industrial water supplies, the development of water resources, rationalization of use, and other measures. Large subsidies for construction of an industrial water supply did not prove necessary, because the relocation process stalled. Measures were instead adopted to respond promptly to changes in the industrial structure: the Subsidy Framework for Small-Scale Industrial Water Supply Expenses, for example, was established in FY 1985 to promote the construction of small-scale inland industrial water supplies to serve locations with enterprises in advanced technologies, such as the IC industry.

Meanwhile, in the interest of rationalizing industrial water use, MITI conducted "surveys of water consumption, by type, and surveys of the rationalization of water use, by region." Research was also conducted on sewage recycling as a possibility for the future. The R&D of comprehensive water recycling systems launched in 1985 (Aqua-Renaissance '90 Project) was one such example. As a result of these efforts, the FY 1999 surveys issued by the Environmental Protection and Industrial Location Bureau's Industrial Facilities Division showed clear improvements in industrial water recovery rates and in water consumption (Table 6).

Table 6 Industrial water demand and unit consumption

Item	1977	1982	1987	1992	1997	Notes
Delivery amount (1 trillion yen)	132	161	200	260	274	
Area of site (10 thousand m^2)	12,506	12,834	13,342	14,623	14,799	
Number of facilities	54,392	55,207	58,154	60,974	55,386	
Amount of water used (million m^3/day)	132	134	137	151	152	
Amount of water recovered (million m^3/day)	39	35	34	36	34	
Recovery rate (%)	70.4	73.8	74.9	76.3	77.9	
Unit of water used (m^3/day/100 million yen)	99.8	83.1	68.7	58.1	55.5	by shipment
Unit of water recovered (m^3/day/100 million yen)	29.5	21.8	17.2	13.7	12.3	
Unit of water used (m^3/day/thousand m^2)	105.3	104.3	102.9	103.1	102.8	by site area
Unit of water recovered (m^3/day/thousand m^2)	31.2	27.4	25.8	24.4	22.8	

Sources Takeda (2011, p. 191); MITI Environmental Protection and Industrial Location Bureau 2000. *Kōgyō Yōsui Juyō Sōtei Chōsa Hōkokusho—Heisei 11 nendo Kōgyōyō Suidō Jigyō Chōsa* [Survey Report on Expected Industrial Demand for Water—FY Heisei 11 Industrial Waterworks Project Survey]

Note The original source materials do not come with explanation, but the Recovery rate was 1—water recovery volume/used water volume. The consumption rates are the amount of water used and amount of water recovered, obtained by dividing the delivery amount and site area

3.2 Strengthening the Regulation of Pollution

3.2.1 Direct Regulation of Pollution: Air Pollution

The year 1970 saw the revision of the Basic Law for Environmental Pollution Control by the "Pollution Session of the Diet" and the enactment of many regulations. In 1971, the Environment Agency was established. Looking at subsequent environmental policy from MITI's point of view, environmental regulations appear to have been implemented to harmonize with economic development.

Direct regulation of environmental pollution centered on air and water pollution while also addressing pollution in the form of noise, vibration, and offensive odors. The regulation of nitrogen oxides (NO_x) was particularly important in the 1970s because the increase in photochemical smog had emerged as a serious issue.

The environmental quality standards enacted under Article 9 of the Basic Pollution Countermeasures Law therefore included sulfur dioxide, carbon monoxide, and suspended particulate matter, as they had before, and in 1973 added nitrogen dioxide and photochemical oxidants. MITI meanwhile strengthened its regulations, for example extending the application of the K-Value Regulations nationwide on the basis of the Air Pollution Control Law (Takeda 2011, p. 225).

Sulfur oxide (SOx) is generated when the sulfur contained in fossil fuels such as petroleum is burned. Sulfur oxide contamination thus became a serious problem with the rapid increase in petroleum-based fuel consumption. The government sought to counter this trend by expanding the area subject to regulation and strengthening the standards in March 1974 and introducing the Total Pollutant Load Control approach in June (Takeda 2011, p. 229). Based on this action, prefectural governments established regulatory standards on totals and were enabled to ask factories and workplaces to comply with fuel usage standards. As shown in Fig. 2, these measures produced such great improvements that by the early 1980s, sulfur oxide was evaluated as hardly a problem any longer.

Meanwhile, the first controls on nitrogen oxide emissions were implemented in August 1973 in accordance with the environmental standards set by the Environment Agency in March 1973. With developments in preventive technologies thereafter, a second and third set of emissions regulations were established in October 1975 and June 1977, expanding the facilities subject to regulation and revising the emission standards themselves. Uniform nationwide regulation went into effect with the fourth set of emission regulations in August 1979 (Takeda 2011, p. 232).

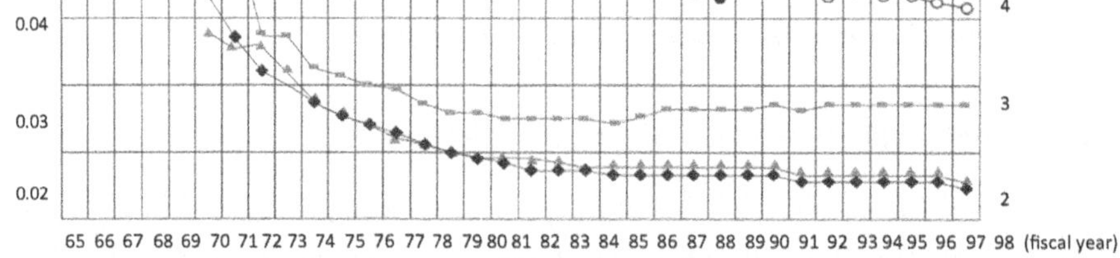

Fig. 2 Changes in air pollution substance concentrations (Takeda 2011, p. 219). *Sources* Environment Agency, *Kankyo hakusho* [Environment White Paper]. Study Group on Constant Atmospheric Monitoring (ed) *Taiki osen jōkyō* [Japan's Pollution Conditions].
Notes Sulfur dioxide, nitrogen dioxide, carbon monoxide: Ambient Air Pollution Monitoring Stations (APMS) annual average value; Dustfall: 7 constant monitoring stations; Suspended particular matter: annual average value

The validity of the environmental standards was questioned with the regulations on nitrogen oxides. The April 1973 report of the Central Council for Environmental Pollution Control, which formed the basis for formulating the standards, was criticized by industry and other sectors for (1) the insufficiency of epidemiological surveys, (2) the underdevelopment of control technologies, and (3) the strictness of the regulations compared with those in other parts of the world. In other words, the stringency of the regulations was called into question from the point of view both of science and of the aptness of the standards themselves. The Industrial Structure Council stated in its December 1977 report that "targets that could not be achieved had been set without any basis" and that "environmental standards should be set to levels that can be realized, not to some ideal value." The Environment Agency reviewed the standards based on the Council Procedure Report and relaxed them in July 1977 in consideration of the request made by Keidanren (Japan Business Federation).

While revising the standards in the immediate term, the Environment Agency also made it known that the new environmental standards would be achieved in 1985 based on the introduction of controls on total volume. This drew opposition from business circles, but controls on total volume were introduced to the Special Tokyo Metropolitan Zone and other areas including the cities of Yokohama and Osaka in June 1981. Reducing auto emissions was difficult because automobiles were so necessary to mobility, so MITI put its effort into developing regulations on other areas in order to achieve the total volumes stipulated in the new controls. Its 1979 regulations applied to trucks and buses, the 1981 regulations targeted light- and medium-weight gas-powered vehicles, and the 1982 regulations established limits on heavy automobiles using gasoline and diesel. Even with such measures, however, regulation of nitrogen dioxide proved limited in effect. Average concentrations, which had remained largely unchanged after 1973, began to worsen after 1986. Results fell short of the standards, particularly with regard to auto exhaust gases.

3.2.2 Direct Regulation of Pollution: Water Pollution

With regard to water pollution, environmental quality standards and effluent standards were adopted under Article 9 of the Basic Law for Environmental Pollution Control. Environmental standards set the criteria that were to be achieved and maintained for the protection of human health and those for the preservation of the living environment. The regulations based on the Water Pollution Control Law set nationwide uniform criteria for wastewater discharged from certain factories, and recognized the more stringent standards set by prefectures. By FY 1975, all prefectures had added their own standards (Takeda 2011, p. 259).

With these regulations, about 70% of Japan's water districts improved or maintained their existing levels of water quality from the late 1970s forward. Pollution worsened in some closed water bodies, however, raising the question of whether total volume controls would also be necessary to prevent further deterioration. Some prefectures had already implemented total volume controls after 1973, based on the conclusion that regulations of wastewater concentration did not readily stop pollution. The Central Council for Environmental Pollution Control's 1977 report, "The total-volume control system in water quality," approved this approach.

Because these measures applied exclusively to factories and business sites, MITI argued that the Environment Agency should consider regulating domestic wastewater as well, rather than imposing the burden only on industry and business. The 1981 proposal by the Central Council for Environmental Pollution Control that a permit system be established regarding company site locations drew particular opposition. MITI sought to ensure that the regulatory measures not be too restrictive of the business activities of small and medium-sized enterprises, and after difficult negotiations with the Environment Agency, a regulatory framework was put into place.

MITI also undertook to raise awareness in order to promote corporate efforts to address pollution problems, and put effort into the development of anti-pollution technologies (Takeda 2011, p. 293). In 1973, the research institutes of the Agency of Industrial Science and Technology undertook R&D on automobile emissions and NOx air-pollution prevention technologies, and the following year began researching technologies related to the prevention of water pollution as well. At the same time, industry, academia, and government joined in the research and development of electric cars and other projects through MITI's National Research and Development Program ("Large-Scale Projects"). MITI also promoted pollution prevention by offering subsidies for the development of pollution-control technologies through the Important Technology R&D Subsidy System, instruction on the formulation of pollution-control plans, and national examinations for pollution-control specialists.

3.2.3 Waste Disposal Law and Waste Management Policy

The Waste Disposal and Public Cleansing Law ("Waste Disposal Law") was enacted in 1970 to address the serious environmental pollution caused by waste disposal and the diffusion of harmful substances. The law distinguished between industrial and non-industrial waste, assigned responsibility for the former to the operator and established disposal systems, and for the latter assigned responsibility for disposal to the municipality. MITI thereby became responsible for providing guidance on industrial-waste disposal and for promoting measures to recycle waste from controlled substances (Takeda 2011, p. 395). Its concrete measures included preparing industrial waste-disposal instruction manuals and establishing the Clean Japan Center (CJC) Foundation in 1975 to develop a national campaign promoting resource conservation and recycling.

The new pollution problem of hexavalent chromium ore (Chromium (VI) Compound Slag) landfill disposal emerged in August 1975, generating strong public concern, as did illegal dumping. In response, the Waste Disposal Law was amended in June 1976, and regulatory measures were added to ensure the operator's liability, but awareness among businesses remained inadequate. MITI began to consider establishing the tentatively named Recycling Promotion Act to (1) develop a recycling system, (2) actively involve the government in the development of recycling technology, and (3) train and support business operators in recycling. The plan was not soon put into effect, however.

Meanwhile, because municipal processing systems were not keeping up with the increase and diversity of general waste, the idea arose of placing the waste-collection burden on businesses. Beginning in 1973, MITI began reviewing this issue in its Waste Recycling Committee and discussed the Polluter-Pays-Principle (PPP) wherein the operators internalize the cost of disposal by including it in the product's price. The committee did not succeed in solving the problem of how the cost burden should be structured. The Waste Recycling Subcommittee of the Industrial Structure Council's Pollution Committee issued an interim report in March 1977 that called for the formation of a resource-conserving industrial structure centered on recycling and emphasized the need for legislative and policy measures to do so. Meanwhile, the concern that PPP systems would become mandatory led to the voluntary promotion of waste-reduction and reuse by industry. As of 1983, about 58% of the 220 million tons of industrial waste generated was recycled, which, compared with the recycling rate of 16% in 1975, represented significant progress. Nevertheless, as the problem of illegal dumping became more apparent, MITI began to offer technical support for the voluntary initiatives of business operators and to promote their awareness through educational activities.

3.2.4 Measures to Address Paper Waste

Measures for dealing with waste paper were regarded as significant means of reducing the burden it imposed on the environment and of securing raw materials (Matsushima 2012, p. 172). Securing raw materials, energy conservation, waste reduction, and protection of forest resources were among the reasons given in the 1981 *Vision* for the emphasis on this area.

Based on the "Measures to promote the recycling and reuse of paper products," which was presented in October 1973 by the Consumer Goods Industries Bureau's Paper, Pulp and Printing Industry Division, concrete policies included the pursuit of legislative measures as well as the establishment of public- and private-sector organizations to undertake promotion campaigns. Legislative measures were not adopted, but the Waste Paper Recycling Promotion Center was established in March 1974 with responsibility principally for (1) public relations and advertising businesses, (2) debt guarantee businesses, and (3) warehousing businesses and the like. The second of these was adopted because of the tiny scale of the recyclers involved, and in 1975, the used paper wholesale business became a designated industry under the Small and Medium Enterprise Modernization Promotion Law (established March 1963). Plans for its modernization were concluded in 1977, principally in order to promote the development of waste-paper standards, sorting containers, and the like. The industry was again given special designation under the same law in 1989 and surveys were conducted on conditions in the industry.

3.3 Environmental Impact Assessment Legislation

3.3.1 Expanding the Preliminary Surveys on Industrial Pollution

A Cabinet Understanding was approved in June 1972 to "pursue environmental assessments in order to promote environmental conservation in public works projects," and from that point forward, environmental assessments were to be carried out based on specific laws and administrative operations. MITI was involved first in the Comprehensive Preliminary Survey on Industrial Pollution where it concerned large-scale industrial development as part of the Factory Location Law, and second in the July 1977 assessments on power development based on the decision of the MITI Departmental Council (Takeda 2011, p. 323).

In areas pertaining to the Factory Location Law, MITI had since 1965 been providing administrative guidance and instruction to companies based on its forecasts of future pollution, in the awareness that to forward the establishment of non-polluting factory sites, surveys had to be conducted before site selection, and the necessary anti-pollution measures taken. This "Preliminary survey on industrial pollution" was an attempt to instruct companies and local public entities on planning the new construction and expansion of factories based on field surveys and on predictions of contamination drawn from both theory and experimentation.

The Law on Industrial Location Surveys and Related Matters was revised in October 1973, reaffirming the role of these preliminary surveys in locating factories with an eye to pollution prevention and strengthening the surveys both in content and systemically. Where pollution prevention was deemed necessary based on these surveys, the MITI Minister was empowered to designate certain districts, with due consideration of the opinions of the Industrial Location Water Council, to require local companies to submit pollution prevention reports and to make recommendations and issue orders as needed.

This use of the surveys required that forecasting accuracy be improved. MITI pursued the development of computerized simulations. In 1969 it began developing improved forecasting approaches to air pollution and in FY 1970 began doing the same with water quality. The 1970s also saw the development of methods to predict the impact of various contaminants, and these were absorbed into the preliminary surveys. In FY 1985, MITI began developing methods to formulate long-term air-management plans (LAMP) to make regional industrial development plans consistent with the preservation of the atmospheric environment. With "high-technology pollution" emerging as a new problem in the 1980s, MITI in FY 1986 created a database of hazardous substances data and usage manuals and decided to revise its environmental regulations according to need. The Law Concerning the Examination and Regulation of Manufacture, etc. of Chemical Substances ("Chemical Substances Control Law") was also revised in 1986 to promote further measures ensuring the safety of chemical substances. Investigations of the environmental impact of high-tech industries continued thereafter.

3.3.2 Power Supply Sites and the Implementation of the Assessments

The Cabinet Understanding, "Concerning environmental conservation measures related to public works projects," was approved in June 1972. MITI did not have jurisdiction over public works but it nevertheless decided to conduct Environmental Impact Assessments on new power-plant construction in the Power Supply Development Plan. The assumption was that these were large-scale developments that would have a significant impact. In July 1977 a MITI Departmental Council Decision was issued on "strengthening environmental impact surveys and environmental reviews of company locations," and in 1979 MITI solidified its plans for surveys and inspections and began carrying out administrative guidance. MITI would carry out environmental inspections after obtaining environmental impact reports from the power suppliers, and then would inform the public about the reports and seek the opinions of local residents, which were to be reflected in the measures ultimately adopted (Fig. 3. See Takeda 2011, p. 337).

The power industry took a cautious stance on the environmental assessment legislation that would establish uniform rules but actively cooperated with MITI's own assessments. In July 1979, however, the Special Committee on Environmental Problems of the Federation of Electric Power Companies raised two issues. First, local residents were concerned that acceptance of the environmental impact survey would inevitably mean approval of the power plant's construction, and this had made it impossible to conduct the surveys themselves; furthermore, certain groups of people had thereby been given a platform for insisting on a zero-impact plan. Second, there was concern that unlimited liability could be imposed on business operators despite the limitations of the forecasting methods. These concerns were consistent with the views that shaped MITI's cautious stance on the enactment of the environmental assessment legislation.

Some years later, in 1997, the Electric Power Supply and Demand Subcommittee of the Electricity Utility Industry Council compiled a report on the environmental impact assessments for power-plant construction. It explained that whereas the public works environmental assessment system required operators to create assessment reports while hearing the opinions of the relevant prefectural governors, power-plant assessments were handled differently. MITI undertook its inspections by utilizing the know-how of administrative inspectors and taking into account the expert opinion of the Environment Inspection Board and completed the inspection after comprehensive surveys had been conducted by the Environment Agency and the relevant prefectural governors in the Electric Power Development Coordination Council. The report pointed out that these inspections prioritized the regulatory system of the Electricity Utility Industry Law and that many exceptions were made to related laws and regulations, but judged the environmental assessments to have been appropriate, given the environmental conservation aim. The report gave particular praise to the fact that the power-plant assessment surveys were more extensive than those based on Cabinet decisions, and that the array of items subjected to predictive evaluation was broader than those of other countries. This latter fact was singled out as being

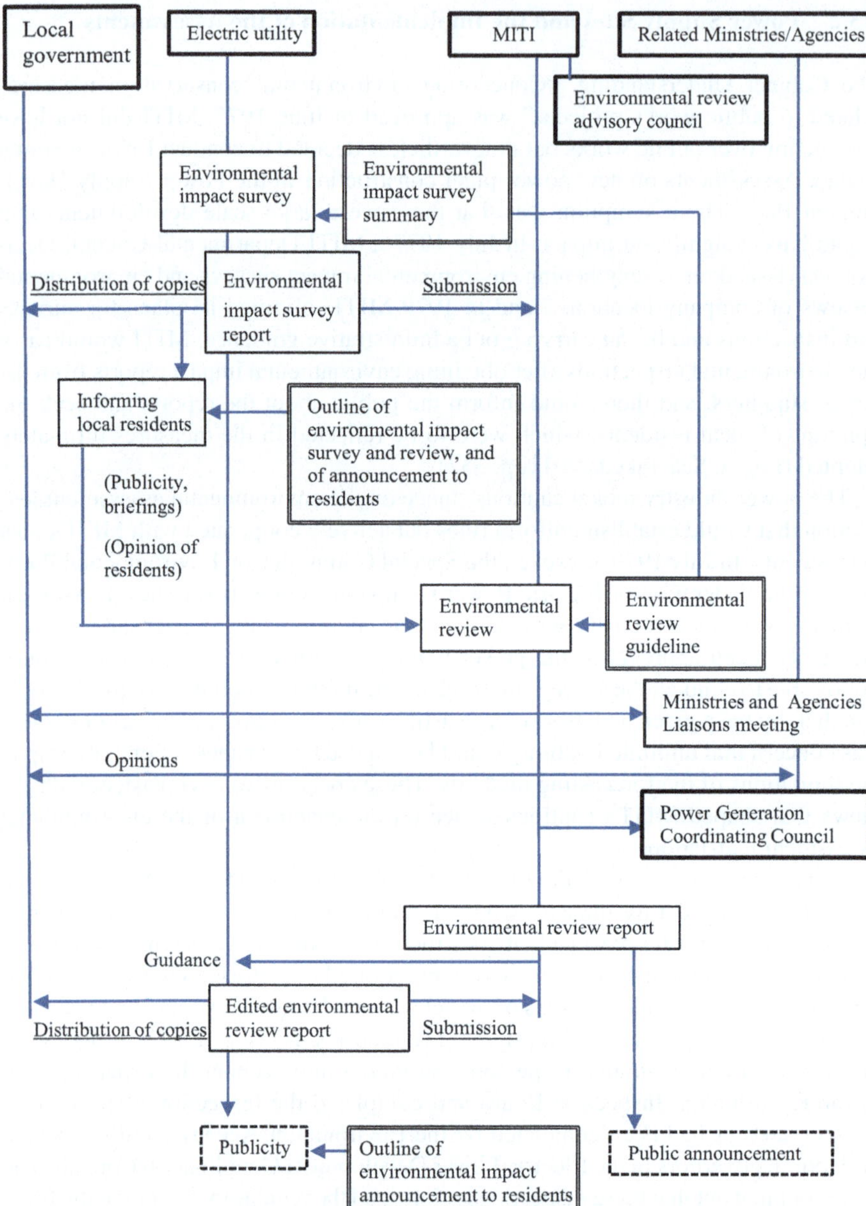

Fig. 3 Outline of the environmental inspection process for power-supply sites (Takeda 2011, p. 344)

particularly excellent. The power-plant assessments were reorganized so as to be included under the Environmental Impact Assessment Law.

3.3.3 Problems Concerning Environmental Assessment Legislation

Meanwhile, the December 1972 interim report of the Central Council for Environmental Pollution Control strongly urged the establishment of environmental assessments and the improvement of the assessment implementation system (Takeda 2011, p. 351). This gave rise to complications between the movement to legislate the assessments and the opposition to that legislation, which remained a political issue for a long time.

Industry was wary for several reasons. First, they feared that power-plant operators would be vulnerable to subjective judgments if the only matters mandated by law were the procedures themselves, and neither the items for evaluation nor the predictive methods had yet been established. Second, they were concerned that seeking and reflecting the opinions of local residents would unduly delay the development of the plants. Third, they argued that environmental impact assessments should be based on comprehensive evaluations of both economic and social impacts, including the effective utilization of land and improvements in public well-being.

In February 1975, MITI summarized the opposition to the Environment Agency's Environmental Impact Assessment Bill as follows: first, the environmental assessment items, forecasting methods, evaluation criteria, and other points in the draft bill were seen as extremely unclear, raising the concern that the burden on business could expand limitlessly based on local residents' demands; second, if the procedures for local residents' participation in siting public works and factories were regulated, that could mean that even a mere procedural error could subject the factory location plan to litigation. While submitting these objections, MITI meanwhile proposed at a May 1975 meeting of the Factory Location and Industrial Water Council that assessments be carried out based on the Factory Location Law. This proposal placed strong restrictions on participation by citizens. The two ministries' drafts of environmental legislation thus differed significantly on this issue.

In other words, following the Cabinet Agreement of 1972, Environmental Impact Assessments were carried out through ministerial administrative procedures, but there were no clear criteria stating which actions and what stages required assessments, and in particular, no procedures were in place for seeking opinions from local residents. Citizen participation was envisioned as a central element of the system, based on the judgment that systems were needed both for the plant operators to conduct self-assessments of the environmental impact and for citizen opinion to be heard.

Efforts were therefore made to establish a direction for the legislation, centered on the Environment Agency. A liaison council was established in 1976 composed of bureau directors from the Environment and National Land Agencies, MITI, and the Ministries of Agriculture and Forestry, Transport, Construction, and Home Affairs, but coordination among them proved difficult. In 1978, the effort to coordinate the various points of view was shifted to the Liberal Democratic Party (LDP), but submission of the bill was still considered premature in April.

The report submitted by the Central Council for Pollution Control in April 1979 said that the system of environmental impact assessments based on ministry and agency administrative guidance and regulations was generating needless confusion, that the variations in procedure were causing a lack of clarity, and that uniform rules were essential. The report therefore called for prompt legislation. The content of the suggested legislation, as compared with the Environment Agency's existing drafts, reflected the consultations that had taken place among the various government offices. Prime Minister Masayoshi Ohira showed strong motivation to enact legislation as suggested in this report. The draft bill of late April 1981 did not include power plants. This was a political decision, based on the opposition of the business world and of MITI to including them in the location assessment targets. However, the bill met with opposition from within the LDP and the exemptions drew the objections of the opposition parties, leading the bill to be scrapped in 1983 without deliberations. Although local governments requested legislation and the government considered resubmitting the bill in 1984, the LDP decided not to submit it for deliberations due to business concerns that lawsuits would multiply. Legislating environmental assessments remained a challenge.

The Environment Agency therefore called for administrative measures that would be based on the main points in the bill. A Cabinet Decision was taken on Implementation of Environmental Impact Assessments in August 1984, and the Environment Impact Assessment Outline was thereupon put in place (see Fig. 4).

In outline, the plants subject to assessment would be those that were either operated or licensed by the national government, that were large in scale, and that had a significant environmental impact, and the operators would create environmental impact statements, taking into account the opinions of the residents and the applicable governor and mayors.

Business operators were not subject to any binding authority, however, so it was expected that they would try to influence the views of residents and others. After nine years of expending enormous energy trying to produce a bill, the end result was that environmental assessments were handled administratively, based on a Cabinet Decision. MITI remained cautious about legislation and ultimately its thinking prevailed.

3.4 Strengthening Policies on Industrial Safety

3.4.1 Promotion of Security Measures for High-Pressure Gas

In the early 1970s, owing to advances in the petrochemical industry, the rules of the existing High-Pressure Gas Control Law were no longer compatible with actual

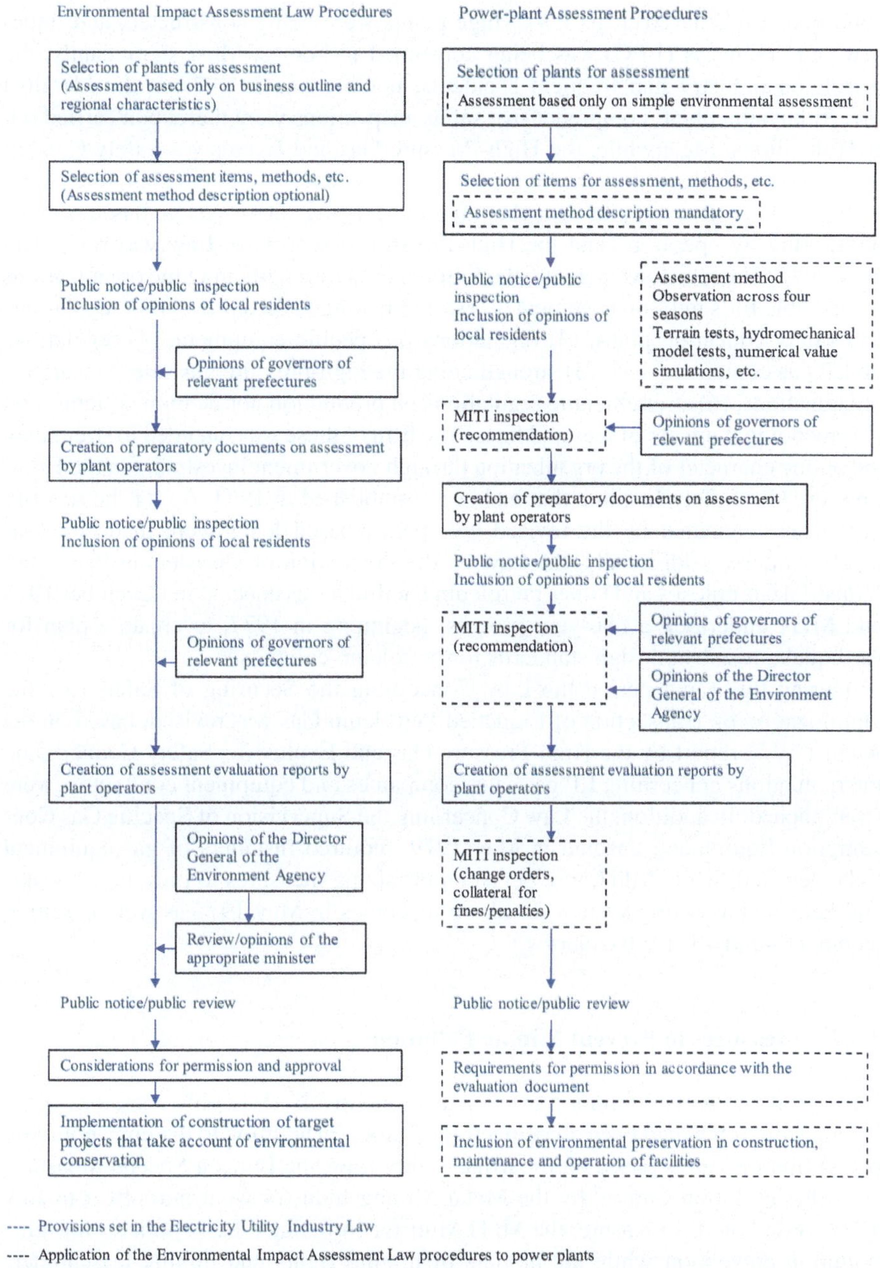

Fig. 4 Environmental Impact Assessment Law procedures and power-plant assessment procedures (Takeda 2011, p. 389). *Source* Environmental Protection and Industrial Location Bureau/Agency of Natural Resources and Energy, On the proposed bill to revise a section of the Environmental Impact Assessment Law and Electricity Utility Industry Law, March 19, 1997

conditions (Takeda 2011, p. 539). Huge plants were being constructed, and liquefied petroleum gas (LPG) was being consumed in homes. Most significantly, the petroleum industry had frequent accidents, notably one in 1973 at the Idemitsu Co., Tokuyama plant; comprehensive safety inspections were thereupon carried out at 16 facilities. Meanwhile, the High-Pressure Gas and Explosives Safety Council issued a report, "Regarding the high-pressure gas security system of the future" (July 1974), which presented plans for changing the existing safety system based on self-monitoring by operators, and the High-Pressure Gas Control Law was revised in May 1975. The revisions included the following: (1) strengthening the organizations responsible for safety management, (2) strengthening hazard prevention regulations and safety education plans, (3) regulations on specific equipment, (4) regulations on LP gas containers, etc., (5) strengthening the high-pressure gas safety insurance organizations, (6) strengthening regulations on production notification systems, and (7) amending the scale of fees and fines. The fifth of these was intended to strengthen the public character of the organization through government investment in the High-Pressure Gas Safety Institute that had been established in 1963. As for the security provisions mandated by the revised law, policy-based loans were made to business operators. Additionally, the Law on the Prevention of Disasters in Petroleum Industrial Complexes and Other Petroleum Facilities was enacted in December 1975 and MITI undertook a two-year process, beginning in 1977, to create a plan for earthquake-resistant design standards for petroleum complexes.

During this same period the Law Concerning the Securing of Safety and the Optimization of Transaction of Liquefied Petroleum Gas was revised, based on the August 1977 report by the High-Pressure Gas and Explosives Safety Council, and the regulations concerning LP gas sales companies and equipment contractors were strengthened. In addition, the Law Concerning the Supervision of Specific Gas Consumption Equipment, enacted in May 1979, required installers of gas equipment to be certified, while MITI, too, began emphasizing measures to prevent gas leaks, and launched a leasing system for alarm machines in May 1977 as well as setting technical standards for the alarms.

3.4.2 Measures to Prevent Mining Pollution

The urgent problem of pollution from metal mines involved not only operating mines but also mines that had been abandoned. Therefore, in addition to the mine pollution prevention measures based on the Mine Safety Law, the Law on Special Measures for Mine Pollution Caused by the Metal Mining Industry went into effect in July 1972. Based on this measure, the MITI Minister formulated basic policies for mine pollution prevention while the holders of mining rights and mining leaseholders formulated their own such plans, and the Metal Mining Agency of Japan (MMAJ) was to accumulate a funding reserve in order to cover the cost of operations to prevent pollution from abandoned mines (Takeda 2011, p. 617).

Meanwhile in 1970, the Mine Safety and Inspection Bureau (Department) had begun conducting a series of surveys of the abandoned heavy-metal mines that seemed in the most urgent condition. MITI took the survey results seriously and decided to establish a subsidy system in 1971 to assist with the costs of construction to prevent pollution at abandoned mines and also subsidized a portion of the costs of such construction at mines run by local public entities. In addition, the July report on the June 1974 inquiries to the Mining Industry Council titled "Policies on accumulated pollution from metal and other mines" said that the existing policies on "accumulated mining pollution" were inadequate and recommended the following concrete measures: (1) the national government should cooperate with local public bodies in cases where no one is responsible for eradicating the pollution, as, for example, at abandoned mines; (2) the financial burden of local public bodies should be greatly reduced; (3) where operators were unable to bear the costs, the national government should take that into account. In response, MITI expanded the mine pollution-control subsidy system for abandoned mines in FY 1973.

In FY 1975, MITI began implementing measures to reinforce metal mining, through guidance and support of design and management, either where the mines in question were large in scale and run by local public bodies, or where the construction required for pollution-prevention was on a very large scale or was technically problematic.

The August 1952 Extraordinary Law on Coal Mine Pollution Recovery and the June 1963 Law on Extraordinary Measures on Compensation Collateral for Coal-Mining Pollution (renamed in May 1968 as the Law on Extraordinary Measures for Compensation, etc., for Coal Mine Pollution) became the legal framework governing pollution policies pertaining to coal mining and was extended several times for 10-year periods. The reason for the extension was the difficulty in completing the process within the time stipulated by the long-term plan. Through its national surveys of the volume of mining damage, conducted over a two-year period beginning in July 1979, MITI ascertained that the mining damage was equivalent to the total mining damage in 1972, and it therefore extended the measures to facilitate pollution abatement. Based on the Coal Mining Council's February 1971 report, MITI aggressively pursued the early and final resolution of the cumulative mining damage. On the premise that rationalization and improvement in administrative and financial efficiency would be taken into account, MITI would undertake to implement the measures systematically and efficiently.

4 The Challenge of Stable Energy Supplies and the Development of Industrial Technology

4.1 *The Two Basic Laws on Oil*

4.1.1 Responding to the Oil Crisis

Prices of crude oil (Arabian Light) more than tripled in less than half a year in the first oil crisis that began in October 1973. This also triggered the transfer of the right to determine crude oil prices from the European and American oil majors to the oil-producing countries. Following the second oil crisis of January 1978, crude oil prices doubled between 1979 and 1981 due to price increases by the Organization of the Petroleum Exporting Countries (OPEC).

These crises made the stable supply and volume of energy a top priority and spurred interest in energy conservation measures and policies for introducing alternatives to petroleum. In the medium term, crude oil prices fell after OPEC lowered the official price by five dollars per barrel in 1983. The soaring price of crude oil had led non-OPEC countries to increase their production of oil, and Saudi Arabia abandoned its role as swing producer (adjusting production) in July 1985. In that sense, the policy question of how to address the crisis was temporary.

Nevertheless, the comprehensive energy policy system that had been developed to decrease Japan's dependence on oil exerted a significant influence on public policy. The policy had three pillars: (1) securing a stable supply of oil, (2) promoting the development and introduction of petroleum energy alternatives, and (3) promoting energy conservation. This represented a shift from the rapid-growth era's pursuit of "abundant, inexpensive, and stable" supplies to "securing a stable supply as the priority policy issue."

In other words, "energy security" (ensuring the stable supply of energy) became one of the so-called 3 E's of energy policy, along with "environment" (adapting it to the environment) and "economy" (utilizing the market principle). This remained the case into the twenty-first century.[4]

As mentioned earlier, the Natural Resources and Energy Agency, established as a MITI affiliate in the July 1973 organizational reform, played the role of promoting a unified energy policy. The organizational reform had been based on the Industrial Structure Council interim report, which had laid out the need for a comprehensive and integrated approach to (1) the expansion of the economy and concomitant increase in demand for energy resources; (2) the changing conditions of resource and energy supplies; and (3) the establishment of comprehensive natural resources and energy policies (Kikkawa 2011, p. 41).

---

[4]Takeo Kikkawa 2011. *Tsūsho Sangyō Seisakushi,* vol. 10 Natural Resources and Energy Policy highlights this point in particular. It was at the end of the 1980s that the emphasis was placed on the second E, "Environment."

4.1.2 The Two Basic Laws on Oil

The Kakuei Tanaka Cabinet, which decided on the Guidelines for Emergency Measures for Oil at the November 6, 1973 Cabinet meeting, called for conserving consumption. At the same time, it took up urgent legislation to prevent unfair profiteering and the spread of inflation due to piggybacking price hikes, and established the Petroleum Supply and Demand Optimization Law and Act on Emergency Measures for Stabilizing Living Conditions of the Public (the so-called Two Basic Laws on Oil) (Kikkawa 2011, p. 120).

The Law on Optimizing Oil Supply and Demand stated (1) that the Prime Minister, following on a decision by the Cabinet, would implement measures to deal with the shortage of oil supplies, and (2) that MITI, following on the said Cabinet decision, was responsible for notifying petroleum contractors of the oil supply targets and of the plans for the production, import, and sale of oil. The authority was given to the MITI Minister to make changes, if necessary; it was also declared that oil consumers should not use more petroleum than the quantities specified by Cabinet order. The MITI Minister was further given the authority to order the implementation of restrictions on sales methods in order to conserve the use of light oil, and likewise to order the sale and delivery of oil to oil dealers to ensure a "supply of petroleum to businesses and activities indispensable for the protection of the people's lives." In this way the government (MITI) was given powerful controlling authority, a reflection of the sense of crisis in the government and related organizations.

Although the emergency measures themselves were removed as of September 1, 1974, efforts to stockpile oil proceeded, and technological development was undertaken in energy-savings and new energy. This will be discussed in greater detail below. The Petroleum Reserve Law enacted in December 1975 required oil companies to maintain oil reserves.

The law was enacted in response to international obligations. The International Energy Agency (IEA), which was established in November 1974, required member countries to maintain petroleum reserves: private oil companies were required to maintain a 70-day stockpile of petroleum, and following the second oil crisis, that requirement was raised to 90 days' worth. Meanwhile, the Japan Petroleum Development Corporation Law was revised to become the Japan National Oil Corporation Law in June 1978 in order to enable national government organs to stockpile petroleum, with the Japan National Oil Corporation bearing responsibility for building the reserve. As demand for LPG rose in the 1980s, LPG reserves also began to be considered a priority, and in 1991, the Petroleum Reserve Law was revised to require private LPG importers to stock a 50-day supply of imported LPG.

The November 1976 Act on the Quality Control of Gasoline and Other Fuels required distributors to be registered and to carry out quality control measures. The Advisory Committee for Energy's Petroleum Subcommittee issued a report in December 1975 titled "About petroleum refining and sales" out of the desire to see the consolidation of primary distributors. Structural reform along these lines was sought because light-oil distribution companies were struggling, and the distribution of low-quality light oil was becoming a social concern. Thus, in the face of the challenge of the oil crisis, policy evolved from the adjustment of demand that accompanied legal measures, to long-term policy making aimed at a stable supply of energy, as for example in the June 1979 Act on the Rationalization of Energy Use.

4.1.3 "The Energy Stabilization Policy of the Showa 50 s [1975–1985]" Report

After the 1973 oil crisis, the first comprehensive examination on how best to implement energy policy was undertaken by the Coordination Subcommittee of the Advisory Committee for Energy beginning in February 1974 (Kikkawa 2011, p. 67). The subcommittee was tasked with considering (1) prospects for the primary energy supply in FY 1980 and FY 1985, and (2) international energy strategy and the securing of financial resources.

The interim report "Energy stabilization measures, 1975–1984" was compiled in August 1975, presenting the four pillars of energy stabilization policy: (1) reduction of dependence on oil and diversification of non-petroleum energy, (2) securing the stability of petroleum supply, (3) promotion of energy conservation, and (4) promotion of research and development of new forms of energy (see Table 7 below). MITI evaluated the measures on supply and demand as a whole and determined the desired allocation of energy conservation and of various supply capabilities from the point of view of achieving a stable supply of energy. This approach differed slightly from prior versions and represented a new philosophy aimed at securing a stable supply of energy through diversification of energy sources and energy conservation. The report was also notable for raising awareness that the cost burden of developing the

Table 7 Changes in domestic energy supply sources

	Primary energy source (%)						Total volume of energy supply
	Coal	Oil	Gas	Hydraulic power	Nuclear power	New energy sources, other	10 billion kcal
1965	27.0	59.6	1.2	10.6	0.0	1.5	168,909
1970	19.9	71.9	1.2	5.6	0.3	1.0	319,708
1975	16.4	73.4	2.5	5.3	1.5	0.9	366,224
1980	17.0	66.1	6.1	5.2	4.7	1.1	397,199
1985	19.4	56.3	9.4	4.7	8.9	1.3	405,323
1990	16.6	58.3	10.1	4.2	9.4	1.4	486,310
1995	16.5	55.8	10.8	3.5	12.0	1.3	543,909
2000	17.9	51.8	13.1	3.4	12.4	1.3	558,651
2005	20.6	49.8	13.9	3.0	11.4	1.3	565,087

Source Odaka (2013, p. 398)

Table 8 Changes in secondary energy distribution

	Secondary energy consumers %					Final consumption amount
	Manufacturing	Distribution and services	Transportation	Household costs	Non-energy uses	10 billion kcal
1965	62.5	7.4	17.6	9.9	2.7	108,537
1970	64.5	7.7	16.2	8.7	2.9	211,226
1975	59.3	9.6	18.4	10.2	2.5	251,083
1980	55.2	10.0	20.8	11.4	2.6	264,541
1985	51.2	10.7	21.8	13.6	2.7	270,545
1990	49.8	11.3	23.0	13.1	2.7	322,870
1995	47.3	12.2	24.1	14.1	2.3	358,795
2000	47.4	12.5	24.1	14.0	1.9	375,740
2005	46.3	12.7	24.5	15.0	1.4	369,975

Source Odaka (2013, p. 419)

oil stockpiles and new energy sources needed for a stable supply of energy would be borne by the beneficiaries.

Furthermore, in relation to downgrading the earlier policy aim of maintaining "low-cost energy," the report pointed out that keeping energy prices low over the long term would weaken the energy industry and thereby compromise the foundations of a stable supply of energy. It further noted that while other countries were beginning to relax their environmental regulations in order to promote energy conservation, one of Japan's national goals remained stronger regulation. In other words, it pointed to a number of contradictions among the various policies and called for consensus to be formed among the people as quickly as possible (Table 8).

4.1.4 The Basic Thrust of Comprehensive Energy Policy

On April 25, 1975, the Ministerial Council on Comprehensive Energy Policy was established to formulate comprehensive energy policies for the future, evincing the Cabinet's strong concern about the issue. The Council's mission was to unite the Cabinet ministers so as to enable formulation of the "Economic Plan for the first half of the Showa 60 s [second half of the 1970s]," which was already in its first year. Energy policy, as one of the underpinnings of the Economic Plan, needed to be considered, and decisions were required on the appropriate economic growth rate with due consideration for the resource and energy restrictions that had followed the oil crisis.

The Council focused most on the issues surrounding the creation of a central body for nuclear-power administration, created to "promote nuclear-power generation."

Having reviewed the Long-Term Energy Supply and Demand Plan and the interim report on comprehensive energy policy, the Ministerial Conference agreed on a policy outline titled "Basic direction of comprehensive energy policy" on December 19, 1975. The basic aim was "to advance a reduction in dependence on imported oil and the diversification of non-petroleum energy as the basis for securing a stable supply of energy." This rested on four conceptual pillars: (1) effective utilization of domestically produced energy and promotion of quasi-domestic nuclear energy, while diffusing the risk by diversifying Japan's overseas energy sources; (2) efforts to ensure the stable supply of oil, which would remain central to the energy supply for the time being; (3) promotion of energy conservation to reduce the demand-side burden on the energy supply; and (4) promotion of new energy development with a longer-term perspective extending beyond the 1980s. The following policies clarified the details: (1) developing domestic resources such as continental-shelf petroleum, hydropower and geothermal power, stabilizing domestic coal mining operations, and promoting LNG and overseas coal development and imports; (2) developing nuclear energy and improving the nuclear energy administration system; (3) strengthening the foundations of the petroleum industry and promotion of 90-day oil reserves; (4) securing the supply of secondary energy such as electricity and city gas; and promoting (5) energy conservation, (6) technology development, and (7) international cooperation. These constituted the government's long-term energy policy initiatives.

4.1.5 Formulation of an "Energy Strategy for the Twenty-First Century"

In August 1976, the IEA reviewed the energy conservation policies of each of its member countries and recommended prompt government implementation of energy conservation in concrete measures, with the necessary budget to fund them. MITI took the opportunity to point out the urgency of the matter: "If the current energy supply and demand structure remains unchanged, people's lives and industrial activities in this country will be extremely unstable with the risk of catastrophic dislocation in the future." The Ministry had begun preparing comprehensive measures for energy conservation in February 1976, and the Coordination Subcommittee's "Long-term vision of industrial structure" included the development of new energy as one of the conditions for realizing a "6% growth-rate economy."

However, although the Ministry sought to pursue policies for "escaping oil dependency," and although the Ministerial Conference, too, saw nuclear power as an important energy alternative to oil, public consensus was likely to be longer in coming. Because of the time involved in obtaining public approval, the electricity industry asked MITI to lower the goals for nuclear-power generation stipulated in the Long-Term Energy Demand and Supply Plan. Within 18 months of the plan's formulation, deviations from it were already under way.

MITI therefore decided to review the plan early in January 1977 and to begin formulating a long-term comprehensive energy policy adapted to the new international energy situation, and the Energy Supply and Demand Subcommittee of the Advisory Committee for Energy compiled the "Provisional prospects for the long-term supply and demand of energy" by June. On that basis, the Consultative Council on Fundamental Energy Issues issued an interim report, "Promoting a comprehensive energy policy that is consistent and effective," that strongly urged the importance of an effective comprehensive energy policy, based on funding and public agreement.

MITI meanwhile solidified its plans to add an Energy Diversification Temporary Measures Act and an Act on Temporary Measures to Promote Change in Energy Sources to the existing Energy Conservation Act (provisional names). The first of these focused on construction of power plants that were not fueled by oil and the second on diversifying industry's demand for energy. MITI regarded these as the "three basic laws on energy" and as the pillars on which to build a long-term energy strategy of reduced reliance on oil and increased savings and efficiency in energy use. Japan's dependency on imported oil dropped from 73.3% in FY 1975 to 57.1% in FY 1980.

About 14 months after the October 25, 1978, interim report, the General Affairs Committee of the General Energy Research Committee clarified the background to the framework described above and compiled a more detailed review of concrete measures in a report titled "Energy strategies for the twenty-first century." This report posed the basic issues as follows: on the demand side was the promotion of energy conservation policies, and on the supply side were (1) securing the stable supply of imported oil, (2) developing and introducing alternatives to petroleum and developing energy technologies, and (3) promoting the siting of power plants.

It also proposed concrete measures on developing and introducing petroleum alternatives (number 2 above), namely, the promotion of (1) nuclear energy development, (2) coal utilization, (3) introduction of liquefied gas, (4) domestic energy (hydro/geothermal), (5) power-source diversification. The emphasis was on the technological development necessary for developing and introducing petroleum alternatives.

Under the category of "developing new technologies," the first priority was promotion of the Sunshine Project: solar cooling, heating, and hot water supply systems (the so-called solar house) were almost ready for practical application, and the report called not only for evaluation and research on improvement through experiments in trial houses, but also other concrete measures such as the construction of solar thermal power pilot plants, and R&D in solar power generation and hydrogen energy technology. It also stressed the need for R&D on nuclear fusion and for international technical and economic cooperation on new energy and called for significant state funding to develop nuclear and new energy technologies.

Thus Japan's energy policy shifted its emphasis after the first oil crisis from promoting an oil orientation to pursuing a stable supply of energy, and from petroleum dependency to a departure from dependency. The new priorities remained following the second oil crisis of August 1979 (see Table 9).

Table 9 The long-term plan for energy supply and demand

		1973 Actual performance			Outlook August 1975			Outlook August 1979	
		FY1973	Converted value (unit:10^{12} kcal)	Composition ratio (%)	FY1985	Converted value (unit:10^{12} kcal)	Composition ratio (%)	FY1990	Composition ratio (%)
Domestic energy	General hydropower (10 K kw)	2,120	18	4.6	2,830	26	3.7	2,600	4.6
	Pump-storage power (10 K kw)	140			1,410			2,700	
	Geothermal (10 K kw)	3 (K kw)	0.06	0	210	4	0.5	730	1
	Domestic oil, Natural gas (10 K kl)	370	3.5	0.9	1,400	13	1.8	950	1.4
	Domestic coal (10 K tons)	2,168	14.4	3.8	2,000	13	1.9	2,000	2
	Subtotal		37	9.5		57	8		
Quasi-domestic energy	Nuclear power (10 K kw)	230	2.4	0.6	4,900	68	9.6	5,300	10.9
	Subtotal		39	10.1		125	17.6		
Imported energy	LNG (10 K tons)	237	3	0.8	4,200	56	7.9	4,500	15.6
	Coal (10 K tons)	5,800	45	11.7	10,240	80	11.2	14,350	9

(continued)

Table 9 (continued)

		1973 Actual performance			Outlook August 1975			Outlook August 1979	
		FY1973	Converted value (unit:10^{12} kcal)	Composition ratio (%)	FY1985	Converted value (unit:10^{12} kcal)	Composition ratio (%)	FY1990	Composition ratio (%)
	New fuel oil, new energy etc. (10 K kl)							3,850	5.5
	Oil (10 K kl)	31,800	296	77.4	48,500	449	63.3	36,600	50
	Subtotal		344	89.9		585	82.4		
Total primary energy			383	100		710	100		
Secondary energy oil conversion (100 million kl)		4.1			7.6			7.16	100

Source Kikkawa (2011, pp. 72–73, 78–79)

4.2 Electrical-Power Development and the Move Away from Oil

4.2.1 Changes in Demand for Electricity and Issues in Electrical-Power Development

The oil crisis triggered new hardships for the electric power industry. Multiple challenges struck simultaneously, including high crude-oil prices, sluggish demand for electric power, a decline in load factors, severe locational and environmental problems, and a sharp rise in financing costs.

Demand for power had been shifting from industrial (large- and small-scale electrical power) to civilian use (electric lights, electricity for commercial purposes) since the 1960s; from 1973–1985, demand for large-scale power decreased in textiles, chemicals, steel, other metals, and mining. The decrease was especially steep in such large consumers of power as the aluminum and ammonia industries. Meanwhile, the large-scale electricity usage by the machinery industry doubled, while demand in the commercial sector and for electric lights also grew steadily (Kikkawa 2011, p. 262).

The changes in electricity demand aggravated the problem of peak summer daytime hours. The load factor of each of the nine electrical power companies fell sharply in the first half of the 1970s and remained low thereafter. The decline in the load factor caused costs to skyrocket and worsened the performance of the power companies. Also contributing to their deteriorating performance was the rising cost of capital, due to soaring fuel costs and declines in the depreciation rates that covered them. Depreciation and amortization costs were the main internal collateral for the electric utilities, and the declining depreciation rate lowered their capacity to self-finance construction and thereby raised their reliance on interest-bearing debt such as corporate bonds and borrowing. Thus the cost of capital began to influence their performance.

As their performance declined, the utilities became unable to sustain a low-cost electricity supply. The nine utilities together raised their electricity rates three times in succession: in June 1974, June to August 1968, and February to April 1980. Hokkaido Power also raised its prices on its own in October 1981. The price hikes were not high compared to the increases in other public utilities, but customers nevertheless spoke of the end of low-cost electricity and the social antipathy to the rate revisions was strong.

Meanwhile, the environmental issues around power-plant location became more serious. From the 1970s into the early 1980s, the implementation of the Electric Power Development Coordination Council's development targets never exceeded the targets themselves. There were significant delays in deciding on locations for thermal power plants in the first half of the 1970s and for hydropower in the late 1970s into the 1980s, and consistently across the years in the case of nuclear power. The Three Mile Island nuclear power-plant accident in March 1979 had a particularly strong impact. In response to the delays of power development, the government adopted the Power Source Location Act and related measures in June 1974.

These included: (1) The Electric Power Development Taxation Law, which imposed a development promotion tax on general-purpose electric utilities, (2) the Law on Special Accounts for Electric-Power Development Acceleration Measures, and (3) the Law on the Development of Areas Adjacent to Electric Power-Generating Facilities, which provided grants for the improvement of public facilities near power-supply sites. These were all aimed at making the process of selecting locations for power plants a smooth one by eliminating the difficulties arising from the fact that any given power plant might bring little direct economic benefit to its immediate area. The policy was expanded in October 1971 with the establishment of a special subsidy system for power plant locations. Power-supply development thus lost some of its autonomy, instead becoming part of broader policy coordination efforts.

4.3 The Energy Conservation Act

Japan's total energy consumption rose almost consistently, but the rate of increase was lower than the rise in GDP, meaning that energy efficiency was advancing (Kikkawa 2011, p. 369). During this period, energy use changed from a 4:1:1 ratio of industrial, civil, and transportation sectors in 1973 to 4:3:2 in the early 2000s. This reflected the high efficiency of energy use in Japan's industrial sector, the result of post-oil crisis energy conservation policy.

The government established a national conservation campaign based in the Headquarters for the Campaign to Care for Our Resources and Energy following on an August 1974 Cabinet Decision taken in response to the first oil crisis. MITI, recognizing the need for energy conservation policy, also considered drastically expanding the existing Heat Utilization Law into an Act on Promoting the Rationalization of Energy. The Act called for targets for reducing unit consumption of energy and for drafting industry-specific implementation plans. The Act was strongly colored by the preference for control that arose out of the sense of crisis, and for this reason did not reach the Diet floor. But improvements in unit consumption were promoted through the special measures later taken in taxation (such as special depreciation of energy-saving equipment) and the creation of loan systems indicated in the basic guidelines of energy conservation policy.

"The need for and challenges of energy conservation policy," compiled in November by the new Energy Efficiency and Conservation Subcommittee in the Comprehensive Energy Research Committee, called for the following: (1) responding to the instability and high costs of energy by reducing the growth in energy demand as much as possible without substantially affecting the economic growth path, and (2) improving all sectors of economic society to orient them toward an energy-conserving model, and (3) promoting legislation and regulations for energy conservation. The Act on Promoting the Rationalization of Energy (Energy Conservation Act) was passed in June 1979.

The basic framework of the act included the creation of guidelines for the rationalization of energy use in factories, construction materials, and machine tools, and guidance when needed to ensure the implementation of the guidelines, but left out the measures with the strongest "control" aspects. The framework for implementing energy conservation policy, although premised on industry's making its own conservation efforts, was thus strengthened to include set guidelines for rationalization and measures for enabling guidance and recommendations to help achieve them.

4.4 Coal and Resources Policy

4.4.1 The Development of Coal Policy

Although domestic coal production shrank in the 1960s, coal's role as an energy resource did not decline. Imports of coking coal, which had rapidly increased in quantity before the first oil crisis, remained high in its aftermath, and imports of fuel coal sharply increased in the 1980s. The shift from domestic to overseas supplies of coal raised the need for structural adjustment policies for the domestic coal industry as the aim shifted from the industry's maintenance and rationalization to its gradual contraction. It also required maintaining a stable supply of overseas coal, and promoting the development and dissemination of clean-coal technology (Kikkawa 2011, p. 207).

Structural adjustment measures on coal began with First Coal Policy in 1963, and continued through eight stages until 2001. In the Third Coal Policy from 1967 to 1969, the target for domestic coal production target was set at 50 million tons per year, and even with promotion of the "Fluid Energy Revolution," various policy instruments were used to try to reach that target.

The Fourth Coal Policy (1969–1972) was the first not to set production targets, indicating that the shift toward the gradual contraction of and exit from the industry was under way. The production targets were revived in the Fifth Coal Policy of 1973–1976 but sharply scaled down to 20 million tons. The Sixth Coal Policy (1976–1982) modified the targets slightly upward due to the oil crisis, a level that was retained in the next stage (1980s).

Meanwhile, summit talks between Japan and Australia, which had an export ban, led to the launching of Australian coal exports to Japan. Japan also sought to stabilize its import supply by offering subsidies and technical cooperation to coal-producing countries (Table 10).

4.4.2 Mineral Resources Policy

The Mining Industry Council Subcommittee on Mining laid out the direction to be taken by policy on mineral resources in its June 1972 "Basic direction of future mining policy" (Kikkawa 2011, p. 235). This served as the foundation for exploration

Table 10 Outline of Coal Policies (IV–VIII)

	Period	Basic plan	Production target	Events
Fourth Coal Policy	1969–1973	Constructing a stable coal output/supply system; aiming for coal companies to restructure or to close if maintenance or restructuring prove too difficult	Scale not specified	Strengthening of anti-pollution measures Mine closures and concentration of mining operations
Fifth Coal Policy	1973–1976	Raising demand and expanding counter-measures in view of the risk that great social dislocation might follow on a sharp contraction in mining	Not less than 20 million tons	First oil crisis Beginning of general coal imports
Sixth Coal Policy	1976–1982	Utilizing coal as much as possible as part of a stable energy supply; maintaining domestic coal production and integrating of foreign coal imports	Over 20 million tons	Second oil crisis Decreasing gaps in prices
Seventh Coal Policy	1982–1986	Aggressively utilizing domestic coal in terms of both safety and the security; maintaining the volume of domestic coal production; supporting the achievement of autonomy in coal mining	Over 20 million tons	Plaza Accord Rising price gaps

(continued)

Table 10 (continued)

	Period	Basic plan	Production target	Events
Eighth Coal Policy	1986–1991	Avoiding concentrated closure, easing the impact on economy and employment, given that the competitive conditions with overseas coal are unlikely to improve, and that a changing role and gradual shrinkage are inevitable for domestic coal	Appropriate levels estimated at about 10 million tons total	End of cooperative agreement on steel industry purchases
Post-Eighth	1992–2001	Gradually reducing domestic coal production to achieve a balance between coal's declining economic role and the burden it imposes on the government, with the final stage of structural adjustment to take place in the 1990s	Specific levels not clarified	Closure of Mitsui Miike mine

Source Kikkawa (2011, p. 213)

and development of mining in close alignment with anti-pollution measures. The Act on Special Measures for Pollution Caused by the Metal Mining Industry was issued to address damage caused by abandoned mines. Reorganization of the Metallic Minerals Exploration Promotion Agency followed, with a 1973 expansion into the Metal Mining Agency of Japan (MMAJ). MMAJ became responsible for an overall policy on mineral resources resting on the following: (1) promotion of domestic exploration, (2) support for the development of overseas resources and cooperation with developing countries on resource development, (3) improvement of the rare-metal stockpiling system, and (4) prevention of mining pollution originating in abandoned mines.

MMAJ's predecessor had since 1964 been conducting detailed surveys of geological structures in order to identify the most stable sources of mineral resources and to discover superior mines. The surveys, which consisted of three stages—regional geological surveys, then detailed surveys, then corporate exploration—were carried out nationwide and are regarded as having achieved significant results. Nine of the survey cases resulted in the development or expansion of mines; the initial regional surveys led to the 1981 discovery of gold deposits in the Hokusatsu/Kushikino area of Kagoshima Prefecture, and became the Hishikari mine run by Sumitomo Metal Mining Co., Ltd.

The major policies for supporting the development of overseas resources included: (1) an overseas exploration financing loan system and debt guarantee system (implemented beginning in FY 1968), (2) overseas geological structure survey system (from FY 1968) and overseas joint geological structure survey subsidy system (from FY 1974), and (3) basic research on resource development cooperation. The overseas geological structure survey subsidy system was designed to subsidize up to one-half the expenses borne by Japanese corporations undertaking surveys in collaboration with foreign corporations. By FY 2005, 71 projects had been conducted under the overseas geological structure survey system and 42 projects under the subsidy system. The basic research was aimed specifically at enabling the government to support mineral-resources development in developing countries, with 180 regions in 46 countries surveyed by FY 2006. These policies for supporting overseas resource development have steadily achieved results.

4.5 *Large-Scale Industrial Technology Development and the "Sunshine" and "Moonlight" Projects*

4.5.1 An Emphasis on Basic Technology

In December 1974, the Agency of Industrial Science and Technology established the Research Group to Formulate Long-Term Strategies for the Development of Industrial Technology as a private advisory body of the director general. Its final report, "Technical development initiatives for the future" (National Institute of Advanced Industrial Science and Technology, ed., 1977), cited the importance of "cultivating basic abilities" both because "Japan has in the past been criticized for using the results of research undertaken by other countries free of charge" and in order to build a framework for following up on breakthroughs in research (Sawai 2011, p. 25). The research group's conclusions were passed on to its successor (Research Group on Long-term Planning of Industrial Technology Development), which was also established as a private advisory body of the director in September 1977. The interim report of August 1980 continued to point to the importance of "basic technology," leading to the launching of the Research and Development Project of Basic Technologies for Future Industries in October 1981.

The recognition that technical problems are not merely matters of technology but part of industrial policy as a whole, and requiring promotion as such, led to the establishment of the Industrial Technology Council, the 1973 successor to the Industrial Technology Commission. The "Progress report on new energy technology R&D," "Summary of promotion of new energy technology R&D," and "On ways of promoting new energy technology development," which were issued almost immediately upon the Council's establishment (in October and December 1973 respectively), produced results in the form of the Sunshine Project. The February 1975 report, "On ways of developing energy conservation technologies," was the occasion for the launch of the Moonlight Project in FY 1978. The interim report of August 1975, "On ways of advancing future industrial technology policy," presented the basic direction of industrial technical policies toward the late 1970s and explained that: (1) Since Japan's industrial technology had reached the level of that in Western countries, Japan could now make the shift from dependency on foreign technology to self-directed technological development, and that (2) whereas Japan's technological development had hitherto been more private sector-led than that in the advanced countries of Europe and America and had mainly focused on improving technologies introduced from overseas, the government's role of developing industrial technology would henceforth become increasingly significant.

4.5.2 The Large-Scale Industrial Technology R&D System

The Industrial Science and Technology Agency launched the National Research and Development Program ("Large-Scale Project") in 1966 (Sawai 2011, p. 130). Based on a November 1966 report by the Industrial Structure Research Advisory Council's Industrial Technology Committee in November 1963, it had been created to facilitate the shift from dependency to self-reliance in technological development, to carry out the government's leadership role in the process, and to formulate a plan for priority technology development and the promotion of research cooperation by industry, academia, and the government. The Large-Scale Project promoted 31 projects before being restructured in FY 1993. Its budget trended upwards until peaking at 16.8 billion yen in FY 1981. It was greatly reduced to 11 billion yen in FY 1984, and then leveled off to about the 15 billion yen level (Table 11).

The Large-scale Technology Subcommittee of the Industrial Technology Council and of the Subcommittee for each project (1) selected the projects and (2) formulated and evaluated plans for their R&D and implementation, while the Large-Scale Industrial Technology Committee (organized by the Agency of Industrial Science and Technology) selected the parties for outsourcing and carried out evaluation of the R&D.

Project leaders included researchers at the National Research Institute and the director and executive director of the Research Association for Mining and Manufacturing Technology. The candidate R&D themes were proposed by the original departments or the testing laboratory based on the needs of the public and of industry. Themes were then selected from among these proposals based on budget and other

Table 11 List of large-scale projects

Project Name	R&D period	R&D expenditure total (100 million yen)	Number of participating companies	Projects targeted for system evaluation	Number of domestic industrial property holdings	Number of foreign patents held
Ultra-high-performance computers	1966–1971	101	8	○	96	21
Desulfurization technology	1966–1971	27	15	○	31	10
New olefin production methods, etc.	1967–1972	12	8	○	7	1
Seawater desalination and byproduct utilization	1969–1977	67	7	○	34	0
Remote-controlled submarine deep-sea oil-drilling equipment	1970–1975	45	19	○	38	1
Electric cars	1971–1977	57	19	○	434	29
Pattern information-processing systems	1971–1980	220	10	○	436	28
Jet engines for aircraft Phase 1	1971–1975	69	3	○		
Resource recycling technology system Stage 1	1973–1975	13	10	○		
Automobile integrated control technology	1973–1978	73	11	○	50	
Direct steel-making with high-temperature gaseous reduction	1973–1980	137	16	○	44	12
Process for producing olefin from heavy oil	1975–1981	138	6	○	17	4
Jet engines for aircraft Phase 2	1976–1981	129		○	24	4
Resource recycling technology system Stage 2	1976–1982	113		○	271	44
Flexible manufacturing system using ultra-high-performance lasers	1977–1984	137	20		234	4
Deepwater oil-drilling systems	1978–1984	150	18	○	109	6
Optical application measurement control system	1979–1985	157	15	○	399	19

(continued)

Table 11 (continued)

Project Name	R&D period	R&D expenditure total (100 million yen)	Number of participating companies	Projects targeted for system evaluation	Number of domestic industrial property holdings	Number of foreign patents held
Production methods for basic chemicals made from carbon monoxide	1980–1986	105	17	○	218	18
Manganese nodule mining system	1981–1989	200	20	○	23	2
High-speed computing systems for science and technology	1981–1989	230	6	○	177	1
Automatic sewing systems	1982–1990	82	29	○	50	
Robots for hazardous environments	1983–1990	155	20	○	29	
Observation systems for resources exploration	1984–1988	109	13	○		
Integrated water-recycling systems	1985–1990	98	22		3	3
Interoperable database computer systems	1985–1991	76	9	○	24	13
Ultra-advanced processing systems	1986–1993	161	21		331	120
Production methods for high performance	1988–1996	97	24		97	1
Propulsion systems for hypersonic transport	1989–1998	280	3		79	6
Technology for deep underground development	1989–1996	77	16		35	19
	1990–1996	98	19		150	34
Applied technology for human sensory measurement	1990–1998	146	25			
Micromachining technology	1991–2000	167	27		495	65
Atomic and Molecular Manipulation Technology (Atom Technology)	1992–2001	139	23		85	23
		3865	479			

Source Sawai (2011, p. 132)

constraints, and a scrap-and-build approach was taken to maintain the projects and the National Research and Development Program as a whole.

The number of participating companies in the Large-Scale Projects came to 479 for a total of 31 projects. Eight of these companies participated more than 10 times. The main companies involved were in general electric manufacturing, general machinery, steelmaking, and the like.

A 1985 evaluation of the Large-Scale Projects by the General Coordination Department Development Program Office concluded that they had four advantages. First, the projects were not restricted by technical subject or field and important or urgently needed technologies could be developed. Second, the program enabled technological development that could not be done by the private sector because of the long lead time and excessive risks involved. Third, the links among industry, academia, and government were advantageous. Fourth, the projects could launch domestic implementation of international research cooperation in areas such as advanced robotics.

However, the evaluation also pointed out the need to respond to the changing environment by upgrading Japan's international standing, improving Japan's technological level, improving the R&D potential of Japanese companies, and raising social interest in advanced and basic technology. To do so, changes were needed in operational areas such as: (1) responding to internationalization, (2) research cooperation with other institutions and systems, (3) strengthening ties with industrial policy, (4) implementing intermediate evaluations, and (5) strengthening of the surveys of technical trends.

By field, the Large Scale Projects were as follows: in the petrochemical industry, "new production methods for olefin" (1967–1972) and "production methods for making olefin from heavy oil" (1975–1981); regarding the shortage of industrial water, "seawater desalination and by-product utilization" (1976–1977); in resource development, "manganese nodule mining systems" (1981–1989). Besides these, projects included: technologies such as "extreme work robots" (1983 to about 1990), expected to be useful in fields such as nuclear power and marine science and disaster prevention; and the first international joint-development project, "propulsion systems for hypersonic transport" (1989–1998).

4.5.3 The "Sunshine" and "Moonlight" Projects

Proposals on solar energy and hydrogen energy were submitted when the Industrial Technology Institute asked for Large-Scale Project themes in February 1973. Project budget limits and time constraints made it hard to pursue them within the Large-Scale Project framework. The Research and Development Office of the National Institute of Advanced Industrial Science and Technology therefore sought other approaches. The Sunshine Project was launched in August 1974 following the Industrial Technology Institute's report to promote research in solar, geothermal, hydro, and coal gas as part of the new energy developments being undertaken by the Institute (Sawai 2011, p. 246).

The Sunshine Project was conceived prior to the October 1973 oil crisis, and based on the philosophy stated in MITI's July 1973 New Clean Energy Technology Development Plan: "The Sunshine Project will replace existing petroleum-based energy systems with permanent clean energy systems by utilizing pollution-free and inexhaustible energy supplies such as solar energy, hydrogen energy and geothermal power.... It is an ambitious national technology development plan to develop the technologies necessary for overcoming the energy crisis that will be caused by depletion of oil resources by the year 2000."

The plan was advanced with the cooperation of the private sector, centering on the Sunshine Project Promotion Committee established in April 1974, but limits to this approach became apparent as the projects moved from the basic research stage to the launching of research at pilot plants. In April 1977, the task of implementing the work was consigned to the Electric Power Development Co. As the effort grew in scale, a more specialized organization became necessary, and the New Energy and Industrial Technology Development Organization (NEDO) succeeded to the role of the Electric Power Development Co.

With the second oil crisis of 1978–1979, the Agency of Industrial Science and Technology hoped that the Sunshine Project would make preliminary contributions to yield about 5% of the total energy supply by FY 1990 (the total at that time was 1.6%). R&D promotion was therefore accelerated. Financial support was provided based on the Law Concerning Promotion of Alternative Energy Development and Introduction of Alternative Energy of May 1980, which secured the budget under a special account.

"About new developments in the Sunshine Project," the August 1982 mid-term report of the Industrial Technology Trial/New Energy Technology Development Committee noted that there had been a gradual relaxation of oil supply and demand. That conclusion was based on the unchanged expectation that the supply of new energy would increase over the long term. Of particular importance was the emphasis on three methods of new power generation: solar power (including amorphous solar cells), which had high potential for practical application; liquefaction/gasification of coal; and large-scale deep geothermal heat. In other words, the emphasis shifted not to photovoltaic generation but to solar thermal power generation. NEDO decided to launch R&D on power amorphous solar cells in FY 1983. This thinking prioritized continuity in the Sunshine Project, but also showed that the sense of urgency tended to fade as energy supply/demand pressures eased (Table 12).

Meanwhile, plans were made for the Moonlight Project based on conservation measures put together by the Industrial Technology Institute in November 1977 and on the report compiled by the Energy Efficiency and Conservation Subcommittee (Sawai 2011, p. 259). The Large-Scale Projects on "waste-heat utilization systems technology" and "Magneto Hydro Dynamics, MHD power generation" were incorporated into the Moonlight Project in FY 1978, its first year. The same year also saw the launching of a new "high-efficiency gas turbine" project. The National Research Institute was in charge of carrying out basic research, while private sector companies directed the systems development. Project implementation took many forms. Before

Table 12 Budgets related to the Sunshine Project (*Unit* = 100 million yen)

Fiscal year	Solar energy	Geothermal energy	Coal energy	Hydrogen energy	Comprehensive research	International cooperation	Other	Total	Special account portion	Coal portion
1974	873	560	435	332	195		46	2,441	172	172
1975	1,091	1,138	857	463	250		156	3,955	253	253
1976	1,419	1,552	912	454	295	18	266	4,916	289	289
1977	1,463	2,563	1,005	520	275	18	335	6,179	1,291	283
1978	2,013	3,181	1,441	590	308	34	562	8,129	2,627	418
1979	3,768	3,548	2,902	690	345	49	634	11,936	4,876	2,507
1980	9,545	8,006	8,552	951	551	679	365	28,649	21,526	7,733
1981	7,961	9,223	13,514	948	1,233	668	112	33,659	26,727	12,634
1982	8,711	9,492	20,637	923	1,067	674	132	41,636	35,414	19,889
1983	8,928	8,248	22,771	492	775	716	77	42,003	36,619	22,059
1984	8,897	6,885	22,411	289	768	71	487	39,809	36,158	21,821
1985	9,169	7,336	25,654	256	663	71	627	43,776	40,754	25,093
1986	8,241	5,976	27,061	227	532	72	102	42,211	39,833	26,562
1987	7,556	5,092	28,794	192	693	66	63	42,456	40,445	28,374
1988	7,471	5,390	22,433	149	496	66	39	36,045	34,456	22,107
1989	6,965	5,383	24,792	121	379	62	113	37,814	36,613	24,486
1990	7,324	5,378	24,901	108	1,784	61	32	39,590	3,869	24,635
1991	7,465	5,237	11,263	107	646	68	30	24,816	24,006	11,037
1992	6,988	4,902	13,281	120	1,084	65	30	26,470	25,779	13,085

Source Sawai (2011, pp. 251–252). Original documents for years up until 1984 are from "Sunshine Plan: The first 10 years"; data on the years after 1984 refer to each year's edition of "The Industrial Technology Institute Yearbook." Totals for 1987, according to Minoru Sawai, were "425,455 million yen." This is obviously an error

NEDO's establishment in May 1980, the Agency of Industrial Science and Technology directly entrusted implementation to companies in some cases, and in others to Technology Research Associations that it organized.

Research on waste-heat utilization technology, for example, relied on the former approach, and development of a high-efficiency gas turbine the latter. The structure of the Moonlight Projects rested on the following six pillars: (1) large-scale energy conservation measures, (2) the development of leading basic energy-conservation technology, (3) international research cooperation efforts, (4) the establishment of and surveys on methods to achieve comprehensive effectiveness in energy-conservation technologies, (5) assistance to private-sector corporate development of energy-conservation technology, and (6) standardization of energy conservation. The first of these included the "New Battery Electric Power Storage System" project (total budget 17.5 billion yen) of 1980–1991 for R&D on storing off-peak electric power in a new kind of battery and then discharging that power during peak hours so as to equalize the load on the system (Table 13).

4.5.4 Grants to the Private Sector for Technology Development

The Industrialization Test Grant system was established in 1975 to provide grants and subsidize part of the expenses incurred by private enterprises for research and development for important technologies (Sawai 2011, p. 295). Priority technology subsidies had been expanding with the growth of additional subsidies for large-scale core technologies, but the budget decreased year by year in the 1980s. In FY 1988, the "priority technology subsidies" were abolished because of steady improvement in corporate technological capability and the extension of the R&D outsourcing system promoted by the government in forms such as the Large-Scale Projects.

Even with the shrinking of "priority technologies," however, various subsidy systems were created in the 1980s, including the Subsidy System for Practical Development of (non-petroleum) Alternative Energy Technology (FY 1980), the Subsidy System for Practical Development of New Power Generation Technology (FY 1981), the Subsidy System for Industry Revitalization R&D Expenditures (FY 1983), and the Subsidy System for Practical Development of Technology for the Rationalization of Energy Consumption (FY 1983). However, because subsidy policies during these years tended to face review or elimination in response to international criticism, the FY 1996 Subsidy System for the Development of Technologies for Creating New Industries suggested reevaluating their effectiveness as tools for addressing the urgent need to generate new industries.

Meanwhile, based on the Law on Research Associations for Mining and Manufacturing Technology (May 1961), the Mining and Industrial Technology Research Association System addressed the issue of efficient utilization of human and financial resources in research through joint experimental research on industrial production technology (Sawai 2011, p. 312).

Table 13 Budget related to the Moonlight Project (*Unit* = 100 million yen)

FY	Large-scale energy saving	Basic technology for energy conservation	International research cooperation	Surveys on establishment of energy saving technologies	Subsidies for development of private energy conservation technology	Standardization of Energy Conservation	Surveys on energy conservation software technology	Other	Total	Special accounts portion
1978	1,185	114	11		451	37		180	1,978	0
1979	1,936	117	26		452	46		399	2,976	205
1980	6,929	202	35		467	57	9	78	7,777	4,655
1981	8,316	208	16		467	56	14	86	9,163	6,207
1982	8,474	198	5	11	669	49		84	9,491	6,466
1983	8,729	186	22	11	527	42		75	9,589	7,145
1984	8,809	233	22	10	438	39		78	9,629	8,052
1985	10,464	227	20	69	195	32		140	11,146	9,761
1986	11,815	195	25	88	123	23		58	12,326	11,300
1987	10,495	172	27	151	119	22		493	11,479	10,719
1988	9,098	154	35	7	236	21		408	9,957	9,271
1989	10,109	155	95	6	360	5		9	10,739	10,118
1990	10,978	102	171	5	303	4		8	11,572	11,035
1991	11,326	100	192	20	253	3		7	11,902	11,404

Source Sawai (2011, pp. 262–263)

The plan was to give such associations corporate status in order to promote collaborative research by industry. The associations operated on a philosophy of mutual aid.

This method was also used in the framework of Large-Scale Projects and Important Technologies, and many research associations were established by the year 2000. The pace of association establishment weakened from the 1990s on, however. A policy document prepared by the Legal Review Committee in April 1993 stated that "technical innovations by companies were rather more hindered than otherwise by collaborative research" and called for a "review of the National Research Institutes, especially of the regional laboratories" and "reviews of the Large-Scale Projects and other R&D by Research Associations and expansion of the subsidy system for industry-university collaborative research."

The special tax measures for promoting R&D included the Increased Research and Research Tax Deduction System established in 1967. This was a tax deduction for a certain percentage of expenses exceeding the previous highest R&D expenditures. A 1973 revision added support for expenses for advanced technical training related to computers and information processing. In FY 1985, the Tax Program for Promoting R&D in Basic Technologies (high-tech taxation system) further extended this system. Tax deductions were recognized for the depreciable assets needed by corporations to conduct test research if they met certain requirements. The Special Tax Credit System for Test Research was established in 1993, making tax deductions permissible in order to promote public and private research and research on innovative environmental technologies.

The Japan Development Bank ("the Bank") established a long-term, low-interest loan system in 1968 to finance new domestic technologies and the promotion of businesses for new products and the commercialization of products.

In March 1980, the financing system was expanded based on the Industrial Structure Council's "Industrial policy of the 1980s." What the Bank had called "financing to turn new technologies into businesses" became "loans for new technology development." The Bank also made improvements such as adding infrastructure construction and acquisition to the targets for financing loans with the goal of "business development" as a preliminary step in corporate planning. Also, in FY 1985, it added funds for technological development (financing for non-equipment uses) to the financing for general corporate technology development ("new technology development").

However, industrial technology promotion lending amounts provided by the Bank declined sharply after peaking at 92.8 billion yen in FY 1992. This was in part because companies expanded their own financing and diversified the sources, both domestic and international, of their funding, but it is also true that the Bank came under pressure to review its traditional policy methods.

4.5.5 Patent Law Revision

The four industrial property rights laws regulating Japan's intellectual property system (Patent Law, Design Law, Trademark Law, Utility Model Law), fully revised in 1959 (effective in 1960), provided the foundation of the subsequent framework. Nevertheless, the rapid increase in applications accompanying rapid growth made it difficult to respond promptly enough either in granting accurate rights or in aligning them internationally. The patent law was revised in 1970 and again in 1975 and 1978, and further reforms took place after 1980 (Nakayama 2013, p. 199).

The 1970 revision began with the 1st Industrial Property Legislation Revision Deliberation Council held in December 1962. The Council put together a report in July 1965 and urged that a revised law be submitted to the Diet, but the proposal was scrapped without substantive deliberations.

In November 1966, the Industrial Property Council was once again consulted and discussion continued. The Council again made a report in November 1968, and in May 1970, the Partial Amendment of the Patent Law was passed. Amendment of the review system, including the adoption of a non-examination system, came under discussion but was not realized, and it was in the 1993 revision that a simplified examination method was adopted in the utility model system. Meanwhile, large institutional measures for prompt vesting of rights, such as the introduction of the Early Publication System and of the Examination-on-Demand System, have promoted large institutional measures toward early vesting, and practical improvements were made for speeding up the appraisal and appeal process and for clarification, including time limits for amendments and the introduction of pre-assessment reviews in cases of appeals after patent refusals.

Moreover, because of the gains Japan made in technical capability due to rapid growth, patents on chemical substances were considered necessary for protection, and the argument was gaining strength that non-patent status could itself be motivating.

Three areas gained access to patents as a result of these changes: inventions of chemical substances, inventions of foods and beverages or of flavors, and pharmaceutical inventions or inventions of manufacturing methods whereby two or more existing pharmaceuticals are combined to make one new one. The multi-claim system permitted multiple patent claims for one invention, and was in use in many countries. However, Japan had been using a single-claim system—one patent per item invented—ever since the patent law of 21 years earlier. While the Industrial Property Council had discussed reexamining the question, as mentioned above, its deliberations were not reflected in the system's revision, but because members of the 1970 Patent Cooperation Treaty (PCT) were required to adopt the multi-claim system, Japan was forced to consider its introduction. In other words, ratification of the PCT challenged Japan to adopt a multi-claim system for the sake of international coordination and the harmonization of the international system as a whole.

Trademark law was also amended in 1975 (Nakayama 2013, p. 243). This was first because the number of applications for trademark registration had by 1973 increased by 5.3 times its level in 1960, the year the law came into effect. Second, Japan was considering joining the Trademark Registration Treaty (TRT), which created an international registration system for trademarks, and shortening of the application process was indispensable for that purpose. The "report on the revision of the trademark system" compiled by the Trademark Subcommittee of the Industrial Property Council System Reform Committee in December 1974 emphasized that the rapid processing of the trademark application system was the most urgent task of trademark administration and that in addition to requiring legal reform and improvements in the operation of the system, the government should ask industry for cooperation in, for example, adopting self-restraint when submitting applications for registrations that are not immediately needed. There were four main revisions of the law, including revisions to the regulations on renewal registration. Attempts were made to speed up the process.

5 Policies to Address Structural Depression in Basic and Consumer Industries: The Large-Scale Retail Stores Law and Small and Medium-Sized Enterprises

5.1 Policies on Industrial Structure Adjustment (The Industry Stabilization Law and the Law on the Structural Improvement of the Textile Industry)

5.1.1 Law on Temporary Measures for the Stabilization of Specific Depressed Industries

Japanese economic growth had been sluggish since the first oil crisis in 1973, and it was during this period that the issue of "structurally depressed industries"—those whose capacity utilization rates and profitability were low over the long-term—became apparent. MITI considered various countermeasures to the problem in new policies targeted for FY 1978, and in December 1977 Prime Minister Takeo Fukuda, recognizing the need for legislation, directed the government to enact or amend the relevant laws. MITI focused on policies to scrap excess capacity and announced a bill in January 1978 (Imuta and Washizawa 1993, p. 23). Its main points were as follows:

(1) The competent minister, with reference to the opinion of the Industrial Structure Council, will prepare a basic stabilization plan for the structurally depressed industries defined by this law, that will stipulate how facilities are to be scrapped in a planned manner and how joint projects are to be undertaken.
(2) In the event that the scrapping of facilities stipulated in this plan does not progress smoothly, the competent minister shall consult the Industrial Structure Council and direct the relevant business entities in the specified industry to undertake jointly the scrapping of plants (mandated cartel).
(3) The competent minister, taking into account the opinion of the Industrial Structure Council, may impose limits or prohibitions on outsiders (those not participating in the mandated cartel) regarding the establishment of new facilities.

(4) Exceptions to the Antimonopoly Law will be made as appropriate to exclude mergers and business transfers in the case of the mandated cartels of businesses belonging to the structurally depressed industry under consideration. In this case, approval of the mandated cartel and mergers must be made in consultation with the Fair Trade Commission.
(5) The State will establish a credit fund for structurally depressed industries, to offer credit guarantees on loans and facilitate the financing needed to implement the scrapping of facilities in accordance with the basic stabilization plan.

As can be seen, the proposal gave MITI great authority, stipulating that the competent minister could issue directives to the relevant industries regarding joint actions such as the scrapping of facilities, and in some cases could prohibit capital investment in such industries, impose fines, and authorize exceptions to the application of the Antimonopoly Law for certain joint actions and mergers.

The Japan Fair Trade Commission ("Fair Trade Commission [FTC]") strongly objected to these proposals. This led to the deletion of the portions on prohibitions of new investment, penalties, and exceptions to the Antimonopoly Law, by decision of the Chief Cabinet Secretary. The resulting Law on Temporary Measures for Stabilization of Designated Depressed Industries ("Industry Stabilization Law") was enacted in May 1978.

The Industry Stabilization Law was intended to be in effect only until 1983. The depressed industries designated by the law were the targeted manufacturing industries: open-arc furnaces, aluminum smelting, synthetic fibers, and shipbuilding. The competent minister prepared a stable basic plan for each designated industry, and established the scrapping method for each case. Instructions for joint action were excluded from application of the Antimonopoly Act with the consent of the FTC. A Trust Fund for Designated Depressed Industries by the Japan Development Bank and private sector investment provided loan guarantees for scrapping facilities (Table 14).[5]

5.1.2 Structural Improvements in the Petrochemical Industry

The oil crisis had a serious impact on the chemical industry and the basic materials sector. The soaring price of naphtha (crude gasoline), which was the main raw material of basic chemistry, pushed down both exports of and domestic demand for major chemical products, leading to growing concerns about overcapacity. From the latter 1970s to the 1980s, therefore, policy became concerned with the scrapping of industrial facilities and the improvement of the industrial structure (Yamazaki 2011, p. 60). Meanwhile, the soaring price of crude oil spurred energy-saving investment

[5]Fourteen industries were designated under this law, and the scrapping of facilities was carried out almost according to schedule. A statistical examination of the effects on profitability and productivity for 886 companies in the mining and manufacturing sector shows that the companies covered by the Industry Stabilization Law yielded greater profitability and productivity increases than those that were not, although the statistical difference remained inadequate.

Table 14 The enforcement status of the Industry Stabilization Law

		Special depressed industry designation	Facilities to be processed (handled/scrapped)	Capacity before processing (1000 tons)	Volume processed (1000 tons)	Ratio (%)	Amount to be processed after plan revision (1000 tons)	Ratio (%)	Amount processed as of the end of 1982 (1000 tons)	Achievement rate (%)	Joint action
Open-arc furnace		1978 7.4	Open-arc or electric furnace	20,700	2,850	13.7	2,850	13.7	2,730	95.4	None
Aluminum smelting		1978 7.4	Electric furnace	1,642	530	32.3	930	56.6	899	96.7	None
Synthetic long-fiber nylon		1978 7.4	Spinning machines	367	72	19.5	74	20.3	73	98.1	Some → None
Textiles	Polyacrylonitrile staple fibers	1978 7.4	Spinning machines	431	73	17.0	85	19.7	96	112.5	Some → None
	Polyeter long fibers	1978 7.4	Spinning machines	350	37	10.5	45	12.8	37	81.5	Some → None
	Polyster short fibers	1978 7.4	Spinning machines	398	68	17.0	78	19.7	71	90.2	Some → None
Ship-building		1978 8.29	Slipways or docks	9,770	3,400	34.8	3,420	35.0	3,580	104.7	None
Alloy iron	Ferro-silicone	1978 11.10	Electric furnaces	487	100	20.5	100	20.5	100	100.0	None
Chemical fertilizer	Urea	1979 1.23	Synthesis, decomposition, granulation plants	3,985	1,790	44.9	1,790	44.9	1,670	93.3	Some

(continued)

Table 14 (continued)

		Special depressed industry designation	Facilities to be processed (handled/scrapped)	Capacity before processing (1000 tons)	Volume processed (1000 tons)	Ratio (%)	Amount to be processed after plan revision (1000 tons)	Ratio (%)	Amount processed as of the end of 1982 (1000 tons)	Achievement rate (%)	Joint action
	Wet-process phosphoric acid	1979 1.23	Reaction plants, filtration plants	934	190	20.3	190	20.3	174	91.6	None
	Ammonia	1979 1.23	Raw material for gas production, purification, synthesis plants	4,559	1,190	26.1	1,190	26.1	1,190	100.0	Some
Textiles	Cotton spinning, etc.	1978 12.18	Spinning frames	1,204	67	5.6	67	5.6	52	77.9	None
	Worsted spinning, etc.	1978 12.18	Spinning frames	182	18	10.1	18	10.1	18	96.2	Some
Cardboard	Containerboard	1979 4.14	Paper machines	7,549	1,147	15.2	1,147	15.2	1,083	94.4	Some

Source Okazaki (2012, pp. 38–39)

and technological innovation, along with the diversification of raw fuel. Under these circumstances, the chemical industry from the 1970s to 2000 shifted the composition of its shipments away from bulk chemicals to fine chemicals.

Meanwhile, in November 1976, MITI organized a study group on the international competitiveness of the petrochemical industry in order to put together the necessary measures concerning it. The final report of July 1978 called for (1) strengthening the petrochemical companies' negotiating position on the price of the raw material naphtha, (2) improving the structure of purchases, for example by turning naphtha imports into a jointly operated business, and (3) diversifying the raw materials used by the industry The second of these led in September 1978 to the establishment of seven chemical ethylene centers by the Petrochemical Feedstock Importing Co. (PEFIC).

With the second oil crisis, the Japan Petrochemical Industry Association made structural improvements based on the final report (January 1981) of the Raw Materials Research Association that was established in October 1979. This will be described in Chap. 3.

5.1.3 Structural Improvements in the Textile Industry

The 1967 Law on Extraordinary Measures for the Structural Improvement of Designated Textile Industries (Structural Improvement in Textiles) was due to expire in June 1974, and the need to consider further policy measures therefore came to the fore (Matsushima 2012, p. 23). In response to consultations with the Textile Industry Council and the Industrial Structure Council in October 1972, a report titled "On textile industry policy in the 1970s" was compiled in October 1973. The report said first that given the signs of change in the international environment (textile industry growth in developing countries), Japan must change its traditional method of relying on lower production costs to enhance competitiveness and instead seek to make higher-value-added products. The trends in demand suggested that luxury, diversification, and individualization were progressing due to rising personal income, but that none of these was expected to increase total demand. The report pointed out the importance of an accurate grasp of information on consumers and of the means of responding to them.

Second, with regard to the Structural Improvement in Textiles Law, the scrapping of excess capacity and the modernization of facilities were still considered necessary tasks. Third, regarding the industry's new trend of responding to environmental changes, the report pointed out the growth of the apparel manufacturing industry and the related fashion industry. In sum, the report located the future of the textile industry not in the pursuit of modernization (in other words, the merits of scale), but rather in knowledge-intensity. This required (1) strengthening information-gathering about consumers, (2) strengthening product development, (3) strengthening inventory management and sales functions, (4) collaborating naturally among industries and processes, and (5) modernizing and rationalizing logistics systems.

The Special Textiles Law was partially revised based on the report, and its name changed to the Law on Extraordinary Measures for the Structural Improvement of the Textile Industry (Textile Law). It was put into effect in May 1974 for a five-year period. Whereas the Special Textiles Law had targeted just four industries, the new law was designed to cover all the textile industries and international competitiveness was removed as one of the aims of the Law. The Law was characterized in particular by its promotion of "the development of new products and/or new technologies" and modernization in order to enable the sound development of the industry. In addition, the Minister was to establish guidelines for structural improvement, assuming the existence of an intra-industry knowledge-intensive group to serve as the business entity. This group would itself formulate a Structural Improvement Program, such as the development of new products, in accordance with the guidelines, and obtain the approval of the Minister. The Textile Industry Rationalization Agency had been established on the basis of the Special Textiles Law and was responsible for purchasing facilities, financing and lending, guaranteeing debt, and other measures. The promotion of new product development was now added to its tasks.

The outlook for the industry under the Textile Law was not necessarily convincing to policymakers or industry. Pressures from imports were increasing, and the textile industry and the small- and medium-sized spinning industries that felt the greatest impact were intensifying their calls for import restrictions. The Bureau of Lifestyle and Industry set up a private advisory body known as the Textile Issue Discussion Group in September 1975 and searched for an appropriate response to the problem. Its November report, "On immediate measures for textiles," pointed to (1) import problems, (2) structural improvement problems, (3) distribution problems, and (4) industry efforts related to year-end financial problems and the need for policy measures. In response, the Textile Industry Council issued its own proposals in its December 1976 "Recommendation on the new textile industry" to the Minister.

The recommendations were intended to adhere to the fundamental direction of the Textile Law while providing thoroughly detailed plans for: (1) clarifying consumer trends, (2) strengthening vertical linkages, (3) emphasizing the apparel industry, and (4) facilitating a smooth transition. These issues were specified in order to reflect the underlying thinking that Japan would not resort to imposing limits on trade because to do so would inevitably undermine Japan's position as a trading nation.

Specific measures for carrying out these recommendations were not immediately developed. Even so, against a backdrop of rising import pressures, policies on cartel-based production and pricing coordination, and zero-interest financing of purchasing funds for excess capacity were advanced in 1979. In addition, based on the Industry Stabilization Law of May 1978, the synthetic textiles industry proceeded with disposing of its excess capacity.

With the expiration of the Textile Law on the horizon, the Textile Industry Council and Industrial Structure Council issued a report in November 1978 titled "On the future improvement of the structure of the textile industry" (Yamazaki 2011, p. 52). On the premise that economic recovery was not going well, that domestic and international environmental requirements were changing, and that the textile industry in general was obviously experiencing excess capacity, the report urged that the textile industry should take the path of: (1) promoting the consolidation of know-how, (2) developing the apparel industry, (3) collaborating on production and distribution, and (4) correcting the excessive competitiveness that characterized the industry. In concrete terms, it suggested that the Textile Law be extended by another five years. The tasks that had been planned when the law first went into effect had basically been followed, and more time was needed for complete implementation of the framework, but the emphasis of the 1979 revision was to shift to promotion of the apparel industry. Based on these revisions, for example, the Textile Industry Structure Improvement Business Association (formerly the Textile Industry Rationalization Agency) established the Apparel Industry Promotion Center and promoted various measures, including development of human resources.

5.1.4 Structural Improvement of the Pulp and Paper Industry

The Industrial Structure Council issued a committee report on the pulp and paper industry in October 1972, titled "The paper and pulp industry in the 1970s," designating the following as policy issues with respect to this industry: shifting away from polluting industries, implementing measures to address resources, improving the supply system and the composition of companies, facilitating distribution, and other issues (Matsushima 2012, p. 131).

The need to resolve the water-pollution problem arose because of the damage to fisheries in 1958 caused by wastewater from paper pulp factories. The resource issue was that, although raw materials were plentiful in the early 1970s, demand was predicted to increase rapidly in the 1980s, meaning that measures to secure overseas resources would be important. It was recognized that Japan would need to participate in the development of resources overseas, through afforestation projects, for example, and to promote the shift of production to locations overseas. Issues such as the composition of firms were related to improving international competitiveness in the face of increasing paper and pulp imports. Many companies were small in scale and struggled chronically with overcapacity, because the paper and pulp industry had not yet been able to secure the advantages of scale. It was therefore necessary to consolidate the investment entities and rationalize investment in capacity, and at the same time, because demand was beginning to diversify, to facilitate distribution.

However, as a result of the two oil crises, the pulp and paper industry experienced an increase in energy costs and a decline in demand (meaning a structural downturn). The Industrial Structure Paper and Paper Industry Committee, in its March 1981 *Pulp and Paper Industry Vision for the 1980s*, singled out the following needs: (1) to effect structural improvement, (2) to change management awareness, and (3) to achieve a stable supply of raw materials. The highest priority in structural improvement was placed on the problem of excess capacity. Solving the problem, according to the *Vision*, would require, firstly, a shift in company consciousness to an awareness of shared interests and moderated behavior, and secondly, advancing on the premise that the companies would carry out these changes on their own, even if public intervention turned out to be required. The background to the emphasis on voluntary change by the companies was that in the pulp and paper industry, the corrugated cardboard industry had been designated to receive government directives through the structural improvement activities that were based on the Industry Stabilization Law, and had carried out facilities adjustment as a result, but had nevertheless seen their business deteriorate. From May 1971, wood-free paper, coated paper, and unglazed grocery paper were struggling enough that they received approval to form a Depressed Industry cartel, but the structural improvement in this industry did not achieve the desired results.

5.2 *Measures to Modernize Distribution*

5.2.1 Establishment of Large-Scale Retail Store Law

Distribution policy after the war placed a high value on the role of the distribution industry in providing employment opportunities. Policies were enacted to protect small and medium-sized retailers, including the Department Store Law (1956) and the Law on Special Measures for the Adjustment of Retail Business (1959) ("Retail Law") (Ishihara 2011, p.27). However, as inflation had become a social problem since the beginning of the 1960s, MITI began to look to supermarkets to play a role in lowering prices and therefore was reluctant to apply the Department Store Law to supermarkets.

In response to the workings of these laws, small and medium-sized retailers began in the late 1960s to seek regulation of supermarkets as "pseudo-department stores." Department stores, which were subject to restrictions on opening branches, also were dissatisfied with the inequality in the application of the law. Meanwhile, liberalization of capital moved forward in the distribution industry, with retail specialty stores designated for liberalization in the second round in 1968. Full liberalization of the retail industry took place in June 1975. This raised concerns about giant foreign retailers entering the market. Thus, distribution policy from the late 1960s to the early 1970s faced an array of challenges: deciding on immediate price policies and consumer interests, modernizing of distribution by nurturing supermarkets, addressing department-store dissatisfaction with the "pseudo-department store" issue, addressing the small and medium-sized retailers' demands for regulations on supermarkets, capital liberalization, and so on.

In August 1972, the Distribution Committee of the Industrial Structure Council compiled a report titled "Retail commerce under innovations in distribution—Toward revision of the Department Store Law," which called for easing the restrictions in the Department Store Law with an eye to consumer interests. The report also said it would be necessary to develop some kind of coordination process given the disparity in competitiveness between large and small-scale retailers. Reflecting this view, the Department Store Law was abolished in March 1973 and replaced with the Law Concerning the Adjustment of Retail Activities by Large-Scale Retail Stores ("Large-scale Retail Stores Law").

The Large-Scale Retail Store Law adopted a building principle according to which large-scale retail stores were defined as those with store areas of 1,500 m^2 or more in the building (or over 3,000 m^2 in specially designated cities) (see Fig. 5. Note that it includes later revisions and supplementary measures). A builder planning a new large-scale retail store was required to notify MITI of a set of stipulated items; the Minister had to be notified for plans for a retail business at the store four months prior to the business start date (Article 5 notification). The MITI Minister was then to judge whether there was any risk of the new store's affecting the surrounding small and medium-sized retailers. Where there was such risk, the Minister would solicit the opinion of the Large-Scale Retail Stores Council, which was composed of academics and others, and recommend reductions in the number of days the store could be open, or the size of its floor-space, and other matters. The Large-Scale Retail Stores Council also had an obligation to hear the opinions of the local Chamber of Commerce and Industry, consumers, retailers, and others that submitted them based on a Ministerial ordinance. The Chamber of Commerce and Industry, when deliberating, was supposed to consult with the Commercial Activities Coordinating Committee, which, like the earlier Department Store Law, was established within the Chamber of Commerce. The Commercial Activities Coordinating Committee consisted of representatives from commerce, consumers, and academic experts. As described above, the Large-Scale Retail Store Law was new in that it adopted a notification system requiring preliminary examination as part of the coordination policy. The preliminary examination was ordinarily literally a notification system, but in more extreme cases, it functioned more like a de facto permission system.

5.2.2 Revision of the Large-Scale Retail Store Law

Efforts to open large-scale retail stores after the establishment of the Large Store Law won local understanding relatively smoothly in districts with few large retailers, which characterized many cases, but intense disputes arose in some areas, gradually highlighting the problems of the Law's approach to coordination (Ishihara 2011, p. 43). In response to the formal process launched after the Article 5 notification, merchants had to seek consultations and discussions. In some cases, the new stores' opponents did not accept requests for preliminary negotiation, and some local governments forced them to engage in preliminary negotiations. However, because preliminary consultations of that kind were not formal procedures under the Large-Scale Retail Law, negotiations were often prolonged and resolutions were sometimes reached through the offer of settlement monies. Unofficial coordination activities took on greater significance.

Moreover, even those large retailers that were not subject to the law (because their stores were under 1,500 m^2 in area) were threatening to general retailers of the 100 m^2 range, leading some local governments to enact ordinances and outline additional controls and regulations. The ordinances calling for voluntary adjustment, pioneered by Toyonaka City in April 1976 and Kumamoto City in November, spread to

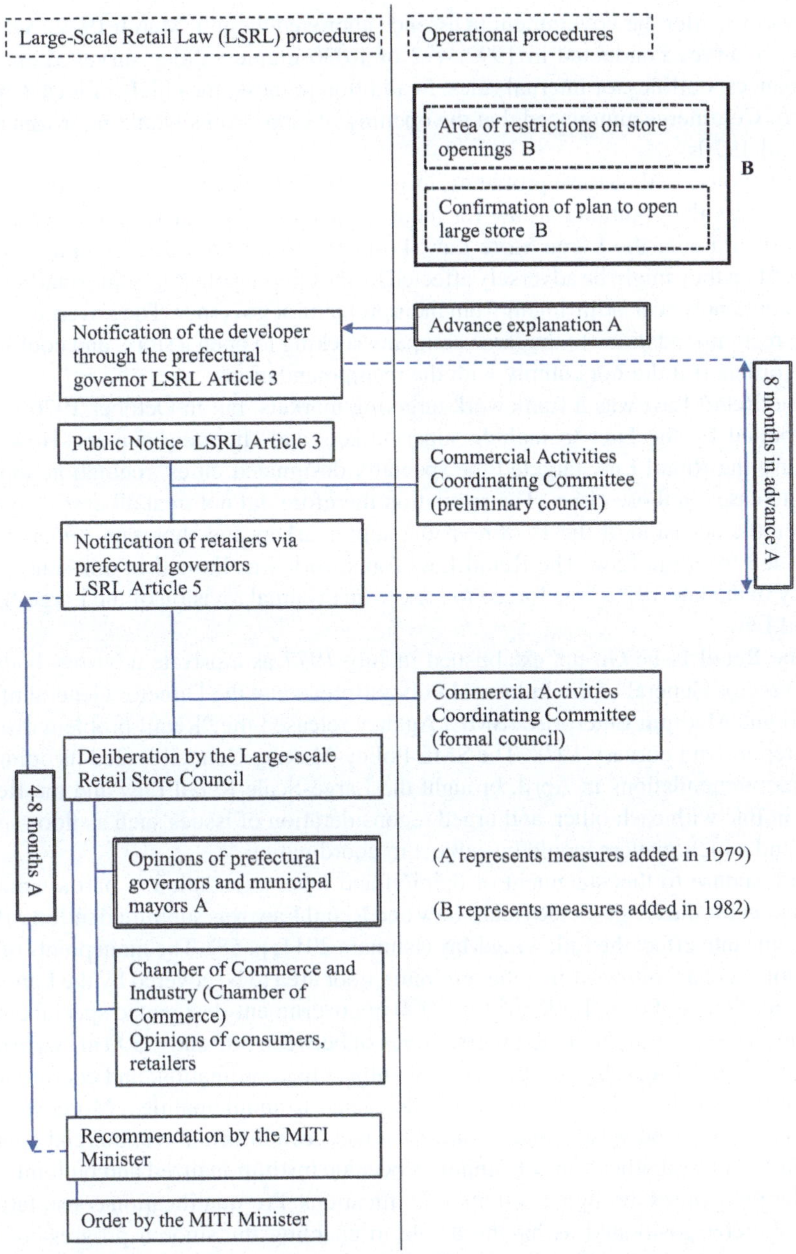

Fig. 5 Procedures for processing store openings, based on the Large-Scale Retail Law (LSRL) (Ishihara 2011, p. 77). *Sources* Partial revision of Ministry of International Trade and Industry Policy Bureau Commercial Section, ed., "The Large-Scale Retail Law Henceforth—The Nature of the Reconsideration of the Revised Law [Report of the Joint Meeting of the Industrial Structure Council, SME Policy-Making Council]. Trade and Industry Survey Group, 1994, p. 126. In the case of the second type of large-scale retailers, replace "MITI Minister" with "prefectural governors."

many cities after the government in essence approved them in March 1977. According to a survey conducted in 1992, 432 of 1,030 municipalities surveyed enacted ordinances, outlines, or internal rules. In addition to these, the chiefs of local Chambers of Commerce announced that the opening of large stores would be frozen after the mid-1970s.

In response to the above problems, in June 1977, the decision was made to revise and address the commercial law for medium-sized stores that were not subject to adjustment under the Large Store Law. If small and medium-sized retailer groups judged that they might be adversely affected by the opening of large-scale retail stores, they could now seek adjustment from their prefectural governor. The governor could issue recommendations to the large company seeking to open a store, and could also issue orders if it did not comply with the recommendations.

The Retail Law was a framework targeting markets, but in October 1976 it was interpreted by the Diet to include supermarkets and shopping centers. However, because the Retail Law targeted the specially designated cities, regulation applied only to cases in those cities. The regulation therefore did not treat all cases equally, and on the occasion of the 1978 revision, supermarkets and shopping centers were excluded from the Law. The Retail Law framework was limited in this sense, and policy in the late 1970s was forced to look to an eventual revision of the Large-Scale Retail Law.

The Retail Issue Group, established in July 1977 as a private advisory body to the Director General of the Industrial Policy Bureau and the Director General of the Small and Medium Enterprise (SME) Agency released the "Retail problem discussion report" in February 1978. The SME Policy-Making Council issued its opinions and recommendations in April, brought the Large-Scale Retail Law and the Retail Law in line with each other, and urged reconsideration of issues such as floor-space area and which matters would be subject to coordination.

In response to this statement of opinion and recommendation, a partial amendment plan for the Large-Scale Retail Law and Retail Law was submitted in June 1978 and came into effect the following May (Ishihara 2011, p. 58). The main points of the revision were as follows. First, the minimum floor area to be covered by the Law was lowered. Stores of over 1,500 m^2 (or 3,000 in government-designated special cities) became Type 1 Large-Scale Retailers. Stores of between 500 and 1,500 m^2 were designated Type 2 Large-Scale Retailers and subject to coordination, and coordinating authority over these Type 2 stores was delegated to municipalities. Moreover, the coordination period was extended, and what had been informal commercial coordination and pre-qualification consultations became institutionalized and built into the regular procedures through a system of notifications. Pre-qualification consultations were thereby positioned as having a role in enabling the smooth progress of the Commercial Activities Coordinating Committee.

However, problems recurred in the actual operation process of this cooperative framework. A preliminary briefing session was held before the pre-qualification Commercial Activities Coordinating Committee, and it became virtually essential to obtain local approval at this stage. Some municipalities began to require agreement at preliminary briefing sessions, and the same problems arose as had occurred before the revision of the Large-Scale Retail Law. It transpired that where agreement was not reached at this stage, subsequent coordination would be delayed or faced difficulty. This revealed the problem of the preliminary briefing session. More important, the preliminary explanatory meeting, which began to play the role of de facto coordination, was the venue for agreement between the applicants for store openings and the local small and medium-sized retailers. Therefore it gradually came to light that the interest of the consumer, who was the actual responsibility of the Commercial Activities Coordinating Committee, might well be hardly reflected at all.

After the revised law came into effect, opposition against the opening of stores began to gain momentum. In response, MITI showed plans for addressing the problem in 1981 and entrusted discussion of the issue to the Council on the Large-Store Problem. The Council's final report announced in January 1982 sought first of all to enforce the law in a restrained manner while continuing to consider consumer interests. It also said that it was necessary to strengthen the functions of the Commercial Activities Coordinating Committee and to devise fair and appropriate deliberation and management of it. MITI handled the administrative regulation of the store-opening process in line with these policies.

However, the opposition movement against store openings quickly made the government aware that coordination through these policies would be difficult. Therefore, in October 1982, the Industrial Structure Council Distribution Committee and the SME Policy-Making Council's Distribution Subcommittee met jointly, releasing their report in December 1983 titled "The basic direction of the distribution industry and policy in the 1980s." The report stressed that whereas the basic policy to this point had been to modernize distribution, treating distribution as an economic system and seeking "economic efficiency," it was instead necessary to see it from the point of view of a social system and to pursue "social effectiveness" as well. It was hoped that business opportunities for small and medium-sized retailers would continue to be guaranteed under the retail-industry coordination process. The MITI Minister's Ordinance of 1984 likewise urged that the restrictions on store openings be maintained while considering the possibility that opening a store in an existing commercial area might enhance the appeal of the area. In other words, it began to foster an objective reexamination not only of the confrontation between large-scale and small/medium-sized retailers, but also of the impact that large-scale retailers might have on a district.

5.2.3 Approaches to Modernizing Distribution

Initiatives for modernizing distribution were based on the Small and Medium Enterprise Modernization Promotion Law, which was enacted in March 1963 with the expectation of improving productivity not only in manufacturing but in distribution as well. It was assumed that the distribution sector's productivity could be improved by rationalizing management, enabling companies to operate on a more optimal scale, and creating joint operations among businesses. The focus on distribution arose at this time because the delay in that area was regarded as one reason for rising prices and also because the aging of commercial centers in existing urban areas was causing land-use and congestion issues in dense urban areas (Ishihara 2011, p. 149).

Most important among these was the impact of distribution on prices. The Industrial Structure Council's Distribution Committee issued successive reports on the subject, beginning with its first interim report, "The current status and issues of distribution organizations" (December 1964). The sixth interim report, "Issues in and the future of the modernization of distribution" (August 1968), stated that the modernization of underdeveloped sectors continued to be important for sustaining growth, and that for the foreseeable future, the principal issues were capital liberalization to create a system that could compete with foreign capital and improvements in distribution productivity as the most powerful approach to the consumer price problem.

In a similar vein, the third interim report, "On turning retail stores into chains" (September 1965), pointed to the effectiveness of the voluntary chain for overcoming the problems of small scale in the retail industry. In "On the distribution activities system" (July 1969), the Subcommittee on Distribution Policy issued a proposal that treated distribution as a single system and stressed plans to upgrade the distribution system as a whole and to improve its productivity. This was because the basic structure of the system was defined as management within the company of (1) operations planning, (2) transactions, (3) physical distribution, (4) finances and financing, and so on. Creating links among companies enabling them to connect with one another would require standardization of product codes and transaction codes, various records and forms, and product packaging. In response, the Committee for Developing the Distribution System was established in September 1970, and in that fiscal year, budget measures were adopted for the basic surveys on the standardization of sales slips, and the Japan Development Bank began financing products related to the distribution system. The Committee began to explore ways to make maximum use of computers in distribution and in September 1971 compiled the Basic Policy on the Distribution System, a set of plans targeted for implementation by 1975.

In addition, the "Distribution in the 1970s" report compiled by the Industrial Structure Council's Distribution Committee in July 1971 followed on these policy priorities and sought (1) an upgrading of the market structure (pursuit of economies of scale), (2) maintenance and promotion of effective competition (optimization of transaction conditions and customs), (3) promotion of consumer interests, and (4) rationalization of the physical aspects of distribution, and so on (Ishihara 2011, p. 172).

Measures were also taken to address the urban problems related to distribution. These mainly concerned the wholesale industry because of the concentration of wholesalers in urban areas. In December 1965, the Distribution Committee of the Industrial Structure Council proposed the construction of "general wholesale centers," facilities where wholesalers could not only share shop-fronts, but also the receipt, dispatch, shipment, storage, and delivery of merchandise. This was followed in 1966 by the enactment of the Law Concerning the Improvement of Urban Distribution Centers, which designated certain areas as distribution business districts and complexes and made it possible to construct truck terminals, freight rail stations,

Table 15 Number of wholesale associations and complexes established

Number established	Pre-1965	1966–1970	1971–1975	1976–1980	1981–1985	Post-1986	Total
Distribution associations	18	47	21	15	7	7	115
Distribution complexes completed	2	20	40	20	14	15	111

Source Ishihara (2011, p. 178). The total number of "complexes completed" also includes four whose completion date is not known

wholesale markets, warehouses, and other facilities within those areas. As of March 2010, the policy of concentrating and relocating distribution businesses had led to the operation of such complexes in 18 cities and 27 districts (Table 15).

Furthermore, instead of regulating supermarket businesses, MITI sought to work with city planning in response to the City Planning Law in 1968 and the Urban Renewal Law in 1969, which treated retailers as urban facilities. This led to "regional planning for the modernization of commercial businesses" in the 1970s (Ishihara 2011, p. 182). This planning was at first delegated to the Japan Chamber of Commerce and Industry (JCCI) by the Small and Medium Business Administration Agency and then in FY 1984 was turned into a government-subsidized project. From FY 1991, it was taken over by the Project for Planning and Implementing the Revitalization of Shopping Streets and funded by the operating gains of the Small Commercial Business Revitalization Fund. Plans were formulated for 241 districts over a period of 21 years.

5.2.4 Policies to Promote Small and Medium-Sized Retail Businesses

The Law on the Promotion of Small and Medium Retail Business ("Small Retail Law") was established in September 1973 with the aim of improving shopping districts, and was aimed at developing shopping districts, creating joint store areas, and modernizing business practices. The Minister heard the views of the Small and Medium Enterprise Modernization Council, on the basis of which he established guidelines for the development of projects with policy support (Ishihara 2011, p. 187). The promotion guidelines aimed to secure consumer interests and modernize small and medium-sized retailers, and in the case of subsidized businesses, included improvement projects such as establishing arcades as part of the station-front infrastructure sought in regional commercial modernization plans.

The Distribution Systems Research Institute was established at the Distribution Economics Institute of Japan to serve as the parent organization for developing the measures related to the September 1971 Basic Policy on Distribution System Development discussed above. The center's aim was the modernization of distribution activities through the development and dissemination of systems related to distribution, and it has since then played a central role in promoting systematization.

Meanwhile, MITI entrusted the Japanese Chamber of Commerce and Industry with the task of standardizing sales slips for department stores in 1974, for chain stores in 1976, and for other kinds of wholesale transactions in 1977. In 1978, an initiative aimed at standardizing the common product code was launched. The number 49 became the international code for Japan when Japan joined the European Article Number Association. The shift from the use of magnetic tape to communications lines for the delivery of data on intercompany transactions followed, and in 1980 the Japan Chain Stores Association standardized the process with the JCA Protocol. In 1982, MITI established the so-called "J-procedure," a transmission control procedure that would be common to the entire distribution industry. This encouraged significant progress in the accuracy and efficiency of distribution transactions.

The Distribution Systems Research Institute mentioned above also played a role in promoting the development of point of sale (POS) systems. JAN (Japanese Article Number) codes were assigned and registered for products, and JAN company code registration was launched as well. In addition, the symbols for displaying JAN codes on barcodes were included in the Japanese Industrial Standards, and it became possible to introduce the POS system. POS experiments were conducted at stores from 1979 to 1980, and the experiments entrusted to the Institute took place in three stages. Following a similar process of trial and error, Seven-Eleven Japan Co., Ltd. introduced the POS system to all stores in 1982, and Ito-Yokado Co., Ltd. followed in 1985, at which point the use of POS systems at convenience stores and supermarkets had become the decisive trend. In 1986, the Small and Medium Enterprise Agency conducted a "POS feasibility study for shopping streets" and began focusing on spreading POS systems to small and medium-sized retailers. The use of point cards in shopping streets also progressed.

With these advances in product management, companies were ready to begin exchanging information via computers, and EDI (Electronic Data Interchange) became possible. The spread of POS and EDI greatly changed commercial transactions. Inventory management, rather than something intuitively based on experience, became based on the objective rendering of the saleability or lack thereof of a given product. This allowed for smaller orders and delivery units, and more frequent deliveries, and also encouraged joint deliveries and the integration of distribution functions. Joint deliveries had already been started by Seven-Eleven in 1976, were adopted by Ito-Yokado in 1985, and spread from there to the general supermarket sector.

5.2.5 Revision of the Law to Promote the Modernization of Small and Medium-Sized Enterprises

Post-WWII policy on small and medium-sized enterprises was based on the Basic Law on Small and Medium-Sized Enterprises, and aimed to realize "improvements in SME growth" and "a rise in the economic and social status of SME workers," by "rectifying the disadvantages that were due to [their] economic and social constraints." It developed policies in the following four categories: (1) advancing the structure of SMEs (including modernizing facilities, making technical upgrades, rationalizing business management, and optimizing the scale of enterprises; (2) rectifying negative business activities (preventing excessive competition, optimizing subcontracting transactions, and so on); (3) implementing measures for small-scale enterprises; and (4) implementing financing and taxation systems.

The SME Council presented a summary of "The state of SMEs in the 1970s and the direction for SME policy" (the 1970s *Vision of SME Policy*) in August 1972, and regarding the 1970s as "an era of change and fluidity," it suggested new policy directions. The changes cited were (1) internationalization, (2) the growing importance of respect for all members of society, (3) the deepening of environmental problems, and (4) the shift to knowledge-intensive industry. The Council's suggestions called for greater emphasis to be placed on "the demand side," "the environment and labor welfare" (in other words, quality of life), and "SME diversity" (Nakata 2013, p. 17). However, in response to the yen's appreciation, the oil crisis, and other dramatic changes in the business environment that began around that time, Emergency Measures for SMEs in Response to the Changes in the International Currency Situation were issued in March 1973, and Comprehensive Measures for the Economy and Emergency Measures for SMEs Regarding the Yen's Appreciation (January 1978) were adopted by Cabinet Decision in September 1977 and January 1978 respectively, and policy began promoting shifts in business type and sectoral adjustments.

In line with these policies, the SME Modernization Promotion Law was amended in 1975, introducing three new points of view (Nakata 2013, p. 174). First, it added the perspective of "improving the quality and stability of the people's lives" to the earlier aim of strengthening international competitiveness. Second, it sought to include social needs such as improving the welfare of workers, raising consumer benefits, preserving the environment, and so on. Third, it encouraged entry into new fields. This enabled policy to promote industry-wide (including upstream and downstream operations) and region-wide structural improvements.

Specifically, the competent minister formulated a modernization plan for each "Designated Industry" based on a survey of its actual situation. The modernization plan included three areas: (1) time-specific targets for modernization of product performance or quality, as well as production costs, and so on; (2) items necessary for achieving the goal of modernization, including development of new products or new technologies, modernization of facilities, optimization of business scale and/or production and management methods, normalization of competition or improvements in business relations; and (3) important items for consideration in the modernization process, including improvements in worker welfare, the advancement of consumer interests, and preservation of the environment. These plans served as the foundation for measures to support SMEs until the Law's abolition in 1999.

5.3 A New Emphasis on Quality of Life: Promotion of Consumer Protection and the Housing Industry

5.3.1 Vision of the Household Goods Industry

In 1968, the Industrial Structure Council's Committee on Miscellaneous Goods and Housing Materials issued a report titled "The future of the miscellaneous goods industry under a liberalized economic system" that emphasized the "export character" of the industry, and laid out the direction to be taken in order to overcome the various challenges of the existing situation (Matsushima 2012, p. 204). On the production side were mechanization and mass production in order to enable the industry to escape its labor-intensive character, and efforts were to be made toward product differentiation. On the distribution side was promotion of modern linkages between production and sales and rationalized marketing systems; management would be modernized. The sector was divided into categories according to the level of mechanization and product differentiation that had been achieved, and policies were considered to address the needs of each one.

In March 1976, the "Vision of the household goods industry from 1975 and the appropriate direction of response" (the interim report of the Industrial Structure Council's Household Goods Committee) changed the name of the industry in question from "miscellaneous goods industry" to "household goods industry" and at the same time shifted the related policy-making aim from promoting exports to promoting enrichment of the life of the people. Based on this change in orientation, the following were cited as challenges facing the household goods industry: (1) stable growth and qualitative changes in people's needs (requiring upgrading, higher performance, individualization and the greater demands for social responsibility); (2) the question of how to respond to environmental changes, namely, the steady advance of international specialization or the rapid growth of developing economies. Overcoming these challenges would fundamentally require relying on self-help, complemented where needed by government measures.

The policy issues for the household goods industry, leaving aside those of specific industries such as Western-style kitchen metal-ware, porcelain, and matches, were modernization and structural improvement and the elimination of excessive competition. The policy measures corresponding to the first of these were the 1963 SME Modernization Promotion Law, based on the 1960 Law on Extraordinary Measures for Sector-Oriented Promotion, the creation of the Structural Improvement Planning System based on the 1969s SME Modernization Promotion Law, and following these, the advancement of plans for knowledge-intensive industries and structural improvement planning by region (1973), the creation of a system for planning entry into new sectors (1975), and the introduction of structural improvement plans for business strategy (1984) and post-structural improvement plans (1992).

Regarding excessive competition, the following frameworks remained in place: the Law on Temporary Measures Concerning the Stabilization of Designated SMEs

(1952), the Small Enterprises Stabilization Law (1953), and the Law Concerning the Organization of SMEs (1957).

Structural improvement projects were implemented using not only the SME Modernization and Promotion Law but also the July 1979 Law on Extraordinary Measures for Regional SMEs ("Production Region Law"). The "Production Region Law" framework was adopted to implement structural improvement projects. The framework of the Production Region Law was such that associations in the production region would undertake research and development for new products or new techniques, the development of demand, and plans for the promotion of projects for human resource development, and these would be submitted to the prefectural government and, if approved, could receive subsidies. The range of MITI's involvement was therefore limited: the framework relied heavily on the cooperation of industrial associations. Responsibility for policy management was shifted from the department of goods affairs to the prefectural governor.

5.3.2 Establishing a Consumer-Oriented System

Following the 1968 establishment of the Fundamental Law on Consumer Protection, related ministries and agencies decided to expand the administration of consumer affairs by increasing the budget for it. MITI established the Consumer Protection Division in 1976, and built up its administration of the area, including through legislative means (Ishihara 2011, p. 326). These included making administrative responses more consumer oriented. In 1965, MITI launched a system for handling complaints related to consumer lifestyle improvement in 1965, setting up a consultation window for people with complaints. The National Consumer Affairs Center of Japan was established in 1970. By 1973, at least one Consumer Life Center had been established in each prefecture, and systems for consumer consultations and complaints were being put into place.

The sharing of the collected information and collaboration among organizations was encouraged, and a network system linking centers for consumer life was established at the 16th Consumer Protection Conference in November 1983. (The Conference was established based on the Basic Law on Consumer Protection, chaired by the Prime Minister, and with the membership of the heads of the relevant administrative units, was charged with determining basic policy related to consumer administration). This resulted in the establishment of the Practical Living Information Online Network (PIO-NET) in December 1987. Meanwhile, MITI also sought improvements in industries' systems for handling complaints. In 1967 and 1968, it offered guidance through industry associations on the establishment of "complaint windows." With the prospect of an increasing number of complaints from consumers, it issued a notice in August 1979 urging the further development of a consumer-oriented system and industry understanding of the need for it.

5.3.3 Optimizing Business Transactions

Policies were developed on door-to-door sales and installment sales, from the point of view of optimizing business transactions (Ishihara 2011, p. 360).

First, the Special Subcommittee on Sales, in the Industrial Structure Councils' Distribution Committee, reviewed special business operations that were on the rise, including door-to-door sales, mail-order marketing, chain stores, and multilevel marketing systems, and in March 1975 submitted a report urging legislation on this area. On the basis of this report, the Law Concerning Door-to-Door Sales was established in June 1976 with the twin aims of promoting fair business practices and preventing damage or loss to consumers. The Law, in keeping with the particular needs of each kind of sales practice, obliged sellers to disclose their name and the type of merchandise being sold and also introduced a "cooling-off system." MITI also organized sales associations to establish the foundations for the sound development of these new sales methods, including, for example, the Door-to-Door Sales Association (established in March 1979) and the Japan Direct Sales Association (established in April 1980), and provided them with administrative guidance.

Consumer issues were mounting, however. In the case of door-to-door sales, consumers who were uncertain or vacillating could not avoid making contracts. The law on door-to–door sales was revised in June 1984, and the cooling-off period was extended from four to seven days. The affected businesses that had initially resisted the idea also changed their view of the matter, learning to provide products that consumers would not choose to return and concluding that their own credibility increased when their sales methods improved. In May 1985, MITI launched an information system on problems in door-to-door sales and worked to prevent the occurrence of such problems by widely disseminating the content of the consultations to the general public and related government offices.

6 Friction with Foreign Countries

6.1 Trade Imbalances and Negotiations with Europe and America

6.1.1 US Criticism of Japan

Japan's trade surplus with the US reached about 10 billion dollars in 1978 and continued to increase thereafter, to about 60 billion dollars in 1987. Although somewhat sluggish in the first half of the 1990s, it again increased to 64 billion dollars in 1998, 73 billion dollars in 1999, and 81 billion dollars in 2000. However, since the EU and China surpluses with the US were growing at the same time, the situation was different than it had been in the 1980s. The US portion of Japan's total exports rose from less than 26% at the end of the 1970s to 35% in 1984 and remained around 30%

in the 1990s. Meanwhile, the US ratio of Japan's total imports remained at about 20% from around the 1980s, rising at most to 24% in 1998.

Against this backdrop, US criticism of Japan had been mounting since 1977, particularly in the US Congress, because imports from Japan were increasing dramatically despite the appreciation of the yen (Abe 2013, p. 53). The January 1979 report by the Jones Task Force on US-Japan Trade (US House of Representatives Ways and Means Committee, Subcommittee on Trade) strongly criticized Japan for being the only country with an excessive trade surplus at a time when most countries were suffering from recession, and asked for efforts to be made to open Japan's market and improve the trade balance. The US also established the Trade Agreements Act of 1979, which detailed the requirements for the Laws on Countervailing Duties and Anti-Dumping.

Meanwhile, the Japan–US Summit meeting in May 1979 issued a joint statement with the subtitle, "A fertile partnership looking to the 1980s." Japan was called upon to maintain economic growth through the expansion of domestic demand and open its market to foreign products. The US would restrict imports if Japan's exports soared too rapidly, and Japan would resolve the issue by voluntarily regulating its own exports. These approaches were maintained into the 1980s.

6.1.2 Full-Scale Trade Friction with Europe

Trade friction also arose between Japan and the members of the European Community (EC), beginning around 1970 (Abe 2013, p. 147). In 1971, Europe, like the United States, was suffering from the rapid increase in steel imports from Japan, and in January 1972, Japan adopted Voluntary Export Restraints (VER) through the Export and Import Transaction Law. These voluntary regulations were renewed repeatedly, continuing in place until the 1990s. In addition to iron and steel, tape recorders and televisions became the target of VERs on exports to Europe from the early 1970s on. This was part of the Japanese government's effort to maintain the international export order during this time.

However, in 1976, immediately after the first oil crisis, the EC became concerned by the flood of exports from Japan—specific items such as steel, autos, ships, and bearings. When a delegation from Japan's Federation of Economic Organizations visited Europe in October of that year, the Europeans harshly criticized the influx of Japanese products. They argued that non-tariff barriers (specifically the technical obstacles to manufactured imports posed by regulations on exhaust gas, the testing process for pharmaceuticals and chemicals, and so on) were hindering the export of European products to Japan and demanded improvement on the part of the Japanese. While the trade friction between Japan and the EC intensified in this way, the value of Japanese exports to the EC came to twice that of the EC's exports to Japan and Japan posted a trade surplus with Europe exceeding 3 billion dollars.

As a result of the delegation's request upon its return home, government-level discussions were held between the EC Committee and the Ministry of Foreign Affairs in November 1976. The same month, the Japanese government submitted responses to the EC complaints, including (1) restraints on the number of automobile shipments, (2) the launching of discussions on the shipbuilding issues, and (3) the importation of agricultural products such as powdered skim milk. The EC reacted with appreciation. Japan also sought to improve areas regarded as non-tariff barriers by omitting the double inspections and certifications. Nevertheless, in February 1977 the EC Committee took steps against the import of Japanese-made ball bearings by unexpectedly imposing an anti-dumping tax of 10–20% for up to three months, making it clear that the EC's approach of sanctions against Japanese products was not brought entirely to an end.

6.2 Simplifying Import Procedures and Maintaining the Export Order

6.2.1 Efforts to Expand Imports

Import promotion policies sought to increase imports not only by developing markets for the sake of leveling the field of competition but also by promoting the penetration of imported goods and supporting import expansion policies. They also sought market-opening policies, including the easing of import regulations, reduction of tariff rates, and the improvement of standards and conformity assessment systems.

The import expansion policies were developed against the background of the late-1960s trade friction with the US and the early-1970s friction with Europe, and the 1971 Comprehensive Economic Policy of Japan marked the first clarification of import promotion policies (Abe 2013, p. 175). Thereafter, export promotion policies, which had been the focus during the period of high economic growth, were transformed into import-promotion measures of a kind not seen in other countries overseas, and energetically advanced until the beginning of the twenty-first century.

The effort put into expanding imports from the latter 1970s resulted in a policy system as of the fall of 1982. The memorandum submitted by the general assembly of the Trade Conference that October was the first comprehensive and detailed description of the system of import promotion policy, and it was carried on and developed in subsequent measures. It urged the need to encourage import expansion through the use of JETRO (the Japan External Trade Organization) and MIPRO (Manufactured Imports Promotion Organization). Events and import fairs were pursued thereafter, with due consideration for the concerns of the Trade Conference.

6.2.2 Exploring Market-Opening Policies

Among the import-promotion policies were policies to open the market (Abe 2013, p. 226). The core of these policies was the relaxation of restrictions on imports, because of the trade friction discussed above. The trade friction of the latter 1970s forward was new in that macroeconomic economic policies and adjustment of exchange rates now became diplomatic issues with the aim of resolving the imbalance of the current account. There is no clear standard on how much of an imbalance causes problems, but structurally speaking, current account imbalances arise because the countries with surpluses continuously achieve levels of industrial development that surpass their domestic demand, while deficit countries continue simply to open their markets to foreign goods, raising the possibility that their industrial development will stall as a result. It was from this point of view that Europe and America called on Japan to increase its domestic demand and open its market from the late 1970s into the 1990s.

Interestingly, the Japanese side was clearly aware of the existence of an array of obstacles relating to importing, even as it passively responded to the external pressures by undertaking market-opening measures. Although Japan's policies did not necessarily result in import expansion, the process became an opportunity to shed light on problems that had been hidden from sight within Japan. Industry circles, including the Federation of Economic Organizations and others, while strongly resisting criticism of industry and business, sought the relaxation of government regulations and hoped to increase their own freedom as corporate actors thereby.

The Japan–US bilateral current account was made an issue in the negotiations between the two countries, although it has meaning only when there are strong restrictions on the exchangeability of currency. The reason was that the US could not deny that the background to the problems was the emotional reaction that arose from the trade friction in specific, but its complaint was that although Japan had grown to become the world's second-largest economy, it did not have a fully open market. Japan, meanwhile, promoted import expansion and market opening, but the problem of the current account imbalance was not easily resolved even in the twenty-first century. To that extent, the measures undertaken by Japan cannot necessarily be regarded as having achieved sufficient results.

In relation to the EC, meanwhile, Japan started government-level negotiations in mid-November 1976 and from time to time attempted to relax import restrictions and voluntarily regulate exports, but these were undeniably ad hoc responses. This was because MITI, as of 1976–1977, was strongly aware that the Japanese market was already fully open in systemic terms.

There were, however, cases in which domestic safety regulations in effect proved disadvantageous for imported goods, and MITI did not go this far into detail in its deliberations. In the view of MITI in those years, the criticism from Europe and the US was fundamentally based on a misunderstanding of the Japanese market. MITI's policies, therefore, were developed basically as attempts somehow to avoid trade sanctions.

6.2.3 Simplifying Import Procedures

Overseas complaints against Japan's import system persisted, and MITI's attitude gradually changed. The change was reflected in the Japanese government's more aggressive promotion of the Tokyo Round.

The New Policy issued in 1979 by the International Trade Policy Bureau and the International Trade Administration Bureau said that, "For the sake of upgrading and improving the efficiency of our own economy, we should not refuse to expand imports," and called for "Eliminating factors that impede the expansion of imports." Inhibiting factors included various inspection procedures, the closed nature of Japanese industry, the practice of cross-shareholding within a conglomeration of businesses, the areas in which distribution was not modernized, and other factors. MITI's stance of simply trying to overcome overseas misunderstandings shifted slightly, and instead of avoiding a response to the current account imbalance, it began advancing import-promotion policies and coordination within domestic industry in order to achieve an equilibrium. In other words, it began firmly pursuing efforts to raise industry to a still more sophisticated level.

An array of programs for promoting imports to Japan were presented in senior official-level consultations between the US and Japan in September 1977. A Trade Facilitation Committee (TFC) was inaugurated to handle problems with trade procedures and to seek out what might be promising US products for export to Japan. The TFC also became the organization charged with fully responding, for the first time, to the complaints made about trade.

The latter 1970s also saw the step-by-step progress on the simplification of import procedures. The first step was the 1977–1978 implementation of a partial revision of the Import Trade Control Order. Among the revisions was that made to Article 21 in October 1977: trade contracts with intermediaries, instead of requiring permits from the MITI Minister as they had previously, now required the submission of notifications to the Foreign Exchange Bank, and where the payments and price of cargo received were both under one million yen, the notification requirement was lifted. The Export Trade Control Order was also revised in October 1978, furthering the simplification of procedures for handling cargo exports and imports. Because this series of amendments to protectionist measures targeted regulations what in reality were hardly implemented, they could not be expected to have a significant effect on import expansion. Nevertheless, they did have meaning in that they allowed Japan to assert that it was opening its market.

6.2.4 Policies for Maintaining the Export Order

The basic thinking of policies concerning foreign trade in postwar Japan was that goods in principle be exported freely, with controls on exports limited to the necessary minimum. The December 1949 Foreign Exchange and Foreign Trade Control Law ("Foreign Exchange Act") adhered to this thinking, restricting the scope of control on exports. Even so, the Foreign Exchange Act was partially revised in December

1980, against a backdrop of rising Japanese exports, to allow for even freer export trade, and revisions were made to a wide array of ministerial ordinances (Abe 2013, p. 301). As a result, although approval would still be required for specifically designated exports and imports, "consignment trade in processed goods" was in principle liberalized, for example. "Payment method regulations" were also changed from the "positive list" method to the "negative list method": that is, where payment methods had previously had to be positively singled out as not requiring approval, under the new system, only those payment methods specifically designated as requiring approval would be subject to controls. However, on the occasion of the Toshiba–Kongsberg scandal, the Foreign Exchange Act was again revised in September 1987 to strengthen export controls on strategic goods to communist countries. Nonetheless, MITI decided to establish the Bulk License System in March 1989, and was promoting the simplification of procedures for bulk export licenses exceeding 200,000 annually.

The 1952 Export and Import Transaction Law aimed to prevent unfair export transactions and to establish an order for import and export transactions (for example, eliminating excessive competition), and to this end, recognized the establishment of export associations and of agreements among businesses. When the law was first enacted, the question was how to deal with problems that occurred in the main exporting sectors, which were composed of relatively small-scale companies producing textiles, miscellaneous goods, light machinery, and so on. Many export agreements were still being signed in the 1970s, the majority of which were agreements on quantity or volume of exports.

Chapter 3
The Global Responsibilities of an Economic Superpower (1981–1992)

1 Keynotes of the Japanese Economy and Trade Policy in the 1980s

1.1 Fiscal Restructuring and Stable Growth

The combination of steep inflation and slow growth rates was a common problem faced by industrial economies in the late 1970s and early 1980s. Japan responded to these issues on the micro level by pursuing policies for "streamlining" businesses, especially through energy conservation, and on the macro level by promoting financial reform.

Companies cut costs by reducing energy use per unit of production and recovered their international competitiveness in tandem with their progress in conserving energy. Meanwhile, adjustments were made for employment in the short term through temporary leaves and transfers as well as the expiration of construction contracts and the dismissal of temporary workers. As these practices spread, the problem of the incompatibility of employment adjustment policies and the need for employment security became evident to both labor and management.

On the macroeconomic side, after the negative real growth of 1974, Japan's growth rate slowed dramatically, and the problem emerged of mounting fiscal dependence on deficit spending. Dubbed "the first year of welfare," 1973 saw a substantial increase in the budget for welfare-related expenses such as free medical care for the elderly. This was followed almost immediately, however, by a focus on "welfare policy review" and a policy reversal that stressed that "even the welfare budget isn't off limits [from cuts]".

The 1980s Liberal Democratic Party administrations of Prime Minister Zenko Suzuki and his successor, Yasuhiro Nakasone, prioritized administrative and fiscal reform. The Provisional Commission for Administrative Reform was established to formulate policies on administrative reform, while at the same time, a "zero-

Committee on the History of Japan's Trade and Industry Policy. RIETI,
Dynamics of Japan's Trade and Industrial Policy in the Post Rapid Growth Era (1980–2000),
Economics, Law, and Institutions in Asia Pacific, https://doi.org/10.1007/978-981-15-1987-1_3

ceiling principle" was adopted with regard to the budget in order to restrain spending increases, meaning that budgets were to be held to the previous year's level (budget for FY 1982) or lower (budget for FY 1983 and beyond). In addition, the government promoted the division and privatization of three public corporations—the Japan National Railways, Nippon Telegraph and Telephone Public Corp., and Japan Tobacco and Salt Public Corp.—and "fiscal reform without tax increases." Tax increases were considered under names such as "sales tax" and "value-added tax," but such measures were judged too difficult to effect at the time, given the instability of the conservative electoral base. It was only in 1989 that the consumption tax was finally introduced. For this reason, simple administrative reforms were needed in order to realize cost savings, and reviews were undertaken of the kinds of authority exercised by the various bureaucratic agencies, along with attempts to relax unnecessary regulations. In other words, Japan pursued neo-liberal economic policies aimed at "small government" of the kind then being adopted by the Thatcher administration in the UK and the Reagan administration in the US.

1.2 Publication of the 1980s Vision

The "Industrial policy for the 1980s" ("*1980s Vision*"), submitted to the MITI Minister in March 1980 by the Industrial Structure Council, represented an effort to formulate a new vision, comparable to the Industrial Structure Research Advisory Council's 1963 report, "Heavy and Chemical Industrialization" and its "Knowledge-Intensive Structure" report of 1971 (Okazaki 2012, p. 1). The *1980s Vision* pointed out that Japan (1) had entered an era of "diversified energy use" through its shift from oil to alternative energy, (2) was developing a multipolar political economic structure centered on the United States, (3) had completed its "catch-up modernization" and was in a new phase of economic growth, and (4) now accounted for 10% of the world's total gross domestic product. Based on the recognition of these changes, the report articulated new long-term "national goals" and laid out the issues involved in realizing these objectives. The new goals were defined as (1) contributing to the international world as an "economic power," (2) overcoming the constraints of being a "resource-poor country," and (3) achieving a lifestyle balance between "vitality" and "comfort."

With these points in mind, Chap. 9 of the *1980s Vision* addressed "the kind of industrial structure demanded by the times," dividing its requirements into four categories: (1) dynamic comparative advantage (based on the development of a technology-intensive, high value-added, technologically autonomous industrial structure), (2) fulfillment of the needs of the people (responding to growing social needs arising from the aging of the population and changes in public consciousness, lifestyle, and so on.), (3) Energy- and resource-conservation, and (4) security (meaning guarantees of economic security). These were combined under the term "Creative Knowledge Intensity" and defined the fundamental task for industrial policy as ensuring that the changes that occurred in the industrial structure in the 1970s be solidified through the exercise of creativity in the domestic development of technology, among other areas. Underlying this outlook was the recognition that Japan had gradually caught up with the advanced economies of Europe and the United States and therefore had to ask itself how to devise policy for the future when it was already at the cutting edge technologically. The *Vision* also reflected an awareness of the problem of how to cooperate with and contribute to the international community. Biotechnology, new materials, new energy, and fifth-generation computers, among others, were suggested as specific new industries that could take the lead in advancing the necessary shift in the industrial structure.

The *1980s Vision* held the premise that these four highlighted needs would be met by the voluntary efforts of businesses, but also addressed the possibility that it might not be desirable from a long-term point of view to rely on market mechanisms alone. It accordingly asserted that industrial policy had a role to play in: (1) realizing an appropriate international division of labor based on the maintenance and formation of dynamic comparative advantage, (2) establishing the foundations for long-term development and economic security, (3) responding to the external diseconomies that accompany corporate activity, and (4) enabling smooth industrial adjustment.

The *1980s Vision* went into detail regarding the concrete measures involved in these industrial adjustment policies. That is, temporary policy intervention was regarded as necessary if friction were to mount over such problems as employment or oversupply in "specific industrial sectors that were shrinking or undergoing conversion to other sectors." This "industrial adjustment" was to be applied in a limited manner and in accordance with the following principles: (1) efficiency, (2) complementarity (complementing the changes taking place through the market mechanism), (3) non-permanence (the adjustment phase was to be temporary), and (4) clarity (the scope of measures were to be limited and the contents clear). The basic approach, which saw industrial adjustment as occurring through market mechanisms but invoked policy intervention as merited in specific cases, was in accord with the Positive Adjustment Policy (PAP) set forth by the OECD in June 1978. In that sense, it represented an early adoption of OECD policy.

This approach to industrial adjustment policy was based on assumptions about the basic materials industries (petroleum refining, petrochemicals, vinyl chloride, and others), the performance of which had been deteriorating due to the increase in raw fuel and energy costs with the twin oil crises of the 1970s. The transformation of the industrial structure required addressing expectations both of decline and of growth. The basic material industries in this period (1) were intensive consumers of energy, (2) had difficulty with product differentiation given the character of general-purpose materials, (3) had large fixed costs which meant that any contraction in operations made the burden of interest payments that much heavier, (4) were at a disadvantage in their bargaining power over prices because of their many large-scale customers, and (5) were extremely capital intensive.

Meanwhile, since the 1970s, as resource nationalism began emerging in various countries, the government had been wary of rises in the basic material industries' import ratios. For this reason, MITI regarded policy on basic materials industries not merely as a set of measures to address recession but as an issue of national importance with bearing on the entire industrial structure and economic security of Japan.

For these reasons, there was a need for coordination of the basic materials sector as a whole, and MITI began exploring policy frameworks for the period to follow the expiration of the Law on Temporary Measures for Stabilization of Specified Depressed Industries ("Industry Stabilization Law"). As will be explained below, the resulting Temporary Measures Law for the Structural Adjustment of Specific Industries (May 1983 "Structural Improvement Law") represented a plan for a shift in industrial structure policies and industrial adjustment policies, including the Antimonopoly Law.

1.3 Yen Appreciation and International Contributions

Prime Minister Nakasone, returning home after his summit meeting with US President Ronald Reagan in January 1985, instructed the Cabinet to set out market-opening measures for the US and to proceed with simplifying import procedures and improving standards and conformity assessment systems in the fields of communication equipment, electronics, timber, medical devices, medicines, and so on. Additionally, on April 9, the Prime Minister issued an unusual "call to the people" on TV, declaring that, "In order to maintain the free trade system, we must open the Japanese market to the utmost extent, 'on the principle of freedom with a minimum of exceptions.'" He called for a radical reduction in government regulations on imports and for entrusting choice, and responsibility for that choice, to consumers. He also called on "each citizen to buy at least $100 worth of foreign products" for the sake of expanding imports.

In October that year, Nakasone launched the "Study Group on Economic Structural Adjustment for International Cooperation," a private advisory group charged with examining measures for converting Japan's industrial structure from export dependence to external cooperation. Its chair was Haruo Maekawa, former Governor of the Bank of Japan. The group was asked to consider measures for (1) medium-term structural adjustment to enable harmonization with the demands of the international economy, (2) maintenance of an appropriate balance of trade, and (3) international cooperation to stabilize and maintain appropriate currency values. The study group's "Maekawa Report" had a significant influence on the subsequent course of economic policy.

The Maekawa Report was compiled within the context of Japan's particular international position in the 1980s. Western countries, which had maintained tight money policies for a long time in efforts to curb the inflation caused by high oil prices, were plagued by zero and negative growth, as well as high unemployment and inflation rates. Interest rates in the US reached their highest level since World War II. The official discount rate hit 14%, which in turn led interest rates to reach 18%. High interest rates worldwide exerted strong deflationary pressures on each economy, hindering economic growth. The burden of high interest payments also had the adverse effect of producing high cumulative debt in non-oil-producing developing countries. The impact on the Japanese economy was also significant: high interest rates in the US led to the depreciation of the yen, complicating Japan's efforts to maintain low interest rates that were designed to stimulate growth, and acting as a drag on the recovery of domestic demand.

As the gap between domestic and foreign economic conditions widened, European and US criticism of Japan's growing exports mounted, creating a need for currency adjustment. In response to the criticism against Japan, the government promoted import expansion and market-opening policies. Repeated efforts were made to resolve trade problems bilaterally, including Japan–US negotiations on steel, automobiles, machine tools, and semiconductors, among others, and industrial cooperation plans with European countries.

However, these measures were not immediately sufficient to resolve the various problems in the world economy, including the worsening of the US trade balance. The Conference of Ministers and Governors of the Group of Five (G5) that met at New York's Plaza Hotel in September 1985 therefore agreed to undertake a large-scale currency revaluation, or depreciation of the dollar, in what became known as the Plaza Accord. The result was a sharp appreciation of the yen. This posed a challenge to the Japanese economy, but the adjustment phase was not long. Japan gradually advanced measures for expanding domestic demand and the economy made progress toward recovery. Based on rising personal consumption and capital investment, the steady growth of this period was the longest in duration after the Iwato boom of 1958–1961 and the Izanagi boom of 1965–1970.

1.4 "The Basic Design of 21st-Century Industrial Society"

The yen appreciation in the latter half of the 1980s brought new challenges to Japanese industry, beginning with the basic materials industries. First, domestic demand stagnated due to the relocation overseas of high-demand industries, the expansion of products and parts imports, and the shift to service industries. Second, domestic market conditions deteriorated due to changes in both domestic and foreign supply and demand and in the price structure. The government therefore formulated the "Law of Temporary Measures to Facilitate Industrial Structural Adjustment" and other measures to support companies and regions whose economic situation had deteriorated markedly for the above reasons, and developed new approaches to shifts in the industrial structure.

Meanwhile, the Planning Subcommittee of the Comprehensive Group on Industrial Structural Adjustment in May 1986 issued a report titled "The basic design of 21st-century industrial society." The report was a response to these new circumstances and pointed out the following new trends (Okazaki 2012, p. 6): (1) The growing interdependence of the world's economies meant that the world was moving from an era centered on the US to one of maintaining order through cooperation and solidarity among major countries; (2) technological innovation and an information revolution, tantamount to a third industrial revolution, were underway (including the trend toward "fusion" among disparate industries and diversification of industry); (3) social consciousness was shifting toward a greater emphasis on a rich spiritual and cultural life. Given these trends, the report cited three tasks for Japan: "international cooperation and international contribution," "the maintenance of industrial vitality based on the exercise of creativity," and "creation of a new lifestyle culture." Among these, "international cooperation and international contribution" was especially important in defining the basic approaches of policy-making and industrial policy. The report called for a fundamental reliance on market mechanisms, much as the *1980s Vision* had, but said that the role of industrial policy was to reduce the domestic friction accompanying industrial adjustment and to respond promptly to the international economic environment. The need to respond to external economic imbalances and international economic friction was highlighted because of the mounting urgency of these problems. In that sense, the underlying thinking of the committee and its policy discussions had much in common with the Maekawa Report issued by Prime Minister Nakasone's private advisory body in 1986.

1.5 Progress in Deregulation

The administrative and financial reform promoted by the Second Provisional Commission for Administrative Reform after the early 1980s constituted a review of policy with an eye to reducing the administrative role. This was symbolized in the July 1982 announcement in the "Third Report" of a "shift away from guidance, regulation, and protection of the private sector by civil administration toward a reliance on the private sector and an administrative emphasis on assisting with the establishment of a direction, and with coordination and complementarity." In line with this policy, the final report of March 1983 recommended concrete deregulation measures concerning banks, property insurance, alcoholic beverage sales, silk threading, the petroleum industry, the freight-forwarding industry, and others. Such deregulation would transform the domestic economic structure through regulatory reform, while also easing international tensions by opening the domestic market.

The Administrative Reform Commission established in July 1983 took over from the Second Extraordinary Investigative Committee to deliberate on the role of government regulation of private activities. The result of this examination was summarized in the February 1985 report titled "Administrative reform for promoting the vitality of the private sector." On the premise that regulation and protection restricts private business activity and preserves inefficient enterprises, the report called for a review of the public sector aimed at promoting "the market and competition principles in the private sector" and eliminating or reducing permits and subsidies. Deregulation was divided into two categories: "economic regulation" that regulated business activity on everything from entry into business, to facilities, quantities, and pricing; and "social regulation" for safety and sanitation. Deregulation was aimed at minimizing the former of the two, but also targeted the latter where administrative divisions had led to duplication. Deregulation was thus clearly positioned to be one of the key points of administrative reform.

Additionally, the April 1986 Maekawa Report, seeking to harmonize with the world on the issue of current account imbalances, advocated limiting exceptions to the free-market principle. It thereby added new impetus to deregulation as a means of responding to economic friction with the outside world. The Second Provisional Council for the Promotion of Administrative Reform, established in April 1987, formed a Public Regulation Subcommittee for a fundamental regulatory review, and based on its deliberations, issued a "Report on the relaxation of public regulations" in December 1988. The Second Reform Council, like its predecessor, had favored administrative reform and an emphasis on private sector vitality. The Public Regulations Subcommittee added an emphasis on improving the quality of life of the Japanese by making structural adjustments of the external imbalances and eliminating the gap between domestic and foreign prices. Regulatory reviews were carried out in seven specific areas: distribution, logistics, information and communications, finance, agricultural products, new businesses, and the inspection certification system and qualification systems. In December 1988, a Cabinet Decision was issued to respect "to the utmost" the report titled "Directions for the Promotion of Deregulation." Meanwhile, because US pressure on Japan was a constant feature during this period, deregulation took place within the framework for implementing the 1989 Japan–US Structural Impediments Initiative (SII) and the April 1993 US–Japan Framework for a New Economic Partnership. A Third Administrative Reform Council was established in October 1990 and its first report, submitted in July 1991, confirmed implementation of the final report of the Second Reform Council, and stated that public regulations would be halved in number within 10 years. Deregulation therefore remained a consistent feature of policy from this point forward.

2 Economic Superpower Status and International Contributions: Responses to Economic Friction

2.1 Export Adjustments—From Market-Oriented Sector-Specific (MOSS) Talks to the Structural Impediments Initiative (SII)

2.1.1 Japan–US Trade Friction and the MOSS Talks

Economic friction between Japan and the United States worsened significantly in the early 1980s, extending beyond sector-specific trade issues, and giving rise to criticism of Japan, such as accusations of unfair trade policy in high-tech industries. While rebutting such arguments, Japan also responded by implementing market-opening measures in six stages from December 1981 to March 1985. However, with the US

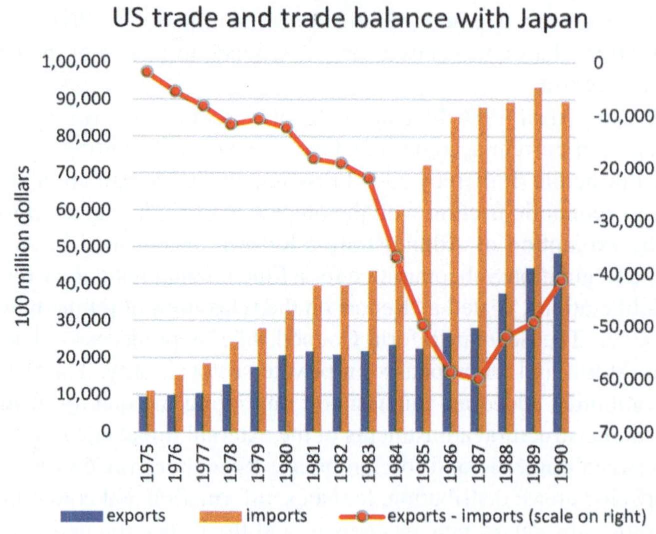

Fig. 1 US trade and trade balance with Japan. *Source* Abe (2013, pp. 54–55)

maintaining its policy of high interest rates and a high dollar value, Japan's trade surplus continued to expand, and the trade friction did not subside.

It was in this context that in the late 1980s the MOSS (Market-Oriented Sector-Selective) talks began. This was an approach to negotiations agreed upon at the Japan–U.S. Summit meeting of January 1985, with the objective of eliminating barriers to entry into the Japanese market by relaxing government regulations and reducing tariffs on individual items of interest to the United States. The MOSS talks took up four industrial sectors: telecommunications, medicines and medical equipment, electronics, and forest products. In October 1986, Japan and the United States announced an agreement reaffirming the "desirability of these discussions for promoting the increase of imports to Japan by achieving unrestricted market access for the United States and other foreign countries."

MITI was involved in the electronics and forestry talks. In the former, "items for implementation" included reducing tariffs on electronics by 20%, eliminating tariffs on telecommunications equipment in which the US had an interest, and other measures. The MOSS talks, citing these positive results, added "transport equipment" as a new sector in May 1986. Auto parts eventually joined the list (Fig. 1).

2.1.2 Responding to US Super-301

In 1988 the United States enacted the Omnibus Foreign Trade and Competitiveness Act of 1988. Previously, the US had addressed unfair or unreasonable foreign trade practices with the harsh measures of Section 301 of the Omnibus Trade Act of 1974.

Section 301 made it possible to call on the government to adopt retaliatory measures where negotiations had not yielded the desired results (Abe 2013, p. 66). The US government had not ever applied Section 301, because depending on how it was exercised, it could potentially constitute a violation of GATT (the General Agreement on Tariffs and Trade). But Congress became more vociferous in calling for it from 1985 on. In September 1985, therefore, the Reagan administration announced its "new trade policy" of firmly opposing unfair foreign trade through the utilization of Section 301. The comprehensive trade law mentioned above, enacted in response to this "new trade policy," made numerous changes, including amending Section 301 and establishing the Super 301 Provisions of the 1988 Omnibus Trade Act. Depending on how they were handled, these changes could have a protectionist impact. In adopting them, therefore, the United States was showing a stronger inclination toward unilateral action.

The amended Section 301 enabled the Office of the United States Trade Representative (USTR) to initiate investigations, based on appeals from interested parties, into whether foreign government measures or policies were "unfair," "irrational," or "discriminatory" and in violation of trade agreements, and to apply sanctions where cause was found. However, because the criteria for judgment were unclear and the USTR was in the role of both prosecutor and judge, the new system did not satisfy the standards of neutrality and fairness. Super 301 required the USTR to submit reports to Congress about cases of foreign unfair trade practices, to undertake negotiations with the country in question with the aim of removing the trade barriers, and to adopt sanctions where the problem could not be resolved within one year.

Super 301 was said to be aimed at Japan, but in May 1989, the USTR designated India and Brazil, along with Japan, as Super 301 "priority countries." In Japan's case, government procurement of supercomputers and satellites and technical import restrictions on forest products were singled out for negotiation. Nevertheless, the decision was made that Japan should not be judged as unfair across the board, and that negotiations should proceed outside the scope of Super 301. Moreover, the Japanese government adhered to its position that it could not participate in negotiations based on a Super 301 designation. As a result, bilateral negotiations were transferred to the Japan–U.S. Trade Committee, which convened in Hawaii in September 1989.

Supercomputers were among the cases under negotiation (Abe 2013, p. 70). Underlying this problem was the decline in market share of the US companies that in 1980 had dominated the world supercomputer market, and the simultaneous rise in market share of Japan's general-purpose supercomputers that had swept into the market in the latter 1980s. Therefore, the main issues under negotiation were (1) the adoption by the Japanese government of preferential policies for domestic products, and (2) the US argument that Japanese companies were making substantial discounts in order to eliminate US companies from the market.

The negotiations resulted in Japan's undertaking to ameliorate the discount issue. Beginning with the budget requests for 1990, its budget plans would reflect appropriate market prices for supercomputers. It also undertook to promote "computer installation procedures" for procurement. There were limits to improving the situation, as evidenced, for example, in the July 1996 lawsuit against dumping, filed by US supercomputer maker Cray Inc., but certain improvements were seen as a result of the bilateral negotiations.

2.1.3 Japan–US Structural Impediments Initiative (SII) Talks

In April 1986, Foreign Affairs Minister Shintaro Abe and US Secretary of State George Schultz agreed to hold talks on the structural problems affecting the economic balance between the two nations. Because cooperation on macroeconomic policy has a limited effect on correcting external imbalances, structural improvements and adjustment at the microeconomic level were deemed necessary by both sides. The talks based on this agreement began in October 1986, and because of the overlapping issues involved, President George H.W. Bush in May 1989 proposed holding Japan–US talks on structural issues in a framework separate from the Super 301 talks (Abe 2013, p. 77).

The Japan–US talks on structural issues were intended "as a supplement to macroeconomic policy coordination, wherein the two parties would identify to each other the structural problems in the two countries that are thought to impede the adjustment of the trade imbalance, and each take steps to resolve these issues." The first meetings were held in September 1989, followed by an interim report issued in the fourth round of talks in April 1990, and a final report in the fifth round in June of that year. The report called for Japan to increase public investment, amend its Anti-Monopoly Law to strengthen it, and other measures.

Not only were the Japan–US SII talks linked to the resolution of specific issues, they also were greatly significant in generating a change in attitude toward negotiations on the part of the US. At the time, the US had conceived of negotiations in which the US would seek systematic increases in US exports to Japan. This marked a change from the Reagan administration approach of regulating Japanese imports.

Japan, however, demanded and achieved two-way talks, in which each country identified problems in the other. As a result, the US realized that the current-account imbalance between Japan and the US was basically a macroeconomic problem. Given its earlier assumption that its trade deficit was due to the closed nature of other markets and that the aim of trade talks was therefore to open those other markets, this constituted an epochal change in perspective. The talks were founded on the recognition that the special economic and social structure of Japan hindered US exports to Japan, but the SII talks of the Bush Administration were limited to seeking a voluntary improvement of procedures on the part of Japan. This was a significant feature of the talks and fundamentally different from the Clinton Administration's "results-oriented" approach that followed in the 1990s.

2.2 Negotiations on Specific Issue Areas Across Many Sectors

2.2.1 The Issue of Voluntary Controls in Automobiles and Auto Parts

The automobile and auto parts issues emerged against a backdrop of structural changes in the US auto market triggered by the oil crisis (Hasegawa 2013, p. 336). US manufacturers had maintained an overwhelming advantage within their market sectors, mainly large passenger cars in the 5,000 cc class, but with the impact of the second oil crisis in 1979, consumer preferences shifted to fuel-efficient compact cars. Under these conditions, imports of small Japanese-made cars rose sharply. Automobile imports to the US in 1979 were up 16.4% over the previous year, with Japanese autos posting a 30.5% increase even as domestic car sales decreased by 10.5%. With the decline in performance by the Big Three and in particular the crisis faced by the Chrysler Corp., the US auto industry, labor unions, and Congress were highly critical of Japan. In 1979, the US Trade Representative (USTR) Rubin Askew indicated that the US government was ready to impose import restrictions on Japanese-made cars. At the January 1980 general meeting of the United Automobile Workers (UAW), UAW president Douglas M. Fraser strongly urged restricting Japanese exports to the US while at the same time calling on Japanese automakers to manufacture locally in the US.

Amid strong protectionist pressures domestically, the Carter Administration in 1980 announced its opposition to imposing import restrictions on Japanese cars or requiring Japan to adopt export restrictions, instead calling for Japanese makers to invest in the United States and for the expansion of US-made autos and auto parts exports to Japan. These issues were then left to intergovernmental negotiations between the two countries. Two administrative-level meetings of Japanese and US auto specialists were held in April 1980. In May, Japan announced voluntary measures in the form of a "Japan–US Auto Package," and the US took this as a positive step. Japan's automakers had not made any clear expression of intent to invest in the US. In light of this, the package included the promotion of Japanese automakers' investment in the US and measures to liberalize the Japanese market. This was intended to address the two principal demands of the US: first, that strict import inspections and standards impeding the export of US-made autos to Japan be relaxed, and second, that the gap be reduced between the taxes imposed on large autos and on small. These measures were not enough to resolve the issue, however.

With the recession deepening in the US auto industry, the UAW in June 1980 and Ford Motor Company in August filed suit with the US International Trade Commission (ITC) based on Section 201 of the 1975 Trade Act. In November, the ITC rejected the lawsuit, whereupon strong anti-Japanese sentiment emerged in Congress: the House actively sought enactment of legislation to restrict imported vehicles, and Congress adopted a joint resolution calling for the US government to respond to the situation. In April 1981, the newly inaugurated Reagan administration responded to the mounting demand for protection by announcing the rebuilding of the automobile industry through deregulation.

In response to the seriousness of the situation, MITI "requested sensible exports" of the Japan Automobile Manufacturers Association (JAMA), and given the judgment that legal restrictions on exports would be undesirable, the automakers began considering plans for self-regulation to restrain exports. On the US side, the ITC indicated that "the increase in imported cars is not the main cause of the slump in the US automobile industry," but the calls for strong regulation persisted nonetheless.

For this reason, the still new Reagan administration clarified that USTR would be the contact point for consultations with the Japanese government, and that while some import control measures were necessary for the domestic automobile industry, the United States should avoid actions that would violate the free-trade principles it advocated, and unofficially signaled that it would leave the regulation of imported vehicles to the voluntary judgment of its trade partner. The Japanese government announced its export projections based on the expected totals of exports of each vehicle maker, and through discussions with MITI Minister Rokusuke Tanaka, sought the reaction of the United States. Based on MITI instructions, it decided to regulate exports to the US for a three-year period from April 1981 to March 1984, and that its initial framework would limit the number of automobile exports to 1.68 million.

The second-year numbers would include the first-year numbers plus 16.5% of whatever growth had been achieved in the market. The condition of the US passenger-car market as of the end of the second year would be evaluated in the third year, and the question of whether to continue with the restrictions would be considered. These Voluntary Export Restraints (VER) continued to be implemented beyond FY 1984, through FY 1991, while the upper limits on exports were raised. Local production in the US by Japanese automakers also advanced from 1981 forward (see Table 1).

Regarding the issue of parts procurement, auto parts became subject to the MOSS talks mentioned above. As the US saw it, even with the premise that auto parts were not subject to institutional barriers such as tariffs, access to the Japanese market was a problem. Surveys were therefore conducted of the relationships between Japanese automakers and auto parts suppliers, and talks followed three times in 1986. The final report, issued in August 1987, called for JAMA to make regular disclosures to the US of procurement data regarding US-made auto parts, to provide US parts suppliers with clear information about contacts, and to promote plans for the expansion of trade in imported auto parts, and to follow up on them.

Technical survey teams and auto parts purchasing missions were dispatched from Japan and US personnel were hired to direct purchasing. Through these means Japan was able to obtain recognition that the relationships between Japanese automakers and parts suppliers were neither closed nor unique, and that they were rational and based on their superiority relative to others in the international market. However, due to differences between Japan and US in parts-procurement practices, the effect of measures for expanding purchasing was limited.

Table 1 Local production by Japanese automakers

Company name	Local manufacturer name	Est.date	Capitalization unit = $10,000	Form	Production start year	Product	Production capacity 10,000 vehicles/year	Number of employees
Honda	Honda of America Mfg., Inc.	1978	57,800	Solo	1982	Accord, Civic	36	6,300
					1986	Engines, drives, systems parts		1,600
					1989	Civic	15	500
Nissan	Nissan Motor Mfg. Corp., USA	1980	37,500	Solo	1983	Datsun, Sunny	25	3,500
Mazda	Mazda Motor Mfg. (USA) Corp.	1985	20,000	Solo	1987	MX-6, Ford Probe	24	3,500
Mitsubishi Heavy	Diamond-Star Motors	1985	19,950	Joint venture with Chrysler	1988	Eclipse, Mirage	24	2,900
Toyota	New United Motor Mfg., Inc.	1984	26,000	Joint venture with GM	1984	Prism, Corolla	20	3,100
	Toyota Motor Mfg., USA, Inc.	1986	54,000	Solo	1988	Camry engines, axles	20	3,000 500
	Toyota Motor Mfg. Canada Inc.	1986	25,000	Solo	1988	Corolla	7	1,000

(continued)

Table 1 (continued)

Company name	Local manufacturer name	Est.date	Capitalization unit = $10,000	Form	Production start year	Product	Production capacity 10,000 vehicles/year	Number of employees
	Canadian Autoparts Toyota, Inc.	1983	1,400	Solo	1985	Aluminum foil		120
Fuji Heavy/Isuzu	Subaru-Isuzu Automotive Inc.	1987	25,000	Joint venture	1989	Legacy, small trucks	16	1,900
Suzuki	CAMI Automotive	1986	15,000	Joint venture with GM Canada	1989	Cartus, Escudo	20	2,000

Source Hasegawa (2013, p. 342–343)

2.2.2 Setting Numerical Targets for Semiconductors

Friction over semiconductors surfaced around 1981, when Japan began adopting voluntary restrictions on its automobile exports to the US (Hasegawa 2013, p. 729). The semiconductor issue arose in the context of Japanese semiconductor manufacturers' rapid advance into global markets in the latter 1970s, particularly in the industry's memory chips sector. The growth was particularly marked in Japan's exports to the US. In February 1983 the US Semiconductor Industry Association (SIA) launched various denunciations of Japan's actions, including a report titled "The Effect of Government Targeting on World Semiconductor Competition: A Case History of Japanese Industrial Strategy and Its Costs for Americans." In June 1985, the SIA intensified its offensive by filing suit under Article 301 of the 1974 Trade Act.

MITI Minister Michio Watanabe and US Trade Representative Clayton Yeutter reached an agreement in principle at a May 1986 meeting, in accordance with which the contents for an agreement were put together in July, including expanding opportunities for entry by foreign semiconductor makers into Japan's market and instituting a monitoring system to prevent dumping. These became the core of the September 1986 US–Japan Semiconductor Agreement. Its most important feature was not incorporated in the agreement per se, but rather in a side letter saying that, "The Government of Japan recognizes the U.S. semiconductor industry's expectation that semiconductor sales in Japan of foreign capital-affiliated companies will grow to at least slightly above 20% of the Japanese market in five years. The Government of Japan considers that this can be realized and welcomes its realization." The US side interpreted this to mean that the Japanese government acknowledged numerical targets, which was to create significant problems in later years.

Following the conclusion of the agreement in March 1987, the United States announced that it regarded Japan to be in violation of this agreement. Its reasons were: 1. that entry by foreign semiconductors into Japan's market was insufficient, and 2. that dumping by Japanese firms in third-country markets was continuing to take place. The announcement said that in order to offset the sales opportunities lost by US industry, the US would impose a 100% tariff (totaling roughly 300 million dollars) on Japanese-made electronic instruments such as personal computers and color televisions, triggering the imposition of these measures in April that year. While continuing discussion with the US, the Japanese government concluded that the agreement violated GATT and proposed bilateral negotiations based on Article 23 Paragraph 1. The US accordingly eliminated the measures that were based on reason 2 above, but those based on Reason 1 remained in place until a new Japan–US Semiconductor Agreement was concluded in June 1991 (Fig. 2).

2.2.3 Measures to Address Steel Industry Trade Friction with the US

In the early 1980s, the US steel industry, whose profitability was deteriorating due to a high cost structure based on the high cost of labor, attributed its sluggishness to

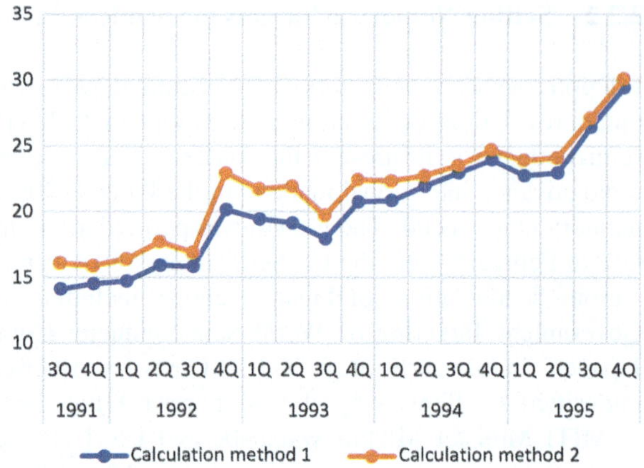

Fig. 2 Share of foreign-made semiconductors. *Source* Hasegawa (2013, p. 886). Original material from MITI (1997, p. 229)

unfair trade practices by Japanese steel-makers and in December 1982 filed for USTR application of relief measures under Article 301 of the Trade Act (Yamazaki 2011, p. 235). Its complaint was not accepted, but the US steel industry continued to raise similar issues thereafter. US–Japan Steel talks began in October that year, following President Reagan's statements that he would be seeking cuts in steel imports and improvement in the competitiveness of the US steel industry.

MITI entered the negotiations while in frequent exchanges of information with trading companies and steelmakers, and in March 1985 concluded the "Japan–US Steel Trade Agreement, Voluntary Restraint Agreement (VRA). "This limited imported products (not including semi-finished products) to 18.5% of the volume of domestic consumption and restricted Japanese steel imports to the US to a 5.8% market share. In principle, the target items were all steel materials, and the target period was the five years from October 1984 to September 1989. The same VRAs were established with other countries, but for Japan, which had sought to maintain a 6% share of the US market, this represented a major concession. Based on this arrangement, MITI issued the following instructions to the domestic steel industry in April 1985: 1. to establish a new export association to cover all the items subject to regulation, and 2. to establish an export cooperation association for exporters to the US in order to conclude an agreement among producers that would cover the items targeted by the regulations. The Association of Exporters of Steel to the US was established in May 1985, and adopted an Export Approval System based on the exercise of the outsider regulations of Article 28, paragraph 2 of the Export–Import Transaction Law, and took responsibility for issuing export certificates and exchanging information among companies and between companies and MITI. MITI considered this a short-term measure, and because the US too was concerned that it constituted a violation of antitrust law in the US, the Antitrust Division of the US Department of Justice also worked in close cooperation with MITI.

The "Association of Exporters to the US" was responsible for frameworks coordinating the volume of exports allotted to each manufacturer. The export quotas set up to control export volumes allowed for the following to some extent: (1) Advance Use, meaning the advance use of the next fiscal year's quota for the prior year; (2) Carry-overs, meaning the carry-over to the following year of export limits which were not reached in the current year; and (3) substitutions of yearly quotas, product types, and exporting companies, in instances of quotas not being met for certain types of products. That Japan's insistence was able to secure this flexibility in operations helped enable the concessions on quantitative targets. In October 1989, a bilateral agreement was concluded to extend the VRA for 30 months. Japan's export quota would be 5.0% for the first 15 months and 5.3% in the second 15 months. While the export quotas were reduced from 5.8%, the flexibility was enhanced. The VRA expired in March 1992.

The above VRA had the following effects, showing the Japan was not simply bearing the burden of export reduction. Japanese steelmakers' exports to the US were extremely profitable at the time when the agreement was concluded, and securing stability in that market was of great importance. In fact, Japan was earlier than other countries to reach agreement with the US in the negotiations for its extension. Moreover, because of the rapid appreciation of the yen, the dollar-denominated steel prices remained unable to keep pace with the rise in prices; sustaining the VRA export quotas was therefore preferable to following the usual path of accusations of dumping. In these ways, Japan's steel industry benefitted from the VRA.

Meanwhile, Japanese steelmakers expanded their exports to Asia to offset the decrease in exports to the US. These included supplying Japanese companies that were entering Asian markets. In the latter 1980s, Domestic demand expanded as well in the latter 1980s. Steelmakers therefore found themselves unable even to fill the quotas set under the VRA, in the final year exporting only just over 50% of the quota volumes. Thus the VRA didnot prove burdensome to Japan's steelmakers. The US steelmakers, however, while standing to benefit from the restrictions on Japanese exports, were unable to achieve sufficient rationalization of their industry.

2.2.4 Machine Tool Industry and Trade Friction with the US

For about 10 years beginning in the late 1970s, the United States' increasing reliance on imported machine tools became an issue (Abe 2013, p. 139; Hasegawa 2013, p. 729). One reason for this increased reliance on imports was the advance of low-priced small and medium-sized Japanese goods, centered on numerically controlled (NC) machine tools, which were well-regarded in the US because of their ability to respond to specific user needs. For this reason, dissatisfaction and a sense of crisis gradually increased among US makers and was expressed at the September 1977 National Machine Tool Builders Association (NMTBA) meeting. MITI was concerned that the dumping issue, already prominent in steel, would spread to the machine tool industry. While working to overcome the opposition of Japan's machine tool industry, MITI implemented an export certification system in February 1978 based on the Export and Import Transactions Law. This "Approval System for exports of horizontal numerically controlled lathes, horizontal and vertical machining centers, and related numerically controlled accessories" was implemented regarding exports to the US and Canada in March. In response, the NMTBA, which had been examining the issue, delivered an objective analysis of the competitiveness of Japan's machine tool industry in May 1981, finding no sign of unfair trade practices on Japan's part or of actions to restrict competition.

US dissatisfaction was not thereby eliminated, however. In 1982, trade friction between Japan and the US entered the field of machine tools when Houdaille Industries, Inc. of the US made an appeal to the president, by way of USTR, to exclude Japanese-made machining centers and numerical control punching machines from the investment tax credit target, based on Article 103 of the 1971 Revenue Act. The relevant associations in Japan put together a document arguing against this action, but letters of opinion continued to be submitted to the USTR. The USTR and US Department of Commerce thus began focusing on Article 301 of the 1974 Trade Act with machine tools as a new target. In February 1983, US Trade Representative Brock expressed to MITI Minister Sadanori Yamanaka his suspicions that Japan's industrial policy constituted an unfair trade practice, and hinted that the US might apply Article 301 in order to rectify the situation.

Meanwhile, the NMTBA continued with its suits. In March 1983, it sought from the Department of Commerce restrictions on the import of foreign machine tools based on Section 232 of the 1962 Trade Expansion Act. Based on a MITI proposal, a Japan–US Industrial Policy Coordination Committee was established and in mid-May 1983 held its first meeting.

Through this committee, affiliated Japanese companies argued that the content of the NMTBA litigation was based on a misunderstanding of industrial policy. No major developments followed in the case until January 1986. This was because analysis of Japan's machine tool industry showing that NC machine tools were a rational product of innovation, and the US machine-tool industry did not have the political power to impose constraints on user choice in the US. However, after deliberations on the NMTBA case resumed in January 1986, President Reagan in May issued a statement calling for voluntary export controls by Japan. Consultations followed several times between the US and Japanese governments, and in November 1986, the two countries came to an agreement on the voluntary regulation of export volumes of six machine tools for a five-year period beginning in January 1987 (Table 2).

Volume export restraints were applied to three types of NC machine tools in line with the Export Trade Control Order of the Foreign Exchange and Foreign Trade Control Law. The three non-NC varieties of machine tools were subject to a monitoring approach, and the volume of exports to the US in fact remained at the same levels as they were when self-regulation began. The voluntary export restraints saw some temporary relaxation in 1988 and 1989, but in December 1991, the restraints on four of the models were extended by agreement for an additional two years, until 1993.

The effect of these restraints was a decline in the volume of NC machine-tools exports to the US from 1985 forward, and because Japanese production and exports both increased after 1988, the rate of increase of exports to the US fell by comparison. Self-regulation was recognized as effective in the sense that it limited exports to

Table 2 Voluntary export controls on machine tools, 1987 (Rate of Reduction)

Machine type	1986 number of units	Original restrictions	July 1987 Revision of restrictions
Machining centers	3,435	2,800 (−18.5%)	2,400 (−34.80%)
NC machine tools	4,456	3,200 (−28.2%)	2,560 (−42.60%)
NC drilling machines	N.A.	250	N.A.

NC numerically controlled
Source Hasegawa (2013, p. 243)

Table 3 Status of implementation of the action program on the assessment process for standards and conformity of imports

	Number of items as of March 1988	Number implemented	Number implemented as of March 1990
Standards and certification areas	81	72	80
Reducing government intervention	33	30	33
Reducing the number of applicable items	10	9	10
Moving from government certification to self-certification	15	13	15
Reducing or relaxing the number of regulations and standards	5	5	5
Other	3	3	3
Comprehensive determinations by the coordination headquarters for standards and conformity	48	42	47
Proactive use of foreign inspection data and organizations	20	18	20
Assuring transparency	7	7	7
Aligning with international standards	11	7	10
Simplifying/speeding up certification (conformity) procedures	10	10	10
Import process areas	10	10	10
Reducing the scope of procedures' applicability	3	3	3
Simplifying/speeding up of procedures	7	7	7
Total	91	82	90

Abe (2013, p. 297)

the US. At the same time, however, the per-unit price of US imports of Japanese machine-tools rose. This was due in part to the yen's appreciation but also reflected the Japanese industry's shift to more sophisticated and higher-value added products.

2.2.5 Japan-Europe Trade Friction and Negotiations

The growth in European imports of general and electric machinery from Japan became an issue in the early 1980s amid the trade imbalance between Japan and the EC (European Community) and the recession in EC countries. In July 1980, the EC Committee issued "EC's trade policy towards Japan—a reexamination" and demanded that Japan adopt voluntary restraints on its exports in exchange for the EC's eliminating discriminatory restrictions aimed at Japanese products (Abe 2013, p. 147). Japan responded by adopting voluntary restraints on exports of the products in question while also continuing to negotiate with Britain's Department of Trade and Industry on industrial cooperation. However, the EC Committee in February 1982 issued a report on economic relations with Japan and expressed its intention of filing suit with GATT on the issue of the openness of the Japanese market. Because the EC was unable to obtain the desired conclusion from the GATT deliberations, the EC Committee twice extended its system of monitoring Japanese imports: once in December 1982 and once in March 1983, adding to its list of "sensitive items" such products as VTRs, light commercial vehicles, motorcycles, and then forklifts, hi-fi equipment, and quartz watches. These monitoring measure were maintained until 1985.

Separately, France introduced its own import supervision system and required a longer period than usual for obtaining model certifications of Japanese-made cars. In October 1982, it decided on "economic relations measures for improving the trade balance," adopting a series of measures that made international access to France's market more difficult, such as requiring the use of French in customs documents, and centralizing in its inland Poitiers office the customs offices handling VTRs. These measures potentially violated GATT in many ways, but in February 1983, MITI announced a three-year implementation of minimum export pricing system on VTRs based on the Export and Import Transaction Law, and released a plan on voluntary export restraints regarding the EC. In addition, in response to the EC Committee's presentation of revisions to its comprehensive list of demands of Japan in April 1984, MITI announced its projections regarding exports to the EC of specific items such as VTRs and communicated its intention to maintain voluntary controls.

The so-called Japan Problem meanwhile deepened in the mid-1980s. Discussions were sought on such issues as improving Japan's distribution system and standards and certification systems, promoting government procurement, simplifying import procedures, and adopting measures to counter illegal products. In response to these demands, which came not only from the US but also from the EC, Japan, as mentioned above, announced in July 1985 a "framework for action programs for improving market access." From November to December that year, Japan and various EC governments held talks on industrial cooperation, and the EC–Japan Center for Industrial Cooperation was established in Tokyo, as proposed by Japan.

This effort at mutual cooperation was expanded through regular consultations on Japan–UK industrial cooperation launched in 1981. The first meeting of the Japan–EC Symposium was held in November 1982 with the theme "Japan–EC Economic Relations and the World Economy—Exploring Paths to Improved Coordination." The EC discussed the trade imbalance and the closed nature of the Japanese market while Japan pointed out the lack of effort on the part of the EC to develop its market in Japan and also the need for concrete explanations of the closed nature of the market. These meetings were to be held about once a year thereafter. At the Second Japan–EC Symposium, it was agreed that discussions on industrial cooperation would be held between MITI Minister Yamanaka and EC Committee Deputy Chair Étienne Davignon on a regular basis. It was in the course of this process that the Japan–EC Industrial Cooperation Center was established in 1985.

2.3 Liberalization of the Domestic Market and Deregulation

2.3.1 Market Liberalization

In the early 1980s, "non-tariff barriers" became the focus of criticism of Japan, beginning with issues related to Japan's import systems. Domestic industry, too, was beginning to raise criticisms of Japan's import systems (Abe 2013, p. 246). The Product Import Measures Council, a new subcommittee of the Import Council at the July 1979 Trade Convention, discussed reviewing trends in product imports, evaluating existing measures to promote imports, and deliberating on import-promotion measures for the future. The subcommittee met five times before June of 1980, and submitted its conclusions as proposals to the Import Council, pointing out problems in import procedures and also puting together an overview to introduce overseas audiences to some particular features of the Japanese market. The May 1982 Ministerial Conference on Economic Measures decided that issues of Japanese business practices and Japan's distribution system would also be taken up by the Product Import Measures Council, and reviews were launched of systems related to imports.

Meanwhile, the Federation of Economic Organizations (Keidanren) issued the "Request Concerning the Improvement of External Economic Relations" in December 1981, and as "measures to further open the market," proposed tariff reduction, the relaxation of unit and volume import restrictions and the elimination of non-tariff barriers, along with the implementation of "various measures effective for promoting imports," such as expansion of product imports and emergency imports.

Keidanren also issued a proposal to the government in December titled "Views on Import and Export Procedures and Inspections" and called for the simplification and rationalization of customs procedures and a review of import inspections. At the same time, the Import Promotion Measures Council established by MITI in October issued an interim report citing the necessity of (1) tariff reduction, (2) relaxation of restrictions on imports, (3) improvement of import inspection procedures, and (4) improvement of other areas such as non-tariff barriers. In December 1981, the government decided on "external economic measures" at the Ministerial Conference on Economic Action and called for concrete policies in the five areas of market opening, import promotion, exports, industrial cooperation, and economic cooperation.

Furthermore, in the Ministerial Conference on Economic Action in January 1982, the government adopted "market-opening policies" focused on measures to improve import inspection procedures. The main content of the measures for the "first step" of market opening included implementation of remedial measures on 67 cases selected from the 99 cases of import inspection procedures that had been under review at the meetings on measures regarding product imports; the addition of nine further improvements for consideration; and establishment of an Ombudsman Office of Trade and Investment (OTO) to handle complaints from other countries related to import inspection procedures. Particular to these measures was that many of them were safety standards of the past that were in effect cases of barriers to entry.

These safety standards had been created not as trade policy but because of particular sectoral needs and were not necessarily intended to shut out foreign products, but many could easily be criticized as over-regulation. Complaints on imports, which used to be brought to the US–Japan Trade Facilitation Committee (TFC), the Product Import Measures Council, and the liaison for each of the agencies and ministries, were now brought to the OTO, which held its first deliberations in February 1982.

However, the United States continued to exert strong pressure on Japan to open its market. Keidanren conducted its own independent investigation and in April 1982 put together its "Proposals on Easing Economic Friction with Foreign Countries," asserting that "Once protectionism spreads, it cannot fail to shake the free trade system and even the liberal economic system itself" and "The way our country can contribute to world peace is by realizing a new role in international society and cooperating with other countries to maintain and strengthen the free-trade system and build stable interdependent relationships." In May, the government decided on its "second step," which was "measures to open up the market."

Import-promotion measures were implemented in the following areas: improvement of import inspection procedures; reduction of tariffs; relaxation of import restrictions; expansion of imports; improvement of distribution facilities and business practices; liberalization of trade in services; and cutting-edge technologies. Thus, the efforts to expand imports, which had been under way since the latter 1970s, were given the force of policy in the fall of 1982. The written opinion of the General Committee submitted to the Trade Council in October was the first example of a concrete and comprehensive system of Import Promotion Policies, which shaped the development of subsequent measures. Suggestions were made about the need to promote foreign countries' export expansion efforts through JETRO and MIPRO (Manufactured Imports and Investment Promotion Organization), leading to events and import fairs with input from the Trade Council (Fig. 3).

(1) Political support measures for importers

*Creation of tax system for promotion of product imports

*Elimination of tariffs on 1,004 items, centered on machinery

(reduction of tariffs on a further four items)

*Expansion and reinforcement of import finance

Expansion and reinforcement of Export-Import Bank (EIB) import financing

Expansion of Japan Development Bank (JDB) import financing system

EIB and JDB financial system for promoting aircraft introduction

Expansion and improvement of the lending system to facilitate the sale of imported goods by small and medium-sized retailers through JASME and JFC

Expansion of direct lending system by Hokuto Financing Corp

*Support for the promotion of sales of imported goods (assistance to *shotengai* shopping districts, etc.)

*Import promotion seminars (targeting regional wholesalers)

*Advancement of import promotion projects in the distribution industry (Comprehensive international distribution centers)

*Expansion and improvement of insurance for prepayments on imports

*Support for partner countries exporting to Japan

・Support by JETRO:

Cooperative projects to support exports to Japan

(policies regarding advanced economies of Europe and the US)

1. establishment of Economic Internationalization Centers)

(providing information on imports on a national scale)

2. inviting business people from Europe and the US

3. dispatching specialists to seek out products to export to Japan

4. dispatching and receiving missions

5. Comprehensive Import Promotion Centers and pilot projects

Provision of surveys and information

1. information on import trade

2. domestic marketing surveys

3. surveys of overseas products

4. creation of US state-specific catalogs of products of export interest

5. other

Support for developing countries

1. invitations

2. guidance for the development and improvement of export products

3. LDC (Least Developed Countries) centers, S/C projects

4. Projects to foster small and medium-sized businesses

・Support by MIPRO:

exhibition projects

projects to introduce quality import products

other

Fig. 3 Comprehensive plan for import expansion (Abe 2013 p.191). *Note* JFC, Japan Financing Corporation; JASME, Japan Finance Corporation for Small and Medium-Sized Enterprises. *Source* A similar chart is found in Tsusansho kōhō (October 2, 1990, p. 8)

(2) Requests to industry for import expansion (314 companies)

(3) Public campaigns for the expansion of imports

Import expansion month (October each year)

Import bazaars and fairs, and exhibitions of all types (JETRO, MIPRO)

Fostering of individual importers, consultation corners for individual importers (MIPRO)

Support of import fairs at department stores, supermarkets, etc.

Projects for import penetration, projects to provide information on import products

Fig. 3 (continued)

2.3.2 Simplification of Standards and Conformity Procedures

The second step, "market-opening policies," was well-received by the US up to a point, but the tensions remained. In the closing meetings of the Japan–US administrative-level trade talks in August 1982, the US said it was ready to ask Japan for bilateral discussions, based on GATT, on Japan's inspection procedures for imports of metal baseball bats. Import systems had previously been a relatively minor problem between the two countries, but the metal bats issue was related to the systems, practices, and ways of thinking of the two nations, and proved a trigger for entering more deeply into each other's domestic systems.

It was in this context that Keidanren in December 1982 submitted to the government its "Recommendations on Improvement of Trade-related Permissions and Inspections." This proposal was noteworthy because rather than adhering to Keidanren's earlier reactive stance regarding economic friction, it suggested a strong recognition that the comprehensive establishment of the "principles of free trade" would be positive for private enterprises. It argued that, since procedures and inspections were "complicated and opaque" and the "confusion around the interpretation and operation of the law" acted as a "bureaucratic barrier," "we should abolish excessive inspections, simplify and unify complicated procedures, and standardize the operation of laws and ordinances, in order to actively promote smoother and speedier distribution."

Against a background of domestic and international criticism, the government in the January 1983 Ministerial Conference on Economic Measures decided on "Market-opening policies" in five areas, of which measures on non-tariff barriers formed a major part. The government also established the Liaison and Coordination Headquarters on Standards and Certification Systems (Headquarters for Standards Coordination) to put together a bulk amendment bill by the end of March for simplifying the standards and conformity assessment system (Abe 2013, p. 270).

Meanwhile, Keidanren submitted to the government its "Opinion concerning the amendment and improvement of trade-related laws and regulations" in March 1983. It argued that:

> From the general viewpoint of the national economy, not just the limited matter of the standards and conformity system for import inspections, we should bring about substantive reform through a change in consciousness regarding trade-related permits and inspections and seek not only to ease the trade friction but also to reduce the burden on the people and simplify and rationalize administrative affairs in order to invigorate the private sector.

The Opinion urged revision and operational improvement of 41 laws and ordinances to encourage firms to become less passive about US–Japan friction.

After consideration by the Headquarters for Standards Coordination, the government decided at the Ministerial Conference on Economic Policy to apply the principle of "nondiscrimination between domestic and foreign firms" with a comprehensive revision of 17 laws including the Electrical Appliance and Materials Control Law so that foreign firms could apply directly for inspections of import products. Various measures, including revision of the law, were undertaken in response to strong demand from Europe and America. But MITI stressed that the revisions were aimed at equal treatment for domestic and foreign firms, not at altering fundamental principles, and that they would not come at the cost of consumer safety. Because the revisions did not bring about an immediate rise in imports, they did not eliminate trade friction either. In February 1984, MITI simplified the standards and conformity procedures so as to accept foreign inspection data, in hopes of gaining the understanding of those countries that were most critical of Japan.

2.3.3 Advancing the Action Program

In 1983, the Product Import Measures Council began reviewing issues concerning the distribution system. The Japanese government took the position that it was reasonable that Japan's distribution mechanisms would be adapted to their home environment, that non-rational systems were in the process of being improved, that foreign exporters should show an understanding of Japan's unique environment, and that Japan was ready to cooperate in promoting that understanding. This was not an argument that foreign critics of Japan were ready to accept, but neither did the critics have a clear position about what precisely was needed to be resolved.

The Product Import Measures Council responded in June 1983 with a report titled "The Japanese distribution system and business practices: analysis recommendations." The Council clarified in detail the particularities of the Japanese system where it differed from European and American systems, and while pointing out a number of features for improvement, also emphasized those that had a certain rationality and explained them to those overseas. Because the current account imbalance was expanding principally as a result of differences in macroeconomic policy, however, the Council's market-opening policies could not necessarily result in a direct expansion in imports.

Prime Minister Nakasone therefore instructed MITI Minister Keijiro Murata in November 1984 to examine the market-opening policies vis-à-vis the United States (Abe 2013 p. 283). The US wanted concrete results in the four fields in which high-level negotiations were taking place (communications equipment, timber, electronics, and medical equipment and medicines). With the focus on how to provide relief to the domestic plywood industry in the face of timber tariff reductions, even weak parts of the Japanese economy were being viewed in terms of market-opening possibilities.

The March 1985 "Report" of the Government's External Economic Problems Advisory Committee" expressed regret that the six-stage market-opening policy of the government was a passive response to overseas requests and urged that the basic "principle of free trade (not including energy and food)" govern economic exchanges with foreign countries. The frameworks confirmed in July 1985 accordingly consisted mostly of items that required aggressive policy involvement to promote the expansion of imports.

The "Framework for an action program for market access improvement" was officially decided on in July that year. Among the basic principles introduced in the general discussion were: (1) that the fundamental perspective of "free trade in principle, with a minimum of exceptions" meant the government should intervene as little as possible, leaving the outcome to consumer choice and responsibility, (2) that Japan should be active in conformity with its own stance of pursuing a new round of talks, and (3) that Japan should be especially concerned to be of use in promoting the economic development of developing nations. Based on these principles, the Framework set out various action plans on the three items: concerning tariffs, restrictions on imports, and standards and conformity in the import process.

Further reforms of the standards and conformity system included: (1) reducing the number of targeted items, (2) furthering the shift from government certification to self-certification, and (3) eliminating or relaxing the number of planning and standards items. This meant that there would be a wide range of regulatory easing for domestic firms as well. MITI actively pursued these reforms in line with government policy.

2.4 Progress on the Uruguay Round Negotiations

2.4.1 Moves to Opening a New GATT Round

GATT, which came into force in 1948, provided a trade order based on the principles of free trade and nondiscrimination and a place for multilateral free-trade negotiations, and contributed to the expansion of world trade in the postwar period. The Tokyo Round of 1973–1979 achieved results in the form of the first real reduction and elimination of non-tariff measures (Imuta and Washizawa 1994, pp. 215–219) and agreements were formed in 12 areas, but protectionist trends expanded on a global scale thereafter. Deregulation therefore remained a consistent feature of policy from this point forward.

Negotiations were challenging at the November 1982 GATT Ministerial Meeting in Geneva, but they resulted in a political declaration on the maintenance of the free-trade system and in the formulation of the "GATT Work Plan" according to which GATT would take up 17 areas, including safeguards, trade in agricultural products, textiles and clothing, dispute resolution procedures, trade in illegal goods, and trade in services (Abe 2013, p. 403). The Williamsburg Summit in May 1983 confirmed the content of the agreement, and Japan began active preparations for a new round. At the November Japan–US Summit, Japan proposed preparations for a new round under Japanese and US leadership and obtained agreement; it also began strengthening its outreach to the EC on the same subject. As these activities proceeded among advanced economies, however, developing economies sought adjustments in the balance of interests. They argued that: (1) the merits of a new round were not clear, (2) past rounds had served the interests only of advanced economies, (3) advanced countries were promoting the liberalization of trade in products from tropical regions. Developing countries were also concerned about negotiations on the liberalization of services, an area in which they were not competitive. Amidst the standoff between advanced and developing countries, the US in 1985 proposed a vote based on the provisions of Article 25.4 to decide whether to hold a special general meeting of GATT. This was followed by a special general meeting in September at which it was decided that a preparatory process would begin, and in November by a GATT regular general meeting decision to establish a preparatory committee. These movements were said to have been influenced in part by the "New Trade Policy" announced by the US in September, which represented the US's expression of intent to continue pursuing trade agreements at the bilateral and regional level. Subsequent coordination with developing countries remained difficult, but against the background of the US "new trade policy" stance, the Uruguay Round began in September 1986.

2.4.2 The Start of the New Round

In previous negotiations, one draft was prepared for the ministerial declaration to initiate negotiations, but the Uruguay Round saw drafts both from hardline developing nations such as India and Brazil and from the advanced economies and the moderate faction of the developing nations. Negotiations were launched with both drafts in parallel. The two differed on whether or not to include new areas (trade in services, measures on trade-related investment, trade issues related to intellectual property). Ultimately, the ministerial declaration (the Punta del Este Declaration) starting negotiations on a new round adopted the new areas, in line with the draft presented by the advanced economies and the moderate wing of the developing economies. The declaration said the Uruguay Round would conclude negotiations on 15 areas within four years, and that it would adopt a "single undertaking" approach. "Single undertaking" meant comprehensive talks requiring agreement on all areas. If agreement could not be reached in any one area, the entire agreement would be rendered moot.

Fourteen of the 15 areas under discussion addressed trade in goods, but classified by content, they covered: (1) improvement in access: tariffs, non-tariff measures, tropical products, natural resources products, textiles and clothing, agricultural markets; (2) negotiation matters: GATT provisions, safeguards (SG), multilateral trade negotiations (MTN), various regulations/provisions (anti-dumping, AD), subsidies and offset/compensatory measures, dispute management rules; and (3) new areas of negotiation: services, TRIPS (agreement on trade-related aspects of intellectual property rights), TRIMs (agreements on trade-related investment measures). Areas of dispute can be categorized as follows: (1) those in which developing countries had many demands to make of advanced economies: tropical goods, natural resource products,

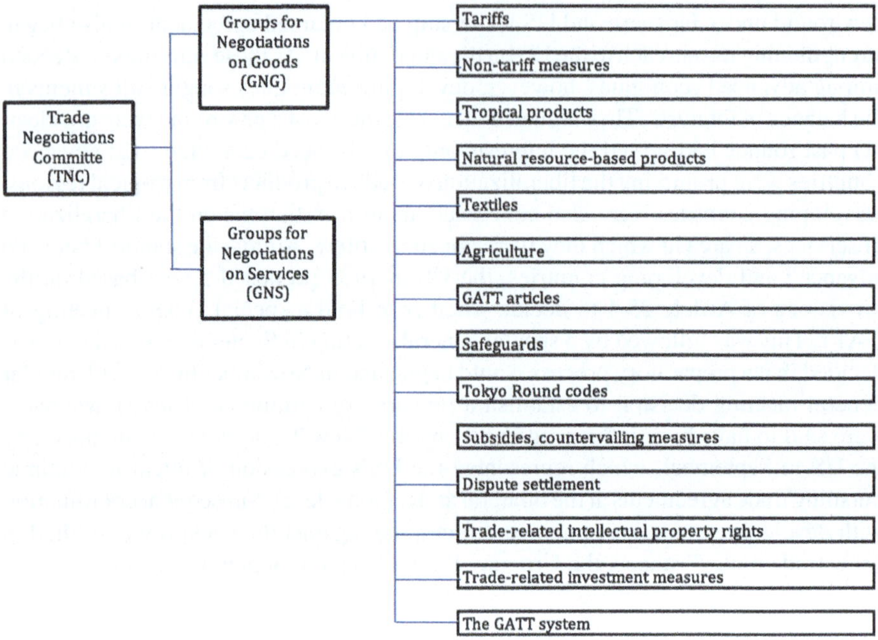

Fig. 4 Organization of negotiations in the new round (Abe 2013, p. 414)

textiles, and safeguards; (2) those with conflicts of interest not only between advanced and developing economies but also among advanced economies: MTN rules and dispute resolution; (3) those in which advanced economies had many demands to make of developing countries, principally regarding the new areas under negotiation (Fig. 4).

2.4.3 The Reduction of Tariffs on Industrial Goods

The addition of talks on agricultural products and new areas reduced the relative weight of the talks on tariffs on industrial goods but they still remained highly significant (Abe 2013, p. 425). The effectiveness of GATT talks in reducing tariff rates in advanced economies only highlighted the non-tariff barriers that affected industrial products. Furthermore, these negotiations centered on the advanced economies, while the percentage of items with a set bound rate in developing countries was low, causing problems when the tariff rate was also high.

The US opposed using the Formula System of prior rounds as the approach to lowering tariffs through negotiation, demanding instead the use of the Request Offer System. The EC proposed using the Formula System for those products on which tax rates were high, and the Request Offer system where tax rates were in the middle range. It was agreed at the December 1988 Montreal Ministerial Meeting that there would be an overall reduction of tariffs as there had been at the Tokyo Round, or in other words a reduction of 33% on a trade-weighted average basis. Determination had not been made on the question of how to achieve these reductions, but in February 1990, an agreement was reached allowing countries to pursue their own approaches. Thereafter, the various member countries explored ways of reducing their own tariffs. The fourth ministerial meeting in Tokyo in July 1993 saw a breakthrough, and four points of agreement were reached on access to markets for manufactured goods. This became the catalyst for achieving a final package in December.

The results of the negotiations on the reduction of tariffs on industrial goods can be categorized as follows: (1) overall reductions, (2) sector approaches, (3) the treatment of high-tariff items, and (4) developing countries. The average overall rate of reduction of tariffs in industrialized countries was 38%. Developing countries had a 20% reduction in the bound tariff rate. Japan's reduction rate was 56%, representing the high end. Also, the proportion of items with tariffs bound at zero was 44% for advanced economies overall: this broke down into 38% for the EU, 40% for the United States, and the prohibitively high 71% for Japan. Discussions on high-tariff items did not produce satisfactory results, but the fourth category saw a significant improvement in the scope of GATT discipline extended to tariffs on developing countries: the percentage of items with a bound rate in developing countries rose significantly from 21% to 73%. Nevertheless, tariff reduction in developing countries remained inadequate.

2.4.4 International Agreement on Textiles and Clothing

The 1974 Multi-Fibre Arrangement (Multi-Fibre Arrangement Regarding International Trade in Textiles (MFA)) separated the framework for trade in textiles from that for the products subject to GATT's general principles. This special framework was developed because the textile industry was highly localized and reflected the particular interests of each country, such as the need to create abundant upstream, midstream, and downstream employment. The MFA covered trade in cotton, wool, and synthetic fibers and permitted more moderate triggering conditions than the normal safeguards (SG) accepted in Article 19 of the GATT.

Member states had deep-rooted criticisms of MFA, charging that it impeded free trade in textiles. In 1982, the GATT Ministerial Conference agreed to consider liberalization and approaches to including textiles in GATT (Abe 2013, p. 434). In the Uruguay Round that began in 1986, the US, EU, Canada, Australia, Norway, and Finland, all active users of the MFA, urged the GATT integration to be as gradual as possible. The most difficult negotiations were to be addressed in high-level administrative meetings in April 1989. The statement that the Ministers "agree that measures on the process of integration into GATT will cover the elimination of MFA-based regulations" confirmed an approach to eliminating the MFA. This issue would later be reviewed as an individual item in WTO negotiations, discussed in Sect. 3 below in relation to the Uruguay Round negotiations.

2.4.5 Issues in Trade in Services

The major areas to be newly negotiated were trade-related investment measures, intellectual property rights, and trade in services. Global trade in services had seen a remarkable expansion, despite the many domestic regulations that remained in effect in all countries in the 1970s and 1980s (Abe 2013, p. 484). This area therefore became part of the agenda for international negotiation for the first time, introduced by the US at the 1973–1979 Tokyo Round. Subsequently, as discussions continued at GATT, the conditions for what would be the Uruguay Round negotiations were also put in place. These included talks on four areas: the application of Most-Favored Nation status, National Treatment status, systemic issues such as the definition of "services," and how the demands of developing countries should be handled.

In the early stages of the negotiations started in February 1987, the major countries exchanged various ideas. The EC proposed a universal approach targeting a wide range of services, from the point of view of ensuring effective market access. It also proposed establishing an organization to monitor discrimination due to domestic regulations. The United States initially wanted liberalization of the service sector overall, but gradually shifted to a sectoral approach to exclude sectors such as shipping. Japan supported the US's orientation, with a position of seeking the liberalization of transportation, tourism, finance, etc. Meanwhile, developing countries generally favored the universal approach, but Latin American and Caribbean countries adopted a sectoral approach. Developing countries also proposed that export promotion and infant-industry protections should be incorporated into the agreement. One of the major issues that surfaced in 1989 in the discussion of individual service areas was whether to adopt a "negative list method," according to which the obligations under the agreement would be applied to all service areas except for specified exceptions, or the "Positive List System" in which the agreement would apply only to those fields specified in it.

Although the United States advocated the former approach of promoting the principle of liberalization, and the EC agreed, developing countries advocated the latter approach, and negotiations proceeded along parallel lines. Similar stalemates occurred in other areas of discussion. In December 1991, the results of all the negotiations were presented in the "Draft final act embodying the results of the Uruguay Round of Multilateral Trade Negotiations" (the Dunkel Draft), with a number of issues in the service sector still outstanding.

As a result of the Uruguay Round negotiations, the "General Agreement on Trade in Services (GATS)," which provided a disciplinary framework for trade in services, came into force as an annex to the WTO Agreement. However, because the promises made by member countries did not involve significant changes in existing domestic regulations, the agreements did not necessarily result in an expansion of market access. While member countries promised internationally to assure transparency of their domestic regulations, they were able to offer legal stability by retreating from the promises made and restricting them thereby.

2.4.6 Japan-Related GATT Disputes

Before the 1970s, Japan's trade policy did not make any use of GATT dispute settlement procedures. That changed completely in the 1980s, however (Abe 2013, p. 503). For example, Japan requested bilateral consultations under Article 23 for the first time, following on Article 22 consultations, in response to a changes made in the tariff classification of the cab chassis by the United States in 1981. In this case, the negotiations did not result in agreement and no panel was set up. Japan also tried to resolve the 1982 VTR dispute with the French government through GATT mechanisms, but a panel was not set up in this case either.

The import restrictions on leather goods that began in 1983 marked the first occasion on which Japan was able to ask for a substantive judgment from the panel. Since Japan had already assumed IMF Article VIII status in 1964, it had no grounds for maintaining its limitations on quantity, and the US asserted that Japan's import restriction measures violated GATT Article 11. Japan tried to justify its quantity restrictions on the basis of social policy needs but without referring to specific exception clauses such as GATT Article 20. Although the Panel showed an understanding of Japan's situation, it dismissed its defense on the grounds that the Panel was limited to considering the problem in light of GATT provisions. The report was adopted at the meeting of the Board of Governors in May 1984, and Japan announced the substantial liberalization of Wet Blue (a semi-finished product of chemical-treated leather). In March 1985, the United States once again requested consultation based on Article 23 paragraph 1 of GATT. This targeted import restrictions on leather footwear. The United States announced the suspension of the procedure in December, following Japan's November announcement to the Board of Directors that it was abolishing its quantity restrictions on footwear. This compromise was brought about by a reduction of tariffs on 149 items by Japan and the US decision to limit its pursuit of sanctions on Japanese leather products. Other panel consultations occurring against the general backdrop of Japan–US economic friction included the 1981 EEC (European Economic Community) complaints against Japan and the US regarding a third-country semiconductor export-monitoring incident.

Japan was not necessarily in a situation to actively apply for panel consultations in the early 1980s, but towards the end of the decade began to refer its disputes vigorously as the complainant country.

The turning point was an EEC tax case on Parts Anti-Dumping (AD). The panel that Japan requested in October 1988 met twice in July and September 1989. The EEC's new AD tax-bypass deterrence prevention rules, in which taxes were assessed ex post facto on parts, were intended to prevent AD taxes on finished goods being bypassed through the so-called "knockdown methods" of importing and then assembling parts. Japan's argument was that the tax on parts was not applied at the point of import and therefore constituted domestic taxes, and that the imposition of those taxes only on imported goods was contrary to Article 3, paragraph 2, 1 of GATT. Also, the exemptions on the taxation of parts, on the condition of increases in local procurement, would promote priority being given to EEC products, which Japan claimed was contrary to GATT article 3.4. The panel report in March 1990 generally approved Japan's claim.

2.4.7 Japan's Economic Cooperation Policies and Asia

One of the pillars of the economic cooperation policy from 1985 to 1991 was the Yen Loan System. Based on the June, 1975 Memorandum of Understanding between the relevant ministries and agencies, the system was solely the responsibility of the Overseas Economic Cooperation Fund (OECF) (Abe 2013, p. 767).

Under this mechanism, the OECF decided on individual lending operations, and the Economic Planning Agency, Ministry of Foreign Affairs, Ministry of Finance, and MITI approved the decisions. MITI advocated the use of yen loan provisions to promote economic and social development in developing countries, its position being that such development would benefit Japanese companies and Japan's national economic interests.

The benefits to Japanese companies can roughly be classified as follows: (1) promoting exports through loan projects procuring material from Japanese companies, and (2) providing ODA loans for infrastructure in order to facilitate investment by Japanese companies. Regarding the first there were two approaches: either secure or expand yen-loan procurement volumes based on "tied conditions" or raise the rate of procurement from Japanese companies in the loan provisions through "untied conditions." providing ODA loans under untied conditions. Although international regimes for regulating the use of tied conditions in ODA (Official Development Assistance) had been constructed over time, they had little influence on Japan's economic cooperation policy before 1985.

However, in 1985 the OECD Arrangement on Officially Supported Export Credits was revised, and the ODA loan system was forced to change its policy based on the Wallen Package agreement of 1987. This was because a discount-rate calculation method was adopted that prohibited many low-interest loans by donor countries, with Japan as its implicit target. In addition, except for exceptional measures, the Helsinki Package of 1991 prohibited the ODA loans with any tied conditions for projects of a potentially commercial nature. MITI strongly argued for maintaining tied conditions but was unable to win acceptance. Japan made the shift to untied conditions at the beginning of 1988.

After the G5's Plaza Agreement of 1985, Japanese companies also began to urge creation of an environment that would support overseas investment. ASEAN countries were inspired by the 1980s success of South Korea, Taiwan, Hong Kong, and Singapore and were seeking foreign capital-driven development strategies. Improving the investment climate could involve either the development of new target countries or advancements in existing infrastructure. An example of an effective case was the ODA loans advanced to Thailand in the latter 1980s. This case was treated as "the Japan ODA Model" in the 2005 interim summary of the Economic Cooperation Subcommittee of the Industrial Structure Council.

2.5 International Harmonization of Intellectual Property Rights

2.5.1 The Intellectual Property Strategy of the US and the Japan–US Problem in the 1980s

Trade in electronics products such as computers, telecommunication equipment, and electronic components saw particularly marked growth within the overall expansion of world trade in the 1980s. US President Ronald Reagan, who regarded the loss in international competitiveness of high-tech products of this kind as a matter of national security, organized the Presidential Commission on Industrial Competitiveness in June 1983. The report stated that "US technological strength is still at the highest level in the world" and that the fact that its strength was not reflected in world trade was "due to [other countries'] inadequate protections for intellectual property." The report therefore proposed promoting enhanced protection of intellectual property rights (Nakayama 2013, p.72).

This point of view was at the core of the Reagan administration's September 1985 "New Trade Policy," and was slated to be pursued in the new Uruguay Round the following year.

Meanwhile, Japan's exports to the US increased sharply in the 1980s, and Japan–US patent disputes were frequent as well. As US industry saw it, the Japanese patent system and its operations presented the following problems: (1) the Japan Patent Office delayed the review of patents and thereby interfered with the opportunities of US companies for entry, (2) the scope of the rights interpreted by the court was narrow and could not be used effectively against infringements of US companies' patents. With these dissatisfactions in industry, the US Senate resolved in July 1989 to demand that the US government investigate 16 items. The Japanese and US governments planned intergovernmental talks to address the patent problem and included it on the agenda of the Japan–US Structural Impediments Initiative talks of 1989–1990 and the US–Japan Framework for a New Economic Partnership in 1993–1994. Japan adopted the following measures: (1) accepting applications in English, (2) shifting to a post-grant opposition petition system, (3) improving the operations of the early screening system, and (4) restricting compulsory licenses on use relations. For its part, America undertook to (1) optimize the starting dates for patent terms, (2) introduce an early publication system, (3) introduce a re-examination system and (4) issue compulsory restrictions on licenses on use relations. However, the necessary revision of the law was delayed by about five years, and a number of issues remained unresolved.

2.5.2 The Uruguay Round and the TRIPS Agreement

After the announcement of its New Policy on Trade in September 1985, the United States promoted the creation through GATT of multilateral rules regarding intellectual property (Nakayama 2013, p. 95). The reason GATT was chosen rather than the UN's World Intellectual Property Organization (WIPO) was first and foremost because of the difference between the two in enforcement mechanisms: GATT had economic sanctions. Second, under GATT it was possible to put together a package deal that included other items of negotiation, and third, America was in an isolated position in the ongoing WIPO negotiations on a patent harmonization treaty.

In response, Japan concluded that its position was basically the same as that of the United States, namely, that improving intellectual property protection in developing countries would be beneficial. The multilateral approach was also desirable for Japan, which wanted to resolve its bilateral issues with the United States in a multilateral forum. Some developing countries, by contrast, strongly opposed the formulation of international rules and called for utilization of WIPO.

Amidst these various considerations and interests, the TRIPS negotiations were launched with the Uruguay Round Ministerial Declaration (Punta del Este Declaration) in September 1986. Of the "submissions" made by the end of 1989 by each country as the starting point of discussion, the US proposal focused on "the developing countries problem," Japan's addressed "the developing countries problem" and the "US problem," and the EC stressed all of them (especially the "protection of geographical indications"). These proposed negotiation items were based on political considerations.

This means that despite the fact that the main concern of the US regarding Japan was "review delays caused by the large volume of applications," it put that issue aside, and Japan, too, abandoned its "First-to-File System" proposal. Both the submission of the agenda and the process of coming to agreement were deeply colored by political resolutions.

Once the overall outcome of the 15 Uruguay Round fields had been agreed upon at the Morocco Ministerial Meeting in April 1994, the TRIPS agreement came into force in January 1995. Despite opposition by developing countries, the TRIPS agreement was achieved based on the adoption of the collective consignment method in the Uruguay Round agreement. Developing countries accepted the agreement as a whole, and multilateral rules were constructed on intellectual property to correspond to the globalization of the economy. Meanwhile, separate from international cooperation in WIPO, the Government of Japan agreed that it would cooperate in a three-way effort with the United States Patent and Trademark Office (USPTO) and the European Patent Office (EPO) in areas such as development of more advanced computer systems. The first meeting based on this agreement was held in October 1983, after which repeated discussions were held, mainly on computer-related topics. Concrete policies for cooperative relationships with developing countries were explored, including (1) bilateral cooperation through the Japan International Cooperation Agency (JICA), (2) multilateral cooperation through WIPO, and (3) a combined bilateral and multilateral cooperation using funds contributed by Japan to WIPO.

2.5.3 Revision of the Industrial Property Rights System

Intellectual property policy from the 1980s on aimed to respond to the explosive expansion in the use of industrial property systems, and proposed revisions to the system emphasized the establishment of an institutional infrastructure that would quickly grant patent rights as a precondition to responding to demands for international institutional harmonization (Nakayama 2013, p. 216) (Fig. 5).

The Patent Law revisions of 1985 involved mainly the introduction of "Domestic Priority." The Paris Convention on the Protection of Industrial Property ("Paris Convention") adopted a "priority rights system" according to which patent applications submitted first to one Convention member country would not be disadvantaged so long as they were submitted to other member countries within one year of the first: their filing would have priority over others made after the "priority date" of the "basic application." In addition, where patent applications were being filed in multiple countries, it would be permitted to incorporate into one application the multiple applications related to a single invention, in order to take into consideration differences in the degree to which inventions were regarded as unitary in different countries. The system was one that would play a tremendous role in the smooth acquisition of comprehensive rights, covering a series of linked inventions without leaving gaps between them.

Japan's domestic application system, by contrast, did not permit reapplication based on applications made in a home country. For this reason, domestic Japanese applicants could not acquire comprehensive rights by adding further inventions to the basic invention, which meant that an imbalance arose between them and non-Japanese who could use the Priority Rights stipulated by the Paris Convention. In order to correct this unfairness, Japan explored the introduction of a domestic Priority Rights system, with the Paris Convention as a model, and ultimately began to recognize applications that asserted priority rights for comprehensive inventions.

While international harmonization was thus achieved, the contents of the patent application became more and more advanced and therefore increasingly complex.

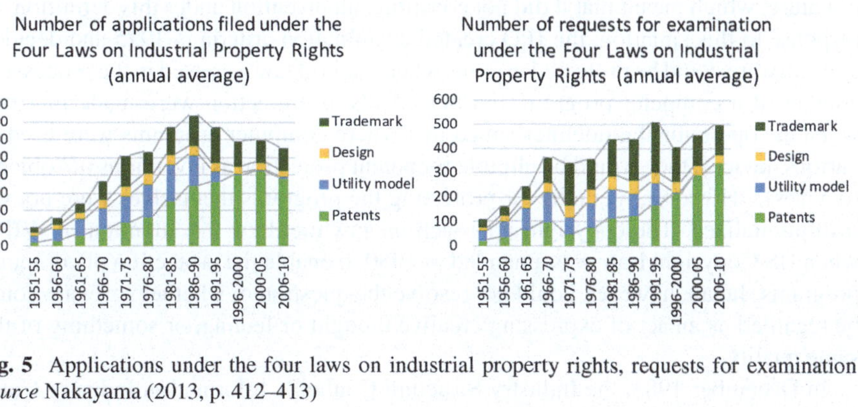

Fig. 5 Applications under the four laws on industrial property rights, requests for examination
Source Nakayama (2013, p. 412–413)

Furthermore, there were strong demands that Japan review its procedural provisions based on international approaches. Following on the December 1986 report of the General Assembly of the Industrial Property Council, the Patent Law was amended in May 1987, with improvements such as the Multiple Claims System.

The Unfair Competition Prevention Law was also amended (Nakayama 2013, p. 249). Japan had no legislation intended exclusively to protect trade secrets, which fell under general laws such as the Civil, Commercial, and Criminal Laws, but demand for civil protection of trade secrets mounted in the late 1980s. First, "trade-related aspects of intellectual property rights including trade in fraudulent goods" were an important item on the Uruguay Round agenda, and included as well were "information assets," at the core of which were trade secrets. In addition to the need for international harmonization, growing employment mobility heightened the need for protection domestically as well. From October 1989, therefore, the Industrial Structure Council's Information Assets Subcommittee reviewed the protection of trade secrets and issued a summary report in March 1990. Revisions to the law preventing unfair competition were enacted in June. The revised law defined trade secrets as "technical or business measures that are useful for production, sales, and other business methods and that are not publicly known." In other words, the requirements for characterization as "trade secrets" were the ability to control secrets, the usefulness of the secrets, and the fact that they were not public. The law established the types of acts related to trade secrets that would constitute unfair competition, and stipulated the right to demand damages.

2.5.4 Systematization of Software Protection

There are two approaches to protecting software: the "Patent Approach" and the "Copyright Approach." In the discussions that took place from the 1970s on, the views of the patent approach were predominantly negative (Nakayama 2013, p. 266). Patent law at the time defined invention as: "the highly advanced creation of technical ideas utilizing the laws of nature." It was hard to regard software as using the laws of nature, which meant that it did not constitute an invention under this definition. In response to this situation, the JPO created examination criteria in 1975 and decided that software could be protected in cases where natural law was used in the processing content of a computer program. Further efforts at protection were made in 1982, when the operational guidelines stated that where computer programs were used in various devices, they would be eligible for patent protection as inventions of "objects (devices)." However, methods for protecting the programs themselves were not yet institutionalized. The copyright approach meanwhile drew the attention of WIPO when US Copyright Law was amended in 1980 to enable the protection of computer programs. Japan, however, could not resolve the question of whether software could be regarded as an act of expressing creative thought or feeling, or something of the same quality.

In December 1983, the Industry Structure Council's Information Industry Committee compiled a report regarding the discussions at the JPO and in international forums. The report pointed to the increasing importance of software and proposed establishing a legal mechanism for clarifying the rights protecting programming, through a modification of the Copyright Law mechanism. The value of a software program is activated only once it is used, and the concept of usage rights was already well-established. The idea, therefore, was to place the copyright law at the center of the new legislation by introducing the concept of usage rights to it.

With the 1984 interim report of the 5th Subcommittee of the Copyright Council, the Agency for Cultural Affairs asserted the literary nature of computer programs, regarding it as sufficient to clarify the point. The Agency for Cultural Affairs garnered support for its proposal from the US Copyright Law clarifying the protection of computer programs. MITI pointed out certain issues, such as the short period of protection, but was unable to generate any support.

Thus, in January 1986, the Act Partially Amending the Copyright Law came into effect, and software received copyright protection as literary products under copyright law. Moreover, the TRIPS Agreement, which came into effect in 1995, stipulated that computer programs "should be protected as literary works prescribed in the Berne Convention for the Protection of Works of Arts and Literature," so the matter was also resolved internationally. Nevertheless, with advances in the sophistication of computer use, the importance of software has only increased, and copyright law is being reconsidered as to whether the ideas themselves should come under its protection.

2.5.5 Improvement of the Operational Foundations of the Intellectual Property System

The 1980s saw not only an increased number of applications for examination but also an increase in the number of patent applications for more advanced technical creations. With the revision of the law in 1987, a multi-item system was adopted to recognize applications claiming multiple uses because of the diverse uses of a single invention. The burden on examiners thus expanded, and so the need to improve the infrastructure for operating the examinations was urgently felt (Nakayama 2013, p. 411).

To that end, the JPO established the "Industrial Property Long-Term Problem Review Committee" as an internal committee in the summer of 1982, and in accordance with its report, promoted the "computerization of administrative processing and searching functions." Given US dissatisfaction with Japan's patent process, US aims were also a factor, so these efforts were also promoted for their applicability to the goals stated in the final report on Japan–US SII talks, which said: "The Government of Japan will use its best efforts to reduce the average patent examination period of Japan to 24 months within five years."

In addition, the Patent Special Account system was put in place in July 1984, and with the financial foundation for the patent system thus established, the introduction and expansion of computer systems were aggressively pursued. Specifically, based on the deliberations of the Headquarters for the Comprehensive Mechanization of the Patent Office established in the Agency in October 1983, a "paperless plan" aimed at the comprehensive computerization of and installation of databases for Patent Office administration was formulated in 1984. These plans were intended to (1) increase the efficiency of the screening process, (2) streamline administrative processing, (3) enhance patent information provision services, and additionally to (4) actively promote international cooperation. They also took into consideration the publication of a "searchable database" and electronic filing. Initiatives also began for outsourcing the application process and otherwise optimizing filing practices. To ensure that the preliminary examinations were complete and that the applications did not reflect only the most positive results of the assessment of the invention, the "public notice ratio"—indicating the degree of efficient acquisition of rights—was introduced as an important index for business for the patent administration process.

3 Coordination of Industrial Policy and the Antimonopoly Act

3.1 Coordination of Industrial Policy and the Antimonopoly Act

3.1.1 Review of Guideline Methods

Until the response to the first oil crisis, MITI and the Japan Fair Trade Commission (FTC) had maintained a policy of "responding to the short-term production adjustments that accompanied economic fluctuations with recession cartels based in principle on the Antimonopoly Law." In the 1970s, MITI introduced a method of creating and announcing the outlook for demand in the short term (the "guideline method"). MITI also came to use this guideline method as a measure for soft landings and as a supply-and-demand stabilization measure after the termination of a recession cartel. The FTC, which became increasingly cautious about approving recession cartels in the latter half of the 1970s, acknowledged the need for such measures, but judged that approach would in some cases trigger "synchronous reduction" (sympathetic production cuts). Thus, in the late 1970s and early 1980s, differences in opinion began to emerge between MITI and the FTC regarding the appropriate response to the problem of recession cartels (Okazaki 2012, p. 227).

The background of this issue was an incident in an oil price cartel. In February 1974, the FTC filed criminal charges against 12 oil dealers and 25 of their company executives, and the Petroleum Association of Japan and four of its officers, for violating the Antimonopoly Act. The charges targeted: (1) Five price cartels formed in 1973 by 12 wholesale companies (price fixing cases) and (2) the production quantity cartels (production adjustment cases) formed in early November 1972 and April 1973 on the basis of decisions by the Petroleum Association.

In September 1980, the Tokyo High Court ruled that the price-fixing cases constituted a violation of the law. It found the production cartels in violation as well, but ruled that the accused were innocent because they were not aware of the illegality of the cartels and had not deliberately violated the law as they had reasonable cause for that unawareness. Appeals were brought on the price-fixing cases, and some of the accused were found innocent by the Supreme Court in February 1984.

In the September 1980 ruling, the point of dispute was the illegality of cooperative measures among companies that took place under "administrative guidance." The defense argued that although there were no provisions for exemptions under the Antimonopoly Act, the Petroleum Industry Law of May 1962 did include content restricting competition promotion policy, and that if the actions were taken in response to MITI instruction under this law, a finding of illegality might be blocked. The ruling said that the actions in this case did not fall in this category while recognizing in general that a "block" of that kind on illegality was possible. In other words, it showed that there were circumstances in which such action would not be judged illegal, (1) if the action fell within the range permitted by the Petroleum Business Law, and (2) if the cooperation measures were conducted under MITI guidance in order to implement adjustments in supply and demand.

Furthermore, the September 1980 ruling on the price agreement found a degree of substantive significance in the requirement "Contrary to the public interest" referred to in Article 2, paragraph 6 of the Antimonopoly Act. With regard to cooperative action based on administrative guidance, the ruling held that the phrase "contrary to the public interest" in principle pertained to violations of an economic order based on free competition protected directly under this law, and that even if the actions formally corresponded to it, the above interests protected by the law, and the interests protected by these actions, were in comparative equilibrium. The ruling recognized exceptional cases in which such actions would not substantively violate the ultimate aim of the law, which was "to secure the interests of the general consumer and promote a democratic and healthy development of the national economy" (Article 1), inasmuch as it indicated the need to interpret the purpose of exempting such actions from the rules regarding "unfair trade restrictions." The thinking was that even if an action constituted a formal violation of the "economic order of free competition," there were cases in which the judgment should be made in terms of the equilibrium with the interests being protected.

With this ruling, the FTC in March 1981 released its "Ways of thinking about the relationship between the Antimonopoly Act and administrative guidance" and MITI set forth its basic views in "Ways of thinking about administrative guidance." MITI's opinion was that the Antimonopoly Law regulated the actions of business operators and was not intended to apply to the acts of administrative agencies, while the FTC stressed that administrative guidance must be undertaken with due care so that it is not the businesses in question who violate the Antimonopoly Act. The two statements revealed the gap between the two parties. The FTC therefore continued to strengthen its cautions against administrative guidance by MITI. The number of authorized recession controls therefore decreased substantially in the early 1980s.

3.1.2 Establishment of the Structural Improvement Law, Based on the Six Yamanaka Principles

The turning point in the relationship between the Antimonopoly Law and industrial policy, including those issues accompanying administrative guidance, came with the coordination that occurred in the process of establishing the Temporary Measures Law for the Structural Adjustment of Specific Industries (Structural Improvement Law). This law was devised to respond not only to the worsening environment after the second oil shock, but also to the emergence of new "structurally depressed industries."

In 1981, the Aluminum Industry Committee and Chemical Industry Committee of MITI's Industrial Structure Council considered measures to rebuild these industries. Their December report evaluated the role of basic materials industries in economic security, and pointed out the need for reviewing the laws and regulations related to it. In February 1982 it presented the idea of enacting a new law on structurally depressed industries to coincide with the expiration of the Industry Stabilization Law. The new law would expand the number of target industries and would also include exemptions to the application of the Antimonopoly Act.

However, as discussed above, the FTC since the oil cartel incident was wary of recession cartels and said that caution was required in expanding the scope of exemptions beyond that of the Industry Stabilization Law. The Special Committee on Basic Material Industry Special Measures for the General Conference on Production Statement and Adjustment established in August 1982 therefore issued an Opinion Brief in December 1982 titled "On measures for basic materials industries." Two aspects of its thinking are revealed in the Opinion Brief. First it advocated shrinking as quickly and smoothly as possible those parts of the industries that were losing their economic viability and showed no signs of future recovery. Second, it advocated measures to address (1) the cost of raw materials and energy, (2) high value-added, technological development, and (3) the consolidation of firms. It also stated that the role of government was to facilitate coordination along these lines.

Given the principles of industry self-help, elimination of measures for preserving industries, and maintenance of the open system, the Opinion Brief emphasized the limited time available for policy intervention. This accorded with the Positive Adjustment Policies (PAP) guidelines of the OECD. Its emphasis on market mechanisms and PAP guidelines reflected not only a response to FTC criticism but also a change in MITI opinion that was gradually clarified in the 1980s, namely, its perspective that industrial policy served as a complement to market mechanisms.

These judgments came together in the principles underlying proposed Industrial Structure Law, which were introduced by MITI Minister Yamanaka in late January 1983, just before the expiration of the Industry Stabilization Law. Dubbed the "Six Yamanaka Principles," these were: (1) contraction and revitalization, (2) mitigation of the impact on employment and regional economies, (3) implementation of comprehensive measures, (4) respect for private-sector autonomy, (5) focus on competition policy and adherence to open systems, and (6) time-limited policy responses

(Okazaki 2012, p. 49). Among these basic principles, the fifth—focusing on competition policy and adherence to open systems—meant "business alliances that did not require exemption from the application of the Antimonopoly Act, but that aimed to lower costs through the advantages of scale within a group." Because MITI recognized that its preliminary coordination with the FTC on the Industry Stabilization Law had not gone smoothly, this plan stated clearly that coordination with the FTC and full discussions between the competent minister and the Fair Trade Commission were to take place (Table 4).

The Industrial Structure Law (ISL) of May 1983 was limited legislation set to expire in June 1988. It shared many features with the Industry Stabilization Law but differed in that it included not only capacity reduction but also optimization of scale and production methods. The designations under the Cabinet Order also differed from the ISL, which could be described as "industry-led" in that it was premised on applications made by business operators to the MITI Minister.

The Minister prepared a basic plan for structural improvement with methods for capacity reduction. It stipulated that the Minister could direct joint action where the autonomous efforts of business were not sufficient to reduce capacity, and it stipulated that the Minister could direct joint action. This instruction was essentially based on the concept of "exemption from applicability" of the Antimonopoly Act. However, the approval system newly established for business alliances did not exempt Ministerial approval from the application of the Antimonopoly Act, but rather was to be carried out within the scope of what was permissible under the Act, determined through consultation with the FTC.

This "specific industries" category covered 26 industries, 11 of which were the same as those covered by the Special Law and 15 of which were new designations (see Table 3). The Industry Stabilization Law had covered shipbuilding, spinning (including cotton and other fibers), and worsted spinning, but the Industrial Structure Law did not. Capacity reduction rates (target rate and completion rate) varied widely from 55–302%. Research confirming the outcomes suggests that the facilities closures and capacity reduction based on the Industrial Structure Law had a positive effect on profitability and productivity.

The Industrial Structure Law was related to the Antimonopoly Act in that it strengthened industrial policy to reflect its complementarity with competition. This was clear in the explanation provided, which stated: "The national economic significance of industrial coordination under the open economic system is that it aims at a shift toward industries that can achieve economic rationalization over the medium-to-long term through efficiencies in management and advantages of scale. It therefore can be harmonized with the Antimonopoly Act, which aims to secure competition" (Okazaki 2012, p. 255). It was thus clarified that industrial policy, while premised on market mechanisms, had the role of supplementing and occasionally reinforcing them, and that competition policy and industrial policy could be compatible with each other on a mid- to long-term basis. The Industrial Structure Law was epochal in that sense.

Underlying this rethinking was the fact that foreign countries in the 1980s were harshly critical of administrative guidance, regarding it as a barrier to imports. MITI

Table 4 Implementation status of the Industrial Structure Law (ISL)

		Relative to ISL: maintained (M) or new (N)	Equipment processed or eliminated	Date of specified industry designation	Target disposal volume (10,000 tons)	Rate,%	Disposal volume completed (10,000 tons)	Rate,%	Joint action designation (D), or none
Electric furnaces		M	Electric furnaces	1983.5.24	380	14	238	63	None
Aluminum smelting		M	Electrolytic furnaces	1983.5.24	93	57	148	159	None
Synthetic fibers	Nylon long fibers	M	Spinning machines	1983.5.24	Completed under old law				None
	Polyacrylonitile short fibers	M	Spinning machines	1983.5.24	Completed under old law				None
	Polyester long fibers	M	Spinning machines	1983.5.24	Completed under old law				None
	Polyester short fibers	M	Spinning machines	1983.5.24	Completed under old law				None
	Viscose short fibers	N	Spinning and refining machines	1983.8.2	5	15	3	66	None

(continued)

Table 4 (continued)

		Relative to ISL: maintained (M) or new (N)	Equipment processed or eliminated	Date of specified industry designation	Target disposal volume (10,000 tons)	Rate,%	Disposal volume completed (10,000 tons)	Rate,%	Joint action designation (D), or none
Chemical fertilizer	Ammonia	M	Raw gas production equipment, raw gas purification equipment, synthesis equipment	1983.5.24	66	20	112	170	None
	Urea	M	Synthetis equipment, decomposition equipment and granulation equipment	1983.5.24	83	36	86	104	None
	Wet process phosphoric acid	M	Reaction equipment	1983.5.24	13	17	21	162	None
	Fused phosphate	N	Electric furnace, open-hearth furnace	1983.6.17	24	32	21	88	None

(continued)

Table 4 (continued)

		Relative to ISL: maintained (M) or new (N)	Equipment processed or eliminated	Date of specified industry designation	Target disposal volume (10,000 tons)	Rate,%	Disposal volume completed (10,000 tons)	Rate,%	Joint action designation (D), or none
	Chemical fertilizer	N	Reactor equipment, granulation equipment and drying equipment	1983.6.17	81	13	88	109	D
Ferro-alloy	Ferrosilicone	M	Electric furnaces	1983.5.24	5	14	14	274	None
	High-carbon ferrochrome	N		1985.1.29	6	10	14	244	None
	Ferronickel	N		1985.1.29	5	12	15	302	None
Western paper and board	Western paper	N	Papermaking machines	1983.10.7	95	11	89	94	D
paper	Container board	M	Papermaking machines	1983.5.24	154	20	85	55	D
Petro-chemistry	Ethylene	N	Decomposition equipment	1983.6.17	229	36	202	88	D

(continued)

Table 4 (continued)

		Relative to ISL: maintained (M) or new (N)	Equipment processed or eliminated	Date of specified industry designation	Target disposal volume (10,000 tons)	Rate,%	Disposal volume completed (10,000 tons)	Rate,%	Joint action designation (D), or none
	Polyolefin	N	Polymerization equipment, granulation equipment, compression equipment	1983.6.17	90	22	85	94	D
	Vinyl chloride resin	N	Polymerization equipment	1983.6.17	49	24	45	92	D
	Ethylene oxide	N	Oxidizing equipment	1983.8.30	20	27	12	60	None
	Styrene	N		1985.1.29	49	26	34	70	None
Other	Rigid PVC pipe	N	Extruders	1983.8.30	12	18	12	100	None
	Sugar refining	N	Decomposition equipment, crystal equipment	1983.9.27	100	3	90	90	None
	Cement	N		1984.5.2	3000	23	3100	103	D
	Electric wires/cables	N		1984.9.26	9	14	9	100	none

Source Okazaki (2012, p. 54–55)

was therefore seeking to explain the concept of Japan's administrative guidance and industrial policy through periodic exchanges of views with overseas antitrust authorities and formal and informal consultations. It was in that context that MITI made an even further shift going into the 1990s.

3.1.3 Establishment of the Law of Temporary Measures to Facilitate Industrial Structural Adjustment

Against a backdrop of external trade imbalances and economic friction with other countries, the Industrial Policy Bureau proposed to the Ministry in May 1986 that an Industrial Structural Transformation Policy be part of the new policy for FY 1986. This was the starting point of what became the Law of Temporary Measures to Facilitate Industrial Structural Adjustment (Okazaki 2012, p. 57). The major policies involved were (1) the creation of industry-specific visions, (2) the promotion of large-scale system development projects, (3) industry-specific administrative guidance aimed at international cooperation, (4) industry-specific employment and regional measures, and (5) legal measures pertaining to specific industries. The last of these aimed to change Japan's industrial structure to further international cooperation. The policy was intended to encourage reductions in domestic production capacity and entry into new business fields for those industries that would be facing significant increases in imports. The Industrial Structure Council meanwhile responded to the same situation in a December 1986 report titled "Specific measures for industrial structural adjustment." It said that foreign direct investment and domestic industrial adjustment had followed on the yen appreciation and stabilization after 1985. This meant the emergence of employment issues and their impact on regional economies, and therefore of a need for a smoother transition for Japan's industrial structure.

With these considerations in mind, the Industrial Policy Bureau summarized its thinking on the new law in January 1987. According to the "Basic Concepts of Twenty-First-Century Industrial Society," although it was to be assumed that industrial structural changes would occur autonomously in response to the market, policy support was needed in those sectors where relying on private-sector efforts alone would cause delays, such as employment and regional revitalization. Such measures included (1) supporting the reduction or consolidation of facilities and business tie-ups where business operators were struggling with a rapid decline in demand due to the rising yen and therefore with excess capacity; (2) aiding venture businesses and new businesses that would be linked to an expansion of new industrial sectors to revitalize areas struggling with employment issues and regional decline.

The specific features of the bill revealed a shift away from the framework of the Industrial Stabilization Law and the Industrial Structure Law. First, while these two laws were supposed to designate specific industries and provide policy support to them, the new law targeted certain kinds of facilities without designating the industries themselves, and granted policy support to each individual operator using such facilities. This shift was in part a response to US criticism that the competitiveness of Japan's exports to the US was enhanced by Japan's industry-specific industrial policies. It also aimed to implement regional measures. The new law was enacted in April 1987 as the Temporary Measures for Facilitating a Smooth Transformation in Industrial Structure ("Facilitation Act").

The Facilitation Act stipulated measures for "specific business operators" and "specific regions." The former referred to mining or manufacturing firms that used "specific equipment" to produce products for which the demand had declined precipitously and the excess capacity was therefore extreme, and where such conditions were expected to persist over the long term. Specific enterprises could receive financial and tax support if the "business adaptation plan" and "business alliance plan" they created themselves were approved by the appropriate minister. Because business adaptation plans were prepared for individual companies, it was judged that there was no need to seek exemptions from the Antimonopoly Act as it applied to business alliances. "Specific regions" meant areas where the closure or contraction of businesses and business activities had occurred on a considerable scale, and where such establishments accounted for a substantial part of the business activities of the region and thus there had been an adverse effect on the local economy and local employment.

Thirteen types of specific equipment (four kinds of steel, six types of fiber, three kinds of nonferrous metals) were designated under the law in April 1987. However, these particular facilities were not necessarily in use by a large number of "specific business operators" whose business adaptation plans had been approved. A March 1988 survey found seven approvals in the mining and manufacturing industries and four in the synthetic fibers industry. Forty-three specific regions were designated in April 1987, and eight more in June. It can be verified that after designation under the Facilitation Law, the designated areas saw greater improvement than other areas in the growth rates of employment and real shipment values.

3.1.4 Creating New Industries and Improving the Business Environment

The Technology Development Policy and Industrial Location Policy were the first of the 1980s policies to be developed with the aim of creating new industries along the lines laid out in the *1980s Vision*. This was followed by an examination of the actual conditions and policy issues in new developments in the service industries (Okazaki 2012, p. 93). R&D, for example, not only saw an expansion in related budgets but also had a role in regional recovery policies (industrial location policy), which led to the establishment in May 1983 of the Law for Accelerating Regional Development Based upon High-Technology Industrial Complexes ("Technopolis Law"). This was followed in May 1985 by the Law for the Facilitation of Research in Key Technologies aimed at promoting experimental research and raising the level of basic technology in the private sector. The law provided, for example, for the use of state-owned laboratories at low cost.

Based on "The key concepts for twenty-first-century industrial society," MITI in the latter 1980s continued to expand and reorganize its systems of support for technology development and industrial location policies while also steadily introducing methods whereby businesses could themselves support the creation and nurturing of new areas of development. For example, under the May 1986 Private-Sector Participation Promotion Law, R&D/Research Core Facilities and information infrastructure began receiving MITI support for the purpose of facilitating experimental research, technical training, information disclosure, and commercialization of basic research. The Law to Promote the Group-Siting of Designated Types of Business Contributing to More Sophisticated Local Industrial Structures ("Key Facilities Siting Law") was established in April 1988. Additionally, various financial support measures were advanced under the Basic Technology Research Facilities Act to support those enterprises that were developing new sectors and to concentrate higher-order industrial functions ("brains") in non-central regions.

These developments notwithstanding, some policy issues carried over into the 1990s. These included inter-ministerial issues, such as the relaxation and legal regulations and review of the nature of business organizations and management, as well as the trade policy issues relating to globalization and stimuli for firms' overseas business activities. All these awaited the progress of government discussions on trade policy and on administrative reform. In September 1988, a globalization unit was established under the Planning Subcommittee of the Industrial Structure Council's General Committee to review these questions, and study groups were organized within MITI to discuss policy issues concerning the nature of business organizations and enterprises.

3.1.5 Policy on Small and Medium-Sized Businesses Aimed at the Transformation and Integration of Operations

"The 1980s and the direction of SMEs and SME policy," composed by the Small and Medium Enterprise Policy-Making Council in May 1980, laid out what was desired of SMEs. This included: (1) a shift in business strategy from quantity to quality, (2) the spurring of creativity and mobility and the nurturing of human resources to that end, (3) new developments through regional groups and groups of disparate industries, and (4) a social awareness of the values and social consciousness of the citizens who sought fairness, stability, and safety (Nakata 2013, p. 70). It thus emphasized a positive assessment of the active majority and a recognition of diversity. In these ways, the distinctive aspect of the mid-1980s was that policies such as these were being developed to support business transformation as an emergency response to the Plaza Accord. Measures were also expanded to strengthen soft management resources, including the promotion of technological development, and to support regional revitalization and concentrations of industry. These policies aimed to steer Japan away from the export-led economy that until the 1970s had pursued the goal of "strengthening international competitiveness," toward "correcting external imbalances" and "promoting domestic demand."

The policy on interaction and exchanges among different industries began as a "Technology Exchange Plaza Hosting Project" in 1981 (Nakata 2013, p. 277). The Small-and-Medium Enterprise Agency also issued a notice in August 1983, titled "Regarding guidance on the establishment and operation associations of disparate industries" and sought an elastic use of the Law on Cooperative Associations of SMEs. These policies became systematized with the April 1988 establishment of the Extraordinary Law Concerning the Promotion of the Development of New Business Areas through a Fusion of the Knowledge of SMEs in Different Industries ("Knowledge Fusion Law"). The temporary legislation, with an intended 1995 expiration, aimed to integrate the knowledge of SMEs in different fields and to open up new fields, so as to enable the improvement and development of SMEs. It not only conceived of business cooperatives as the initiators of integrated projects, but also made as targets of its policy the business and industry associations composed of SMEs and individuals and businesses conforming to them. For the enterprises targeted by these policies, financing was made available in the form of subsidies from the General Account, special cases of financing for advancement, and special loans for the promotion of SME fusion (undertaken by the Central Bank for Commercial and Industrial Associations).

In the seven years of its operation, the "fusion method" did not result in more than 309 cases of accredited partners, and the number of participating companies remained under 2300. Considering that 20,000 firms were participating in the inter-industry exchanges in 1987, it appears that it was hard to proceed beyond the stage of these exchanges. Even so, however, there were over 300 cases of conversions made to new fields (Nakata 2013, p. 312).

Meanwhile, the yen appreciated to unprecedented levels. Imports of textiles and miscellaneous goods, already present from Korea, increased from Taiwan and Singapore as well, and the action program that followed on the Plaza Accord began to be felt as well. All of these changes in the environment in the 1980s had a severe impact on SMEs. The Law on Temporary Measure for Business Conversion of SMEs had been in effect for 10 years and was approaching its expiry. MITI therefore announced "Special Adjustment Policies for SMEs" in November 1985, saying that there was a "need to plan for the business stability of small and medium-sized enterprises and for a smooth conversion of business operations." The SME Agency, too, released a report titled "Special Adjustment Policies for SMEs" in December, and made clear its intent to forward legal measures for business conversions. The Small and Medium Enterprise Modernization Council in December 1986 issued the "On SME policies for responding to changes in the international economic environment," in which it pointed out that SME business conversions would not only contribute to employment, but would also contribute to the stabilization and revitalization of regional economies and thereby the national industrial structure as well. A change in perspective was under way, in other words, such that policies to enable business conversions were not to be regarded as something unavoidable and backward-looking, but rather as important national policies that would contribute to employment and the development of regional economies.

The February 1986 Law on Temporary Measures for Business Conversion by Designated SMEs (Business Conversion Law) was time-limited legislation set to expire in March 1988. Its aim was to serve as an emergency measure to facilitate the business transformation of SMEs in response to the "remarkable changes in trade structure and other circumstances in recent years" that had been triggered by the yen's appreciation following the Plaza Accord. Specific SMEs covered by the Business Conversion Law could obtain financial, credit, and tax support if they devised a "business conversion plan" and received approval from their prefectural governor. The effectiveness of the mitigation measures was evident in the increased rate of use: the number of target industries increased from 116 to 203, and loans totaling about 407.6 billion yen were made in the seven years the law was in effect.

These measures were in line with development policies aimed at promoting SMEs as local industries from the vantage point of regional revitalization. SMEs were regarded as key players in regional economies. It was hoped and expected that they would have the potential to develop endogenously, and that they would bring stability and improved welfare to the lives of people in rural areas.

Attention was therefore also paid to small and micro enterprises. Industries and occupations in which family and business activities were blended were regarded as requiring specific support. The distinctive features of this support were (1) that prefectural governments formulated a vision for local industry promotion in order to solve regionally specific problems in cooperation with cities, towns, and villages, (2) that local industrial promotion projects were launched to foster the capability to develop new products, to develop demand, and to develop human resources, and (3) that third-sector Local Industry Promotion Centers were established and regarded as a core institution for SME promotion. The Business Conversion Law took its place in the development of these new policies.

In addition, the Law on Temporary Measures for SMEs in Specified Areas ("Specific Regional Law") was established in November 1986. It applied to SMEs in specific areas, stipulating that where suppliers carried out projects to adapt to the new economic environment, it would be possible to provide support subsidies and thereby to stabilize economic activity in specific areas (Nakata 2013, p. 848).

The Business Conversion Law was revoked in December 1991, and the Special Regional Law was revoked as planned in February 1993. Twelve thousand adaptation plans were approved under the latter between December 1986 and December 1991. Of the 216 municipalities designated in the legislation, 134 shipped more industrial goods in 1991 than they had in 1985. The ratio of job offers to job seekers increased during the same period in 159 municipalities.

3.2 Industrial Adjustment and Structural Improvement

3.2.1 Structural Improvement of the Petrochemical Industry

The Material Problems Study Group, established by the Japan Petrochemical Industry in October 1979, issued its final report in January 1981. The report sought improvements in the following areas: (1) the inability of petrochemical companies, under the Petroleum Business Law, to import naphtha freely, (2) the imposition of oil taxes and customs duties on raw materials, namely naphtha, (3) the obligation to stockpile naphtha. In July 1980, MITI also set up an advisory body to the Director General of the Basic Industries Bureau to study the problem of raw materials in petrochemicals from a long-term perspective. Both the public and private sectors explored ways of avoiding the impact of soaring petroleum raw material prices (Yamazaki 2011, p. 60).

Meanwhile, the precipitous rise in naphtha prices, driven by the second oil crisis, was having a serious impact on the petrochemical industry. Amidst a sharp decline in domestic demand in 1980–1981, imports of petrochemical products from North America rose significantly. This was because the price gap between naphtha and ethane, which is contained in natural gas, began to widen, causing a decline in the international competitiveness of naphtha-dependent Japanese petrochemical products relative to resource-rich countries such as the US and Canada, which used ethane as a raw material. With declining profits because of rising raw material prices, and rising fixed costs due to lower utilization of capacity, it was inevitable that Japanese petrochemical companies would respond to the pressure of cheap imported goods in the domestic market by competing more intensely with each other. The Basic Industries Bureau issued the "Regarding measures on naphtha, raw material in petrochemicals" as a Decision of the MITI Departmental Council and pursued the following measures. (1) Petroleum refining and petrochemical companies were to decide on quarterly planned quantities and to notify MITI of plans to import anything in excess of them: naphtha imports covering excess in demand would not be regarded as violating that limit. (2) Domestic naphtha prices would be determined in conjunction with import prices. (3) After FY 1983, domestically produced naphtha would be treated as tax-exempt, like imported naphtha.

Regarding the problem of excess capacity, the June 1982 report by the Industrial Structure Council found that the outlook for the petrochemical industry was harsh and called for the following systems to address it: (1) Joint production by petrochemical companies and consignment of production, (2) joint investment, (3) joint purchases of petrochemical raw materials, (4) joint imports of petrochemical products (5) the rationalization of logistics, (6) joint sales, (7) establishing rules for the reduction of excess capacity and capital investment, and (8) joint research and technology development. The examination of individual products undertaken by the Industrial Structure Council's Chemical Industry Committee was expected to advance corporate consolidation. The Industrial Systems Subcommittee proposed the following in its December 1982 submission, "On industrial systems development in the petrochemical industry": (1) Set product-specific numerical targets for reducing excess capacity and make progress on them by grouping companies; (2) promote rationalization and concentration based on the grouping of companies; and (3) carry these out under a new law replacing the Industry Stabilization Law. Petrochemical companies proceeded to establish product-specific joint sales for the moment. In November 1981, 17 companies divided into four groups to set up joint-sales companies, the establishment of which reflected capital ties and geographical considerations. However, joint sales was not a sufficient means for resolving the problem of excess capacity.

With the enactment of the Industrial Structure Law in May 1983, the petrochemical, ethylene manufacturing, and polyolefin manufacturing industries sought designation as "specific industries" and received that designation in June. The vinyl chloride resin industry received the designation as well. The reduction of excess capacity was carried out jointly according to government instruction. The ethylene oxide and styrene monomer industries, by contrast, adopted a policy of pursuing capacity reduction at the discretion of each company. The industries that pursued joint capacity reduction saw a high achievement rate. Policy promoted the consolidation into higher-efficiency facilities, leading to a concentration of production into large plants producing 300,000 tons or more annually. Meanwhile joint sales also began to be effective in reducing costs, but price competition was unavoidable. Solutions continued to be explored: for example, in December 1986 each company put together an action program and tried bundling what had been manufacturer-brand products into one common brand (Tables 5 and 6).

The special designation under the ISL was lifted in September 1987 in those industries where the reduction of facilities had borne fruit, but because ethylene demand increased rapidly beginning just at that time, MITI was concerned about the reemergence of excess capacity. It therefore sought to maintain appropriate investment by introducing the "Declare System" (advance reporting system). The target industries

Table 5 Overview of petrochemical industry facilities closures under the industrial structure law. Unit: 10,000 tons/year, %

	Capacity prior to capacity reduction A	Target capacity reduction volume B	Capacity reduction ratio B/A (%)	Real amount of capacity reduction C	Achievement rate C/B (%)	Remaining capacity
Ethylene	635	229	36.1	202	88.2	433
Polyolefin	413	90	21.8	85	94.4	328
Vinyl chloride resin	201	49	24.4	45	91.8	156
Ethylene oxide	74	20	27.0	12	60.0	62
Styrene monomer	180	47	26.1	34	72.3	146

Source Yamazaki (2011, p. 76)

Table 6 Concentration of ethylene production through capacity reduction

	Before capacity reduction		After capacity reduction
	Reported capacity	Active capacity	Active capacity after reduction
Number of factories	18	16	14
Production capacity (1000 tons/year)	6347.7	5352.8	4316.4
Number of plants	32	20	14
Over 300,000 tons	11	11	8
200,000–299,999 tons	3	3	5
100,000–199,999 tons	8	4	1
Under 100,000 tons	10	2	0
Production capacity per plant (1000 tons/year)	198.4	267.6	308.3

Source Yamazaki (2011, p. 77)

were ethylene and polyolefin, and investment adjustments based on this method were implemented beginning in November 1987 and March 1988, respectively.

3.2.2 Conversion to Non-mercury Methods in the Soda Industry

The soda or alkali industry was making enormous capital investments to convert to non-mercury production following the pollution controls laws of the 1970s. Supporting this endeavor was regarded as a policy issue (Yamazaki 2011, p. 110). However, it was becoming difficult to promote these efforts due to the increasing cost of raw fuel in the oil crisis. In May 1977, MITI provided financial and tax support under the plan of completing the conversion of all facilities by the end of the fiscal year, but only two-thirds of the conversion from mercury electrolysis to asbestos diaphragm electrolysis was completed by the end of that period. This was because businesses had seen marked deterioration and also because the asbestos diaphragm electrolysis method was inferior in terms of quality. Faced with these obstacles, MITI presented a plan to the 1979 Mercury Pollution Control Promotion Meeting to support the development of the ion exchange membrane method that offered quality at the level of the mercury method and thereby to complete the conversion by the end of 1984. The conversion was completed in June 1986. This was an unprecedented achievement anywhere in the world. In a context of rising public unease and opposition to pollution and mercury contamination, the soda industry faced deteriorating market conditions. Offering lateral support to the industry, MITI overcame the friction with it and was able to induce the industry to make the shift in manufacturing method.

3.2.3 Structural Improvement of the Aluminum Smelting Business

The aluminum smelting industry was typical of energy-intensive industries, and based on the November 1977 interim report of the Aluminum Industry Committee of the Industrial Structure Council, a plan was in place to shrink its production system through a freeze on its facilities and other measures (Yamazaki 2011, p. 286). It was therefore designated a "structurally depressed industry" in February 1978, and measures were adopted for it based on the Industry Stabilization Law. The basic plan for stabilization was put together in January 1979 and called for scrapping or suspending 530,000 tons of its domestic smelting capacity (suspension to continue until June 1983) to reduce capacity to 1.1 million tons by the end of FY 1979. This constituted a significantly greater reduction than that called for in the 1977 report. The tariff quota system was also utilized to support structural improvement. The application of tax-free or low tax rates up to a certain amount of imports guaranteed a supply of low-priced imported goods in order to maintain a competitive environment by applying a high tax rate for imports exceeding this limit. However, it aimed to allow time for the rationalization of the refining sector by placing the burden for high tariffs on the aluminum industry as a whole. (The plan was in effect for two years beginning in FY 1978).

However, the second oil crisis in 1979 aggravated the situation, and the existing plans were judged inadequate. This was because inexpensive imports were flowing into Japan from the stagnant world aluminum ingot market, exacerbating the domestic industry's troubles. The aluminum subcommittee began studying the matter in April 1981. Its review of structural improvement measures based on an annual production capacity of 1.1 million tons was presented in its October report titled "The Aluminum Smelting Business and Related Measures Going Forward." The report held that domestic supply should be maintained from the point of view of maintaining the demand–supply adjustment function and bargaining power, namely, ingot imports. Furthermore, by maintaining and developing the superior technology that had been cultivated, the industry was expected to be able to develop new materials or participate in overseas development projects. It proposed reducing production to about 700,000 tons a year by 1985, and said that in order to do so, the following structural improvement policies were necessary: (1) Reduction of electricity costs, which accounted for 40% of smelting costs, (2) reimplementation of the tariff rebate system, and (3) promotion of the development and import of semi-domestic products.

The specific countermeasures called for in the report included concentrating production in high-efficiency facilities, as proposed in the May 1983 structural improvement plan formulated under the Industrial Structure Law, and cost reductions through the elimination of transport complexities on the logistics side. Capital investment for revitalization included conversion to coal power in order to reduce electricity costs, and other investment in facilities to reduce the cost of energy and raw materials, as well as investments leading to higher-quality products such as high-purity aluminum. The plan went smoothly, with shutdowns covering 9,300 tons in facilities completed by the end of May 1983, and 530,000 tons worth scrapped as of April 1984. Despite the large scale of the scrapping, however, capacity utilization remained stagnant, and the market environment remained harsh.

In December 1984, the Nonferrous Metals Industry Committee (renamed from the Aluminum Committee in April that year) compiled its own report (also titled "The Aluminum Smelting Business and Related Measures Going Forward"). Determination of the appropriate capacity for the smelting industry emphasized the following criteria: (1) that it carry out the minimum production necessary for guaranteeing a stable supply to the domestic market, (2) that it retain the technical base necessary for developing overseas projects, and (3) that it secure a supply of the high-purity bare metal for which import substitutions were not easy to access. This led to a plan for a 350,000-ton system, and the report called for realizing this by FY 1988. MITI in response put together a basic plan for structural improvement in line with these recommendations, and as concrete measures, prohibited the installation or expansion of electrolytic furnaces excluding those used for experimental research, and promoted business alliances aimed at concentrating production in high-efficiency facilities and at joint sales and purchasing, joint transportation, and so on. It also maintained the tariff regime, but with the market-opening action program announced in July 1985, the government was forced to cut the 9% tariff on bare metals to the 1% level of the United States in January 1988. That meant that it would be difficult to maintain the 350,000-ton regime. After this, corporate efforts in the aluminum industry focused on cost reduction and high added value in the rolling process, and with regard to the supply of bare metals, sought out stable supplies through long-term import contracts and development projects intended for import to Japan. However, with the search for a stable supply of bare metal, the major producers lost their ability to control prices in the international market of the mid-1980s, and the increase in competitive suppliers reduced their raison d'etre.

3.2.4 Structural Improvement Policies for the Electric Furnace and Ferrosilicon Industries

The electric furnace and ferrosilicon industries also implemented structural improvement policies in response to long-term supply and demand problems (Yamazaki 2011, p. 220).

In the ordinary steel electric furnace industry, 27 out of 58 companies were operating one electric furnace as of 1983; in other words most were micro operations and their facilities were aging. Small bars and small- and medium-sized steel accounted for 80% of electric furnace industry products and were low value-added products. Most were intended for the construction industry, which was dominated by on-the-spot and commercial transactions. In the early 1980s, earnings dropped due to excess competition, and the industry began exploring structural improvement measures. The "cartel faction" in the industry suggested ways to try to reduce capability across the industry but also hoped for coordination from the government on capacity reduction, while others such as Tokyo Steel Manufacturing Co. argued that the reduction should take place through bankruptcies. Policy coordination was expected to be complicated in this industry.

Twice before February 1980, the Non-Integrated Steel Producers' Association had considered the question of electric furnaces and MITI addressed it as well for three months beginning in April 1981, through the Flat Electric Furnaces Facilities Subcommittee of the Industrial Structure Council. The subcommittee proposed extending the "basic stabilization plan" to June 1983. Because the scrapping of plants under the Industrial Stabilization Law invited if anything an expansion of capacity through the rationalization efforts of electric furnace makers, the development of steelmaking technology, plant upgrades, and so on, "corporate restructuring and consolidation" was added to the plan upon its extension. As a result, the formation of groups within the electric furnace industry advanced under the initiative of blast furnace manufacturers.

The ordinary steel electric furnace industry received ISL designation again in May 1983. MITI convened the Steel Industry Committee of the Industrial Structure Council in July that year and proposed a "Basic Plan for Structural Improvement." Capacity reduction, business alliances, and capital investment for revitalization aimed to lower production costs and establish a stable foundation suitable to open economic system. The business groupings planned a concentration of production in high-efficiency plants as well as joint sales of products and other measures.

Demand for electric-arc furnace (EAF) steel recovered around 1987 especially in the construction industry, and although the plan's extension was postponed due to the expiration of the Industrial Structure Law, the industry had by then seen a reduction in personnel and a consolidation of firms, so that the results of structural improvement were evident. The number of workers in the industry in 1987 was down to almost 40% of its 1982 levels, while the number of companies had decreased from 78 in 1975 to about 50 in the early 1990s. Likewise, the number of electric furnaces was down from 146 in 1978 to 93 in 1988. Some electric furnace manufacturers were thus able to increase their market share rapidly. Since the construction of new electric furnaces had been frozen for 10 years under the Industrial Stabilization and Industrial Structure Laws of 1978 and 1983, Tokyo Steel and others that operated the most advanced electric furnaces were able to acquire a greater share of the market.

3.2.5 Structural Reform of the Cement Industry

The cement industry also suffered serious deterioration in performance after the second oil crisis. The Cement Association of Japan set up a Structural Problems Study Group in October 1982, which conducted repeated investigations. Its February 1983 interim report cited as basic problems: (1) stagnation of demand, (2) excessive production capacity, (3) expansion of the distribution sector (posing logistics problems for cement and related industries), and (4) excessive competition in cement. Recommendations included (1) scrapping of excess capacity, (2) gathering cement makers into groups, and (3) responding aggressively to the needs of related industries. The

Association decided in April to adopt the recession cartel formulation and to undertake structural improvements based on the Industrial Structure Law (Matsushima 2012, p. 302).

A third-sector recession cartel was approved in August 1983. This time, it set limits not only on production amounts but also on sales quantities. As a result, improvement progressed most markedly in regions where the price decline had been particularly sharp. Cement was recognized as a designated industry under the second Industrial Structure Law in April 1984, and a basic plan for its structural improvement was formulated in August. Its contents included (1) reducing capacity by 30 million tons of equipment, equivalent to 23% of the cement clinkers' annual production capacity as of March 1984, with "reduction" in principle, meaning "scrapping," and (2) undertaking joint sales and logistics management, through the establishment of companies for joint operation. Thirty-one million tons were scrapped by March 1986. A plan for company groupings was put together in January 1984 and joint operating companies were established.

Although some advances were achieved, import pressures increased due to the appreciation of the yen after 1985, and capacity utilization remained at 72% even after the scrapping of plants. It was not easy to dispel concerns about excess capacity, so the cement industry sought the application of the "Facilitation Act" when it came into being in April 1987. "Cement kilns" were designated as "specific facilities" under Article 4 in October and capacity reduction continued. Rationalization through the mechanism of joint operating companies also continued. The plant scrapping and production freezes proceeded as planned, covering 10.71 million tons by the end of March 1991. Additionally, the final report of the Japan–US SII talks in February 1990 indicated plans for an increase in public investment, and in May 1991, the Cement Industry Fundamental Issues Committee, a private advisory body of the Director-General of the Consumer Goods and Service Industries Bureau, decided to cancel the industry's designation under the Facilitation Act.

Regarding the joint venture company, the committee indicated that it was hard to judge whether the various activities to secure the foundations of the business—unifying sales systems and organizations, securing profits, and holding assets—were sufficient. In line with the committee's judgment, the joint operating companies chose either to dissolve or to continue to attempt greater rationalization. Of the five original groups, two were dissolved. The Committee pointed out in its May 1994 report titled "The Cement Industry Going Forward" that "unification of sales had not progressed" since August 1984, that cooperation on reducing costs had not progressed since the dissolution of the two groups, and that profits were therefore deteriorating further. It proposed measures for the dissolution and merger of the joint operating companies. An announcement was made terminating the policy that had envisioned organizing the entire industry into groups, and thereafter, the industry's reorganization took new paths based on the merger of large firms to respond to internationalization, technological development, and environmental policy.

3.2.6 The 1980s *Vision of the Paper and Pulp Industry*

The *1980s Vision of the Paper and Pulp Industry*, compiled by the Pulp and Paper Industry Committee of the Industrial Structure Council in March 1981, said that because of the two oil crises, the paper and pulp industry was facing rising energy costs and reduced demand. It pointed out three issues: (1) structural improvement, (2) reform of business consciousness, and (3) securing stability in raw materials (costs). The most important area for structural improvement was the issue of excess capacity (Yamazaki 2011, p. 135). This was linked to the second issue above. It was understood that the reason excess capacity remained despite the low capacity utilization rate that followed the first oil crisis was that businesses were adhering to their rapid growth-era assumption that excess capacity would be resolved through economic growth and demand recovery. In other words, the assumptions of the rapid-growth era had become entrenched. The *Vision* advocated a shift in business attitude toward sharing and moderation, and said that the change should be voluntary even if it required some degree of public intervention. A third challenge was the emerging fears of a raw material shortages, because Japan was dependent on foreign countries for half its pulpwood in 1980. The Committee called for (1) urgent implementation of development imports centering on overseas afforestation, (2) stabilization of the supply of domestic pulp material, (3) and expansion of waste paper collection use and promotion of supply and demand stabilization.

The fundamental problem was structural improvement. Although the paper manufacturing industry did not meet the requirements of the Industrial Stabilization Law, businesses were still under pressure from the high cost of raw fuel and reduced demand. As an emergency measure, wood-free and coated paper were granted permission in May 1981 to form a recession cartels, which remained in place until the end of February 1982. This was the first such case for printing paper. Unglazed grocery-paper businesses formed a recession cartel in June 1982, the second in that sector since 1978. The waves of structural recession were spreading throughout the paper manufacturing industry.

MITI therefore strengthened its policy of restraining expenditure on capital investment, and in February 1982, organized a Paper Supply and Demand Council (renamed "Paper Demand Council" in 1992 and abolished in 1996). The Industrial Structure Law was also applied to the paper industry, because of its substantial excess capacity. In August 1983, 44 companies in the paper manufacturing industry (excluding the newspaper manufacturing industry) submitted a request to MITI and in October the industry was given the "specified industries" designation, with a basic plan announced in October that set the goal of structural improvement by FY 1988. The main content was to reduce facilities and equipment by 950,000 tons (capacity reduction rate of 10.6%) by September 1986. In November 1983, MITI also issued instructions under Article 5.1 of the Industrial Structure Law on joint action limiting or prohibiting new establishments and the expansion or rebuilding of facilities.

Designation under the Industrial Structure Law was not limited to paper manufacturing. Corrugated fiberboard manufacturing, already covered by the Industrial Stabilization Law, was also designated under the Industrial Structure Law in May

1983. In August, a basic plan was established for structural improvement by 1988 through the suspension of 385,000 tons, focused on paper machinery. Parts of the plan were revised in March 1984, with production capacity to be reduced by 1,537,000 tons (a reduction rate of 19.8%) by a target date of June 1987.

The paper manufacturing industry's designation ended in March 1988 due to the economy's recovery. The plan for corrugated fiberboard ended in June due to the cancellation of the Industrial Structure Law. Adjustment was not abandoned, however. Against a background of strong demand in 1988, the paper industry saw successive plans for expansion, but the Paper, Pulp and Printing Industry Division of the Consumer Industries Bureau required each company to report its capital investment plans to the Ministry. The "Declare Method" referred to these announced plans in the expectation that each company would adjust its own plans voluntarily. This approach remained in place until March 1991.

3.3 Basic Industries, Consumer Goods Industries, Coal Industry, and Others

3.3.1 Introduction of Energy-Saving Equipment and Policy Support for Technological Development in the Steel Industry

In the early 1980s, the government supported the introduction of energy-saving plants. The Iron and Steel Industry was subsidized in two ways: through financial assistance by way of the Japan Development Bank loans and through taxation support (Yamazaki 2011, p.187). However, since major steel manufacturers' dependence on bank loans declined, it was the "investment tax credit" established in 1978 and the "tax system for energy measure promotion" established in FY 1981 that was most useful for the investment in equipment. The support aimed at the introduction of advanced facilities that would enhance energy utilization in accordance with "The Energy Infrastructure Advanced Facilities Investment Promotion Tax System" of 1986. The support applied to investment in either (1) advanced energy utilization manufacturing equipment or (2) advanced energy utilization equipment additions. The first was for the energy-consuming production facilities to introduce machinery and other equipment that would improve the manufacturing function, institute automated or continuous production processes, or improve manufacturing or assembly methods in other ways. High-performance steelmaking rolling mills are typical of such facilities, including high-temperature continuous casting equipment, high-temperature direct-feed rolling equipment, roll-cooling continuous grinding machines, automatic adjustment thick-plate cooling equipment, and so on. Typical of the second were equipment for rationalizing fuel combustion as a heat source, recovering and utilizing waste heat, preventing loss of heat or power, rationalizing heating, cooling, and electric heat, and low pressure-loss waste-power recovery

Table 7 Rate of penetration of major energy-saving equipment in the steel industry (1996)

%	Japan	South Korea	United States	United Kingdom	Germany
Coke dry quenching equipment	85	50	0	0	33
Top recovery turbines (TRT)	100	100	12	0	24
Converter gas recovery facilities	100	25	11	18	0

Source Yamazaki (2011, p. 196)

devices, devices for the storage of by-product gases, and dry coal distillation devices using waste heat (Table 7).

The introduction of energy conservation equipment through tax system supports resulted in the active introduction of coke dry quenching equipment (CDQ), top pressure recovery turbines (TRT) in blast furnaces, and converter gas recovery facilities. The improvement in the rate of penetration of energy-recovery facilities led Japan's steel industry to become the world's leader in energy efficiency.

With regard to technical development support, MITI in the 1980s and 1990s expected a growing need for (1) product differentiation through superior quality and cost reduction, and technological development leading to the development of new demand, (2) basic and creative research and development bringing advances to the cutting edge worldwide, (3) global environmental measures, alternative energies, and measures for waste disposal and recycling. In collaboration with manufacturers, MITI in November 1990 established a Research Group on Steel Production Information Infrastructure Technologies and provided support such as the compilation of development plans in the first two areas.

For more direct technical development support, steel, nonferrous and ferroalloy manufacturers jointly established a Research Association for New Foundations in Smelting Technology in 1982 with the aim of developing energy-saving smelting technology. It received subsidies for basic research under the "Shared Infrastructure for the Development of Energy Substitutes for Petroleum" adopted by MITI as a policy target in FY 1982. This Association pursued development in two tracks during this period: (1) direct steel and iron ore smelting reduction processes, and (2) molten slag sensible heat recovery technology. The first arose from a recognition of the limits of the existing blast furnace method. The use of coke as a blast-furnace reducing agent was important both for diversifying energy sources and for addressing the problem of aging plants. In addition, as capacity reached excessive levels, it was expected that flexible operations could be realized with the blast-furnace approach, which would contribute to energy-source diversification by using ore and coal in powder form.

Full-fledged development was triggered by a report from the Basic Materials Industries Council in 1987. Independent development of smelting reduction technologies by various makers was supported with national subsidies beginning in 1988 through the Japan Iron and Steel Federation, which established a Committee on the

Development of Smelting Reduction in April. In 1993 support went to test plant operations, and 2000 was chosen as the target year for launching practical applications of the technologies. From FY 1995, the Japan Research and Development Center (JRCM) served as the nucleus for collaboration between industry, academia, and government on technological development, and research on practical applications of basic technologies was undertaken according to a 10-year plan.

MITI had been issuing guidelines on production volumes since 1966, but these were abolished with the mounting overseas criticism of Japanese trading practices and administrative guidance in the latter 1980s.

3.3.2 Conversion of the Textile Industry to an Advanced Industrialized Industry

As the Law on Extraordinary Measures for the Structural Improvement of the Textile Industries ("Textile Industry Law") approached the next expiration date, the continued slump in domestic demand, excess capacity, high cost of raw fuel, and import pressures for the most part remained unchanged. A Joint Committee of the Textile Industries Council's Coordination Committee and the Industrial Structure Council's Textile Committee issued a report in October 1983 titled "About the Textile Industry in a New Age." The report expressed the view that new development of an "advanced economy-type industry" could be launched through the efforts of the textile industry (Matsushima 2012, p. 59).

What was meant by "advanced economy-type industry" was that "Advanced economies have broad markets that are highly sophisticated and diverse, with high potential for industrial technology and cultural creativity and abundant human capital, and the industry that can fully utilize that latent strength can maintain its dominance internationally." The report considered the existing production contraction, low profitability, and capacity reduction to be the result of structural factors in the industry. These included: (1) stagnant demand due to structural changes, and at the same time rapid progress in individualization, diversification, and upgrading, and ever-shorter fashion cycles, with the result that the industry was forced to shift to high-variety, small-lot production; (2) new competition with foreign countries with the emergence of developing economies; (3) the difficulty of securing young workers.

On the other hand, signs of revitalization were also evident, including: (1) the advance of vertical linkages among different industries in various forms around the planning and development of new products, and (2) advances in innovation such as combining the results of technology developments at each level of the textile industry, including yarn, woven fabric, dyeing, and so on, to create new products.

Development into an "advanced economy-type industry" offered the industry new directions: (1) becoming an "information- and technology-intensive industry that would satisfy lifestyle and cultural needs" supplying "not only the necessities of daily life but rather social goods and goods that represent value and that satisfy human sensibility" and (2) becoming a "system-type industry based on utilizing the industry as a whole...[to] supply products that could meet actual demand through the smooth distribution of information, and by linking product planning and high technology, could meet the consumer needs for high quality." Besides this, a third area was discussed, namely, the path to an "international industry based on utilizing an international division of labor." Various measures were presented to foster these types of development, including measures for aggressively promoting structural improvement in the apparel sector. The decision was made to extend the Textile Law for five more years and the Law was enacted in May 1984 (Table 8).

Through repeated extensions, the Textile Law was in effect for 15 years from 1974 to 1989 and consistently advanced policies aimed at knowledge consolidation. The results came in the form of projects for product development centers, equipment leasing, business improvement, and so on.

Textile firms formed knowledge-consolidation groups, which created business plans and promoted improvement projects with the Minister's approval; large companies with planning experience and capability also participated in these groups. Over the 15-year period, 77 knowledge-consolidation projects and 30 joint-facilities projects were approved by the Minister. The total cost of these projects was 102.7 billion yen, of which 66.4 billion yen came from upgrade financing and 6.7 billion in the form of debt guarantees by the Textile Industry Rationalization Agency for funds raised by the firms themselves.

3.3.3 New Trends in Policies on Consumer Industries

Industrial policy reflected the intensifying calls from the 1980s on for Japan to expand its domestic demand, and many issues in consumer life and culture were explored under the heading, "consumer industries policy." This also reflected the shift in priorities then taking place in policy making, from production to quality of life. The establishment of the Life Culture Forum in November 1985 was the opportunity to make this shift manifest. The Forum, which was distinctive in its use of freely grouping experts, clarified the basic concepts and significance of a renaissance in "life culture" and made recommendations to the relevant sectors (Matsushima 2012, p. 248).

The Forum met in four stages, producing proposals titled "Creating a beautiful, comfortable, and worthwhile lifestyle" (first recommendation, May 1986); "Design: the point of view of fashion" (second recommendation, June 1987); "Toward a rich information environment—life culture and information" (third recommendation, June 1988), and "Movement and life culture—towards the creation of a new lifestyle of mobility" (fourth recommendation, June 1989). The fourth proposal said that, "The improvement of social infrastructure such as networks and means of transportation to accompany increasing social mobility naturally begins with improving safety measures. Administrative responses appropriate to Japan as a lifestyle power are needed in other areas of people's lives as well, namely leisure, education, medical care, welfare, and public services." It went on to raise concrete issues such as the reduction of work hours, realization of a long-term leave system, and corporate support for free-time activities.

Table 8 Structural improvement projects in the textile industry, industry comparison

1974–1988	1989–1993	1994–1998
Projects by structural improvement groups		
① Projects related to development of new projects or new technologies (obligation of establishing product development centers)	① Projects related to development of new projects or new technologies	① Projects related to new products or new technologies (including design-related)
② Projects related to modernization of facilities/plants and equipment	② Projects related to modernization of facilities/plants and equipment	② Projects related o modernization of facilities/plants and equipment (including leasing of facilities)
③ Facilities-leasing projects	③ Facilities-leasing projects	③ Projects on the improvement of scale or mode of production
④ Projects on the improvement of scale or mode of production	④ Projects on the improvement of scale or mode of production	④ Projects on the rationalization of sales or inventory management (information networks projects, etc.)
⑤ Projects on improvements of business	⑤ Projects on improvements of trade/transactions	⑤ Projects on improving scale of business
⑥ Projects on industrial relations measures	⑥ Projects on industrial relations measures	⑥ Other structural improvement projects
⑦ Other structural improvement projects	⑦ Other structural improvement projects	· Projects related to business improvement
		· Projects for securing or fostering human resources
Commercial and industrial associations facilitation projects		
	① Projects related to the development of new products or new technologies	① Projects related to the development of new products or new technologies
	② Projects for the securing or fostering of human resources	② Projects for the securing or fostering of human resources
	③ Projects related to the provision of information	③ Projects related to the provision of information
	④ Projects related to establishing facilities to contribute to the business rationalization (joint projects such as distribution facilities; information infrastructure facilities; facilities leasing projects)	④ Projects related to establishing facilities to contribute to the business rationalization (joint projects such as distribution facilities; information infrastructure facilities; facilities leasing projects)
	⑤ Other projects related to the facilitation of structural improvement	⑤ Other projects related to the facilitation of structural improvement

Source Matsushima (2012, p. 105)

Although these recommendations did not immediately result in policies, they were reflected in the administrative organization of the Consumer Goods and Services Industries Bureau. For example, based on the first recommendation, a New Office Advancement Committee was established in August 1986 in the Household and Miscellaneous Goods Division, which was in charge of office furniture. The Committee was to serve as a private advisory body to the Directors General of the Consumer Goods and Services Industries Bureau, the Industrial Policy Bureau, and the Machinery and Information Industries Bureau, and to examine ideas for the ideal new office and policies for promoting it. Its focus was not the production of office furniture, but rather the office using that furniture. This represented a new, demand-driven perspective. Its December "Proposal on the promotion of the new office" treated the office as one of the venues of people's lives, in other words, or as "a place for human life," "a place at the core of the information era," "a place expressive of corporate culture," and "a place at the frontier of internationalization." "What we are calling the 'New Office' is an office that is comfortable and functional, that is to say, a place where it is possible for the worker to live an intellectual and comfortable life, where companies can ensure high-quality production, and where management attitudes and ways of thinking are manifested. We appeal to the world, including corporate executives and office workers, to bring it to reality." In April 1988, the Committee summarized "Guidelines for making the new office" and put this in concrete terms with the key points for realizing a comfortable and functional new office. This was followed in May 1992 by an interim report by the Daily Goods Division titled "Creating the ideal office of the future—a people-friendly office is a place where wisdom can be created." This report, also known as the "Second Guideline for New Offices," represented a shift to a psychological approach, including discussion of the ideal organization. As interest shifted to this direction, MITI withdrew its involvement and transferred the campaign to a private organization called the New Office Promotion Association established in June 1987 (incorporated in March 1989).

3.3.4 Promotion of Projects for the Development of New Housing

As a successor to the 1975 "House 55 Plan," which had been a joint project of the Ministry of Construction and MITI for high-quality, low-priced industrialized housing, MITI independently launched the New Housing Development Project in 1979 (Matsushima 2012, p. 347). This plan, which covered seven years from FY 1979 to FY 1985, consisted of developing (1) systems technologies for the care of the elderly and physically handicapped, (2) systems technologies for variable living spaces, (3) systems technologies for the utilization of basements, (4) systems technologies for natural energy-based housing, and (5) technologies for improving the durability of building materials for homes. The New Housing Development Committee was set up as a private advisory body of the Director of Consumer Industries Bureau and deliberated on possible directions of development. Fourteen groups, composed of 56 companies, participated in the development. Significant results were seen in (1)–(4)

of the above plans. In addition, MITI established a third project, the New Materials and Equipment System Development Project for Apartment Houses (the "21st Century Condominium Plan") in FY 1984.

The Cabinet Decision on the Fourth Comprehensive National Development Plan in June 1987 aimed for a deconcentration of people and institutions in Tokyo and a shift to decentralized multipolar land use. The Industrial Council on Housing and the Urban Industry Committee then conducted a new review. According to the interim report presented in May 1988, a supply of housing was needed that would be appropriate for the era's diversification of values and individualization of lifestyles, and that would meet the need for further cost reduction. MITI thereupon launched the New Industrialized Housing Industry Technology and Systems Development Project, its fourth solo project. With a seven-year plan beginning in FY 1989, it focused on (1) developing designs for living spaces and performance simulation systems, (2) developing high-performance building materials, housing equipment, and factory production technology, and (3) developing comprehensive energy-use systems for residential use. The first of these targeted the development of methods and systems capable of predicting and making calculations for moist heat, air, sound, light, and other environmental and housing functions (Fig. 6).

The publication of the *Vision for the 1990s* meant that new developments were sought in housing-industry policy. The Roundtable on Ideals in Housing and the Housing Industry, a private advisory body of the Director of Consumer Industries

	Project Name	Objective	Content
Shifting from quantity to quality in housing	House 55 Project 1976-79	To supply low-cost, quality detached residences	Supply of 100 m^2 houses in the 5 million yen (at then values) (jointly with the Ministry of Construction)
	New Housing Development Project 1979-1985	To upgrade the quality of detached residences	Development of technology for elderly- and physically handicapped-care systems Development of variable living space systems Development of residential systems using natural energy Improvement of the durability of residential building materials
Upgrading quality and supplying housing in metropolitan areas	Development of new materials and new appliance systems for housing complexes 1984-1990	To supply quality urban housing complexes	Development of improved durability technology R & D in technologies to improve habitability Development of energy use technology
	Development of new factory-built housing industry technologies and systems 1989-1995	To improve and upgrade production technologies and systems for factory-built housing	Development of space design by residents, development of performance simulation systems Development of technologies for high-functioning building materials, residential equipment and factory productivity
Responding to the diversity in housing needs	Development of housing that creates value in lifestyle 1994-2000	To make proposals for comfortable, low-cost housing	Improvement in the value of housing stock compatible with lifestyles Research and development for technologies harmonizing with the environment
	Development of technologies for resource-recycling housing 2000-2007	To construct resource-recycling housing	Development of 3R-compatible housing systems Development of comprehensive high-efficiency energy systems

Fig. 6 History of housing technology development projects. *Source* Study Group on the Housing Industry of the Future [Kongo no Jyutaku Sangyo no Arikata ni Kansuru Kenkyukai] 2008. New Paradigms for the Housing Industry (Report for METI)

Bureau, was established in December 1993 and in June 1994 produced a report titled "Toward a Decade of Housing Industry Reform." The report pointed to three directions for reform: a shift from a "luxury orientation" to an "authenticity orientation," from "housing as an asset" to "housing for function," and from "dispersed housing" to "housing integrated with the townscape." A new Development Project for Housing That Creates Lifestyle Value was launched in FY 1994 to forward technological developments for the following: (1) improving and creating a housing stock of value, (2) meeting the needs of new lifestyles, (3) harmonizing with the environment.

The above-mentioned vision and technology development projects targeted prefabricated housing in particular. The ratio of prefab housing to total construction starts grew steadily from 7.3% in 1973 to 18.0% in 1992 and then remained in the 15.0% range in the latter half of the 1990s, meaning that construction could proceed at a certain rate. In addition, the development of prefabricated houses was also effective for triggering the development of a wide range of related material industries.

3.3.5 New Issues in Distribution Policy

The joint deliberations of the Distribution Committee and the SME Policy-Making Council Distribution Subcommittee from October 1982 forward resulted in a December 1983 report titled "1980s Distribution Industries Vision" (Ishihara 2011, p. 200). The report pointed out that a variety of retail formats were emerging as regional communities came to be seen as living spaces or societies with their own distinctive appeal, and as consumer needs became more individualized and diversified. In this sense small and medium-sized retailers were not losing their competitiveness in every instance. At the same time, *shotengai*, or shopping districts, which played an important role in creating a new commercial culture appropriate to the history and traditions of their cities, continued to need modernization. The report found that their functions could be reevaluated and that there were grounds for suppressing the entry of large stores to those areas. Issues to be addressed by policy included: (1) responding to the diversification of consumer needs, (2) supporting SME development to produce a vigorous majority, (3) strengthening the collaboration between commercial and urban policy, (4) actively responding to the emerging information society, (5) securing human resources, and (6) determining the role of distribution in an internationalized society. The report also recommended actively expressing the value of local commerce by changing the terminology from "shopping space" to "living space," and suggested that this could be put into concrete form with the concept of a community mart. Accordingly, a Community Mart Center was established in March 1985 with funding from associations of small and medium-sized retailers.

The Forum on 21st Century Distribution was established in April 1987 as a private advisory body of the Director of the Industrial Policy Bureau to discuss ideal distribution structures looking ahead to the 21st century. The Forum submitted a report in July that year. The Forum had considered how the distribution industry could contribute to the harmonization of foreign economic relations with economic growth centered on domestic demand, and whether policy support could be given to that end. It also discussed the expansion of personal consumption, employment creation, revitalization of regional economies, the expansion of imports, and contributions to international society. This report introduced fresh ideas in distilling the challenges of the distribution industry to two: transforming itself into a creative life industry and building open distribution mechanisms.

Meanwhile, with escalating economic friction with the US, negotiations were expected to focus in part on the barrier to imports posed by the laws on large-scale retail and by distribution practices. The demand for improvement in these areas became an important factor in setting the direction for distribution policy. This will be discussed in detail in Chap. 4.

3.3.6 Safety Improvements and Product Standardization

In November 1983, the 16th Consumer Protection Conference (established under the Consumer Protection Fundamental Law) decided to create a system linking the various Consumption Life Centers into a network (Ishihara 2011, p. 336).

Another focus of consumer-oriented administrative responses was product testing. The product-testing activity of the Industrial Manufacturing Inspection Institute was enhanced in accordance with the 1973 Consumer Product Safety Law, and in 1984 the Institute was integrated with the Textile Products Inspection Institute, forming the MITI Inspection Institute. Where the Institute had mainly conducted inspections of exports in the past, the reorganization accompanied an expansion of work related to consumer administration. In 1995, the MITI Inspection Institute was renamed the National Institute of Technology Evaluation, promoting further improvements in product testing and collaboration with prefectural Consumption Life Centers and other groups.

The Consumer Products Safety Law designated certain products as requiring safety regulation. Safety standards were determined at the national level, and those items could not be sold without the S-mark (for Safety) indicating that they were in conformity with the standards. Fifty-six items received this designation at the end of FY 1992. However, the US government, which was criticizing the closed nature of the Japanese market in the 1980s, raised the issue of this safety standard system and argued that it should be liberalized to the level of the American market. Keidanren also wanted simplification and rationalization of the safety requirements along American lines.

In March 1983, the government's Standards and Certification System Liaison and Coordination Headquarters decided on a comprehensive review of the standards and certification system in response to requests from the GATT Standard Code. As a result, foreign and domestic companies became able to obtain the same registration and approvals. With the amendment of the law in December 1985, government approval was still necessary, as before, for products designated Type 1, meaning products for which it was hard for business operators alone to guarantee the quality. Other designated products, however, were classified as Type 2 and were shifted to a system of self-evaluation and approval based on confirming a product's conformity with the standards. This made it possible to affix the S-mark to Type-2 products by notification to the Minister.

Meanwhile, with regard to relief for victims of accidents, the Tokyo District Court's August 1978 ruling on subacute myelo-optico-neuropathy and the Fukuoka District Courts Ogura Branch ruling on the Kanemi Rice Oil Disease Incident of 1968 both imposed heavy obligations for care on the manufacturer. The court rulings made evident the inadequacy of consumer protection laws and the need for such protection and became a major influence on the establishment of the Product Liability Law. At the same time, industry and MITI were both concerned that prioritizing consumers could endanger the survival of companies, and legislation did not make much progress. Nevertheless, in the event of an actual accident, there was no choice but to forward negotiations between the parties. It was becoming clear that there was a limit to the degree to which enterprises could rely only on judicial precedents and that the government could not continue to neglect the issue.

3.3.7 Responses to the Growth of Service Industries

Government administration respecting service industries was not so much a matter of responding to administrative needs as of exploring what the demands on administration were in a context of service-sector growth. The Commercial Affairs Division of the Industrial Policy Bureau was established in July 1973 and its jurisdiction described in MITI's Order of Organization included the term "service industries" for the first time. The Commerce and Service Industries Affairs Office was established in July 1978. A Study Group on Service Industries was organized immediately after its establishment to begin considering policy responses (Ishihara 2011, p. 407). The results of its investigations were summarized in the Industrial Structure Council's report, *The 1980s Vision*, which characterized service industries as supplementing the production activities of the various industries of the manufacturing sector. That was the extent of the attention paid them at that time, and no specific policy developments were made with regard to them.

In October 1984, the Senior Officer for Service Industries was established in the Commerce Policy Division of the Industrial Policy Bureau, and a Ministerial Office was established to focus on service industries. The organizational revision followed on the recommendations in a report by the Service Industry Study Group, a private advisory body of the Director-General of the Industrial Policy Bureau. The January 1985 report, titled "Hybrid Innovation: A New Era for Service Industries," made the point that newly emerging housework and health care services reflected the diversification of people's values and attitudes and that significant development was to be expected in these "new service industries." MITI began treating this sector as comprising "new businesses" that had not appeared in earlier classifications of industry, and took measures such as forming organizations for the operators, considering policy, and offering financial support, to give potential for growth to these novel and innovative industries.

It was after the September 1989 submission of the *1990s Vision* that MITI began to form related measures from this new point of view.

4 Promotion of Domestic Demand and the Vitality of the Private Sector

4.1 Towards an Advanced Information Society

4.1.1 Problems in the Liberalization of Data Communications

Following the March 1980 report "Ideal approaches to industrial policy in the 1980s," the Information Industry Committee of the Industrial Structure Council compiled an interim report in December, which said that a comprehensive and high-grade shift to information systems was essential to the survival of Japanese industry. It urged the need to boldly anticipate the next decade or two and recommended the following measures (Hasegawa 2013, p. 47): (1) development of an information architecture and the infrastructure necessary to it, (2) proactive advancement of technological development, and (3) active development in the international arena.

The Information Industry Subcommittee report of June 1991, titled "The information society and information industries in the 1980s and approaches to measures addressing them," called for "removal of institutional constraints that hamper the smooth progress of the shift to an information [society and economy]" and called "the elimination of use restrictions on communication lines… an urgent task."

In August that year, the Telecommunications Policy Roundtable, a private advisory body of the Minister of Posts and Telecommunications (MPT), recommended the liberalization of data communications, the introduction of market principles to the telecommunications field, and a review of the organizational structure of the public corporation Nippon Telegraph and Telephone Corp. (NTT). In August 1983, the MPT put together the Value-Added Networks (VAN) Bill for liberalizing the use of communication lines for data management (Hasegawa 2013, p. 650). There was strong opposition to the MPT bill, however, beginning with calls for the elimination of the regulations. Coordination among the parties proved difficult. Ultimately, the MPT gave up the VAN bill and aimed to prioritize revision of the Public Telecommunications Law, while MITI decided to propose VAN liberalization for SMEs. Based on coordination between the two ministers, it was decided that the MPT Ordinance (Second Line Liberalization) would be followed.

Along with this, MITI decided to develop measures to support the practical application of new media, but because significant restrictions remained on the institutional infrastructure related to telecommunications, "freedom of entry," "freedom of business activities," and "freedom of use" were necessary. A review of telecommunications systems led to the establishment of the three laws of telecommunications reform in December 1984: the Telecommunications Business Law, the Law on Nippon Telegraph and Telephone Corporation, etc., and the Law Concerning the Infrastructure for the Related Laws."

4.1.2 Establishment of the Basic Technology Research Facilitation Act

The Information Industry Committee examined the basic policy on information industry policy in the latter half of the 1980s in response to new circumstances such as the privatization of Nippon Telegraph and Telephone Corporation and released a report in January 1985 titled "Recommendations for the Realization of an Advanced Information Society." The key issues for addressing the problems expected to arise with information technology were: (1) human resource development, (2) ensuring computer security, (3) open information, (4) making the shift to information systems according to local circumstances, (5) establishing laws for an advanced information society, and (6) standardizing information equipment and systems.

The framework established by the Law on Temporary Measures for the Promotion of Specified Machinery and Information Industries was nearing its expiration date in June 1985. At the same time a review of its measures was needed given the friction with the United States and Europe (Hasegawa 2013, p. 72). The Study Group on Prospects for Technological Development and the Industrial Structure Council released reports on Industrial Technical Policies at about the same time. MITI sought to reflect their recommendations as far as possible and accordingly made budget requests for the following: (1) to supply risk money, (2) to promote joint research for the purpose of strengthening collaboration between industry, academia and government, (3) to promote international research cooperation, and (4) to disseminate research information. MPT also envisioned the establishment of a special corporate telecommunications promotion organization. After coordination at the government and ruling party liaison meeting in December 1984, the decision was made to consolidate the ideas of both ministries and establish the Japan Key Technology Center for Special Accredited Corporations, and the Law for the Facilitation of Research in Key Technologies was enacted in May 1985. New legislative measures were established with cooperation between MITI, which acknowledged the need to promote policy development of high-tech industries based on legislation, and MPT, which was considering a telecommunications advancement promotion bill.

The pillars of the law included measures such as the low-cost use of state-owned testing laboratories and the flexible handling of patents in international research cooperation, and the establishment of a center for promoting basic research on technology. The main tasks of the center, which was established in October, included (1) investment, (2) lending, (3) joint research mediation, (4) invitations to foreign researchers, (5) provision of basic technology information, (6) research.

In FY 1985–1994, the center worked on a total of 99 projects, with expenditures rising from 2.2 billion yen in FY 1985 to 22.4 billion yen in FY 1991. It handled 305 loans (to 324 companies) totaling 60.9 billion yen between FY 1985 and FY 1994. However, the number of investment projects adopted remained in the single digits after FY 1988, and from the same year, the number of mining and manufacturing projects and telecommunications projects remained at only one to three each fiscal year. Owing to these circumstances, the center was dissolved in 2003.

Meanwhile, in October 1986, the Machinery and Information Industries Bureau established a Roundtable on Future Perspectives on the Machinery and Information Industries, which issued an interim report in August 1987 titled "On the ideal form of the machinery and information industries: Aiming for international cooperation." The interim report pointed out that the machinery industry had a significant share of the international market and was heavily dependent on exports and said that, given the trade friction, declining profits due to the yen's appreciation, and so forth, the machinery industry needed to find ways to coexist and share prosperity with other countries. This required, first, the establishment of appropriate corporate behavior in the international economy, including exporting in harmony with the world market, establishing local production, facilitating international partnerships, and so on, and, second, it meant developing technologies and new business areas, principally centered on domestic demand, in order to maintain the industry's vitality. Concrete measures were considered with the following three principles in mind: (1) an emphasis on market mechanisms, (2) respect for the concept of progress through competition, and (3) contributions to realizing free trade.

International cooperation was thus named a policy objective, and the role of the government was limited to improving the environment so that companies' voluntary efforts could have the desired effect and supplementing corporate activities by providing timely and appropriate information. This vision of policy was manifest in the *2000s Vision for the Information Industry* put together in June 1987 by the Information Industry Committee's Subcommittee on Long-Term Perspectives and in the June 1989 report of the Machinery Industry Committee of the Industry Structure Council titled "The future outlook of the machinery industry: Looking to the year 2000."

4.1.3 Promotion of Fifth-Generation Computer Development Project

The Fifth-Generation Computer Development Project was carried out with a budget of 57 billion yen over 13 years beginning in FY 1982 (Hasegawa 2013, p. 666). Because Japanese computer technology had caught up with that of Europe and the United States, Japan changed its policy goal to spearheading the development of basic computer technology. The development of the fifth-generation computer was addressed in the new policy of 1979 and the concept was honed based on a three-year investigation of the plan. The aim of the plan for the preliminary phase, from April 1982 to March 1985, was the "the successful development of the world's first successive inference machine (inference function in hardware form) and operating system written in logical programming language." The results of this research were presented to the Second International Conference on Fifth-Generation Computers in November 1984. R&D in the preliminary phase was carried out in four fields and resulted in such achievements as the Personal Sequential Inference Machine (PSI), Parallel Relational Database/Machine (Delta), Sequential Inference Machine Programming and Operating System, SIMPOS), and successive-logic programming language (Kernel Language, KL 0, Extended Self-Contained Prolog, ESP).

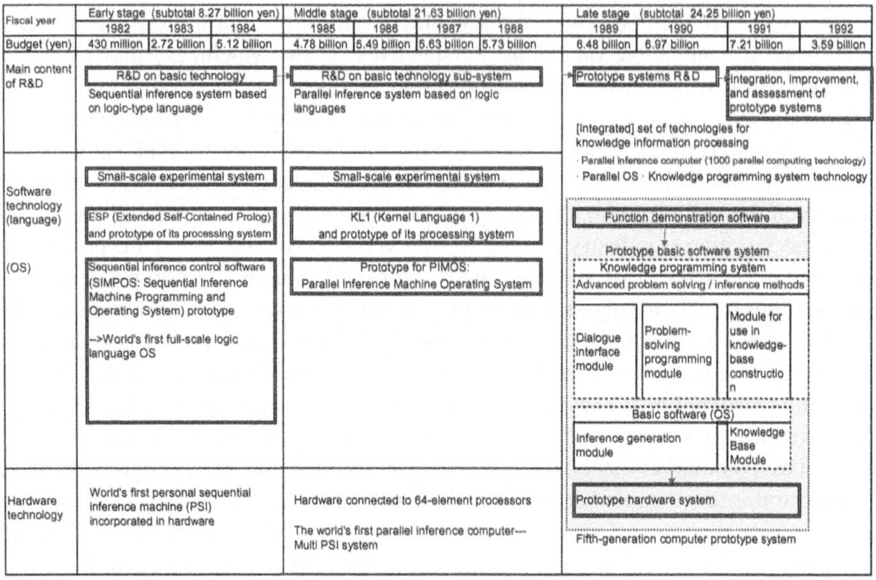

Fig. 7 R&D projects for fifth-generation computer prototype systems. *Source* Hasegawa (2013, p. 720). Based on information in the Institute for New Generation Computer Technology 1992. Outline of the fifth-generation computer project, pp. 10–11

In the medium-term plan of FY 1988, the emphasis shifted to the development of parallel-type inference technology, as yet an unexplored technical field. Beginning in FY 1988, MITI also carried out the Future Personalized Information Environment Development project (FRIEND 21), for R&D on the human interface, but its implementation was shifted to private organizations. The TRON (The Real-time Operating-system Nucleus) project was also launched in June 1984 (Fig. 7).

The Information-technology Promotion Agency (IPA) project was drastically expanded from 1985 on as the core agency responsible for using information technology to improve the efficiency and effectiveness of telecommunications. To increase the efficiency of software production, a budget was assigned to the "Construction of a system for industrializing software production "(Σ system) and the "Σ project" was launched. This was aimed at automating and mechanizing the hitherto labor-intensive software development process and greatly improving its productivity. The Σ project was a five-year plan beginning in FY 1985 with a total budget of 25 billion yen, but in FY 1989 the project shifted to the commercialization stage and MITI withdrew its involvement. Sigma System Co., Ltd. was established in 1990 and proceeded with the effort using IPA-related assets.

4.1.4 Turning to International Cooperation

The shift towards international cooperation was clarified in the interim report of August 1987 titled "About information industry mechanisms for International Cooperation." This occurred against a background of Japan–US trade friction on machine tools and automobiles. The August 1984 interim report of the Industrial Machinery Policy Roundtable (private advisory body of the Machinery Information Bureau) had also shown concern for international cooperation and harmony by revising what had been a strong emphasis on export growth.

In response to the friction with the US on machine tools, MITI implemented an export approval system in February 1978 based on the Export and Import Transaction Law. This initially calmed the dissatisfaction of US industry, but not the more general US frustration. In response to a lawsuit filed by Houdaille Industries in the United States in 1982, tensions over machine tools entered a new phase.

Ultimately, President Reagan announced in May 1986 that the US was seeking voluntary export restrictions from Japan, and several talks were held between the two governments, resulting in a November 1986 agreement that Japan would voluntarily restrict its exports of six machine tools to the US for a period of five years beginning in January 1987. The restrictions were temporarily relaxed in 1988 and 1989, but voluntary restraints were agreed to again in December 1991 at the US request, and a two-year extension to 1993 was applied to four types of machine tools.

In addition to trade friction over machine tools, the Toshiba–Kongsberg Scandal involving Toshiba Machine Co.'s violations of COCOM and trade friction over the export of bearings forced policy on industrial machinery to reflect the need for international cooperation.

Concern over trade friction was also strong in the automobile industry. Industrial policy in this field was formulated from the point of view of the need for international cooperation, based on the Roundtable on the Future Perspective of the Machine Information Industry's August 1987 report "Outlook and issues of the automobile industry." The report pointed out the need to create a market environment dependent on domestic demand in order to resolve trade friction and called for reviews of various regulations involving road infrastructure improvement and automobile-related taxes. That the shift to a domestic demand-led economy needed to be regarded as a policy issue was evident in other statements as well, appearing in the reports of the industry-specific roundtables sponsored by the Machinery and Information Industries Bureau's Director General during the process of setting policy for the 1990s.

The July 1989 report titled "Aiming for an advanced automobile society in the 21st century — Summary of the Roundtable on Automobile Issues" (by the Roundtable established in November 1988) cited development of a domestic demand-led industrial structure as a mid- and long-term challenge. Meanwhile, however, some machine-industry sectors were struggling due to a lack of international competitiveness. Projects addressing domestic demand challenge in the early 1980s included energy-related engineering projects such as investment in petroleum stockpiling and in alternative energy. It was anticipated that investment would increase not only in national land development but also in fields such as environmental conservation systems, water-supply and sanitation systems, and medical welfare systems. Regarding the international challenge, the focus was on engineering sectors that were expected to invest in production plants and urban development in oil-producing countries. However, the forecasts for market expansion were revised downwards significantly, which, in combination with external considerations, meant that aggressive policy development was not undertaken in these areas.

4.1.5 Promotion of Unmanned Factories and the Robot Industry

One of MITI's policy emphases regarding industrial machinery in the 1980s was promotion of the robot industry (Hasegawa 2013, p. 208). MITI had long been interested in the "development of technology for unmanned machine plants" and regarded the following as interconnected areas where unmanned technology-based mechanical systems were related to the machine industry overall: conserving energy, upgrading safety, and diminishing the need for dirty and difficult work. Functionally integrated commercialization, the "systematization of industry" taking place in the industrial structure, and the human costs of overseeing the legal safety requirements were also considered. Of these, the most serious were the need to improve the work environment and respond to emerging labor shortages.

MITI therefore prioritized the robot industry as one of the up-and-coming advanced-technology industries alongside the aircraft, nuclear, and information-processing industries, and therefore advanced measures were implemented to promote it. It established a leasing system through the fiscal investment and loan program, utilized tax measures to institute a "special depreciation system for important multi-function machine equipment," and activated special loan systems for industrial safety and sanitation equipment, as well as a modernization fund loan system for SME plants and equipment, and so on. On the technical side, it launched a seven-to-eight-year plan beginning in FY 1983 for the development of a "robots for extreme environments" through the Large-Project System of the Agency of Industrial Science and Technology. Interest in the robot industry was due in part to an expectation that robot use would be applicable not only in manufacturing industries but also in other industries such as nuclear power and welfare.

4.1.6 Quality Assurance for Nuclear Equipment

Following the Three-Mile Island Nuclear Power Accident in 1979, the Presidential Special Investigation Committee in the US called for strengthening measures to improve quality assurance. In Japan, the Nuclear Power Station Quality Assurance Review Committee was established as a joint advisory body of the Director-General of the Agency of Natural Resources and Energy and the Director of the Machinery Information Bureau (Hasegawa 2013, p. 451). The committee analyzed the 154 domestic accidents and failures that were reported between 1966 and 1979 under the

Electric Utilities Industry Law and the Nuclear Reactor Regulation Law (Law on the Regulation of Nuclear Source Material, Nuclear Fuel Material and Reactors), and found the following. First, while quality assurance activities had definitely improved, the annual number of accidents or failures remained steady at about 20 with the increase in the number of nuclear reactors, and there was room for improvement in order to gain public confidence. Second, the time between periodic inspections had been lengthened. Third, many imported items in the equipment had failed.

A separate report presented by the Review Committee in September 1981 pointed out that for further improvement of Japan's quality assurance system, "it was necessary to refer to the excellent aspects of quality assurance in other countries, and also to examine the approaches to quality assurance that take advantage of the characteristics of our country." The specific suggestions for improvement included: (1) establishing a denser exchange of information within the industry, (2) strengthening the design check through verification tests and reliability analyses, (3) strengthening guidance and management all the way through to the subcontracting company's level, (4) strengthening oversight of general commercial products and items purchased from overseas, (5) strengthening education and training for maintenance workers, and (6) making comprehensive maintenance manuals and improving and strengthening the quality assurance diagnosis system. While quality assurance improvement "should be done by the industry as a whole," the Committee said that "the nation, too" should play an active role, and it proposed formulating unified standards and guidelines on quality assurance activities.

Further measures to prevent problems at power plants were promotion of the development of nuclear-power generation support systems that could quickly predict and respond to problems and also of advanced light-water reactor technology. In April 1987, the Committee for the Promotion of Reactor Advances was established and "Subsidies for Equipment Development Expenses for Improving Nuclear Power-Generation Reliability" were offered for technical development. However, despite the importance of improving the reliability of nuclear power generation, the development budget was greatly reduced after FY 1985 due to adverse fiscal circumstances and not all the funds were allocated.

4.1.7 The YXX Plan and Joint Development in the Aircraft Industry

YXX aircraft development had been under review since the late 1970s (Hasegawa 2013, p. 486). The August 1985 interim report issued by the Aircraft and Machinery Industry Council in consultation with MITI suggested that portions of the development expenses, especially those with high risks, should be subsidized, with the development entities being supplied with compensation for interest payments. A draft amendment to the Aircraft Industry Promotion Law was established in April 1986, changing the aim of the law from "the promotion of the aircraft industry through encouragement of domestic production of aircraft, etc." to " the promotion of the aircraft industry through the encouragement of international joint development." Concurrently, subsidies were made available through the International Aircraft Development Fund (IADF) established in May. The main distinguishing points in its financial support were first, that financing was made available on terms that required only limited security rather than the full security previously required of each company. Part of the risk, in other words, was borne by the fund, and the project was given the character of an initial large-scale venture. Second, the principal would be recovered in proportion to the volume of sales (the "Fokker system"), and model certification would be acquired in 1992. Development costs were high, however, even though fuel prices rose no higher than expected, leading to a review of the project. In March 1994, Boeing released a development plan for the 737-X development, forcing the suspension of the YXX. Despite the results, both tangible and intangible, achieved through joint development, the project made Japanese developers recognize the risks and difficulties involved in civil aircraft development.

Meanwhile, in July 1990, the Industrial Structure Council released its report on "Trade and Industry Policy in the 1990s," which sought aggressive development of new aircraft industry projects. MITI surveyed the development of supersonic transport machines already under way and of small civilian transport aircraft and considered upcoming policy issues, along with exploring methods of joint development for the 1990s. But none of them got underway.

4.1.8 Exploring Space Industry Policy

The history of space development in Japan originated in 1955 with The University of Tokyo Institute of Industrial Science research on solid rockets and the development of space observation rockets. Thereafter, the government began promoting space development, and MITI launched the promotion of the space industry (Hasegawa 2013, p. 53).

However, policies promoting the full-scale and sustainable development of the space industry began only after the Space Industry Office was established in the Machine Information Bureau in September 1979. Space-industry policy at this time did not yet have a specific focus. The Roundtable on the Basic Issues for the Space Industry was established as a private advisory body of the Mechanical Information and Commission Director-General in order to develop a vision for space-industry promotion in line with the realities of the existing industry. The report issued by the Roundtable in April 1981 pointed out the following problems: (1) a fragile technology base, (2) a limited space-industry market, and (3) institutional issues. Regarding the first, the Roundtable was concerned that, although Japan had succeeded in launching a satellite within a short period of time, it was behind in acquiring fundamental technology, chiefly because it depended on technology from the United States.

The search for a space-industry policy based on these recommendations continued until FY 1984. However, given the ongoing fiscal reconstruction, the policy planning lacked precision. It was progress in the commercialization of space that enabled new possibilities to emerge despite the somewhat stalled policy development, and the fact that private enterprises hoped to participate in the use of communication satellites following the establishment of the new Telecommunications Business Law. Plans for utilizing space were put on the path to reality with the January 1984 US announcement of plans for a space station. In the latter 1980s, a comprehensive space industry was promoted in the following areas: (1) "Promotion of resource remote sensing" (satellite observation of the ground surface from space), (2) development of a resource exploration observation system for mounting a polar orbit platform, (3) development of an unmanned space experiment system (space experiments/observation free flyer) that began in FY 1986, and so on.

4.2 The Challenge of Next-Generation Technology Development

4.2.1 "The Road to Becoming a Technology Nation"—*Vision for the 1980s*"

The March 1980 *Vision for the 1980s* summarized the results of an examination of technology policy explained in its Chapter 6, titled "The Road to Becoming a Technology Nation" (Sawai 2011, p. 31) and cited the following as required for the technology of the 1980s: (1) overcoming energy restrictions, (2) qualitatively improving living conditions and enriching regional communities, (3) promoting more creativity- and knowledge-intensive industries, and (4) taking on the challenge of next-generation technological innovation. These were regarded fundamentally as tasks for the private sector, but there remained areas in which the government was needed to carry out R&D or to play the role of project organizer. Thus, the goals or philosophy of industrial-technology policy looking toward the 1980s was "creative autonomous technological development" to support the country now become an economic power after overcoming the two oil crises.

Established in December 1983 as a private advisory body of the Director-General of the Agency of Industrial Science and Technology, the Study Group on Technical Development Perspectives compiled a report in September 1984 that stressed stronger collaboration among industry, academia, and government. It also pointed to the importance of independent technology development. In other words, the deeper the pursuit of basic research, the greater the uncertainty became, creating a unique role for the government itself in providing support through measures such as subsidies, loans, and taxation. In 1987, MITI also launched a Research Group to Study Trends in Technological Innovation and Prospects for New Markets, which compiled its own report in June. A MITI report the same year titled "Liven up, Japan!" said that fields such as microelectronics, new materials, and biotechnology were undergoing a technological revolution comparable to a "third industrial revolution." Basic research would be essential in order for Japan to be at the center of that revolution, and the role for industrial technology policy was accordingly likely to expand.

The Industrial Science and Technology Agency published an "Industrial technology white paper" in 1988, the first since the Agency's establishment in 1948. Its aims were as follows. First, as technology development began to expand to the extent that it no longer remained within the framework of original bureaus and divisions, industrial technology policy would henceforth be developed without regard for interministerial and interagency boundaries. The second aim was to transform Japan from a "processing center" to a "center of creative knowledge." With these aims, the White Paper pointed out issues such as low government investment in R&D, a lack of research in basic technology fields, and the need to promote international exchange and international cooperation. The White Paper placed a heavy emphasis on the impact of basic technology research and on the fact that "the growing accessibility and resonance of science and technology" were making steady advances.

4.2.2 The Establishment of a New Research and Development System for Next-Generation Industrial Basic Technology

The importance of basic technology was pointed out in the final report of the Study Group on Long-Term Planning for Industrial Technology Development in October 1981, and an R&D Program on Basic Technologies for Future Industries was established that October to develop concrete measures for it (Sawai 2011, p. 165). This system, which aimed to promote R&D with broad cross-sectoral impact, was based on different principles from those of the Large-Scale, Sunshine, and Moonlight Projects that had targeted sector-specific technological development. The new system was intended to cultivate the "buds" of technology until the development was a "young sapling" that the private sector could research and develop on its own strength. Using terms like "bud" and "sapling" as slogans, it aimed to promote R&D based on linkages among industry, academia, and the government. A biotechnology roundtable, High-Performance Polymer Materials Council, and Fine Ceramics Roundtable were established by private corporations. Through repeated discussions between these roundtables and the related MITI divisions, and with the participation from the national laboratories and universities, the outlines for next-generation-themed projects were decided. The roundtables became the parent organizations of the groups established to implement the technology development (Table 9).

The projects selected in 1981 spanned 12 subjects in three fields: new materials, biotechnology, and new functional elements. The field of new materials saw R&D of fine ceramics and other materials; biotech focused on the promotion of bioreactors. The budget increased steadily from 2.7 billion yen in FY 1981 to 6.4 billion yen in FY 1985, and funds were thereafter maintained in a special account at the 60–70 billion yen range. Many of the first-round projects initiated in FY 1981 were reaching their end dates in FY 1988, and were examined by the Planning Subcommittee of the Industrial Structure Council's Next-Generation Technology Development Committee established in April 1988. The report issued by the Subcommittee in June found the following problems: (1) adverse effects on "take-home research" by private enterprise, (2) insufficient links with university researchers, (3) delays

Table 9 Next-generation industrial infrastructure projects

Sector	Theme	Period	Total project costs (100 million yen)	Number of patents	
				Applications	Registered
New materials, ceramics	Fine ceramics	1981–1992	113	110	
New materials, polymer materials	High-efficiency polymer separation membrane material	1981–1990	42	29	13
	Conductive polymer material	1981–1990	29	18	14
	High crystalline polymeric material	1981–1990	24	54	11
	Silicon polymer material	1991–2000	37	473	
New materials, metal composite materials	High–performance crystal controlled alloy	1981–1988	39		
	Composite material	1981–1988	46	5	3
	Ultra-resistant environmental advanced materials	1989–1996	112	47	12
New materials, optoelectronic material	Photoreactive material	1985–1992	20	72	44
	Nonlinear opto-electronic materials	1989–1998	47	170	37
Biotechnology	Bioreactor	1981–1988	30	161	
	Cell mass culturing technology	1981–1989	34	71	
	Recombitant DNA utilization technology	1981–1990	31	17	7
	Functional protein aggregation application technology	1989–1998	46	39	4

(continued)

Table 9 (continued)

Sector	Theme	Period	Total project costs (100 million yen)	Number of patents	
				Applications	Registered
	Composite carbohydrate production utilization technology	1991–2000	40	33	
New functional elements	Environmental resistance enhancing element	1981–1985			
	Superlattice element	1981–1990	37	36	14
	3D circuit element	1981–1990	65	78	23
	Bio-element	1986–1995	24	108	43
	Quantization functional element	1991–2000	53	169	47
Superconductivity	Superconducting material; superconducting element	1988–1997	269	687	
Software	New software structure model	1990–1997	24		

Source Sawai (2011, p. 166)

in developing internationally, including participation of overseas companies, and (4) quantitative evaluations without qualitative or secondary-outcome evaluations. It also proposed themes for the next round of next-generation technology development, including diversification of research methods, and ways to involve universities. It suggested enlarging the scope of "bud"(technical seeds) to "sapling" (R&D before the application stage) to include the "fostering of seeds and seedlings (examining the possibility of practical applications)." Superconductivity and software were added to the covered fields, and more basic research and interdisciplinary and business-related themes were selected in FY 1988. These included, for example, the development of superconducting materials and superconducting elements.

4.2.3 Fostering Bioindustry

Biotechnology includes technologies that advance medical care, improve breeding, produce useful substances, and clarify biological processes by manipulating the functions of living organisms, including their substance, information, and energy. Biotechnology had already been applied to fermentation and brewing, but the discovery of the role of microorganisms expanded its applications to other fields such as antibiotic production and sewage treatment (Table 10).

Expectations for this field increased in Japan relative to that of the United States, which was at the forefront of biotechnology development and applications. According to a survey conducted by MITI in FY 1982, several tens of new companies had launched biotechnology R&D every year since 1980, as compared with three to five companies each year in the 1970s. In 1988, the MITI Bioindustry Office report summarized the prevailing situation and the issues in each field. According to that report, Japan's chemical industry led the world in amino acid production technology. Amino acids and their derivatives have various properties (ampholytic, chelating action, surface activity, bactericidal/antimicrobial, antioxidant, and so on), and their polymers have properties not found in other substances, such as biocompatibility and biodegradability. The report anticipated that these characteristics would lead to the development of new product areas and industrial fields (Yamazaki 2011, p. 344).

With the rising expectations for biotechnology, the Japanese government, too, began to focus on its development. In July 1982, the Bioindustry Promotion Committee was established within the Basic Industries Bureau and in July 1983 put together the following reports: "How to secure biological resources such as microorganisms" and "Safety concepts when using the results of recombinant DNA technology for industrial production." The former detailed the requirements for securing the necessary biological resources for technology development and industrialization of biotechnology. Since Japan was seeking systematically to secure a large number of microorganisms, animals, and plants, laboratories needed to be improved to that end. Concrete support of technical development included the 1981 establishment of the Next-Generation Basic Industrial Technology R&D System, which covered biotechnology among other areas. Three projects were initiated in its first year. One of them, research on glycoconjugates, was established jointly by the Science and Technology Agency, the Ministry of Health and Welfare, the Ministry of Agriculture, Forestry and Fisheries, and MITI, and the research was advanced by the private sector Research Association for Biotechnology with the cooperation of the Research Institute for Polymers and Textiles, the National Chemistry Laboratory for Industry, the Fermentation Research Institute, the Electrotechnical Laboratory, and the National Research Laboratory of Meteorology, as well as joint research from universities recommissioned by the research associations. R&D projects in MITI's National Research and Development Program ("Large-Scale Project") were also launched, as was research based on the 1983 Law for Accelerating Regional Development Based on High-Technology Industrial Complexes ("Technopolis Law"). A number of regions received support by using biotechnology as the pillar of their

Table 10 Economic impact of biotechnology in 2000 (*Unit* billion yen, %)

Biotechnology areas	Production (value)	Gross value-added production	Industrialization rate
Rice, wheat	519	381	9.51
Vegetables	297	164	8.70
Non-edible cultivated crops	497	400	77.70
Dairy	327	111	25.00
Beef/cattle products	146	37	22.80
Fisheries	118	71	2.97
Dairy products	590	150	20.70
Bakery, confectionery	1.370	507	32.00
Sugar	108	13	10.00
Seasonings	251	73	15.00
Starch and sugars	177	30	26.02
Mixed feed	637	58	30.00
Alcoholic beverages	1,113	662	19.84
Ethyl alcohol	164	49	80.00
Petrochemical basic products	317	44	8.32
Other petrochemical products	753	116	14.50
Pesticides	142	33	30.00
Medicine	3,151	1,564	40.00
Surfactant, Cosmetics	466	155	20.00
Other chemicals	479	149	12.37
Petroleum products	463	79	1.65
Nonferrous metal ingots	300	50	5.62
Computers	188	80	3.00
Electronic appliances	287	103	5.00
Water supply systems	479	303	24.00
Sewer systems	420	238	50.00
Waste systems	471	349	15.63
Total	15,003	6,312	11.80

Industrialization rate = Replacement rate × Realization rate (Replacement rate = ratio of conventional technology replaced by biotechnology; Realization rate = possibility of developing alternatives to conventional technology).
Source Yamazaki (2011, p. 369)

town planning, meaning they used legal frameworks for community development by integrating industry, academia, and residents around the nucleus of a cutting-edge technology. From FY 1988, MITI strengthened its emphasis on revitalizing regional economies through biotechnology: it produced a manual about introducing this technology, established a Biotechnology Instruction Staff System, and with the aim of developing the potential of traditional brewing industries, it mediated in obtaining financing from the Japan Development Bank and others.

With the expansion of the above policy supports, Japan's R&D expenditures in the 1980s increased, mainly in advanced technologies. From 6.0 trillion yen in 1981 to 8.9 trillion yen in 1985, the average annual growth rate was 10.4%. Although the scale itself was small, growth in the field of recombination, in particular, was remarkable. The number of recombinant DNA experiments increased from 284 in 1980 to 4,813 in 1986. The number of related patents also reached 800 in 1986, 13 times that in 1981.

4.2.4 Development of New Materials

The targets of MITI policy in the new materials category were fine chemicals, new metallic materials, highly functional polymer materials, composite materials, and others. By function, these included electrical functional materials, lightweight structural materials, thermal functional materials such as heat-resistant materials, and optical functional materials such as optical fibers. In March 1984, the Industrial Structure Study Group, a private advisory body of the Director-General of the Industrial Policy Bureau, explored the policy issues, including estimating the expansion of new materials-related markets looking ahead to the year 2000. Regarding fine ceramics in particular, the Fine Ceramics Basic Problem Council, a private advisory body of the Director-General of the Consumer Goods and Services Industries Bureau, announced in May 1984 its anticipation of an expansion in the market from 630 billion yen in 1983 to somewhere between 2.8 and 5.0 trillion yen in the year 2000 (Yamazaki 2011, p. 411).

The makers pursued the development of new materials in the 1970s through the establishment of laboratories and production and processing facilities, and by 1984 the excitement was such that it was dubbed "Year One of the New Materials Age." Beginning in 1985, the Basic New Materials Policy Office tried every year to capture the current state of the industry, issuing questionnaires to firms with the possibility of entering the market. As of 1985, 92 enterprises had entered the market, producing a total of 556 products; by 1988, the number had risen to 302 companies and 1,882 items. Entry from the chemical industry was the most frequent, followed by glass and stone, nonferrous metals, and steel. Materials manufacturers accounted for about one-third, but in the late 1980s, user industries—general machinery, electrical machinery, transportation machinery, and precision machinery—were becoming the core of new materials development. Reflecting these trends and classified by function, new materials with mechanical functions accounted for 40% or more of the total. Practical applications found in the 1988 surveys included artificial kidneys, IC packages, and others, and all were underway for ten to twenty years and were technically mature fields. There were also delays in practical applications of new materials such as fiber reinforced metal (FRM), which were less mature technologically and entering markets where the existing materials were competitive in price and performance. The issues highlighted by these materials were the need for differentiation or market-creative product development.

Meanwhile, the Basic New Materials Study Group, a private advisory body of the Director-General of the Basic Industries Bureau, in 1988 again summarized the possibilities for technological innovation in new materials. For example, in aircraft development, the development of new materials was expected to address the problems of large size, high efficiency, high speed, improved safety, and noise reduction. In space development, new materials were being considered for spacecraft, space stations, and artificial satellites. Possibilities were also being considered for utilizing new materials in regular consumer goods such as residential, medical, clothing, and food items.

In October 1989, the Basic Materials Study Group summarized the market size outlook for 2000 and the promotion challenges of the new materials industry in a report titled "About the future direction of the new materials industry." Market size in each new-materials field was expected to expand greatly and to contribute to high economic growth for related businesses. The group cited as challenges the further promotion of technological development in basic research fields, and pointed to the need to assure the reliability of new materials in practical uses, promote joint research and evaluation by the public and private sectors, and promote research into practical applications.

Apart from this, in April 1988, MITI launched the Minerva Plan Promotion Roundtable, which gathered experts to develop common basic technologies across industries, centered on the Nonferrous Metals Division of the Basic Industries Bureau (Yamazaki 2011, p. 322). The Roundtable held that nonferrous metals was a particularly noteworthy sector that could supply important materials supporting ultra-advanced innovations for the advanced technology and information society of the 21st century, and the development departments of major companies were brought together into working groups established for each material. In April 1989, a report titled "Minerva 21" was compiled as a vision for the development of nonferrous metals-related technologies in the twenty-first century. Dramatic improvements in new technologies were anticipated in fields such as optical communication-related technology, high-speed transportation methods such as high-performance aircraft, space development, nuclear energy development, advanced medical equipment, and chemicals, and the report called for advances in the materials to be used in these areas. Thereafter, in the 1990s, environmental and resource energy problems were explored, and with regard to the development of nonferrous metal materials, the

"New Minerva Metal Materials Future Perspective" compiled in 1991 sought to elucidate those areas for which high social expectations could be predicted and to induce research and development in those fields (Table 11).

4.2.5 Grant Aid for Private-Sector Technology Development

Meanwhile, various technical subsidies were created in the 1980s even as the number of government-led projects shrank. These were the Subsidies for the Practical Development of Technology for Energy Alternatives to Petroleum in FY 1980, Subsidies for Practical Development of New Power Generation Technology in FY 1981, and Subsidies for Industry Revitalizing Technology Research and Development in FY 1983, with the addition in FY 1993 of the Subsidy Program for Practical Applications of Technology Related to the Rationalization of Energy Use. Overall, however, from the mid-1980s on, subsidy policies tended to be abolished or reviewed due to criticism from abroad.

The Tax Program for Promoting R&D of Basic Technologies ("High-tech Tax System") was established in 1985. This allowed tax deductions for research and investment depreciation of assets that companies needed for research if they met certain requirements.

The Japan Development Bank meanwhile renamed the loans for "turning new technologies into businesses" as "new technology development" loans, and adopted improvement measures. These included adding to the JDB's list of financing targets facilities construction and acquisitions, the purpose of which was the preliminary stages of corporate planning for the "commercialization" of new technologies. Also, in FY 1985, it began to include funding for non-equipment-related loans in its general financing of corporate technology development ("new technology development"). However, the loans made by the Bank to advance industrial technology declined sharply after peaking at 92.8 billion yen in FY 1992.

4.3 New Regional Development Policy

4.3.1 Development of a New Location (Siting) Policy

Location policy in the 1980s developed under new ideas and marked a change from earlier policy. The new concepts included the Technopolis Plan, the Research Core Plan, the Key Facilities Siting Plan, the Office Arcadia Plan, and others (Takeda 2011, p. 53).

These new attempts were made because of the limitations that emerged in existing location policies, which had tried to disperse industry into non-urban regions based on the Inducement for Industrial Relocation plan. According to a mid-1980s survey, even though the dispersal plan had led to some relocation out of urban areas into the

Table 11 Minerva 21 technologies

	Characteristics, Uses	Issues
High specific-strength alloy (Al–Li alloy)	Aluminum alloy characterized by high specific strength. Aerospace development, super high-speed transportation network, high-performance machine tool development, urban restructuring	Highly active lithium alloy technology, melting/casting process, recovery technology
Intermetallic compound	Nb, Mo, Ti–AI intermetallic compounds having high strength, acid resistance, corrosion resistance, and abrasion resistance in a high-temperature environment. Aerospace development	Crystal control technology, diaphragm technology etc. Atomic level innovation
Rapid solidification technology	Technology to eliminate casting defects such as segregation and tissue abnormality accompanying solidification. Electronics, aeronautical and aerospace fields that require high-performance and high strength	Development of special melting technology, steel tightening technology, special cooling equipment
Titanium new smelting/dissolving method	Light-weight, high-strength, high-corrosion-resistance material. Stainless steel etc.	Reduction of the production cost of titanium ingot, development of continuous smelting method · new dissolving method
Application technologies for high-temperature superconducting material	Development of materials with superconducting properties. High-speed railways /ship, power generation systems, etc.	Development of superconducting material, development of application technology
Rare metal purification technology	An important advanced electronic material and superconducting material, for use in ultra-advanced technology sectors	Development of new refining method, laser separation method, etc.
Advanced recycling technology for useful metals	Precision alloys, dissimilar metals, impurities removal technology required for microfabrication processing	Development of automatic sorting, separation, and recovery technology, and dissolving, smelting technology

(continued)

Table 11 (continued)

	Characteristics, Uses	Issues
Nonferrous metal alloy design technology	Efficient alloy technology to meet advanced processing needs	Atomic-level alloy technology
Technology for evaluating new nonferrous metal materials technology	Reliability of new materials suitable for environment such as ultra-high speed, extreme resistance temperature, high temperature etc. Evaluation technology of safety	Establishment of materials evaluation technology incorporated in the material itself and in society

Source Yamazaki (2011, p. 337)

"induction areas," the industrial sites themselves were in a downturn and beginning to approach the limit of their viability (Table 12).

The Technopolis Plan ("Technopolis Plan"), which was the first under the new policy, was based on the March 1980 Industrial Structure Council report titled "About the nature of trade and industrial policy in the 1980s." The report called for promoting the introduction of cutting-edge technology industries and raising the technological level of existing regional companies. The aim in doing so was to foster the autonomy and revitalization of regional economies as technological cores. This was the "Technopolis 90 Construction Initiative." It aimed at "town"-building based on organic combinations of industry (advanced technology industries such as electronics and machinery), academia (research institutes such as engineering universities and private central research institutes), and living space ("warm" communities). Based on this concept, and on consultations with the Ministry of Construction, Ministry of Agriculture, Forestry and Fisheries, the National Land Agency, and others, the Law for Accelerating Regional Development Based Upon High-Technology Industrial Complexes (the "Technopolis Law") was established in April 1983. The purpose of this law was to promote industrial development based on advanced technology, mainly by local governments and enterprises in regions that did not have a high degree of industrial concentration, and to contribute to the revitalization of regional economies and the balanced development of the national economy. It was distinctive in that it delegated to the prefectures the selection of the areas themselves, and limited the involvement of the central government.

In August 1983, MITI announced policies on How to Proceed with the Technopolis Development Initiative" and on this basis sequentially approved the development plans formulated by the prefectures. Of the 26 selected regions, 20 were approved to start by FY 1986. A survey conducted in 1990, which was the target year of the 20 regions, found that while research projects had been undertaken actively, the results were not reflected in technological improvements among the SMEs in those regions. Research institutes such as universities were advancing technological developments that did not meet the needs of the companies in their regions. In light of these problems, MITI in March 1991 changed its target year to 1995 and made

Table 12 Industrial location vision for the 21st Century: plans and actual status

Item	Plan			Actual status	
Annual growth rate	5.7–6.3%			4.5% (1976–82 real growth rate)	
Factory relocation target	In 1985, reduce the factory site area in the relocation promotion area by about 30% from 1974 level			25.4% decrease in the 23 wards of Tokyo and the cities of Osaka and Nagoya	
New expansion targeted to the relocation districts	On a cumulative basis from 1976 to 1985, site about 70% of new facilities (by area) in the target relocation districts			65.6% on a cumulative basis from 1976–82	
Factory shipment value by region in cases where target was met		1974	1985	1982	
	Relocation promotion areas	23%	11%	18.1%	Conversion from Tokyo 23 wards and the cities of Osaka and Nagoya
	Previously undeveloped areas	53%	59%	57.9%	Conversion to 27 prefectures
	Relocation target areas (for induction)	24%	30%	24.0%	
	Pacific Belt region	69%	60%	67.3%	
Industrial base	Factory site area	150,000 hectares	220,000 hectares	157,000 hectares	Converted to factories of over 30 employees
	Factory water recovery rate	64.90%	70%	73.80%	

Source Takeda (2011, p. 48)
Source data from MITI Local Environmental Pollution Bureau Industrial Relocation Section 1985, p. 12

additions to its guidelines on technology advancement in regional firms that made up local industries, the establishment of new firms based on advanced technology, the individuation of regions, and the spread of advanced technology to areas outside the Technopolis. It also added new functions such as "play" to the categories of industry, academia, and residential community. The 1999 survey revealed the limits of these plans, finding that the outcomes of the high-tech industries were not particularly prominent in the designated areas. Although certain regions had seen their efforts bear fruit and were ready to turn those results into businesses, overall the policy outcomes in the 1990s were not as intended. The Technopolis Act developed into the Law for Facilitating the Creation of New Business in December 1998 (Fig. 8).

The second Research Core Plan sought to address the economy's shift to service industries and the hyper-concentration of economic activities in Tokyo by aiming at the regional dispersal of service and administrative sectors, and based on the 1986

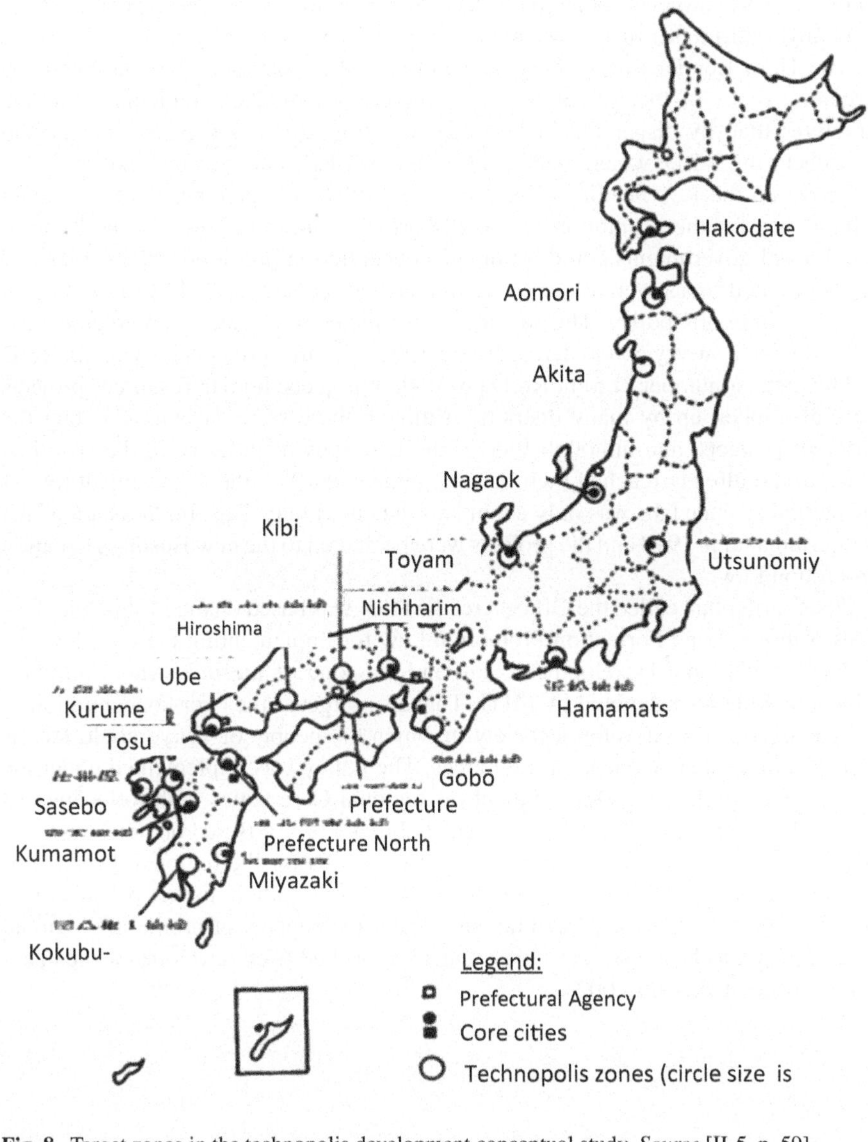

Fig. 8 Target zones in the technopolis development conceptual study. *Source* [II-5, p. 59]

Private Participation Promotion Law, it developed Research Cores, meaning specified facilities utilizing the capabilities of private-business operators. Although the project was intended to support the gathering of research and development functions in regional cities that already had a high degree of urban functions, the development was limited by the strict conditions that were imposed. In order to shift to a domestic demand-led economic structure, this concept focused on building regional economic structures by dispersing service industries and higher-order functions such as manufacturers' R&D projects, and to build regional economic structures responsive to the economy's shift to services and software.

The Third Key Facilities Location Plan targeted a wider area than the relatively large-city focus of the Research Core. The aim was to build regional economic structures that, by dispersing higher-order functions such as service industry and manufacturing R&D, would help lead to a demand-led economic structure.

Based on the Key Facilities Location Law, MITI in September 1988 presented "Guidelines for the promotion of specific project concentrations" on the basis of which local governments could formulate concentration promotion plans. Many of the designated areas were close to, or overlapped, areas that had been the targets of the Technopolis policy. The two location policies were clearly complementary. According to a survey conducted in March 1994, the three projects involved in R&D had the largest number of joint R&D promotion projects; human resources projects were also taken up by many districts. Although there were variations among the different projects, and although four of the ten types of industry in the specified projects had already reached their original targets in 1993, the achievement rate of the natural science labs was only about half the target rate. The "brain location" act was terminated in 1998 and the projects were passed on to the new Business Creation Promotion Law.

The fourth plan, called the Office Arcadia Plan, was based on the Multi-Polar Patterns National Land Formation Promotion Law for implementing the Fourth Comprehensive National Development Plan and was one of the industrial workplace relocation policies promoted by MITI. This also targeted the over-concentration in Tokyo and aimed to develop a society in which the people of Tokyo could feel as relaxed and affluent as those in rural areas. The policy was implemented under the Law for Comprehensive Development of Regional Core Cities with Relocation of Office-Work Function ("Local Hubs Act," February 1992). Based on this law, MITI decided to construct Office Arcadias to serve as hubs for the regional dispersal of industry. In principle, these were limited to one business hub district per local hub city. By 1994, six areas had been targeted under the concept of promoting regional cores, and six as business core cities, and 16 areas had been developed as business complexes by February 2002.

In addition, services such as location information were provided to foreign companies that were considering investment or advances into Japan. This was intended to contribute to the development of a domestic demand-led economy to ease international economic tensions. In addition, the Rural Area Industry Promotion Law of June 1971 had resulted from the fact that the "introduction of industry" had not produced the results of other industry relocation policies, and with the conviction that it was necessary to respond to changes in the industrial structure, the 1971 Law was renamed in June 1988 as the Law on the Promotion of Introduction of Industry into Agricultural Regions and the range of industries to be thus introduced was expanded.

4.3.2 Review of the Pollution Health Damage Compensation System

Under the Law Concerning Pollution-Related Health Damage Compensation and Other Measures ("Public Health Law") enacted in October 1973, the compensation system for damage to health from pollution targeted the results of air and water pollution. People whose health was damaged by pollution were eligible for compensation if their claims were approved by prefectural governors or the mayors of major cities (Takeda 2011, p. 303). The compensation system came into effect due to a broad national consensus that included industry, against the background of the court ruling in the Yokkaichi Pollution Trial. It was not originally easy to clarify the causal relationships between pollution and disease for individual patients, so in order to avoid confusion, such as multiple lawsuits, the policy was adopted of providing relief if certain requirements were met. It was a system that enabled fairly practical decision making.

Under this system, compensation was paid to the "victim" with charges levied on polluters by group according to the degree to which they contributed to the pollution. However, the problem inherent in the design of the system itself became increasingly obvious in the course of its operation.

One of the problems was that even in cases in which the air quality improved markedly due to pollution regulations, the area designated under the Pollution Law was not removed from the coverage, but rather was expanded. As mentioned above, environmental regulation had had a considerable impact on air pollution, excluding nitrogen oxides. Nevertheless, the designated areas were expanded and the number of certified patients continued to increase. The industries bearing the cost of the compensation were therefore dissatisfied. There was further dissatisfaction because mobile units such as automobiles, although believed to be important sources of pollution, were excused from the funding burden. Needless to say, these views were opposed by those seeking relief for damages, and opinions were especially strong on the unresolved issue of nitrogen oxide.

MITI therefore reviewed the system with a view to improving it. The focus of its reconsideration was improvement of the certification requirements, clarification of the requirements for removal of the regional designation, and rationalization of the cost burden.

The Environmental Health Committee of the Central Council for Environmental Pollution Control (Central Pollution Council), meeting in November and December 1982, declared the need to reexamine the system from a neutral position, and momentum for improving it gradually gained strength, until finally in October 1986, the Environmental Health Committee compiled a report calling for the following: (1) Complete release of the designated regions, (2) continued compensation to those already certified, (3) projects related to prevention of health damage based on contributions from the sources of pollution, especially in the old designated areas. The amended law was enacted accordingly in September 1987. As a result, in March 1988, all Class 1 regional designations were canceled, and the emphasis of the pollution health damage compensation system shifted from offering after-the-fact relief to seeking means of preventing damage in the first place.

4.3.3 Rationalization of Administrative Regulations on Safety

In the latter 1980s, the High-Pressure Gas Safety Institute, a private corporation, was established as the core institution for the voluntary adoption of safety practices. It undertook various projects and made progress in eliminating the duplication of regulations. The business world, meanwhile, was critical of what it regarded as the slow pace of reform (Takeda 2011, p. 588).

In September 1989, the Roundtable on High-Pressure Gas Safety Policy, a private advisory body of the Director-General of the Industrial Location and Environmental Protection Bureau, undertook a review of the deregulation of safety policy on high-pressure gas and in July 1991, it advised the High-Pressure Gas and Explosives Safety Council on "How to formulate safety measures for high-pressure gas in the future." The November report issued a strong call for a shift to voluntary safety controls, and the High-Pressure Gas Control Law was revised on this basis. The revisions strengthened the regulations concerning consumption of high-pressure gas, enabled prefectural governors to make recommendations and issue orders to strengthen business safety measures, and advanced the simplification of procedures.

Deregulation was promoted thereafter as well. In April 1997, the Partial Revision of the High-Pressure Gas Control Law and the Law Concerning the Securing of Safety and the Optimization of Transaction of Liquefied Petroleum Gas came into effect, and the High-Pressure Gas Control Law was renamed the High-Pressure Gas Safety Law. This renaming was in accordance with the rationalization and simplification of various regulations such as permitting self-inspection or inspection by private companies and shifting portions of the sales business to a notification system. Regarding liquefied petroleum gas, plans were also made to rationalize regulations for businesses that established high-level safety systems. Measures included shifting from a licensing to a registration system for sales businesses and establishing a centralized monitoring system. The change, which advanced voluntary safety activities, represented a major shift in the approach to safety regulation.

4.3.4 Measures to Address Mine Drainage at Metal Mines

The costs of treating mine pollution were in principle to be borne by the mine companies that were the polluters. However, the August 1980 Mining Industry Council's proposal titled "Measures for mine drainage in the future" pointed out that these costs could not be met by raising prices and that the burden would only place greater pressure on the businesses and reduce the will to develop new mines. Because of this, the Council suggested that some of the burden be assumed by local governments (Takeda 2011, p. 647). MITI accordingly revised the system in FY 1981 to make the cost of treating environmental contamination eligible for subsidies. MITI also strengthened its measures against pollutant accumulation at mines, based on the Mining Council's proposal of September 1982 regarding problems such as increasing construction volumes and the unexpectedly high cost of clean-up at the former Matsuo Mine. The second Basic Policy Plan on Mine Pollution Prevention Projects Related to Specified Spent Facilities went into effect in April 1983.

As mentioned above, problems with the new system became evident in the course of addressing mining pollution. This was especially true because no technologies emerged that could assure a complete clean-up, and the obligation to bear the burden of others' clean-up costs in addition to their own acted as a restraint on mining businesses and caused problems for the financing system as well. It was in the 1990s that solutions to these problems began to emerge (Fig. 9).

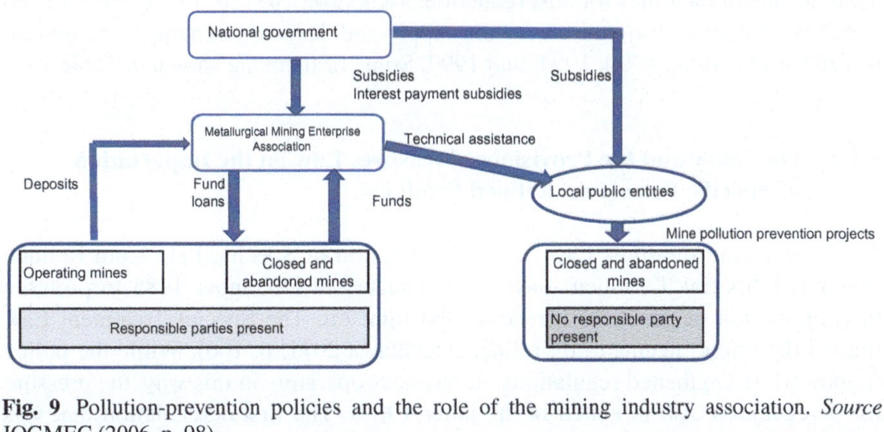

Fig. 9 Pollution-prevention policies and the role of the mining industry association. *Source* JOGMEC (2006, p. 98)

5 Making Progress on Extrication from Dependence on Oil

5.1 Policies Prioritizing the Stable Supply of Energy

5.1.1 On the Long-Term Outlook for the Supply and Demand of Energy and an Overall Evaluation of Energy Policy

The energy supply in the 1980s proved different from what had been predicted immediately after the oil crisis. Oil supply decreased from the 1970s to the first half of the 1980s, but from the late 1980s into the early 1990s it increased again with the fall in crude oil prices. The dependence on the Middle East, which had supplied 90% of Japan's post-crisis crude oil imports, fell to 67.4% of the total in 1987. The proportion of natural gas in the primary energy supply rose. Domestic coal output meanwhile declined from 50.0 million tons in 1961 to 1.29 million tons in 2008. The quantity of imported coal began exceeding that of domestic coal in 1970 and in 1988 passed the 100-million ton mark. From the 1980s on, consumption of coal increased because of strong demand from the electric utilities.

Stable supply was already on its way to becoming the top priority for natural resources and energy policy but was pushed even more in that direction by the second oil crisis in 1979. As the impact of the crisis faded, however, new directions began to be explored. In April 1983, MITI held an Advisory Committee for Energy Roundtable on Basic Issues to undertake a comprehensive examination of energy policy, including the issue of energy costs. The Roundtable summarized its findings in an August 1983 report titled "On the long-term outlook for the supply and demand of energy and an overall evaluation of energy policy," in which it declared that "Although it is more essential than previously to assure a secure supply, we also need to actively address the demands of the times for cost reduction" (Kikkawa 2011, p. 77). Between 1980 and 2000, the long-term outlook for the supply and demand of energy were revised in 1982, 1983, 1987, 1990, 1994, and 1997. Some of them are shown in Table 13.

5.1.2 Oil Policy and the Provisional Measures Law on the Importation of Specific Petroleum Refined Products

The Provisional Measures Law on the Importation of Specific Petroleum Refined Products ("Special Treatment Law") was enacted in December 1985 to promote the importation of gasoline, kerosene, and light oil. The Special Treatment Law limited the import agents to oil refiners (Kikkawa 2011, p. 166). While the policy framework strengthened regulations on business operators in this way, the pressure for deregulation also mounted in the latter 1980s. The first deregulation that was carried out from 1987 to 1993 was triggered by a report of the Committee to Consider Basic Issues in the Petroleum Industry established in November 1986 under the Petroleum Council. The Committee's report was issued in June 1987 under the title "On the Petroleum Industry and Oil Policy Looking Towards the 1990s." This led

Table 13 The Long-term outlook for the supply and demand of energy

		1973 Actual performance			Outlook August 1979		Outlook November 1983		Outlook June 1994	
		FY 1973	Converted value (unit:10^{13} kcal)	Composition ratio (%)	FY 1990	Composition ratio (%)	FY 1995	Composition ratio (%)	FY 2000	Composition ratio (%)
Domestic energy	General hydropower (10 K kw)	2,120	18	4.6	2,600	4.6	2,400	5	2,220	3.3
	Pump-storage power (10 K kw)	140			2,700		1,950			
	Geothermal (10 K kl)	3 (K kw)	0.06	0	730	1	350	1	100	0.2
	Domestic oil, Natural gas (10 K kl)	370	3.5	0.9	950	1.4	190	not available		
	Domestic coal (10 K tons)	2,168	14.4	3.8	2,000	2	1,800–2000	not available		
	subtotal		37	9.5		9		not available		not available
Quasi-domestic energy	Nuclear power (10 K kw)	230	2.4	0.6	5,300	10.9	4,800	14	4,560	12.1
Domestic, Quasi-domestic subtotal			39	10.1		19.9		not available		not available
Imported energy	LNG (10 K tons)	237	3.2	0.8	4,500	15.6	4,000 (including domestic natural gas)	12	5,400	12.8
	Coal (10 K tons)	5,800	45	11.7	14,350	9	12,800 (including domestic coal)	18	13,400	16.6

(continued)

Table 13 (continued)

	1973 Actual performance			Outlook August 1979		Outlook November 1983		Outlook June 1994	
	FY 1973	Converted value (unit:10^{13} kcal)	Composition ratio (%)	FY 1990	Composition ratio (%)	FY 1995	Composition ratio (%)	FY 2000	Composition ratio (%)
New fuel oil, new energy etc. (10 K kl)				3,850	5.5	1,900	4	940	1.6
Oil (10 K kl)	31,800	296	77.4	36,600	50	25,000	48	31,600	53.4
Subtotal		344	89.9		80.1		not available		not available
Total energy supply (oil conversion (100 million kl))	4.1	383	100	7.16	100	5.3	100	5.91	100

Source op. cit. [Kikkawa 2011, pp. 72–73, 78–79, 82–83, 94–95]

to revision of the restrictions on refining and selling that applied even in normal times on the basis of the Petroleum Industry Law and the Gasoline Retail Business Law. Thereafter, the process of deregulation remained ongoing. The mid-1990s saw demands for the further pursuit of a stable supply of petroleum products and for improvements in efficiency, and attempts were made to introduce the principle of competition even in import sectors.

In the refining and sales fields, the United States demanded the liberalization of imports of petroleum products into Japan in the 1980s, and Japanese petroleum distributors were in fact beginning to try importing petroleum products. In March 1985, the Petroleum Council conducted its first policy review since the end of World War II of refining methods in oil-consuming areas. The Special Treatment Law aimed to promote the importation of volatile oils, kerosene, and diesel, and obliged importers to set up various facilities. For this reason, it restricted import activities to refineries, and so although it also promoted and liberalized imports, it acted as a restraint on competition by limiting those who could be engaged in importing. This area, too, however, saw deregulation after 1987.

Where stockpiling policy was concerned, relaxing the private burden of maintaining oil reserves in the late 1980s proved a challenge. A November 1987 report by the Comprehensive Energy Survey Group and the Petroleum Issues Subcommittee of the Petroleum Council called for (1) a 50-million kiloliter stockpile of oil based on the International Energy Agency's requirement that all member countries hold oil stocks equivalent to at least 90 days of net oil use, (2) reduction, in stages, of private oil reserves by a total of 70 days, and (3) gradual abolition of the stockpiling of the petroleum raw material naphtha. The second of these recommendations was implemented in FY 1993, and the national stockpile also reached its target amount in 1997.

5.1.3 Structural Adjustment of the Domestic Coal Industry

As the supply of overseas coal began to increase, the Seventh Coal Policy (1982–1986) maintained its earlier target of 20 million tons, but the end of the road for structural adjustment measures was already beginning to be apparent. Following the yen appreciation triggered by the September 1985 Plaza Accord, the steel industry in June 1986 forced a reduction of domestic coal prices to those of imported Australian coal. The power industry, which was the last to collaborate with the efforts, also announced in November 1985 that it would cut its purchases to two-thirds as of November 1985. The structural adjustment measures for domestic coal that had relied on collective cooperation thus began to approach their end point (Kikkawa 2011, p. 214).

The Eighth Coal Plan (1987–1991) concluded that a gradual reduction of domestic coal production was inevitable, and that an annual production of about 10 million tons was appropriate. The Post-Eighth Coal Policy (1992–2001) had in its purview a phased-out end to the policy.

5.1.4 Maintaining a Stockpiling System for Rare Metals

"Rare metals" is the generic name for metal elements that either have low crustal abundance or that are difficult to extract. Because production of rare metals was limited to a handful of countries such as Russia and South Africa, a rare-metal stockpiling system was established on the instruction of Prime Minister Zenkou Suzuki in December 1980, under the supervision of the Economic Security Council-related Cabinet Meetings established under the Chief Cabinet Secretary. MITI also took the opportunity to set up a special subcommittee on economic security issues within the Coordination Committee (Kikkawa 2011, p. 247). The Subcommittee's April 1982 report, "Aiming at the establishment of Economic security," called for the immediate creation of a rare-metal stockpiling system on a national level. In 1983, a stockpiling system was started for seven of these metals: nickel, chromium, tungsten, cobalt, molybdenum, manganese, and vanadium.

Policy developed after that from the stockpiling system to a strategy of security of rare metals. In December 1984, the Special Subcommittee on Comprehensive Measures for Rare Metals, in the Mining Subcommittee of the Mining Council, compiled a report titled "The Aims of the Comprehensive Measures on Rare Metals: Technological Innovation, Industrial Revitalization, and Economic Security." In addition to expanding stockpiling plans and promoting countermeasures to address supply disorders, the report also suggested promotion of exploration and technology development.

5.2 Pursuing Non-petroleum Power Supplies

5.2.1 Shifting Away from Petroleum

Declining business performance and serious power supply and environmental issues weakened the independence of the electric utility industry. As mentioned in Chap. 2, the initial target values set by the Electric Power Development Coordination Council in the 1970s and early 1980s did not exceed the actual numbers achieved. Decisions on utility locations were delayed but the policy itself was expanded and required further adjustment. This weakened the autonomy of the industry, but despite coordination at the policy level, decisions on location, as described above, did not always proceed as planned (Table 14).

While delays arose in developing power-generation sites, progress was made in shifting the composition of the power supply away from oil. The shift came about first through a strong emphasis on developing nuclear energy, and second through curbs on the development of oil-fired power generation and through an aggressive development of LNG (liquefied natural gas) and coal-fired generation.

It was nuclear power that became the favorite policy approach of the effort to move away from oil (Kikkawa 2011, p. 314). Two conditions boosted its development: first,

Table 14 Rate of growth in output and electric energy generation by nine major power companies, %

		Nuclear power	Thermal power	Hydropower	Geothermal power	Total
Power generation equipment output	1974–1985	23.8	4.0	4.5	25.5	5.6
	1986–1994	5.7	2.3	2.5	7.8	3.0
	1995–2000	2.0	2.7	1.9	6.6	2.4
Amount of power generated	1974–1985	30.2	0.7	1.8	–	3.7
	1986–1994	5.9	4.2	−1.8	–	4.1
	1995–2000	3.4	0.0	4.2	10.2	1.6

Source Kikkawa (2011, p. 315)

Japan's nuclear-power generation had entered the stage of full-scale commercialization in the late 1960s. Second, although uranium imports were necessary at the outset, expectations for the possibility of gradually lowering that dependency increased with the establishment of the nuclear fuel cycle. The development of nuclear power had been hindered, however, by people's unease and doubts about safety. The government and the electric power industry made efforts to dispel these concerns. In October 1978, the Nuclear Safety Commission was established as an entity separate from the Japan Atomic Energy Commission and became responsible for safety regulations for nuclear power generation. Meanwhile, in January 1979, MITI became responsible for the administration of safety regulations on nuclear reactors. It adopted an approach to the establishment of reactors consisting of a first safety review to be conducted when the Ministry was issuing its approval, and a second "double check" by the Nuclear Safety Commission. The government and the industry also started working on establishing a nuclear fuel cycle and practical applications for fast-breeder reactors, which furthered the feasibility of nuclear development.

Attention was also focused on the use of LNG, because no supply issues had arisen in LNG during the successive oil crises. Support for the introduction and use of natural gas as an alternative to oil came in the form of the May 1980 Law Concerning Promotion of Development and Introduction of Alternative Energy (hereafter the "Alternative Energy Law"). The issues in introducing LNG were considered to be the following: (1) securing a stable supply, (2) developing distribution facilities such as liquefaction terminals, LNG tankers, and receiving terminals and supply facilities, and (3) creating and organizing demand. The emphasis was placed on reducing these barriers to upfront investment. With support in these forms, five companies (Tokyo Electric, Tohoku Electric, Kyushu Electric, Kansai Electric, and Chubu Electric) converted a significant portion of their fuel for power generation from petroleum to LNG between 1974 and 1985.

However, because of the enormous capital investment required by the construction of receiving terminals for LNG, the use of imported coal was also taken into consideration. The customs CIF (Cost, Insurance, and Freight) price of standard overseas coal first fell below the standard price of domestic coal for electric power-generation use in FY 1977, and from 1983 on, remained consistently cheaper. From the late 1970s to the early 1980s, five electric power companies (Hokkaido Electric, Chugoku Electric, Shikoku Electric, Kyushu Electric, and Tohoku Electric) increased coal's ratio of the total fuel used for power generation.

5.2.2 Advances in the Development of Nuclear Power

Nuclear power is superior from the point of view of energy security because it is not much affected by changes in the international situation, and because carbon dioxide is not emitted in the power generation process, meaning that it helps prevent climate change. It was also expected to prove less costly than other methods if it operated steadily at a high rate of capacity utilization. In other words, nuclear power seemed able to meet the needs of energy, economy, and environment—the "3-Es" of energy policy. It was, however, highly risky if adequate safety measures were not in place, and spent nuclear fuel was both difficult and costly to dispose of.

In the early 1980s, nuclear-power generation in Japan advanced rapidly. However, the March 1978 Three-Mile Island accident in the US and the April 1986 Chernobyl accident in the Soviet Union made it hard to find sites for nuclear power plants in the 1980s. Furthermore, between 1986 and 1994, the establishment of the nuclear fuel cycle did not proceed as planned. Nevertheless, in May 1986, a portion of the Law on the Regulation of Nuclear Source Material, Nuclear Fuel Material and Reactors (Nuclear Reactor Regulation Law) was amended, and in November 1984, a new Japan–US Atomic Agreement was concluded to establish the foundations for starting the nuclear fuel cycle. In March 1992, Japan Nuclear Fuel Industry Inc. began the operation of a uranium enrichment plant.

While these efforts were made to expand the use of nuclear power, safety assurance measures were also added every time a serious accident occurred. Following the accident at Three-Mile Island, steps were taken to improve safety measures in 52 areas, including safety standards, reviews, and design, as well as operations management and research on disaster prevention and safety. Following the accident at Chernobyl, the Nuclear Safety Commission established a special committee in May 1986. It issued a report in May of the following year, which judged prompt revisions of existing safety regulations unnecessary because Chernobyl's design and structure differed from that of Japan's power plants. The report nevertheless pointed to the lessons learned and asserted the need to improve nuclear disaster prevention measures, foster safety awareness, and promote international cooperation to address the accidents.

5.2.3 Energy Conservation Measures in Every Sector

As part of the effort to realize policy objectives, the 1979 Law Concerning the Rational Use of Energy ("Energy Conservation Act") required certain factories and business sites in the industrial sector to submit periodic reports on energy use, and to make and submit mid- and long-term plans and to appoint energy managers (Kikkawa 2011, p. 403).

The Alternative Energy Law was enacted in May 1980, ushering in the age of oil-substitution policy. At the time, the policy was aimed at resolving the instability of Japan's fragile energy supply base and at addressing the instability of the international oil situation. The political instability in OPEC countries encouraged these legislative measures, as dependence on oil imports reached nearly 100% in 1977, with dependence on the Middle East for 80% of that supply. MITI's thinking on concrete measures also played a role in the establishment of the Alternative Energy Law. That is, the Law was predicated on expectations of the promotion of the following concrete steps: (1) alternative energy development including overseas coal, hydropower, and geothermal, (2) alternative energies in the industrial sector through fuel conversion and the promotion of coal-fired power plant construction, (3) solar energy in public facilities, (4) nuclear power development, including the establishment of the nuclear fuel cycle, and (5) technological development in alternative energies, including coal liquefaction, solar energy, geothermal energy, and so on.

It was estimated that three trillion yen would be needed to fund these measures on alternative energy, over a period of 10 years beginning in 1980. The fruits of the endeavor would ultimately go to the consumer, so it was decided that the funding should be requested of the consumer. This was accomplished through an expansion of the uses of the Promotion of the Power Resources Development Tax and the Petroleum Tax. Ten-year goals were set for alternative energy, and the use of coal, nuclear power, natural gas, hydropower, and geothermal energy was promoted. These measures were not accompanied by penalties but took the form of guidelines.

Chapter 4
Long-Term Depression and Economic Structural Reform (1991–2000)

1 Keynotes of Japan's Economy and Trade and Industry Policy in the 1990s

1.1 The 1990 Trade and Industrial Policy Vision of the 1990s

1.1.1 Collapse of the Bubble and the Prolonged Recession

Betraying the optimistic expectations that had followed on the bursting of Japan's economic bubble, the Japanese economy suffered a long-term recession in the 1990s. Economic growth rates fell to 1.9% in 1992 and below 1% the following year. The steady growth of exports and the trade surplus (which reached over 100 billion dollars) during these years suggest that the recession was largely the result of a marked slump in domestic demand. Japan's solid export record drew mounting criticism from abroad. Meanwhile, a lack of tax revenues meant fiscal rebuilding was interrupted and deficit spending mounted once again. Nonperforming loans, which were aftereffects of the bubble's collapse, acted as a drag on the economy, in spite of steep drops in interest rates. The so-called convoy system of financial administration, which had accompanied financial liberalization, came under review, while the volatility of financial institutions and the question of how to manage their bankruptcy became major issues. If anything, the low interest rates greatly limited the possibility of using other economic stimulus measures. The economy remained stagnant.

Moreover, in February 1993, Japan saw a growing trade surplus along with rapid yen appreciation after a long period of stable exchange rates. On August 17, the currency hit a record of \$1 = ¥100.40, after which it depreciated slightly heading into the new year. This yen appreciation caused a drop in the revenues of corporations in export industries. In response, firms cut back on employment. Consumer morale dampened accordingly, spurring a slump in consumption. Large companies were

Committee on the History of Japan's Trade and Industry Policy. RIETI,
Dynamics of Japan's Trade and Industrial Policy in the Post Rapid Growth Era (1980–2000),
Economics, Law, and Institutions in Asia Pacific, https://doi.org/10.1007/978-981-15-1987-1_4

forced to restructure, closing factories and reducing staff by the thousands, and unemployment became a pronounced issue. In April 1993, the government devised emergency economic measures, investing more heavily in public works, reducing taxes to promote acquisition of real estate, and taking measures for fiscal expansion. In September, the official discount rate was reduced to 1.75, a record low.

Although these policies effectively slowed the decline in business conditions, they had little ripple effect: the first half of 1993 presented promising economic developments, but the yen's rise stalled the economy again, leading to a scarcity of demand on a scale not seen in the postwar period. Production dropped and the year ended with little prospect of a recovery from the deflationary conditions. Japan was meanwhile adopting economic policy changes for international reasons: in July 1993, Prime Minister Kiichi Miyazawa met with US President Bill Clinton, who agreed to a framework—previously discussed at the April summit—for comprehensive discussions of economic issues between Japan and America. This framework rested on three pillars: (1) reduction of Japan's current account surplus and America's budget deficit, (2) the opening of negotiations and discussions by sector and structure, and (3) cooperation on environment and technology. Furthermore, the final draft agreement of the GATT Uruguay Round was adopted on December 15, and in April 1994, was signed at Marrakesh by 125 countries and regions, replacing GATT and leading to the establishment of the World Trade Organization (WTO) on January 1, 1995. The establishment of the WTO meant the maintenance and promotion of global free-trade systems, but America, in matters of economic policy, continued to favor bilateral negotiations like the above Japan–US economic talks. This inevitably led to the formation of bloc economies and to trade discrimination against those outside those blocs.

From 1995–1996, the world economy as a whole continued expanding, due to the significant growth of developing economies, especially in Asia, but Japan remained in a slump. Although 1995 appeared to usher in recovery, albeit a slow one, the Great Hanshin Earthquake of mid-January led to a sharp appreciation of the yen, which rose to the vicinity of 80 yen to the dollar, and Japan's economy again lost its vigor. Imports of products and raw materials soared, accelerating deflation or the so-called price destruction; the unease about employment continued unabated, and the specter of deflation began to haunt Japan. The "Survey of economic trends" by Keidanren indicated that there were many causes for concern after 1994, including the rise in value of the yen, the stagnation of capital investment, the persistence of excess employment, and the business world's negative outlook on the economy.

Moreover, the bad debts held by financial institutions and the fall in land prices that had given rise to them acted as a heavy drag on economic recovery. The instability of the financial sector led to the collapse even of financial institutions that had been regarded as "beyond doubt." The 1994 failures of the Tokyo Kyowa Bank and very secure credit cooperatives were followed by the revelation that the city's largest credit union, Cosmo, was going bankrupt. One month later, in August, the Ministry of Finance announced a rescue package for Hyogo Bank, the largest of the second-tier regional banks, and for Kizu Shin'yo Kumiai, the largest of the credit cooperatives.

The yen returned to $1 = 100-yen levels in August of 1995, and in September, the official discount rate was reduced to 0.5%, another record low. These changes, along with large-scale policies for boosting the economy, enabled Japan to avoid going deeper than the already historic depths of this business cycle. That same month, however, the off-the-book losses of Japanese banks' overseas branches were brought to light, greatly undermining trust in Japan's financial system and leading to the so-called Japan Premium. Thus, Japan's economy saw many changes, but after the bursting of the bubble Japan was unable to take advantage of opportunities for recovery. This led in the fall of 1997 to the outright failure of the Sanyo Securities Company, the Hokkaido Takushoku Bank, and Yamaichi Securities.

1.1.2 The *Vision of the 1990s*

The *Vision of the 1990s*, compiled by the Industrial Structure Council in July 1990, summarized the goals of industrial policy as the following: (1) contributing to international society and undertaking reform on an international scale; (2) realizing a relaxed and affluent life for the people; and (3) securing the foundations for long-term economic development (Okazaki 2012, p. 13).

The first goal emphasized structural reform based on a recognition of the following realities: (1) emerging friction among Western nations following the collapse of the socialist sphere in Eastern Europe; (2) emerging friction not only in trade but also in investment, technology, and finance, as well as in structural areas such as national systems and customs, due to growing international economic exchange; and (3) the growing unease about Japan's economic power owing to Japan's increased presence in the world economy and a distrust that extended even to Japan's social structure and culture. However, the *Vision*'s stress on international friction in explaining the need for structural change indicates that there was a lack of awareness that the industrial structure would become a hindrance to growth. In other words, Japan was still subject to the constraints of the bubble era.

The second goal articulated in the 1990s *Vision* recognized the so-called paradox of affluence: that although the consumption of goods and services had become more sophisticated, basic living conditions, including free time, work environment, living space, and consumer choice, were deteriorating. The *Vision* pointed out that the issue lay in Japan's "corporate-type society" and its prioritization of production over lifestyle, and stressed that resolving this problem would require a shift to a "people-oriented industrial policy."

The third goal assumed a medium-term shift in Japan's industrial structure toward a "service economy," meaning an increase in the service industry's share in the national economy. Another dominant feature of the *Vision* was its consciousness of ongoing "globalization," which had become a clearer trend over the course of the 1980s.

The *Vision of the 1990s* was therefore significant in that it initiated the call for a reform of institutions and practices in order to overcome economic friction. The formation of this *Vision*, like those stressing heavy and chemical industrialization, knowledge intensity in the 1970s, and creative knowledge intensity in the 1980s, helped create a common understanding of the issues.

Nonetheless, the 1990s *Vision* was slightly different in character from its predecessors, because of its emphasis on changing lifestyle rather than on new candidates for growth industries. The new *Vision* did not attract widespread attention, however. People may have been unwilling to embrace it because it suggested that the rapid growth era and the stable growth that had followed were coming to an end. None of the *Visions* formulated after the 1980s conveyed a sense of purpose comparable to that of their predecessors, and the curtain was thus drawn on the era in which industrial policy meant the development of specific industries.

Changes were evident, too, in the kinds of issues that MITI regarded as policy priorities. The issues raised in the *1990s Vision* crossed bureau lines within the Ministry, so committees were established for bureaus to study and address these issues jointly. It therefore became established practice in the 1990s for the various bureaus to address policy-making collaboratively. Even the Basic Industries Bureau, which had a particularly strong identity of its own, became open to tackling issues that cut across bureau boundaries, like the development of advanced technologies and recycling, with an emphasis on energy conservation, safety, and the environment.

1.1.3 The 1994 "Subcommittee Reports on Basic Issues"

With economic structural reform emerging as the government's chief goal from around 1993 and 1994, many policy issues surfaced that transcended basic trade and industrial administration. MITI began actively developing policies to address them. The basic purpose of reform was to transform Japan's economy into a domestic demand-oriented economic structure aimed at rectifying external imbalances, to which end policy was directed to the development of social capital, deregulation, and administrative reform. MITI's tasks were: first, to define the new areas needing social capital and to clarify the responsibilities and financing involved in that social infrastructure; second, to formulate a basic direction and principal policy issues from the point of view of establishing an environment for inter-industry businesses; and third, to put together a vision of the industrial structure of the future.

The Industrial Structure Council's Fundamental Issues Subcommittee, established in October 1992, issued an "Interim report" in June 1993, "Interim recommendations" in November 1993, and a final report titled "Industrial structure of the 21st Century" in 1994 (Okazaki 2012, p. 15).

"Interim recommendations" addressed the need to overcome the prolonged economic recession, while also acknowledging the fact that Japan was facing mid- to long-term structural problems in three areas. (1) On the macro side were mounting foreign criticism of Japan's dramatic current account surplus; concerns about the hollowing out of industry due to the relocation of industry overseas in response to the appreciating yen; and the inadequacy of social capital and living standards even as Japan faced a demographic shift to an aging society, impeding the achievement of an affluent lifestyle and suppressing the development of new industries.

(2) On the micro side were government regulations, restrictive business practices, and the institutional impasses and fatigue of existing mechanisms. These inhibited entrepreneurial spirit and the growth of new industries and hindered access to the Japanese market, thereby limiting consumer choice for low-cost and diversified products. (3) Regarding Japan's industrial structure, concern focused on the coexistence of highly productive industries in highly competitive markets with inefficient, uncompetitive industries protected by entry regulations. This was also a factor in the price differential between the domestic and overseas markets.

The following were needed to address the microeconomic issues: (1) relaxation of government regulations, putting in concrete terms the suggestions of the Interim Report on Deregulation ("Hiraiwa Report"), produced by the Economic Reform Study Group under Prime Minister Morihiro Hosokawa; (2) a review of private-sector practices restricting competition, which meant strengthening the enforcement of cartel and unfair trade regulations under the Antimonopoly Law and expanding the system of litigation by private parties; and a new institutional framework appropriate for the twenty-first century, involving reform of the corporate, employment, and financial- and capital-market systems. Specifically, this would require (1) "bringing partial fluidity to employment" through reform of the Commercial Code, the introduction of multiple tracks for the labor market within corporations, and expansion of the broader labor market; and (2) reform of the financial system based on the recognition that Japan's huge savings were not being effectively utilized for the potential demand for funds, due to insufficient diversity of financial services, competition among financial institutions, and the poor functioning of the corporate bond and stock markets.

As is evident, the Interim Recommendations saw the economy as a system composed of several subsystems and, recognizing the diversity of international economies, called for comprehensive reform of Japan's economic systems.

The Interim Recommendations were significant first for their fundamental point of view that the relaxation or elimination of regulations would not suffice for improving market functions, and that an institutional framework supporting market mechanisms was therefore required; they urged the implementation of policies to that end. In other words, the Interim Recommendations represented a position fundamentally different from those that called for correcting market failures through a partial substitution of policy measures for market functions. The Recommendations also expressed a new approach to policies on industrial structure. The premises underlying the Recommendations differed from those of the oil crisis and the high-yen recession eras. First, whereas policy had previously targeted capital-intensive basic materials industries, a wider range of industries, including machinery and non-manufacturing industries, were now included in its scope. Second, because the assumption had been of a domestic market with low import-penetration levels, the previous approaches to price recovery were joint operations and the elimination of excess capacity, but as the premise shifted to an internationally open market, companies were seen as having to come to their own judgments about making adjustments to production. Third, whereas it had been possible in the past to anticipate which growth industries might replace declining industries, it was no longer clear what such growth industries would be. The policies on industrial structure adjustment therefore did not call for direct government participation as they had in the past but instead emphasized the need for corporate restructuring and the establishment of an environment that would enable the creation of new industries.

The September 1994 "Industrial structure of the 21st century" was based on these Interim Recommendations and served as a manifesto on industrial policy from the 1990s to the 2000s. The report clarified the new position as follows:

> Henceforth, rather than accepting various systems and regulations as given, we must strengthen market functions by bringing neutrality to the system. This requires an emphasis on setting general rules, deregulating, and rectifying practices in the private sector, and then implementing various assistance measures as necessary. We must also strengthen the idea of actively engaging in the formation of an efficient market based on principles of self-help.

The perspective of the Industrial Structure Council and MITI on the role of industrial policy had clearly shifted from an approach of responding to market failures to one of enhancing market functioning through institutional reform.

2 Changes in Economic Structure and Regulatory Reform

2.1 The Revised Antimonopoly Act and the System of Business Laws

The June 1993 Interim Report by the Fundamental Issues Subcommittee marked a major shift in the issues addressed by policies on industrial organization. As mentioned in the previous section, the Report pointed out that in order to promote creative business activities, an environment had to be created that would do away with obstacles to market competition, or that would strengthen the capital market's function of curbing such obstacles. International issues, specifically the Structural Impediments Initiative (SII) talks, also generated a need for policies on industrial organization, and MITI pursued organizational restructuring and established various research groups to strengthen research, analysis, policy planning, and design functions in order to address the desired economic structural reform (Okazaki 2012, p. 291).

The first of these involved a review of the holding-company regulations under the Antimonopoly Act (AMA) and of the regulatory system pertaining to shareholding by large companies. Successive proposals in the mid-1990s called for abolishing or reviewing Sect. 9 of the Antimonopoly Law (regulations on pure holding companies) and 9–2 (restrictions on stock-holding by large companies) on the grounds that they were obstacles to business strategy development. From around 1994, the Government planned a review of antitrust policies as part of its overall policy of deregulation, and the Cabinet Decision titled "On the promotion of deregulation" included a review of appropriate regulations of holding companies and guidelines on venture capital in FY 1994. Furthermore, in response to the "deregulation action program" scheduled for formulation by the end of FY 1994, the business community demanded the abolition of Sects. 9-2 of the AMA, arguing that it constrained the development of domestic business by restricting acquisitions of companies through mergers and acquisitions of shares and by limiting the establishment and nurturing of subsidiaries with the aim of diversification.

Following a review of Sects. 9 and 9-2, the Corporate Law Study Group, established by MITI, submitted the "Recommendations on the pure holding- company regulation and the review of holding regulations on large-scale companies" in February 1995, including: (1) the realization of efficient corporate organization appropriate for diversification and multinational development, as well as smooth personnel and labor management, (2) harmonization with international legal systems, and (3) expectations that corporate governance would avoid friction in organization and personnel matters. It also stated that the elimination of regulations on large companies' shareholding would (a) facilitate investment in new businesses, and (b) enable the smooth restructuring of industry. The report accordingly concluded with a strong call for the revision of existing articles that hindered these effects.

The government issued a Cabinet Decision on a "deregulation promotion plan" in March 1995, and the Antitrust Law Enforcement Order was revised in April, limiting the number of large-scale corporations subject to Article 9-2 shareholding restrictions. In November, the FTC also established the AMA Chapter 4 Revision Review Committee and started discussing the holding company problem, producing a report in December with reconsiderations it regarded as appropriate. Although the FTC bill formulated at this time was not realized, the government's interest in economic structural reform grew rapidly with the establishment of the Ryutaro Hashimoto Cabinet in November 1996, including MITI's program for realizing the reform of corporate organization. A cabinet decision to that effect was made in December and the revised bill was enacted in June 1997.

Although Article 9's general rules on excessive concentration remained, the types of prohibited holding companies were clearly delineated in the amended AMA. Prohibitions were imposed in cases where there were (1) large-scale corporate groups or separate large-scale companies in each of a sizable number of major business sectors; (2) businesses with close non-business financial ties to large-scale financial companies; or (3) different powerful operators in each of a considerable number of major business fields that had mutual relevance to one another. Additionally, regulations under Sect. 9.2 were considerably relaxed. Specifically, holding companies were exempted from the provisions applied to large companies. In other words, the "total stockholding rule" was not applied to holding companies and their subsidiaries. Also expanded were the types of shares exempted from application of the law.

These two revisions had the following significance from the point of view of company group management. First, while Article 9 applied only to holding companies, holding companies were excluded under Article 9.2 and the stocks of wholly owned subsidiaries were newly exempted. This meant that in cases where large-scale companies expanded their enterprises through the establishment or acquisition of wholly owned subsidiaries, they might not be subject to either section. Exceptions were also made in cases where joint venture companies were established for purposes such as joint research and where venture capital lists acquired shares from entrepreneurs in the form of subsidiary businesses.

The FTC pointed out that the lifting of restrictions on holding companies was an "amendment designed to turn certain types of excessive regulation into the minimum regulation necessary under the Antimonopoly Act," expressing its interpretation of the AMA revision as consistent with overall deregulation. From MITI's perspective, the lifting of restrictions on holding companies was intended to contribute to the promotion of economic structural reform by expanding the range of possible types of corporate organizations, thereby creating new businesses and improving the efficiency of existing businesses. In addition, the review of the regulations on shareholding by large-scale companies was regarded as contributing to the revitalization of the economy by eliminating the restrictions on large companies and generating the growth of venture businesses. Underlying these ideas was an awareness of the decline in Japan's economic vitality due to declining competitiveness and a reduced labor force accompanying a low birth rate and an aging society; and of the need to create an environment for businesses that would be internationally appealing and that would enhance corporate creativity and vitality.

Among efforts to reform the economic structure was the need for a review of Commercial Law regulations on merging and splitting companies. This was to be separate from the AMA amendment review and would include the review of provisions for splitting off companies and establishing the so-called company split system (Okazaki 2012, p. 318).

The Industrial Structure Council's Basic Issues Subcommittee report published in June 1994 included the following as policy issues: "policies providing for corporate splits," "simplification of merger procedures" and "simplification of business transfer procedures" under Commercial Law. In response to this report, MITI established a Commercial Law Study Group, which met for discussion repeatedly. In July 1996, MITI issued a "Research Report on the Merger System under Commercial Law" and a "Research Report on Issues Relating to Corporate Splits." The former (1) called for the abolition of the general meetings to report mergers and, in order to compensate for any insufficiency of information that would result, considered to require more thorough disclosures about mergers; (2) highlighted the need for advertisement of the contents of the merger so as to enable creditors to decide whether there were any points of dispute, but the process would be simplified; (3) considered the introduction of simplified merger procedures, and so on. These points were realized beginning in 1997 with the amended Commercial Law (adopted in June, implemented in October). Meanwhile, the Study Group on Corporate Law, reestablished in September 1996, reported on the results of its deliberations in July 1997 in "Towards the reform of systems related to corporate organization: Report of the Study Group on Corporate Law." Some of its recommendations led to the establishment of a share exchange system through the August 1999 amendment of the Commercial Code.

As shown in Table 1, the changes made in the direction of MITI policy in order to harmonize industrial policy with the AMA led to a decrease in the number of cases of "exempted cartels," previously a major means of exercising industrial policy. Few rationalization cartels were instituted as of 1980, and in parallel with this, cases

Table 1 The number of exempted cartels

Type	Underlying laws	Applicable industries	Number of cartels			
			1970	1980	1990	2000
General cases	AMA24-3 recession cartels	General production	0	1	0	0
	AMA24-4 rationalization cartels	General production	10	1	0	0
SME-related	Laws related to the organization of SME associations	Industry associations	364	267	174	0
	Act on temporary measures concerning the stability of specified SMEs	Commercial associations	105	0	0	0
	SME stability law	Commercial associations	105	0	0	0
Trade-related	Import and export act	Export transactions by exporters	133	44	28	0
		Export-oriented domestic transactions by producers and dealers	68	15	11	–
		Export-oriented domestic transactions by exporters and export associations	5	0	0	–
		Import transactions by importers	4	4	1	–
		Trade associations	8	7	3	–
		Subtotal	218	70	43	0

(continued)

Table 1 (continued)

Type	Underlying laws	Applicable industries	Number of cartels			
			1970	1980	1990	2000
Manufacturing-related	Temporary measures law on specified industrial structure improvements	Specified industries	–	8	–	–
	Act on temporary measures for the promotion of the machinery industry	Specified machinery industries	16	–	–	–
	Act on temporary measures for the promotion of the electronics industry	Specified electronics industries	1	–	–	–
	Act on temporary measures for the promotion of specified machinery and information industries	Specified machinery and information industries	–	1	–	–
	Act on temporary measures for fertilizer price stability	Fertilizer manufacturing industry	2	3	–	–
	Act on temporary measures for textile industrial equipment	Specified textile industries	3	–	–	–
	Subtotal		22	12		0

Source Okazaki (2012, pp. 238–239)
Note AML Antimononopoly Act; – shows lack of stipulations permitting cartels or lapse of laws

of Exclusions of Application of the Antimonopoly Law outlined in the Temporary Measures for the Promotion of the Machine Industry and Temporary Measures Law for the Structural Adjustment of Specific Industries ("Structural Improvement Law") were completely absent as of 1990. Cartels relating to small business relationships and Export and Import Transaction Law were also abolished by 2000. The relationship to the AMA is clear in the fact that the principle of competition became the underlying philosophy guiding policy.

2.2 *Respect for Corporate Autonomy and the Role of Government*

2.2.1 "New Market Creation Program (Program 21)"

Promoting the creation of new industries became a pillar of comprehensive economic policy in February 1994, and MITI in response announced the "New Market Creation Program (Program 21)" in March (Okazaki 2012, p. 128). The basic concepts were: (1) to respect the subjective judgments made by economic entities under market mechanisms, (2) to administer cross-sectorial policy responses to problems not resolved by the efforts of individual enterprises, and (3) to define "market sectors responding to social needs." These referred to sectors where potential domestic demand might be strong, but where either autonomous development pathways were lacking, or the market mechanism was imperfect due to external factors or the public nature of the sector. The task was to develop policies to support these sectors. Programs were presented in concrete terms for eight promising fields, based on projections of the future and related measures. These programs were steadily implemented, with an emphasis on actively connecting and cooperating with the other related ministries and agencies.

The June 1994 "Report of the Subcommittee on Basic Issues," issued a decision to devise prototypes for the policy system for creating new industries and improving the business environment, with the "Program 21" concept in mind. The number of promising fields was expanded to 12, and the cross-sectorial issues facing Japanese industry were presented as follows: (1) the need to pursue systematization, with an aim at mutual and synergistic development of hardware and software services; planning, development, procurement, production, sales, and distribution; public and private sector, and so on, (2) the need to pursue a global division of labor, and (3) the need to increase productivity in non-tradable goods and to reduce the domestic and foreign price gap. The foundations for this thinking date back to the July 1990 *Vision of the 1990s*. The ideas of "emphasizing market principles and self-responsibility" and "developing integrated policies internally and externally" aimed at international expansion were the inheritance of the basic stance of the *Vision*, and the inevitable need for the extension of industrial policy administration had, moreover, already been pointed out in the *Vision* as well.

The new business support measures emphasized as policy issues were promoted through the expansion of loan systems by government financial institutions, improvements in the operation of the Law on Temporary Measures to Facilitate Specific New Businesses, and improvements of the environment for funds through a strengthening of the operations of various support organizations. To strengthen support for research and development, the Ministry of Education and the Science and Technology Agency cooperated on budget increases in FY 1995. Efforts to develop new industrial infrastructure to serve as the foundation for new business and new industry development were carried out through improvements in the operation of related laws, beginning with the Private Participation Promotional Law (hereafter, the "Private Promotion Law"). In addition, the Science and Technology Basic Law was enacted in November 1995, aiming at planned support for science and technology, while support for venture companies was procured through financing, the securing of human resources, and similar measures.

2.2.2 The Law on Temporary Measures to Facilitate Business Innovation

In response to concerns over the growing gap between domestic and foreign prices and about the hollowing out of industry in the first half of the 1990s, the Industrial Policy Bureau began, around October 1994, to conceive a new law aimed at structural adjustment. The project pointed out that overseas relocation was advancing even in key industries such as processing and assembly, in which Japan had previously been internationally competitive in productivity and technical capability. This change had come about because of (1) increases in basic costs due to poor regulation and trading practices, the appreciation of the yen, and the persistence of inefficient industries, and (2) the rapid growth of Asian countries and severity of international competition. The Industrial Structure Council's Subcommittee on Basic Issues echoed the view that regulations and institutions were impeding the shift of the industrial structure.

Based on this recognition, the Law on Temporary Measures to Facilitate Business Innovation ("Business Innovation Law") was enacted in March 1995 (Okazaki 2012, p. 74). The core of this law was the Business Innovation Plan. "Designated enterprises" were able to obtain approval by submitting business innovation plans alone or jointly to the appropriate minister. Specific business operators were classified within "specific industries," meaning industries belonging to mining or manufacturing sectors where production and employment were likely to decrease due to changes in the domestic and foreign economic environments, or due to retailers or wholesalers closely related to them, or in other words those engaged in a business specified by Cabinet order. As in the facilitation law, companies were eligible for support, and the rates of increase in performance (Total Factor Productivity (TFP) and labor productivity) of designated companies increased from 1996 on, showing rates of improvement different from those of non-designated companies.

2.2.3 Action Plan for the Reform and Creation of Economic Structures, and the Creation of New Industries

Subsequently, the second Hashimoto Cabinet, established in November 1996, made the "five reforms" its top priority (Okazaki 2012, p. 155). The five were: (1) administrative reform, (2) economic structural reform, (3) financial system reform, (4) social security structural reform, and (5) fiscal structural reform. Education was later added as a sixth area for reform. Importantly, economic structural reform emphasized the creation of new industry sectors as the key to dealing with hollowing out of industry. Prime Minister Hashimoto instructed MITI Minister Shinji Sato to formulate and promote economic structural reform plans to restore the vitality of the Japanese economy in order to put this policy in concrete terms. MITI was to be at the center of this effort and to give instructions for coordinating with the other ministries and agencies. Minister Sato accordingly gathered the staff of the Headquarters for Industrial Structural Conversion and instructed them on coordinating their work with the other ministries. Through these efforts, the Program for Change and Creation of Economic Structure was created by Cabinet Decision in December.

This program acknowledged the need for institutional reform, and with regard especially to the imminent aging of Japanese society, conceived of 15 new industrial fields, and presented an overall view of economic structural reform as a means for creating these. The contents of the program were: (1) rectification of the high-cost structure, (2) reform of various systems relating to corporations, (3) reform of the labor and employment system, (4) improvement of social infrastructure that contributed to economic structural reform and improvement of efficiency in its utilization, and (5) maintenance and development of regional industry and of the skills needed to support manufacturing. Among these, the first required drastic deregulation, improvements in the commodity futures market, improvements in business practices, and systems reform for standardization. The second emphasized the need for optimization of managerial resources such as human resources and capital, by strengthening the development of spin-offs and group management, and reorganizing corporate structures through business restructuring such as mergers and joint ventures, which required reconsideration of the Antimonopoly Act's regulations on business combinations and of company merger procedures.

In line with this Cabinet Decision, a further Cabinet Decision was taken in May 1997 called the "Action Plan for Innovation and Creation of Economic Structure," in which concrete projections and policies were presented regarding each of the 15 new industries (Okazaki 2012, p. 159). It was assumed that these fields, which employed approximately 10.66 million people at that time and had a market size of approximately 198 trillion yen, would grow to 18.27 million employed and 561 trillion yen by 2010. The three sectors related to medicine and welfare, lifestyle, and information and communications were expected in particular to contribute greatly to the expansion of employment (Table 2).

The Keizo Obuchi administration, established in July 1998, froze the Special Measures Law on Promotion of Fiscal Structural Reform approved by the Hashimoto Cabinet in December 1997 but carried on other reforms. The Economic Strategy

Table 2 Forecast on employment and market size in new industry fields (1996)

Industry sector	Employment (10,000 people)		Market scale (trillion yen)	
	Current	2010	Current	2010
Medical, welfare	348	480	38	91
Lifestyle	220	355	20	43
Information and communications	125	245	38	126
New product technologies	73	155	14	41
Distribution, logistics	49	145	36	132
Environment	64	140	15	37
Business support	92	140	17	33
Oceans	59	80	4	7
Biotechnology	3	15	1	10
Urban environmental improvement	6	15	5	16
Aerospace (private sector)	8	14	4	8
New energy, energy conservation	4	13	2	7
Human resources	6	11	2	4
Internationalization	6	10	1	2
Housing	3	9	1	4
Total	1066	1827	198	561

Source Okazaki (2012, p. 166). Source data from the Cabinet decision titled "Programs for changing and creating the economic structure" 1996

Council, reporting directly to the Prime Minister, was established in August, and decided on a policy of drawing up "plans for doubling living space" and "plans for revitalizing industry." To this end, deregulation was needed in the 15 new sectors that were to lead the Japanese economy, as well as support for new businesses. MITI played a central role in formulating the industrial revitalization plan. As far as economic structural reform was concerned, MITI would therefore be responsible for a cross-sectional approach to the various sectors administered by each department in the Ministry.

The industry-related legislation for creating and developing new business was based on the May 1998 Law Promoting Technology Transfer from Universities to Industry ("TLO Law"), and support measures were devised with the aim of transferring the results of research, as the law's name suggests. Meanwhile, the December 1998 Law for Facilitating the Creation of New Business led to (1) direct support for the establishment of individual businesses and companies, (2) promotion of business activities by SMEs using new technologies, and (3) measures based on three points of improvement of the business environment, utilizing regional industrial resources. The same law was amended to add support measures for venture companies in December 1999.

Meanwhile, the economic revival plan stressed the need to raise productivity. The lack of improvement in productivity was ascribed to distortions in the corporate production and accumulation structure that had resulted from the inefficient investments of the bubble era. The supply side needed to be addressed and systemic reforms posed to support the processing of excess capacity and to bring innovation to business organization. Following deliberations by the Council for Industrial Competitiveness established in March 1999, the Law on Special Measures for Industrial Revitalization was enacted in August. Its aim was to raise productivity through the efficient utilization of existing management resources in Japan. To achieve this, the decision was made to support business restructuring, the opening of new areas of business (targeting entrepreneurs and SMEs), and research activities. Designated businesses would be able to receive special exceptions to the Commercial Law and special measures on financing and taxation.

2.3 *Promoting Deregulation*

2.3.1 Implementing Plans to Promote Deregulation

Deregulation proceeded also under the pressure from the United States in the form of the Structural Impediments Initiative of 1989 and the US–Japan Framework for a New Economic Partnership established in April 1993. The Provisional Council for the Promotion of Administrative Reform, established in July 1990, confirmed the implementation of the Second Administrative Reform Council's Final Report, and proposed to reduce public regulation by half over a period of 10 years (Okazaki 2012, p. 196).

Deregulation was sought also from the point of view of reforming Japan's long-stagnant economic structure. Following the Third Administrative Reform Council Report of January 1994, the government established the Administrative Reform Promotion Office in the Cabinet to undertake important matters concerning implementation of administrative reform in government and other necessary related matters. Based on the same report, an Administrative Reform Committee was established in the Prime Minister's Office in December 1994 with the role of monitoring the implementation of policies aimed at (1) promoting regulatory improvements related to private sector activities, and (2) promoting improvements in administrative systems and operations. The administrative reform councils of the Extraordinary Administrative Investigative Committee and Third Council were in the position of responding as advisers to the Prime Minister, whereas this committee was an organization that actively and autonomously carried out monitoring and deliberations.

With the support of powerful organs such as these, a medium-term deregulation promotion action plan was formulated. In March 1995, the Cabinet issued the "Deregulation Action Program" Decision, a five-year plan covering 1995–1999. This plan addressed 11 sectors, establishing a deregulation implementation schedule for each: (1) housing and land, (2) information and communication, (3) distribution and related activities, (4) transportation, (5) standards, certifications, imports, and so on, (6) finance, securities, and insurance, (7) energy, (8) employment and labor, (9) pollution and waste products, (10) environmental protection and dangerous goods, disaster prevention, and security, and (11) others. Deregulation was applied to a total of 1,091 items, and with the establishment of new regulations, a fixed period for review was sought. However, the planning period was revised within three years, by FY 1997, because of the rapid appreciation of the yen (Fig. 1).

The administrative reform committee issued a "Final opinion" ahead of the December 1997 expiration of the planning period, which the Cabinet adhered to in its decision entitled "Promotion of Deregulation." This dictated the continuation of the deregulation plan. Another Cabinet Decision, "Three-year Program for the Promotion of Deregulation" ("New Plan") was released in March 1998. Two months earlier, a deregulation committee composed of private-sector experts was established under the Administrative Reform Promotion Headquarters. The "New Plan" was distinctive in that it included the idea of switching from administration based on "regulation in advance" to one of "after-checks." Whereas the former was characterized by "direct regulation of citizens and businesses," the latter was a form of administration in which "the government establishes clear and concrete rules and the private sector is permitted to act creatively and freely as long as it observes those rules." Deregulation did not end with this shift, but the plan was significant in showing the need to clarify the rules and strengthening the system of after-checks based on them; and as suggested by the Deregulation Committee, which in April 1999 was renamed the Regulatory Reform Committee, it aimed to advance the thrust of policy from deregulation to regulatory reform.

The deregulation policy described above led to changes in the number of licenses as shown in Tables 3 and 4.

2.3.2 Product Standardization and Safety Improvements

Based on the December 1997 Cabinet Decision titled "Follow-up on the 'Action Plan for Innovation and Creation of Economic Structure,'" which sought to minimize government regulations, the Standard Certification Committee was established the following June in the Industrial Structure Council. The Committee prepared a report in January 1999, which sought to utilize the power of the private sector for inspection and verification work (Okazaki 2012, p. 196; Ishihara 2011, p. 341). In August, revised versions of 11 of the 18 laws using MITI's Standards and Conformity Assessment System were established, and the government's certification system based on the Consumer Product Safety Law was abolished. Preliminary regulations were minimized while emergency orders regarding the distribution of dangerous products were maintained, and measures for post-checks were enhanced, whereby businesses became responsible in principle for ensuring the safety of their products. Government's role was to form the safety rules.

On the laws revising portions of MITI-related laws to improve regulations on private activities and rationalize administrative affairs

1. Purpose of the laws

Aiming to relax regulations on private-sector activity and simplify and rationalize administration:

Undertake a general review of MITI-related laws

↓

Promote deregulation

Reform the economic structure

2. Content: 16 laws including 14 revisions and 2 repeals

○ Review of export procedures

Repeal of two laws -- the Export Inspection Law and the Export Design Law -- based on the improvements in Japan's technical level

○ Rationalization of regulations on changes in corporate organization

Establishment of regulations on approval of status of licenced business operators in cases of mergers or the establishment of businesses so as to reduce burden pertaining to changes of corporate organization.

- Laws concerning the establishment of pollution-prevention organizations for designated factories (status of those filing notifications on pollution prevention, etc.)
- High-Pressure Gas Safety Law ("Class 2" producer status and others)
- Laws related to confirming the safety of liquefied petroleum gas and the optimization of the transactions (LPG dealer status)
- Aircraft manufacturing business law (approved businesses status)
- Arms manufacturing law (arms producer status)
- Gravel Sampling Law (gravel sampling businesses status)
- Quarrying Law (quarry business status)
- Law on securing gasoline quality etc. (gasoline distributor status)
- Electricity Business Law (status of installers of electric facilities for business use)
- Electrical Appliances and Materials Control Law (Class B electric appliance producer status, etc.)
- Gas Business Law (Class 2 gas equipment producer status)

○ Review of regulations

- Law Related to Rationalization of Energy Use (Energy Conservation Law) (review of obligation to submit report of energy administrator appointment)
- Electricity Business Law (review of the required period within which an electric utility must commence business)
- Electricity Business Law (abolition of Minister's approval of licenses for chief engineers)
- Electricity Business Law (delegating to the private sector the task of licensing chief electrical technicians)
- Electricity Heat Supply Business Act (review of pre-use inspection of pipelines)
- Electricity Business Law (abolition of business commencement notifications)

Fig. 1 Laws on Deregulation. *Source Tsusansho Koho*, Fig. 3.1, April 1, 1995 [II-2, p. 327]

Table 3 Changes in the number of licenses, by purpose, 1986–1998

Type		Purpose						Total
Licenses, etc.		Citizens' life and property	Welfare	Resources/environment	Business activities	Industry promotion	Other	
Strengthening of regulations	Repeal of regulations	11	0	16	10	0	0	37
	Establishment of new regulations	499	35	222	307	3	16	1082
Relaxation of regulations	Repeal of regulations	433	213	19	1797	0	41	2503
	Establishment of new regulations	322	131	28	1804	109	73	2467
Other	Repeal of regulations	56	39	41	464	139	233	972
	Establishment of new regulations	118	185	57	293	400	437	1490
Total	Repeal of regulations	500	252	76	2271	139	274	3512
	Establishment of new regulations	939	351	307	2404	512	526	5039

Source Okazaki (2012, p. 206)

Table 4 Number of licenses, by Ministry/Agency

Ministry or agency	Number of licenses	
	Dec., 1985	Mar., 1999
Prime minister's office	27	32
Fair trade commission	26	28
National public safety commission	81	139
Financial revitalization commission	–	1003
General affairs agency	29	35
Hokkaido regional development agency	26	31
Defense agency	26	31
Economic planning agency	26	45
Science and technology agency	218	308
Environment agency	149	221
Okinawa development agency	27	34
National land agency	81	100
Justice ministry	146	196
Foreign ministry	37	47
Finance ministry	1116	844
Education ministry	310	394
Health ministry	936	1322
Agriculture, forests, and fisheries ministry	1263	1376
Ministry of international trade and industry	1870	1726
Transport ministry	2017	1505
Postal ministry	265	381
Labor ministry	532	682
Construction ministry	742	976
Home affairs ministry	104	125
Total	10054	11581

Source Okazaki (2012, p. 203)

Regarding the issue of business responsibility and redress for victims of accidents, as mentioned in Chap. 2, the Consumer Protection Committee had repeated discussions since the 1970s on product liability from the perspective of consumer redress. Some in industry and in MITI regarded any priority given by administration to consumers as jeopardizing business, and little progress was made on legislation, but the government could not continue to neglect the issue, as it was forced to handle actual accidents. The result was the *1990s Vision*'s recommendation that a product liability system be taken under consideration, and when the Product Safety Division of the

Industrial Structure Council recommended introducing the product liability system as a comprehensive product safety measure in November 1993, MITI decided to proceed with preparations for legislation. Discussions were carried on for two years within the Ministry and by the Product Safety Division on such difficult issues as what constituted corporate responsibility, the extent of consumer responsibility, and how to set the standards. Rulings gradually became more objective, which spurred further legislation. The Product Liability Law was established in July 1994, stipulating that product liability claims could be brought where there was (1) a defect regardless of intent or negligence, (2) damage, and (3) a causal relationship between the two. This constituted a major revision of the principle of negligence established in the 1896 Civil Law, but given the increased likelihood that product quality labeling would receive greater emphasis due to the law, product liability law proceeded without government regulation, on the principle that responsibility resided with the business operator.

Seen as part of the deregulatory trend, this form of consumer administration did not regard consumers as weak players in need of protection, but rather positioned them as economic entities equivalent in strength to business entities, and therefore minimized preliminary regulation and instead called for consumers to take responsibility for themselves. It therefore also increased the need for information disclosure so that consumers could make appropriate decisions. This became a driving factor in the establishment of the Consumer Affairs Agency in September 2009.

2.3.3 Service Industries

The *1990s Vision* released in September 1989 reiterated the importance of the service industry (Ishihara 2011, p. 430). The goals for the service industry in the 1990s were defined as: (1) the upgrade of labor productivity, (2) promotion of human resource development in fields such as the information service industry and the leasing industry that contribute to advances in manufacturing as well as improving labor productivity, and (3) establishing the environment for development to respond to the upgrade and diversification of the lifestyle needs of the public. The latter included services to support women, such as elder care and child and household care services.

In connection with the deregulation presented by the Hiraiwa Report of the Economic Reform Study Group in November 1993, MITI in 1995 established a Soft Industry Roundtable under the Director-General for Commerce and Distribution Policy, which issued its report in May 1996. It defined "soft industries" as a group of industries with the main objective of providing intellectual value and services. According to the report, the specific fields where growth could be expected were (1) business support, (2) information and communications, (3) human resources, (4) welfare, (5) lifestyle and culture, and for these to develop, development of a market environment based on the principle of competition. MITI was thus seeking ways to contribute to the development of the service industry outside the jurisdiction of the Ministries and Agencies, while adhering to the government policy of deregulation and regulatory reform. However, while these administrative processes promoted a competitive market approach, they also had limitations in that they delayed the development of policies for improving productivity.

2.4 *Abolition of the Large-Scale Retail Stores Law*

2.4.1 Negotiations with the United States and the Large-Scale Retail Stores Law Issue

Amidst worsening economic friction with the United States, the Office of the United States Trade Representative (USTR) asserted the existence of non-tariff barriers in Japan. Regarding distribution, the US urged improvements in the Law Concerning the Adjustment of Retail Business Activities by Large-Scale Retail Stores and in business practices that were seen as barriers to import expansion. The "Report on relaxation of public regulations, etc.," submitted by the Temporary Administrative Reform Promotion Council in December 1988, included the following findings on the Large-Store Law: (1) that "preliminary explanations" should be limited to preliminary explanation of the plan for opening a store, (2) that the Commercial Activities Coordinating Committee, composed of the commercial businesses, consumers, and experts, should adopt standard time limits for preliminary deliberations, (3) that criteria for closing times and number of days off should be determined from the point of view of improving convenience for consumers, and (4) that excessive regulation by local governments should be alleviated. In December 1988, the Cabinet issued a decision to undertake implementation of these suggestions, but in the *1990s Vision on Distribution* compiled by the Distribution Committee and the SME Policy-Making Council in June 1989, MITI decided to incorporate recommendations concerning distribution into its new administrative reform proposal and to work out countermeasures (Ishihara 2011, p. 99).

While this review of the Large-Store Law proceeded domestically, the question of how to optimize operation of the Large-Store Law was also taken up in the discussions on the Structural Impediments Initiative ("Structural Consultations") that began in July 1989. In the final report of the Structural Consultations submitted in June 1990, the Large-Store Law was addressed as the first among the items for deregulation, with the decision that deregulation measures would be undertaken in the following three stages: (1) immediate measures (measures for optimization of operations and so on), (2) legislative reform for submission in the next ordinary Diet session, and (3) review after the revision in the Law stipulated in (2) above. The first stage, launched in May 1990, included: shortening the coordination and processing period of establishing new shops, special measures on spaces for buying and selling imported goods, establishment of store area limits in which coordination was not required, relaxation of the scope of regulation related to closing hours and number of holidays, and improvements in the transparency of the coordination and processing procedures for opening stores. These measures, mainly intended to shorten the coordination process, constituted a concrete form of the policy suggested in the *1990s Vision on*

Distribution, but, with the incorporation of the content on imported items, were also a response to the Structural Impediments Initiative.

Another joint meeting was held between the Industrial Structure Council's Committee on Distribution and the Subcommittee on Distribution of the SME Policy-Making Council to discuss revision of the law. Their December Interim Report sought the following revisions: that store-opening coordination should take place within one year and that the store-opening notification and preliminary explanations contained in the store-opening coordination and processing procedures should be abolished. The Report further urged that the goal of "local explanations" should no longer be to reach agreement with the community, but rather to notify the community of the content of the plans. Other suggested revisions included abolishing the Commercial Activities Coordinating Committee, replacing it with hearings of opinions from consumers, retailers, academic experts, and others by the Large-Scale Retail Stores Council (Large-Store Hearings), and making it allowable to ask local chambers of commerce and other organizations to consolidate the opinions of local stakeholders as needed. The recommendations also called for relaxing special measures on places where imported goods could be sold and for urging local government bodies to exercise restraint in issuing regulations.

The revised law was promulgated in May 1991 (and implemented in January 1992) based on the interim report and was divided into three categories: (1) expanding the area (space) limits for each type of store, (2) expanding the scope of the Large-Store Hearings, and (3) undertaking a review after two years (Ishihara 2011, p. 110). The abolition of the Commercial Activities Coordinating Committee meant that a weighty responsibility was imposed on the judgments issued by the Large-Store Council. For this reason, the Large-Store Council revised its review procedures in November 1991. The revisions maintained the aim of protecting small and medium-sized retailers, as before, but also sought to respond to the diversification and internationalization of consumer needs. In addition to the revised law, the Special Law on Exceptional Measures Concerning Floor Space for Import Sales was established, according to which the Large-Store Law would not apply when the total selling space for imported goods was 1,000 square meters or less (Fig. 2).

The Industrial Structure Council established a Basic Issues Subcommittee in October 1992 to launch a review of the revised law, submitted the final report in June 1994, and sought further relaxation of the regulatory standards in the Large-Store Law. These decisions were based on the mounting view that the reduction of small and medium-sized retailers was due increasingly to structural problems rather than to the advancement of large-scale stores. Moreover, the abolition of the Commercial Activities Coordinating Committee meant that the opposition movement of small and medium-sized retailers lost its home base and that calls for stronger regulations were increasingly eclipsed. Meanwhile, before the two-year review required by the revised law, the joint conference meeting in November 1993 issued an interim report in January 1994 titled "How to undertake the review of the revised Large-Store Law." Many different views were reportedly presented in the joint conference on the need, or lack thereof, for the Large-Store Law, but given that the coordination procedures under the Law were proceeding smoothly after the revision, it was judged that there

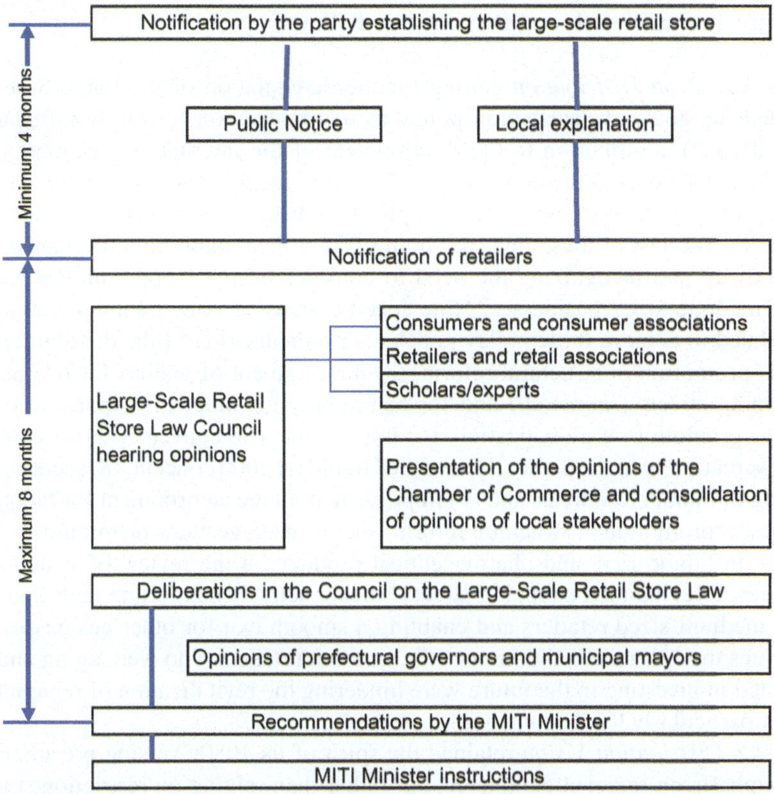

Source: Ministry of International Trade and Industry, Industrial Policy Bureau, Distribution Industry Division , ed., "The future of the Large-Scale Retail Store Law -- How to consider its revision [Industrial Structure Council and SME Policy-Making Council Joint Conference Report]." Industrial Research Council Foundation, 1994, p. 127. Regarding cases of Type II Large-Scale Retail Stores, "Prefectural Governor" replaces "MITI Minister."

Changes to the Large-Scale Retail Store Law

(1) Increase in retail space area for each type of store (related to Article 3)

(2) Expansion of range of opinions to be heard by the Large-Store Council (related to Article 7)

(3) Optimization of self-regulation by local public entities (related to Article 15-5)

(4) Review to be undertaken after 2 years (related to Article 2 of Supplementary Provisions)

Fig. 2 Store-opening procedures under the Large-Scale Retail Store Law for Type 1 Large-Scale Retail Stores (January 31, 1992 to May 3, 2000). *Source* [II-4, p. 114]

would be little merit in abolishing the framework itself. Although the coordination issue had receded, the choice was made to retain the legal framework itself. Even so, in part because of Japan–US friction, the Large-Store Law was gradually dismantled.

2.4.2 Shifts in the Direction of Distribution Policy

The *1990s Vision on Distribution* calling for the deregulation of the Large-Store Law defined the goals of distribution policy as: (1) realization of a truly affluent consumer life, (2) contribution to the development of the international economic society, (3) contribution to the construction of vibrant local economic society, and (4) securing management resources for an appealing distribution industry (Ishihara 2011, p. 229). The last of these involved both making the competition mechanism work effectively and recognizing the need to consider business opportunities for small and medium-sized businesses. Nine specific areas of policy administration were stipulated to achieve these policy goals: (1) rationalization of the distribution system, (2) promotion of structural reform, (3) development of visions for revitalizing shopping streets (*shotengai*) and for community-building, (4) expansion of imports, (5) promotion of globalization, (6) improvement in convenience for consumers, (7) creation of high-quality life and the HighMart 2000 concept, (8) securing and training of human resources, and (9) improvement in the environment for labor. Among these, "promotion of structural reform" included suggestions on minimizing regulations on liquor, rice, and pharmaceutical products in the review of systems and practices. "Revitalizing shopping streets" meant actively supporting ambitious small and medium-sized retailers and enabling a smooth exit for older businesses. This indicates the *Vision*'s recognition of the fact that retailers who were aging and not interested in investing in the future were hindering the revitalization of regional commerce, particularly local *shotengai*.

The *1990s Distribution Vision* retained the spirit of its 1980s version precursor with its emphasis on regional commerce, but rather than relying on restrictions on large stores, it sought to actively develop regional economies while also encouraging the recovery of small and medium-sized retailers. The clear decrease in the number of small-scale retail stores raised doubts about the effect of the regulations based on the Large-Store Law and suggested that new support measures for regional commerce were needed.

Policy changes developed more rapidly after the SII talks. These changes were evident in the 1991 revision to the Large-Scale Retail Store Law and the Special Law on Floor Space for Import Sales, but also in the establishment of the Law on Special Measures Concerning the Promotion of Commercial Zone Improvement, the Private Participation Promotion Law, and the Law on the Promotion of Small and Medium-Sized Retailers. The third of these was conceived as seeking a new cooperative relationship between large stores and small and medium-sized retailers, with large-scale shopping centers as the paradigm. This aim was realized all at once after the final report on the SII talks sought significant increases in Japanese public investment. "Commercial zones" regulated "facilities offered for the use of entities that run a considerable number of businesses" (commercial facilities) and "a variety of facilities that promote the convenience of customers and other local residents" (commercial infrastructure) as "integrated facilities." Municipalities were to formulate a concept, submit it for the approval of the prefectural governor and report it to the appropriate minister, and then receive support. This approach gave municipalities the initiative in formulating the basic concept. It represented a new approach that would later be carried over into the City Core Revitalization Law and other policies. However, inasmuch as the basic direction of policy was determined by specific Ministers (of MITI, Construction, or Home Affairs), it focused on developing large-scale facilities, attracting an array of businesses, and maintaining roads and parks and so on. In other words, the national government envisioned plans for the major remodeling of urban areas through large-scale investments in "hardware," but it was hard for municipalities to conceive plans on so large a scale. Thus, from the very planning stage, national government assistance in budget-planning and expert assistance proved indispensable.

The commercial zones defined under the Act were classified as either "Advanced Commercial" or "Regional Commercial Revitalization" zones. In July 1996, a third type was added, namely, the "City Core Revitalization Zone." Regional Commercial Revitalization Zones received the greatest number of approvals, and the physical infrastructure intended to underpin not only retail but also commerce more generally, aimed in part at modernization of the retail sector. Nevertheless, understanding of the problems facing cities was as yet undeveloped and the tendency persisted to promote conventional approaches to retail.

2.4.3 Revision of Business Practices and Structural Reform

As mentioned earlier, business practices were also among the non-tariff barriers emphasized by the United States as contributing to the trade imbalance (Ishihara 2011, p. 240). In June 1990, the Joint Meeting of the Industrial Structure Council's Distribution Committee and the SME Policy-Making Council issued recommendations on reviewing business practices. These were based on the principles of (1) transparency of business practices, (2) the elimination of business practices that impeded the rationalization of business operations, and (3) a consideration of international perspectives. Specific items for review covered a broad array of issues, including rebates, returned goods, suggested retail prices and manufacturer's invoice prices, and retail field service staff.

The report reflected not only a consideration of US concerns, but also the expectation that distribution businesses in Japan would be better able to expand internationally it they improved their business practices. In June, MITI announced a "Policy for the Improvement of Business Practices." According to FY 1995 surveys, about 30–40% of companies were working on improving business practices before the introduction of the guidelines, while only 10–20% decided to do so afterwards. It was in this context that the changes to business practices such as "ex post facto" price setting by resin makers and processors, described below, were undertaken.

Meanwhile, in February 1991, the Joint Committee of the Industrial Structure Council Distribution Committee and the SME Policy-Making Council's Subcommittee on Distribution established a Planning and Research Subcommittee Logistics Working Group to consider the problem of small-lot deliveries of consumer goods. In September that year, the Joint Committee established a Logistics Subcommittee for the comprehensive discussion of logistics issues, and in October, it created a working group on SMEs to examine logistical problems particular to SMEs. The working group's report pointed out that small and medium-sized wholesalers were losing strength vis-à-vis their business partners because of the growing emphasis on flexibility, which meant demands for more frequent deliveries, shorter lead times, smaller orders, and stricter delivery times. The report suggested the need for policy measures such as infrastructure improvements and subsidies to improve the efficiency of individual business operators. The resulting May 1992 Law Concerning the Promotion of Efficient Distribution Systems in SMEs stipulated that cooperatives and other commercial groups were to prepare efficiency plans according to the basic guidelines set by the appropriate minister, and that grants and loans for their support would be provided to those that were approved. These efficiency improvements were limited to physical distribution operations such as the receipt of goods, storage, distribution processing, shipping, and ground shipping, because logistics was now recognized as fundamental to the process of making distribution more systematic. As compared with the policies on retail, these policies aimed to induce businesses to participate in these endeavors, something that was itself understood as a means to modernization.

Thereafter, in June 1995, the Joint Committee compiled a summary of "the current situation and issues in Japan's distribution" and presented a distribution vision for the twenty-first century. The post-bubble recession only strengthened the demand for internationalization, and although deregulation was making progress, the hollowing out of core urban areas was becoming more pronounced. The report pointed out that this was a problem that transcended the issues of commerce and related directly to maintaining the vitality and liveliness of urban areas. The report called for policies both "from the point of view of seeking greater efficiency" and "from the point of view of social needs."

2.4.4 Abolition of the Large-Scale Retail Stores Law

In June 1996, the US government expressed dissatisfaction with the direction of Japan–US negotiations on photographic film. In January 1995 it asked the WTO to consider whether the Large-Scale Retail Law was a violation of the General Agreement on Trade in Services (GATS), which had come into effect in January 1995 after the establishment of the WTO. Although the Japanese government attempted counterarguments, a May 1997 Cabinet Decision called for investigation of the Large-Store Law, based on the fact that over two years had elapsed since the review of the latest revision (Ishihara 2011, p. 131). It is not clear when the policy of abolishing the Large-Store Law was adopted in the joint meeting of the ISC Distribution Committee and the SME Policy-Making Council's Subcommittee held that month, but the remarks published in October implied that the law should be abolished. The memo raised the question of whether the current legal framework could respond to the diversification of consumption activities accompanying changes in lifestyle. It also discussed how to respond to transportation and environmental problems caused by the opening of large stores, and how to take decentralization into account in coordinating the issues related to the opening of large stores.

Underlying the exploration of a new framework was the idea that complete liberalization of large-store openings would be undesirable but that on the European and US model, location regulations could be implemented from the point of view of urban planning and land use (the guidance method). This can thus be interpreted as replacing the Large-Store Law's aim by securing business opportunities for small and medium-sized retailers through urban planning while continuing to maintain some degree of regulation on the opening of new stores. This shift to an urban-planning aim required the understanding and cooperation of the Ministry of Construction. Daily negotiations ensued at the secretariat level, while MITI considered concrete policies for finalizing the abolition of the Large-Store Law, revising the City Planning Act, and addressing environmental and other issues. A report requesting the abolition of the Large-Store Law was submitted in December. Although commercial associations initially submitted dissenting opinions, industry opinion gradually accepted the premise that the Law would be abolished and shifted toward assuring that the new framework function effectively. The Partial Revision of the City Planning Act was passed in May 1998, and the Law Concerning the Measures by Large-Scale Retail Stores for Preservation of Living Environment and the Law on Improvement and Revitalization of City Centers were enacted in June. With the enactment of the first of these, the Large-Store Law and the Special Law on Selling Space for Imported Goods were both abolished.

2.4.5 Three Laws on Community Development

The City Center Revitalization Law, Revised City Planning Act, and Act on the Measures by Large-Scale Retail Stores for Preservation of Living Environment, all established in 1998, aimed to promote a shift away from the Large-Store Law's controls on competition, toward a greater reliance on the principle of market competition (Ishihara 2011, p. 261).

The City Center Revitalization Law was based on a report compiled in August 1997 by the Joint Committee of the ISC's Distribution Committee and SME Policy-Making Subcommittee on Distribution, which emphasized the need for legal measures to address the hollowing out of city centers. It cited the need for multifaceted measures involving multiple government agencies, approaches that extended beyond isolated targets to address the links between them, respect for the distinctive character and autonomy of different places, and development of entities responsible for urban planning rather than the existing more scattershot approach. The law was implemented under the joint administration of 13 ministries and agencies. Its framework was as follows: the appropriate minister was to establish basic policy, municipalities to prepare basic plans based on that policy, and those implementing the projects stipulated in the plan to submit "specific project plans" and apply for certification by the appropriate minister. The "implementer" was to be a "certified initiative promoter," meaning a "Town Management Organization (TMO)." These would be funded by commercial and industrial associations or the Chamber of Commerce, by special companies or local public associations composed chiefly of SMEs based on Cabinet Orders, or by contributions from a public service corporation. By obtaining certification, the TMO could obtain support from the national government. However, there were problems with this approach. Although municipalities launched TMOs to compete to obtain subsidies, many proposals were merely summaries of the existing business plans of various departments and had little new autonomous input. The framework of the law, while in step with the trend toward decentralization, increased the burden on local governments rather than otherwise. In some cases, therefore, local governments devised makeshift plans that could not produce any outstanding results. In April 2003, the TMO Roundtable of the SME Agency acknowledged that the TMOs were not necessarily making smooth progress; the Board of Audit also took up this issue in FY 2003. It was pointed out that neither the financial basis nor the necessary human resources for TMOs were sufficiently well developed and that TMO principles were not yet well understood.

The revised City Planning Act put into concrete form the policy goals that followed on the abolition of the Large-Scale Retail Law, namely those of encouraging and locating large-scale stores in accordance with urban planning methods. Based on this concept, the designation of special-use districts by Cabinet Order was liberalized to allow local public organizations to make the determinations for themselves, the point being to introduce large stores based on the actual circumstances of the area. The special-use areas, however, were not included in the purview of the suburban siting of large-scale stores in the model of the suburban shopping center promoted in the 1980s. The special-use area concept was therefore ineffective in suburban areas. In 2000, the Ministry of Construction revised the City Planning Act again to limit development not only in agricultural districts but also in areas not subject to land-use zoning. It was hard for municipalities to impose strict regulations on their own, however, and the advance of suburban development continued.

Although the Large-Scale Retail Store Location Law may be understood as a successor to the Large-Store Law, its purpose was completely different. The aim of the new law was not the securing of business opportunities for small and medium-sized retailers, but the maintenance of the living environment of area residents. MITI was asked to indicate what criteria should be included for the operation of this law, and SMEs asked that it incorporate in its consideration the matter of supply-and-demand adjustments. These expectations were not met, however; it was clear that the guidelines for criteria were not adjustment measures. At the Joint Committee meeting in November 1998 where the draft of the guidelines was compiled, two other points were at issue: how far the "living environment" extended, and the extent of traffic problems. Both were questions of how to require new stores to take the local environment into consideration. Joint Committee documents show that the emphasis was on making it the obligation of store owners to consider, on a voluntary basis, factors beyond just the three that were clearly regulated, namely traffic, waste, and noise. Companies were to develop their own responses to the issues. The new Large-Scale Store Location Law completely eliminated supply-demand adjustment measures, instead encouraging new shops to take environmental problems into consideration and to actively take on not only legal obligations but also issues of social responsibility and social contribution.

2.4.6 Review of the Three Laws on Community Development

The Joint Committee began evaluating and reviewing the three laws that comprised the community development system in April 1998 soon after their establishment (Ishihara 2011, p. 291). The further decline of central city areas spurred their work. Their December report indicates their viewpoint in reviewing the three laws and the direction of future town planning. The concerns highlighted by the Committee included: lack of attention in the Revitalization Law to the consolidation of urban functions, problems inherent in the basic planning and operations of the TMOs, the tendency under the City Planning Act to overlook broad regional perspectives while readily approving suburban development. The report accordingly stated that "sustainable municipal finance" and "preservation of the community" were important elements of the so-called *machi*, meaning "town" or "community," and to these ends, called for efforts aimed at "developing compact and vibrant communities." This thinking emphasized consolidation in urban cores rather than suburban development. Meanwhile, the Ministry of Land, Infrastructure, Transport and Tourism (MLIT) also held a conference in November 2004 on the revitalization of city centers, and in February 2006, the Council for Social Infrastructure issued a report titled "Urban planning for a new era." These recognized the need to review policies, and favored suppressing suburban development in terms of both urban planning and building regulation, as well as consolidating urban functions, including residential functions, in city centers.

Thus, in May 2006, bills revising the City Planning Act and the City Core Revitalization Law were passed. Land-use principles that had attracted facilities for large numbers of customers were changed; recognition was given to basing location decisions on urban-planning procedures that reflected local decision-making. In the amendment to the City Core Revitalization Law, approval for basic plans was to come from a higher level, namely the Prime Minister; a City Core Revitalization Headquarters was established in the Cabinet, and the government took the initiative as a whole. This symbolically indicated that the age had ended in which urban commercial policy, a major pillar of distribution policy, was developed in isolation from plans for ideal urban areas.

2.5 *The End of the Textile Policy*

2.5.1 New Developments in the Textile Industry Toward a "Lifestyle Culture" Model

A review of the role of the Law on Extraordinary Measures for the Structural Improvement of the Textile Industries ("Textile Law") was undertaken by the Textile Industries Council and the Industrial Structure Council before the Law's third expiration date, which was set for 1989. The report entitled "Ideal Policies for the Future of the Textile Industry" (November 1988) showed how the situation was understood

(Matsushima 2012, p. 73). First, the report pointed out that imports were increasing rapidly amidst a slump in exports, due to (1) "the upgrading of demand, diversification, short cycles, and spread of textile uses to all aspects of life," (2) the yen's appreciation and the advance of Asia's newly industrialized economies (NIEs), and (3) the continued advances in technological innovation and the shift to information systems. The report argued that the direction the textile industry needed to take was "to build a new demand-oriented response system and to shift toward a "lifestyle-culture" industrial model." To this end, three problems needed to be overcome: (1) progress needed to be made in structural improvements to build a new demand-oriented supply system; (2) the industry needed to upgrade its product planning, information gathering, and dissemination capacity in order to respond to the trend toward fashion that was evident in more sophisticated demand and in diversification; (3) the industry needed to boldly make the most of the fruits of the rapid developments in technological innovation and the importance of information systems. A demand-oriented supply system is a rapid-response system that highlights actual demand and shortens the lead-time in delivering supplies. It is designed to enable the supply of products to correspond to actual demand at low cost in a timely and flexible manner.

This report represented a change in that it did not use the term "structural improvement," but instead called for "active promotion of structural adjustment." It was expected to promote both structural improvement and a smooth "industrial adjustment" at the same time. Structural improvement itself took on a new meaning. That is, it pointed to the "importance of forming groups, through links among multiple firms, that could complement each other with the various functions (linkage production units (LPUs)) needed for a system of supply-chain management in order to respond flexibly and aggressively to a market characterized by diversification and large-variety, small-lot, short-cycle production (Matsushima 2012, p. 78).

Previously, the stress had been on enhancing the distribution of information in industries whose manufacturing processes were divided from each other, but this concept envisioned cases in which companies that had already created vertical linkages among different industries would now go further and play mutually complementary roles. The "Textile Resource Center" was conceived as a means to support infrastructure improvements for building systems of demand-oriented supply. It was expected to gather information on textile materials, designs, and related areas and to enhance the function of transmitting information to textile production regions. This constituted a new understanding of the need for policy responses to the problems facing the textile industry. The law was revised in March 1989 and came into effect in April. The Textile Law was extended for a further five years.

The 1989 amendment featured the establishment of a Textile Resource Center to help build a system for demand-oriented supply. Measures promoted by the Textile Industry Rationalization Agency included the building of a database in the association and the provision of information to a network of textile resource centers based in each of the regions. This method, called "SR-NET Tokyo," was completed in March 1990. Even so, the costs of collecting information on ever-changing fashion were high, and the networks were not able to adequately meet the demands of industry.

The SR-NET Tokyo accordingly lost its role when in 1997 the "Textile Fashion Information Avenue" took its place. LPUs were designed to be reform enterprises based on group linkages and Minister approval, but Commercial Associations used the framework as well, and carried out plans for a smooth structural reform. From 1989 until 1994, there were 47 structural reform enterprises based on LPUs, and 9 Commercial Association plans. There was also one plan for joint facilities, adding up to a total of 57 projects underway with Ministry approval. The total cost of the projects was 47.8 billion yen. Moreover, under this fourth Textile Law, the facilities registration system was abolished, and as of December 1991, the certificates in use were slated for abolition by October 1995.

2.5.2 Policies for Expanding the Textile Industry Market

In advance of the expiration date of the fourth Textile Law, the General Affairs Committee of the Textile Industry Council and the Textile Subcommittee of the Industrial Structure Council compiled a report titled "Ideal policies for the future of the textile industry" in December 1993 (Matsushima 2012, p. 95). While ongoing reductions in the production were observable in response to increasing imports, the industry still employed about 2.8 million people, was the core industry in some regions, and enjoyed a surplus in trade. The report took note of this.

Specifically, the report pointed out that (1) among "its many problematic elements" were the difficulty of acquiring a highly skilled labor force, and as a sector reliant on manual labor, land, and energy, the textile industry in Japan was not cost-competitive compared with those of other countries. However, (2) it was "blessed in demand terms," the Japanese market's being not only large but also highly sophisticated in its demand for quality and design. Finally, (3) industries that were closely related to textiles, namely the textile machineries and the electronics industries, were world class. However, (4) it faced the problems of "an industrial structure that encouraged price-based competition." Accordingly, in order to discover a new direction for creative development while making the most of conditions 2 and 3, the Japanese textile industry needed to aggressively build markets "by undergoing structural reform to shift the paradigm from price competition to product differentiation." This would also enable the expansion of international markets, in the view of the councils. The report proposed three strategies to this end. The first was "structural reform for market-driven rather than producer-driven manufacturing. Second was an industrial structure that would nurture creativity, and third was strategy on a global scale. The first of these was comprised of concrete measures to develop, produce, and sell the products the market was seeking. Realization of these strategies would require complementary measures by the government, and while continuing to mention the need for structural improvement in areas including distribution, the report also recommended extension of the Textile Law. The revised law was thus passed in March 1994 and came into effect in April. The name of the law was changed on this occasion to the Law on Extraordinary Measures for the Structural Improvement of the Textile Industries ("Textile Industry Law").

The Textile Industry Law, again extended for five years and almost tantamount to a fifth Textile Law, carried on the basic framework of the fourth Textile Law, and structural reform projects were carried out by linked groups and groups like Commercial Associations. However, the measures that were focused on production sectors, such as the establishment of demand-oriented supply chains, also took into account the reflections on the system that were added in the process of reviewing the law. Market-driven policies took greater priority, along with the need for structural improvement, including in the distribution sector. The points that were revised through the Textile Industry Law included: (1) the addition of design development to new product development, (2) the addition of facilities or equipment leasing to facilities modernization, and (3) the addition of projects for the rationalization of marketing or inventory control. These revisions were intended to respond to the needs of enterprise groups. Furthermore, assistance measures had previously been limited to finance and debt guarantees, but to these were now added subsidies for developing information networks and new aid systems including subsidies for the promotion of local industry. With the expansion of structural improvement projects and subsidy measures, the number of structural improvement projects came to 96 under the Textile Industry Law, while the number of projects to facilitate structural improvement came to 24, for a total of 120 projects. Total costs, meanwhile, including private procurement, were reduced to 15.1 billion yen.

2.5.3 A Vision for the Textile Industry of the Twenty-First Century

The administration of textile policy began to change little by little as the date of the Law's expiry approached. That was because the Hashimoto Cabinet, established in January 1996, sought a move from industry-specific administration to cross-industry policy frameworks, which meant that the report issued by the general meeting of the committees of the Textile Industry Council and the ISC's Textile Committee differed from those that had previously sought extensions of the law (Matsushima 2012, p. 113).

The report understood the changes in the competitive environment to mean the advent of a new age defined in three ways: a market-led era, an era of competition on a global scale, and an era of new frontiers. "Market-led" meant that the initiative in industrial activities would shift from the supply side to the demand side, and that the development of industries could be secured only through completely rational and innovative activity in the market. According to the report, the existing textile industry was not as yet responding as needed to the advent of this new age, and four problems in this area were only becoming more serious. First was the failure to respond to the market-led era: due to the "lack of clarity in risk-taking, a divided, multi-step structure, and the synergism of both of these," the high-cost supply structure was being preserved as was. The industry was moving appropriately in the "market-in" direction, but "rapid response" remained an issue. Second, the response to large-scale global competition was inadequate, and the need for development on an international level was becoming manifest. While Japan was a key center for high-cost planning and development, the report found that Asia was already in the process of acquiring an enhanced role as a production and development base through international expansion. Third was the need to take on the challenge of new frontiers, as discussed above, and fourth was the slow pace at which reform was under way in textile-production areas.

The report pointed out the reforms considered necessary to resolve these issues, but its most important feature was its premise that these reforms would to a considerable degree be realized through the actions of individual firms in the market. At the same time, the report also pointed out that "given that the market itself is a system, a certain degree of policy intervention is needed to correct the weaknesses in that system or to upgrade that system," and that policy was needed in a complementary role. It was therefore judged that textile-industry policy should not be carried out in the form of individual measures but rather as an overall policy approach.

The impact of the existing Textile Industry Law over the four-year period from FY 1994 was that roughly 1% (1,000 enterprises) out of all textile businesses. Judgments such as the above were based on the fact that the ripple effects were limited in reforming the industrial structure of the industry as a whole, and that "the current issues of the textile industry are widespread, reform methods correspondingly diverse, and the a priori preparation of fixed packages of particular long-term reform measures would have the effect of limiting the potential for policy support for the textile industry." The decision was therefore made not to extend the framework of the existing law but rather to abolish it.

In response, the government decided in February 1999 on the Bill of the Law Concerning the Abolition of the SME Corporation and submitted it to the Diet. The Law, which came into effect in July, was aimed at strengthening SME policy so as to comprehensively and efficiently promote measures for small and medium-sized enterprises, and aimed to establish a comprehensive SME corporation team including the Small Business Credit Insurance Corporation, the Small Business Corporation, and the Textile Industry Structural Improvement Business Association. The entity promoting structural improvement was restructured into this, and textile industry policy would henceforth be developed within the framework of SME policy and cross-industry industrial policy.

2.6 *Revision of the Small and Medium-Sized Enterprise Basic Law*

The premise of the Small and Medium-Sized Enterprise Basic Law ("the Basic Law") enacted in 1963 was that the disparities among small and medium-sized enterprises and the changes brought about by trade liberalization were affecting small businesses and that SMEs needed to plan for growth and development through their own autonomous efforts. At the same time, the directions for policy were deemed to be "to rectify the disadvantage of economic and social constraints" (improve the business environment) and to "promote the voluntary efforts of the SMEs" (support for improvement of management). Through these approaches, both "improved productivity" (raising physical productivity) and "improved trading conditions" (upgrading of actual value) could be achieved. Improvements in productivity were expected through such measures as the modernization of equipment and expansion of scale, whereby transaction terms and subcontracting could be improved and excessive competition prevented.

However, the economic and social environment surrounding small and medium-sized enterprises had changed greatly since the establishment of the Basic Law (Nakata 2013, p. 72, p. 1207). The May 1990 interim report "SME policy in the 1990s" issued by the Small Business Policy Council Planning Subcommittee addressed (1) "the role expected of small and medium-sized enterprises," (2) "small and medium-sized enterprises in the 1990s," and (3) "directions for SME policy." The first of these stressed "small business as the source of creativity" and the second stressed the need for SMEs to reflect and serve potential demand. These ideas were new in that they suggested that small and medium-sized enterprises might themselves foster the creation of new markets. The third called for policy to support enterprises' self-help efforts and for a review of the question of whether competition-restricting cartels were not resulting in protection for vulnerable sectors. The Basic Measures Review Subcommittee, established at the SME Policy Council in October 1992, also presented the "Issues and future directions for SME Policy" in June 1993. It sought a policy system that would (1) strengthen the management base, (2) support structural reform, and (3) develop measures for small-scale businesses, and these in themselves were not a clear expression of a change in policy, but presented what would be part of the discussion that later led to the revision of the Basic Law. Apart from this, a report on industrial structure reform ("21st-century industrial policy report"), conducted by the Basic Issues Subcommittee of the Industrial Structure Council's General Committee in June 1994, made two important points regarding SME policy. First, regarding the debate over the hollowing out of industry, the report stated that changes in the domestic and foreign economic environment and in the comparative advantages of the industry were leading to overseas relocation and import substitution. These in and of themselves should not necessarily be regarded as problems, according to the report, because they meant that the industrial structure was becoming optimized in a global sense. Second, it strongly urged the promotion of deregulation. In other words, new movements were being made to reform the protective policies that had previously prevailed regarding SMEs.

Based on these arguments, the SME Policy Study Group was established as a private advisory group to the Director-General of the Small and Medium-sized Enterprise Agency in July 1998, issuing a mid-term report in November 1999 and a final report in May that called for a review of policy ideals and systems. It cited the following as problems in the former Basic Law system. The first problem was the variance between the reality and the policy concept, which had been based on the idea of correcting the disparities in the so-called dual structure. Second, the policy approach that had been effective in the past had been maintained, hindering the flexible or effective allocation of funds. Third, new policies had been added to existing policies, leading to complex and highly segmented measures that were hard for users to understand. The report also stated that it was no longer inappropriate to treat SMEs uniformly as weak players. Rather, they should be expected to play an active role in creating a dynamic Japanese economy by demonstrating mobility, flexibility, and creativity. This, too, called for a shift in perception. The active roles SMEs could play were envisioned as incubators for market competition, innovators, creators of attractive job opportunities, and developers of regional economies. The first of these referred to stimulation of market competition through the business activities of many small and medium-sized enterprises, which would promote "economic metabolism," or an organic self-sustaining process. Specific policy goals to give these roles real significance were the improvement in the conditions of competition, assistance for SMEs' self-help efforts toward founding businesses and introducing innovations to management, and finally, maintenance of the safety net.

Then-SME Agency Minister Katsuhiko Tokita said that, "MITI was pursuing rationality in policy. The SME Agency, too, was intent on clarifying principles and policies that would shift our footing both officially and substantively from a so-called social policy-driven SME policy toward a forward-looking industrial policy."

In June 1996, the SME Policy-Making Council, with enquiry from Prime Minister Obuchi, established a cross-sectorial subcommittee and proceeded with a review. Its interim report came out in August, and its final report, "A new SME Policy for the 21st century" (the 1999 Report) in September. Fundamentally, this aligned with the final report of the SME Policy Study Group cited above and strongly reflected the concepts of a market orientation and of deregulation. The content, which addressed the changes of the 1990s with policies oriented to the twenty-first century, included: (1) changes in the macro-economic environment, (2) changes in values and lifestyles, (3) the advance of globalization and changes in industrial structure, (4) changes in relationships among enterprises, and (5) changes in industrial integration and in distribution structures. The first of these pointed out that the income levels of those working in SMEs had risen alongside the overall rise in income levels, and that gaps in income were no longer evident, but that at the same time, with the maturation of the economy, growth itself had fallen, and that increases in added value, efficient use of capital, and upgrades in the quality of labor had all become important for the new age. The fourth focused on the growing fluidity of the division of labor among subcontractors and the trend toward decreasing numbers of subcontractors. The fifth presented the constraints on the autonomous development of regional localities, and concerns about the increasing weakness of industrial integration, which was at the foundation of *monozukuri*, or Japan's distinct manufacturing craftsmanship. It was expected that SMEs would serve as incubators for market competition, as innovators, as creators of appealing jobs, and as developers of local economies and society. The policy concepts for putting this into concrete form were to be based on "respecting and activating the market mechanism," meaning first, to facilitate the conditions for competition in which SMEs would play an active part; second, to reinforce progress by SMEs toward innovation and creativity; and third, to establish a safety net. The second and third points were especially recognized as expressing something new.

The New Basic Law was based on the above circumstances. In broad outline, it carried on the new philosophy laid out by the council's report: (1) the shift in principle, (2) the change in policy systems, (3) the diversification of policy methods, and (4) the expansion of the range included in SMEs. The first shifted away from rectifying the gaps among SMEs to expectations that the SMEs would serve as sources of economic development and economic strength. The second called for shifting to the pursuit of advantages of scale, and from compensating for disadvantages to pursuing novelty and originality, as well as for the strengthening of the foundations of management, and maintenance of a safety net. The third represented a shift from loans and organization-building to greater diversity in policy approaches, including methods that stressed direct financing and supplementing soft resources. The fourth included a review of definitions to bring them into line with economic realities and measures for raising capital standards.

Thus the policy principles regarding SMEs advanced in keeping with the goals of economic structural reform.

3 Pursuing Rules-Based Multilateral Coordination

3.1 The Conclusion of the Uruguay Round and Launching of the WTO

3.1.1 Uruguay Round Negotiations

The Uruguay Round agreement was reached in December 1993 after seven years of talks. The outcomes of the round were the following (Abe 2013, p. 403). First, whereas previous rounds had centered on tariffs negotiations, the Uruguay Round formulated rules in new areas such as intellectual property rights and trade in services. It also broadened the scope of discussion to include the textile and agricultural sectors, which were not yet sufficiently covered by GATT rules. Second, resisting the tides of protectionism, bilateralism, and regionalism that emerged in the latter 1980s, the Uruguay Round supported the idea of free trade as the fundamental principle of international commerce. Third, the scope of dispute settlement was expanded and expedited under the WTO, dramatically improving the functioning of dispute resolution. Fourth, due to the role played by the WTO, the following changes in the resolution of international disputes were observed: whereas GATT's procedure for dispute resolution was fundamentally a political one, the WTO's approach placed a relatively high priority on resolving disputes by interpreting the law, meaning a shift from political to judicial decisions.

The specific issues discussed during this period (Abe 2013, p. 425) included the Multi-Fiber Agreement (MFA). As noted in the previous chapter, the meeting of senior officials in April 1989 stated that "[Ministers] agree that measures on the process of integration into GATT cover the abolition of regulations based on the multilateral textile agreement (MFA)...." In other words, it established a path to the elimination of the MFA. Additionally, the WTO Agreement on Textiles and Clothing recognized "transitional safeguards" (TSGs). These differed from the safeguards (SGs) of the 10-year period when textiles were integrated into GATT. They were intended to address market confusion in domestic textile industries that resulted from surges in imports during a transitional period. In 1993–1994, MITI rapidly developed procedural rules on TSG-triggering measures. This was because, whereas the SGs had never been triggered before, the textile industry was now beginning to suffer from import pressures to a degree that MITI policies had to be changed.

In March 1995 the industry requested that TSG measures be implemented and MITI judged that there was sufficient evidence to do so, but as of the November decision, imports of the target items were stabilizing and even appeared to be contracting. The TSG measures were therefore put off. Japan in fact never launched the TSGs, and when the Textile Agreement expired at the end of 2004, textile trade was integrated into GATT.

From the mid-term review to the final stage, anti-dumping (AD) also emerged as an issue that could affect the success of the entire round. Interest in anti-dumping began to build internationally after the summer of 1989. This was because of mounting conflict over how to make the international rules of the 1979 Tokyo Round's Anti-Dumping Code (1979) function in light of the national laws of the member countries. At the end of the negotiations in December 1991, the GATT director-general presented the Draft Final Act Embodying the Results of the Uruguay Round of Multilateral Trade Negotiation ("Dunkel Draft"), which emphasized the director-general's arbitration solutions to individual points of contention. Although the draft was accepted because of the priority member countries placed on the Uruguay Round, the contents of the Draft AD Agreement became a political controversy within the US from 1992–1993, and a number of amendments were made before agreement was ultimately reached.

The rules governing the various entity requirements and procedural requirements for invoking AD measures were also given specificity and clarity. Because Japan was, among developed countries, exceptionally subject to anti-dumping complaints, it was particularly concerned to see the international rules strengthened with regard to the operation of AD laws, and its contributions to the realization of the new agreement were significant.

3.1.2 Developments and Setbacks in the WTO System

The Uruguay Round presented new issues. Where previously trade issues had dominated, the Uruguay Round raised matters that were entangled with domestic systems, and with the dramatic increase in the number of parties participating, the multilateral negotiations that were to follow on the inauguration of the WTO were expected to be challenging (Abe 2013, p. 535).

The main roles of the WTO, launched in January 1995, were: (1) to forward the implementation of the Uruguay Round consensus, (2) to provide a forum for multilateral trade negotiations, (3) to manage dispute settlement procedures, (4) to administer the trade policy review mechanism, and (5) to coordinate global economic policy planning with the International Monetary Fund (IMF) and the World Bank. The first was the biggest task for the WTO immediately after its inauguration. The WTO was involved with the implementation of the obligations incurred under the WTO Agreement, including member state compliance with reporting obligations, implementation of concrete promises (the revision of domestic laws and tariff reduction), and matters on which member states had agreed to ongoing negotiations. Efforts were therefore made to introduce highly transparent institutional mechanisms so as to enable monitoring, and this was achieved.

In accordance with the regulations set by the Marrakesh Agreement establishing the World Trade Organization, an inaugural ministerial conference in Singapore was scheduled, and from early 1996, WTO member states began coordination on what that meeting would address. Japan had four items on its agenda: (1) inspection of the implementation status of the Uruguay Round agreement, (2) further liberalization, (3) the introduction of new areas for discussion, and (4) deliberations on admitting China, Taiwan, Russia, and other countries to the WTO. Japan's position on expanding WTO target areas was in common with that of other developed countries, producing a heated battle with the developing countries that opposed expansion. The developing countries firmly maintained the stance that the Singapore Ministerial Meeting was an opportunity to discuss implementation of the Uruguay Round Agreement. Through the negotiations on the content of the ministerial conference, agreement was finally reached on launching discussions of investment and competition, and it was confirmed that the WTO would not begin work on labor standards. This was in line with Japan's expectations and represented a significant achievement. The greatest achievement of the Singapore Ministerial Conference was the WTO Information Technology Agreement (ITA), which resulted in the December 1996 Ministerial Declaration on Trade in Information Technology Products. In principle, tariffs would be reduced in four stages, affecting 200 products according to tariff classification such as semiconductors, computers, computer software, telecommunications equipment, semiconductor manufacturing equipment, and others. The reductions would begin in July 1997 and the tariffs would be completely abolished by January 2000. The ITA negotiations differed slightly from prior tariff negotiations in that they did not have a mercantilist character. Rather, there was general agreement on the idea that tariff elimination would be desirable for all member states, and negotiations were concluded quickly.

The Seattle Ministerial Conference of November 1999 aimed to launch a new round beginning in the year 2000 and to agree on the scope and method for those negotiations, but this was not achieved. This was because "problems with the decision-making mechanism" arose in the preparatory process, and because compromise was not reached either among the leading developed countries or between the developed and developing countries on "conflicts over specific points at issue." The "problems with the decision-making mechanism" arose because the increasing presence of developing countries in the preparatory process meant more time spent on coordinating among the member states. There was a backlash against the traditional mode of determining the agenda through small-group "Green Room" discussions led by the advanced and newly emerging nations. In addition was the fact that anti-liberalization and anti-globalization protests by NGOs, labor unions, and others grew more extensive than anticipated. This, too, contributed to the failure of the negotiations.

The Doha Ministerial Conference that followed in November 2001 succeeded, after various difficulties, in launching a new round. It narrowed its objectives and gave greater consideration to transparency and efficiency in the format of the meetings. The Declaration released in November represented agreement on achieving a new round on a wide range of areas, including (1) improvements to market access (agriculture services, tariff negotiations on industrial goods, and so on), (2) improvements to existing WTO rules (strengthening discipline of anti-dumping and other measures.), (3) responses to various twenty-first-century issues (rules on investment and competition, trade and the environment, e-commerce, and other measures.). The declaration said that this broad agenda would be subject to the consensus rule and that the Round would be completed by January 2005.

The new Round was named the "Doha Development Agenda" to show the importance ascribed to developing countries. The negotiation aimed at outcomes for reducing poverty and achieving economic growth. By eliminating such items as the WTO Agreement's "implementation issues," protection of intellectual property rights with the TRIPS Agreement (Agreement on Trade-Related Aspects of Intellectual Property Rights), and the advanced nations' high tariffs and export subsidies on agricultural goods, the Doha Round was intended to do away with impediments to development. Investment and the environment were therefore added to the areas discussed in earlier rounds, including agriculture, non-agricultural products, and anti-dumping, resulting in extensive and comprehensive negotiations to respond to new needs such as the needs of developing countries. However, negotiations stalled at the 5th Ministerial Conference in Cancún, Mexico, in September 2003, and extension of the original January 2005 deadline became unavoidable. The WTO General Council in August 2004 sharply narrowed the negotiating agenda, and the sixth Ministerial Conference in Hong Kong that followed in December 2005 adopted a declaration that took full account of developing countries. Nevertheless, the WTO was forced to extend the negotiation deadline once again. The lack of momentum among the negotiating countries, the standoffs on individual areas of negotiation, and the difficulties in coming to decisions have all been attributed to these repeated deadline extensions, and the cumulative effect was to cast doubt on the workings of a world trade system centered on the WTO.

3.1.3 Advancing Rule-Based Criteria in Trade Policy

Throughout the Uruguay Round negotiations, an International Economic Affairs Division, Tariff Division, and Temporary General Trade Negotiation Office dubbed the "GATT Office" were placed in the International Economic Affairs Department of the MITI's International Trade Policy Bureau (Abe 2013, p. 529). In 1990, the Office for Trade Policy Review was established in the International Economic Affairs Division. It was tasked with responding to such matters as the US National Trade

Estimate Report on Foreign Trade Barriers. It aimed to point out foreign practices and customs that from Japan's point of view acted as barriers to trade, not by establishing arbitrary standards as America had done, but by citing international rules under GATT and other agreements. The Report on Compliance by Major Trading Partners with Trade Agreements ("Unfair Trade Report") published in June 1992 was epochal in its clear rejection of the US's results-oriented criteria in favor of "rules-based criteria."

In addition, a Fair Trade Center was established as an affiliate of the Japan Foreign Trade Council, Inc.'s Trade Research Center just prior to the start of the Uruguay Round. The Center built close cooperative relationships with the Tariff Division of the International Economic Affairs Department and provided a place for information sharing and the exchange of opinions with domestic export industries. It also endeavored to build cooperative relationships with academia.

The shift to a rules-based trade policy by MITI and others and the cooperative system developed with domestic industry and academia were organically linked to each other and offered the systemic underpinnings for active participation in WTO negotiations and utilization of WTO Dispute Settlement Procedures.

Regarding specific issues, the panels that Japan requested of GATT on the EEC's AD parts and components regulations were held twice, in July and September 1989. The Panel Report was distributed to the parties in March 1990, mostly approving Japan's claims. The EEC's new rules were intended to prevent the avoidance of AD taxation on finished goods by imposing a retroactive tax on parts that were imported and assembled using the so-called knockdown method. Japan argued that the EEC's parts taxation was a domestic tax because it was not imposed at the point of importation, and that to apply it only to imported products constituted a violation of GATT Article 3, paragraph 2, Sect. 1. Additionally, the exemption from the parts tax based on local procurement rates would give priority to the use of EEC products and was therefore contrary to GATT Article 3.4.

Additionally, in May 1991, the EC Board of Directors approved AD taxation on audiocassette tapes, and Japan consulted with the ADP Committee (Committee on Anti-Dumping Practices) but the consultations did not result in an agreement. Japan therefore requested the establishment of a panel in October 1992. During this period, MITI made it clear that it would steer its trade policy toward multilateral, rule-based criteria, away from bilateral trade management through so-called gray measures, and it showed no hesitation in doing so in this audiocassette case.

3.1.4 Conditions for Utilizing WTO Dispute Settlement Procedures

The first time Japan appealed to the WTO's dispute settlement procedures was with regard to US automobile customs duties (Abe 2013, p. 589). This was part of a long-standing dispute between the two nations regarding autos and auto parts. The New Economic Partnership Framework talks of July 1993 had not come to terms on the interpretation of numerical targets, and following the repeated breakdown of negotiations, the US announced a proposed list of sanctions in May 1995. Japan responded immediately by requesting WTO consultations in May, based on GATT Articles 4 and 22-1 (Understanding on the rules and procedures governing the settlement of disputes). In June, bilateral talks between Japan and the US began in Geneva based on WTO dispute settlement procedures. Here, too, there was no agreement in the two positions, but MITI Minister Hashimoto asked US trade representative Mickey Kantor to push back the US deadline for sanctions, and with the presentation of an "overview" of a voluntary plan by five Japanese automakers, the Japan–US autos and auto parts negotiations reached agreement.

Japan thus rejected "result-oriented standards" and pursued "rules-oriented standards" as had already been declared in the "unfair trade report." This showed both the domestic world and Japan's trade partners that Japan would adhere to this stance even in specific cases, which had great significance for Japan's trade policy. It also made a strong impact by showing that the negotiations were to Japan's advantage because the dispute settlement procedures that had been strengthened by the establishment of the WTO proved effective against the US position of pursuing negotiations based on Sect. 301 trade sanctions. Subsequent negotiations confirmed the value of Japan's stance. For example, in May 1995, America's Eastman Kodak Company filed suit under Sect. 301 over a film case, but Japan succeeded through WTO proceedings in having these claims dismissed. These results were significant for Japan's trade policy in that they demonstrated that legal procedures could offer protection. From 1997 forward, the number of US demands for unilateral market opening shrank drastically, and economic friction between the two countries diminished.

There were many other examples of anti-dumping incidents, but the resolutions that were based on WTO dispute settlement procedures represented a shift from reliance on conventional bilateral diplomacy to legal approaches based on multilateral procedures. The cases that went to the WTO were by and large AD-related issues with the steel and auto industries as the principal targets and the US as the main country in dispute. This was because Japan used the WTO's procedures to curb such US protectionist tactics as AD measures. It also reflected the fact that Japan was utilizing the WTO's procedures to monitor industrial policy measures related to automobiles.

3.1.5 Activating the Import Relief Law—Japan's Transition from Target to Petitioner

GATT's trade liberalization, centered on tariff reduction, gave rise to domestic protectionist pressures in developed countries, which manifested themselves in the quest for trade barriers that could replace the tariffs (Abe 2013, p. 657). The active use of trade remedy actions (principally AD measures) and voluntary export restraints (VERs) were found especially useful. It was easier to use AD measures to develop technical methods for calculating higher duty rates than to invoke the Countervailing Duties (CVD) Law. This made protectionist action easier, and whereas safeguard measures had to comply with the WTO's non-discrimination rules, AD measures could be used to target imports only from specified countries.

From 1980 to 1989, the number of AD investigations worldwide totaled 1,648; Japanese products were the targets of the highest number of these, at 161. Between 1990 and 1993, however, Japan was the target of 38 cases out of a total of 683, and of 61 out of 1,253 cases from 1995 to 1999. In other words, Japan's position vis-à-vis AD petitions changed around 1990.

Meanwhile, Japan had held back on initiating import relief measures until the late 1990s. This reflected Japan's position as an exporting nation, as well as the facts that agricultural and textile products were excluded from GATT's trade liberalization framework and that Japan preferred resolutions based on voluntary export restraints vis-à-vis its partner countries. Early in the twenty-first century, however, reforms were made with a view to increasing the initiation of petitions. The shift came with the 2001 petition for safeguards on three agricultural products (green onions, shiitake mushrooms, and tatami mats). That Japan sought to protect agriculture by pursuing safeguard investigations and interim measures was new in and of itself, but it also became the catalyst for the reform of Japan's domestic systems. This series of amendments demonstrated the penetration of a legalistic attitude on these issues, with an emphasis not only on the transparency and predictability of the investigative procedures but also on their efficiency and timeliness.

3.2 Regionalism and Japan

3.2.1 The Alteration of APEC

In principle, the GATT framework included most-favored-nation (MFN) treatment, but some exceptions were allowed, including two types of Regional Trade Agreement (RTA): Free Trade Agreements (FTAs) and Customs Unions. The number of FTAs gradually increased, and began to threaten the relevance of the WTO. This regionalism, emergent from the late 1950s to the 1970s, began expanding in the 1990s (Abe 2013, p. 712).

For example, the United States' basic trade policy from immediately after World War II to the 1980s was to construct a non-discriminatory multilateral trading system. The US only permitted the 1950s establishment of the EEC and EFTA (European Free Trade Agreement) in Europe due to the Cold War priority of promoting the economic development of Western countries. However, the US's negative attitude toward regionalism began weakening in the 1980s. The United States signed an FTA with Israel in 1985 and with Canada in 1989, signaling a shift from multilateral and gradual liberalization utilizing GATT to regional liberalization using FTAs. Thus, in the mid-1980s, the United States pursued three courses: multilateral and gradual liberalization through GATT, regional liberalization using FTAs, and the unilateralist improvement of access to specific markets in specific countries. The United States also sought to conclude an FTA with Asian countries including Japan. It was unable to do so, however, because Japan was cautious about the impact of bilateral agreements on GATT and on the position of Asian countries. Nevertheless, the US continued to maintain a regionalist course and concluded NAFTA (North American Free Trade Agreement) with Mexico and Canada in the first half of the 1990s.

East Asia did not do much to follow the regionalist course of Europe and the US until the late 1990s, instead defending the non-discriminatory and multilateral GATT trade regime. Asia-Pacific Economic Cooperation (APEC) was an example of this stance. APEC, the concrete form of which was based on deliberations in the Japanese and Australian governments, declared a principle of "open regional cooperation" at its first Ministerial Conference in November 1989 and announced its intent of curbing the move to bloc economies. APEC was originally formed on the understanding that European and American regionalism were functioning as de facto forms of protectionism and that steps needed to be taken to avoid Asian markets' shrinking as a result. In other words, APEC was not conceived as either an FTA or a customs union.

However, APEC members did not necessarily share this philosophy. APEC's role therefore began changing around 1993 and 1994. The United States showed a strong interest in expanding the East Asian market and liberalizing trade, but its suggested approach as APEC Chair in 1993 was that of an FTA rather than adherence to the GATT framework. Thereafter, although the Bogor Declaration issued at the November 1994 Indonesia summit still confirmed an anti-regionalist stance, APEC lost its role as a venue for negotiating collective liberalization. Instead, at the Osaka Ministerial and Leaders Meetings of 1995, APEC adopted the concerted unilateral action (CUA) approach. CUA was the product of a compromise between the United States, Canada, Australia, and New Zealand, which sought binding liberalization, and the countries of Asia, which preferred greater national autonomy. Japan, though arguably an advocate of further liberalization, struggled because the Agriculture Ministry did not want to liberalize beyond the levels agreed to in the Uruguay Round. Nonetheless, the 1996 meeting in the Philippines issued a positive message with regard to the ITA (Information Technology Agreement) that spurred member countries to work on advancing the Early Voluntary Sectoral Liberalization (EVSL) originally raised at the Osaka meeting of 1995. Still, negotiations remained extremely difficult, and by 1998 any possibility of achieving agreement had vanished. On the contrary, doubts were raised about promoting liberalization based on an APEC framework. Nevertheless, the APEC meetings continued, and in the early twenty-first century, a wide range of issues such as countermeasures against terrorism, global warming, and energy were added to the scope of its deliberations.

Meanwhile, the EVSL's failure in 1998 led East Asian countries to seek out an FTA approach. Japan's stance on FTAs was negative on the whole because it placed its confidence in the GATT/WTO regime and on rules-based negotiations. However, with the conclusion of Japan–US semiconductor talks in 1996 and the easing of the trade friction between the two nations, there was less need to adhere to a rules-oriented trade policy. Japan accordingly held FTA consultations in 1998. Despite Japan's emphasis on GATT, MITI concluded that it should actively pursue not only multi- but bilateral relationships as well, because the most active developments of the period were occurring in the FTAs and customs unions advanced by the US and the EU. Japan's FTA with Singapore marked the first concrete result of the new policy.

Based on consultations held in March 1999, MITI actively pursued the agreement, which was concluded in January 2002. It then reached an agreement in principle with Mexico in March 2004 and established a path to advancing an FTA there.

3.2.2 The Asian Industries Development Plan Based on Economic Cooperation

The Asian Industries Development Plan, adopted as an economic cooperation measure, aimed to transmit to ASEAN (Association of Southeast Asian Nations) countries the Japanese development strategies that had given rise to industrial policy. It was distinctive in that it existed outside the constraints of the ODA (Overseas Development Assistance) framework. MITI promoted the so-called New Aid Plan of 1985–1991, which emphasized technical cooperation, and from 1992–1996, advanced policies for upgrading ASEAN industries.

The latter differed from the earlier New Aid Plan in several ways. First, it developed a method called policy cooperation that sought continuous dialogue between the governments; second, it did not rest on bilateral assistance but on turning policy into concrete forms through links with the ASEAN Economic Ministers Meeting (AEM), an ASEAN multilateral organ; and third, while the "New AID Plan" in reality covered the so-called ASEAN 4—Thailand, Malaysia, Indonesia, and the Philippines—the later version aimed to promote ASEAN market integration.

According to MITI's 1993 report, "ASEAN industrial development vision—industry policy recommendations," the need to upgrade ASEAN industry arose because the ASEAN 4 were losing their competitiveness to China and Vietnam in labor-intensive sectors. Even though the policy covered countries other than the ASEAN 4, it aimed to increase the ratio of capital-intensive fields that would realize high added value in these four countries as a whole. Specifically this meant (1) fostering supporting industries, meaning the parts industries required for assembly-type manufacturing; (2) implementing a development-oriented industrial policy; and (3) improving the systems for intellectual property rights.

Policies targeting areas outside these four countries were advanced through the ASEAN Economic Ministers, with an annual AEM–MITI meeting established in November 1991. Although the meetings involved multiple negotiating partners, the most important parts of the AEM–MITI mechanism were (1) the bilateral policy talks at the vice-ministerial level, and (2) the Working Group on Economic Cooperation in Cambodia, Laos, and Myanmar (CLM–WG). The second of these reflected ASEAN ideas of building a production network of assembly-related manufacturing industries in other countries centered on the ASEAN 4, which were making the shift to so-called supporting industries. This made it difficult to coordinate among the various interests regarding which production sectors should be introduced to which country. The CLM–WG, which was established as an AEM–MITI organ in 1994, held many talks, and in 1998 evolved into the AEM–MITI Economic and Industrial Cooperation Committee (AMEICC) or Japan–ASEAN Economic and Industrial Cooperation Committee). Ultimately, a division of labor was developed between the region and the Japanese companies, which boasted an overwhelming share of assembly-related manufacturing in ASEAN.

Following the 1997 Asian monetary crisis, the system of untied yen loans was revised. Japanese-company exports were promoted through untied yen loans based on international bidding, and a new system of tied loans was created. The first consisted of two policies: (1) dividing the consulting portions of the infrastructure construction project, such as decisions on design and use, from the provision of the yen loan, which would have no conditions attached to it; and (2) treating the yen loans as untied but using diplomatic efforts to urge that Japanese companies win the bids. However, from 1999 forward, this second approach came under criticism, principally from the US, at the OECD Working Party on Export Credits and Credit Guarantees and other meetings, and in 2004 Japan was forced to agree to arrangements for more transparent information sharing. The tied loans, meanwhile, were based on the Hashimoto Cabinet's promotion of "special interest-rate loans for environmental projects" after 1997. This approach was adopted because environmental issues were assuming importance in developing countries. The loans supported proposals with little commercial application, and to which the OECD Arrangement on Official Supported Export Credits (the "Helsinki Package") would not apply.

3.3 *Trade Friction and Multilateral Coordination*

3.3.1 US–Japan Framework for a New Economic Partnership

With the drastic international changes that followed on the end of the Cold War in 1989 and the collapse of the Soviet Union in 1991, the United States found it harder to sustain the generous stance toward Japan's policies that had prevailed during the years of greater East–West tension. The Clinton administration, while maintaining the traditional route of pursuing free-trade ideals and strongly determined to open markets in other countries, pursued a "results-oriented" trade policy with respect to Japan.

The shift from the "procedural emphasis" of the Reagan and Bush eras reportedly took place at the direction of President Clinton himself at the beginning of March 1993 in preparation for the Japan–US summit meeting the following month. At the talks, Prime Minister Kiichi Miyazawa clearly opposed the new approach as an example of managed trade. Deputy Assistant to the President Bowman W. Cutter reviewed the policy, including it in May's "Japan Paper." In June, it was presented to Japan as a draft for the comprehensive economic consultations that were to become the US–Japan Framework for a New Economic Partnership (Abe 2013, p. 89). The "Japan Paper" enumerated macroeconomic objectives, including the reduction of Japan's current account surplus based on GDP ratios and "sector-specific and structural negotiations." MITI and the Japanese government completely rejected this approach, especially the setting of numerical targets. However, in July, the "Miyazawa Letter" suggested a compromise, which led to the announcement later that month of the Joint

Statement on the Framework for a New Economic Partnership Between Japan and the United States.

The new US–Japan Framework consisted of three pillars. The first concerned macroeconomic issues, the area regarding which the US, in the July agreement, had requested a clarification of concrete goals. The Framework called for Japan to reduce its current account surplus by promoting domestic demand-led economic growth and market opening. Ultimately, this did not become part of the negotiations on specific items. The second pillar was a proposal for sector-by-sector discussions and negotiations, or "sector-specific agreements." These addressed five areas: "government procurement," "regulatory reform and competitiveness," "other major sectors (automobiles and auto parts)," "economic harmonization," and the implementation of "existing agreements." The sector-specific talks were the centerpiece of the negotiations. The third pillar was "cooperation on a global scale." This was aimed at formulating 15 action groups in the five fields of environment, technology, human resources development, population, and AIDS, with action plans for Japan and the United States to respond with a shared understanding of the problems at hand (Fig. 3).

The talks were wide-ranging, but certain basic principles emerged: First, the Clinton administration maintained its "results-oriented approach" and "objective criteria" to the end. Second, the talks required compromise by both countries. In this sense, the Framework followed the direction set by the SII talks, and some of the items reflected Japan's interests. However, the US consistently saw the Framework talks as intended to seek action from the Japanese. America therefore insisted, with regard to certain US measures that Japan considered problematic, that they were non-negotiable despite the principle of resolving disputes through negotiation. Third, the scope of negotiations was limited to those areas to which government could respond. Like the second attribute above, this reflected Japan's stance and was often opposed by the US.

3.3.2 Difficulties in the Auto Negotiations

At follow-up discussions to the high-level Market-Oriented Sector-Selective (MOSS) talks that started July 24, 1991, the US proposed replacing the MOSS Agreement-based surveys of auto parts with a new survey of sales opportunities for automobiles in the Japanese market. The decision was made to implement this as a type of voluntary purchase expansion plan (Abe 2013, p. 109; Hasegawa 2013, p. 357) because even by the early 1990s, the US automobile industry's predicament and the trade imbalance between Japan and the United States had not improved. The plan did not satisfy the US, however, but became one of the issues addressed in the later Framework talks. The focus of the Framework talks was the large gap between the two sides on what constituted "government reach" and "objective criteria." Both governments were supposed to endeavor to agree on "appropriate objective criteria" to evaluate the achievement of the goals, but the US had proposed that the Japanese government adopt numerical targets. The Japanese government, however, only encouraged voluntary action by the automobile industry, and remained opposed to setting concrete

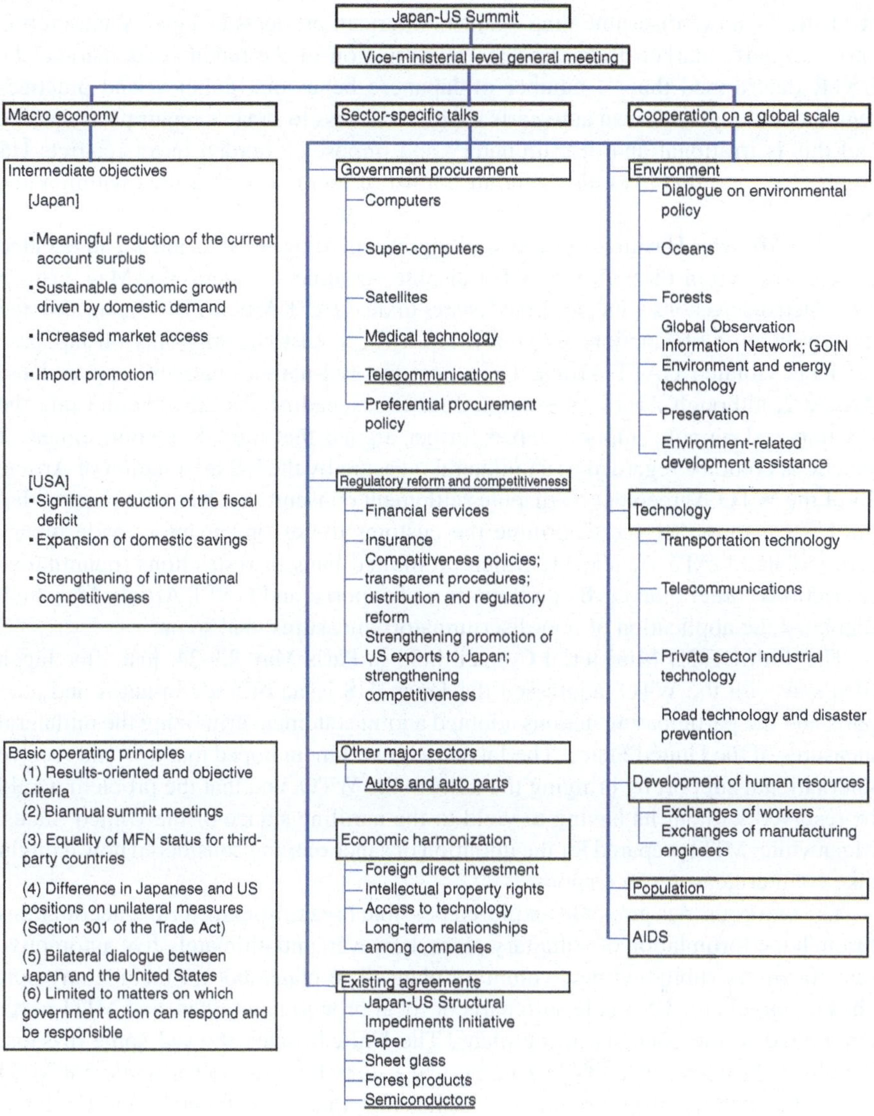

Fig. 3 Composition of the US–Japan Framework for a New Economic Partnership

numerical targets, because a basic principle of the negotiations had been to limit "the talks to matters of government responsibility," and the Japanese government regarded numerical targets as beyond its reach.

Talks were suspended due to this disagreement, and with the repeated breakdown in negotiations, US Trade Representative Kantor launched investigative procedures aimed at imposing sanctions on auto repair parts under Sect. 301 of the 1974 Trade Act. The Clinton administration decided to impose sanctions against Japan on May 10, 1995, and at the same time announced that it would file a complaint with the WTO accusing Japan of discriminating against American products in Japan's automobile and auto parts market. Regarding the investigation of the repair parts market, the USTR determined that "a number of Japanese behaviors, policies, and practices regulate or deny American auto parts suppliers access to Japan's repair parts market, and this is irrational and discriminatory and imposes a burden on or restricts US commerce" and that it would "announce a list of retaliatory measures within a few days."

MITI Minister Hashimoto expressed regret regarding the list, and Japan decided to seek resolution through the WTO dispute settlement system. On May 17th, it requested discussions with the United States under GATT Article 22-1. Japan asserted that application of sanctions in the form of a 100% customs duty only on Japanese products violated GATT Article 1 on most-favored-nation treatment and violated Article 2, although Article 2 exempted tariffs exceeding the 2.5% bound rate the US imposed on auto imports. Japan further argued that the US announcement of sanctions could be regarded as a unilateral measure by the US in violation of Article 23 of the WTO Agreement on dispute settlement consent; that Kantor's request that the US Customs Service determine the customs duties on Japanese-made luxury cars violated GATT Article 11, which prohibited bans or restrictions (quantitative restrictions) other than tariffs on imports and exports, and GATT Article 13, which regulated the application of non-discriminatory measures; and so on.

The 34th OECD Ministerial Council held in Paris May 23–24, just after Japan filed suit with the WTO, addressed the Japan–US issue of trade in autos and auto parts and the participating nations adopted a joint statement criticizing the unilateral measures of the United States. The Japanese government hoped that it would receive international support by bringing the talks to the WTO, and that the problem would be resolved without its having to yield to the hardline stance of the United States. Meanwhile, MITI prepared for the initiation of sanctions and considered how it might take countermeasures in response.

The two countries gradually explored possible breakthroughs for the negotiations through the formulation of voluntary plans, however, and ultimately five automotive manufacturers submitted new voluntary plans. The plans did not include any purchasing targets for US-made auto parts or local procurement rates, and MITI never committed to the contents of the plans. The United States showed some dissatisfaction with the absence of clear numerical values for automotive parts, but MITI adhered to its refusal to provide any further information. Ultimately, the US interpreted the plans on its own, enabling settlement of the issue for the time being. MITI succeeded in avoiding triggering sanctions under Sect. 301 of the Trade Act, maintaining the principle of confining negotiations to areas for which the government was responsible.

The auto- and auto-parts negotiations proved difficult because the US remained fixed on setting numerical targets as against Japan's proposed "corporation approach" of promoting inter-industry cooperation. Agreement was reached in June 1995 based on a voluntary plan by Japan's leading auto manufacturers. The plan allowed for a five-year term for such Japan–US measures as expansion of foreign automobiles' access to the Japanese market, expansion of purchases of foreign-made auto parts, and deregulation of inspections and procedures, based on confirmation of (1) compliance with international trade rules including the WTO Agreement and (2) elimination of numerical targets and the establishment of the principles of free trade and free-market economics. After the agreement, the number of imported cars sold in the Japanese market steadily increased. The US remained dissatisfied, however, because in the economic downturn after 1997, European car sales increased. Concerned about the decline in exports of foreign-made automobile parts to Japan and about the repair parts market, the US requested further deregulation. Although Japan proposed launching new talks in December 1999 before the expiry of the 1995 measures, the United States demanded the measures' expansion and extension, and the two sides failed to reach an accord. The 1995 agreement expired in the year 2000.

3.3.3 Numerical Targets and Semiconductor Negotiations

Japan and the US concluded a five-year agreement in June 1991 concerning market-opening measures for semiconductors, which was one of the major issues between the two nations (Abe 2013, p. 122; Hasegawa 2013, p. 146). The two pillars of the agreement remained the same as those in the old Semiconductor Agreement: (1) expansion of access to the Japanese market for foreign semiconductors and (2) prevention of the dumping of Japanese semiconductors in the US market. There were changes in content, however. Specifically, the US industry "hoped" that the market share of foreign semiconductors in Japan would exceed 20% by the end of 1992, and the Japanese government recognized this expectation, but the two governments agreed that this did not constitute a guarantee of market share or a target range of maximums and minimums. The US interpreted this to mean a de facto acknowledgment of undisclosed numerical targets, and repeatedly asserting that sanctions would be imposed in the event of non-fulfillment of the "promise," hinted that Sect. 301 would be applied. Nonetheless, under the new agreement, foreign semiconductor access to the Japanese market steadily improved. The share of foreign semiconductors increased from 16.5% in the third quarter of 1991 to approximately 30% in the fourth quarter of 1995. When the agreement's deadline approached, the United States sought another new agreement, but Japan insisted on the termination of the agreements. Meanwhile, in May 1996, the Japan Electronics and Information Technology Industries Association presented a proposal titled "Future industrial cooperation on semiconductors" to the US Semiconductor Industry Association (SIA), in which it advocated the establishment of a World Semiconductor Council (WSC). In June, the Japanese government proposed to the US government the establishment of a Global Government Forum (GGF) regarding semiconductors. Japan had, that same month, obtained agreement for a multilateral forum from the EU, which was critical of Japan–US bilateralism. Japan's approach was successful, and when the new semiconductor agreement expired in late July 1996, it was replaced by a framework of multilateral cooperation built chiefly on the support of Japan's public and private sectors. Japan and the United States agreed to the establishment of the WSC and called on other countries to establish the GGF. A decade of bilateral agreements on managed trade ended amid the shift toward multilateral cooperation based on WTO rules and market principles.

3.3.4 Steel and Anti-Dumping Suits

At the beginning of the 1990s, negotiations were pursued on establishing a multilateral steel agreement (MSA) through the GATT Uruguay Round, but the talks that started in July 1990 ended in stalemate (Abe 2013, p. 107; Yamazaki 2011, p. 258). With the failure of the MSA and the revocation of the Voluntary Restraint Agreement (VRA), US steelmakers, faced with deteriorating earnings, reasserted their protectionist stance on trade and from January to June 1992, the major US steelmakers filed 84 large anti-dumping and countervailing duties complaints. Complaints and appeals continued thereafter, and in February 1999, the US Department of Commerce issued a provisional decision on dumping that in reality initiated sanctions against Japanese steel products. The following April, following its determination that illegal dumping was occurring, the US imposed anti-dumping duties on Japanese steel. The Japanese government regarded these measures as violating WTO rules in that they (1) overestimated the injury to US industry, (2) overvalued the dumping margin, and (3) were based on unfair investigative procedures. In October 1999, Japan submitted an appeal to the WTO. The Final Report of the WTO Panel in February 2001 basically accepted Japan's argument and found the US dumping margin and damage determination in violation of the Agreement. Nevertheless, US companies continued to file complaints in the 2000s.

As mentioned above, Japan had ultimately acceded to America's demands in the negotiations that predated the "results-oriented model," although remaining opposed to them. Nevertheless, in the Framework talks from 1993 forward, Japan took the stance that it would not enter negotiations on issues raised in the context of Sect. 301 and strongly opposed the introduction of "objective criteria." The difference in interpretation between the US and Japan over numerical targets in the US–Japan Semiconductor Agreements of 1986 and 1991 generated strong resistance on Japan's part. Still, the auto and auto parts settlement had a significant impact because the announcement of a purchasing plan by Japanese manufacturers complete with numerical values had enabled the US to save face, and in that sense, the Framework talks followed a pattern of reaching agreements that were deliberately ambiguous.

Furthermore, the Clinton administration's unilateral (Sect. 301-based) and bilateral (negotiation-based) approaches to trade negotiations were in clear contradiction to the multilateral (GATT Uruguay Round) thinking that the US was advocating in other spheres. The 1995 reorganization of GATT into the WTO was a blow to America's unilateral and bilateral approaches. However, it was just at that time that the trade friction between Japan and the US began to subside.

3.3.5 Japan–EU Trade Friction Subsides

The integration of the European Union (EU), which was launched when the February 1992 Maastricht Treaty went into effect, strengthened Europe's international negotiating power. Economic relations with Japan moved from confrontation toward cooperation, with trade friction between Europe and Japan gradually subsiding. This was in part because of the prolonged recession in Japan that followed the bursting of the bubble (Abe 2013, p. 166).

A good example was the resolution of the issue of auto exports. Since before the integration, the EU had been apprehensive that the import of Japanese-made automobiles would disrupt European markets, and sought Japanese cooperation during the period leading up to complete liberalization (up to 1999). The EC Committee and MITI came to agreement in July 1991: the EU committee promised that it would not impose measures restricting the import of Japanese automobiles, and MITI in turn undertook (1) to monitor export trends during the period of transition, and (2) to clarify that, of the total projected demand for automobiles in the EC market (including former East Germany) as of 1999, Japan expected exports of 1.23 million automobiles, and that it would monitor auto exports to align with this expectation.

Japan–EC cooperation advanced rapidly. In 1994, the EU abolished discriminatory quantitative restrictions (QR) against Japan, and Japan and the EU commenced talks on regulatory reform and on a Mutual Recognition Agreement (MRA). The EU Ministerial Conference of May 1995 adopted new policies regarding Japan (*Europe and Japan: The Next Steps*) and announced the building of a relationship based on "political dialogue and cooperation," but on the economic front most noteworthy was the "Joint report on Japan–EU trade promotion measures" presented by the EC Committee and MITI at the November 1994 EU Ministerial Conference. It was a summary of trade promotion measures being advanced by Japan and the EU, and represented recognition on the EU's part that Japan's import promotion policies were contributing to imports from the EU. Further, the report on joint promotion of industrial cooperation made clear the contributions of (1) the Japan–EU industrial policy/industrial cooperation dialogue ([a] industrial cooperation on such existing sectors as household appliances, office machinery and computers, and auto parts; [b] the exchange of policy opinions regarding markets with promise for the future and deregulation; and [c] the establishment of an information policy working group); (2) JETRO's work on industrial cooperation; and (3) the establishment of the Foreign Investment in Japan Development Corporation (FIND). In this way, the economic relationship between Japan and EU advanced firmly on the path toward improvement.

3.4 Import Expansion and Market Opening

3.4.1 Import Expansion Policies

The July 1989 G7 Grande Arche Summit in Paris sought new responses to trade friction, including the clear statement in its declaration that trade surplus countries had a responsibility to increase imports. In January 1990, the Japanese government announced a three-year comprehensive import expansion policy and it began implementing this plan beginning in April (Abe 2013, p. 190). The pillars of the plan were: (1) implementation of tax incentives to promote manufactured imports;

(2) elimination of tariffs on 1,004 industrial products; (3) substantial expansion of policy financing to expand imports, (4) a "$100 million grass-roots import promotion project" sending experts overseas through JETRO for long- and short-term periods through JETRO and expanding the national budget to establish and maintain economic internationalization centers in every prefecture.

The first of these had been considered within MITI from about the mid-1980s. The Finance Ministry opposed the idea, saying that it would not benefit consumers to give preferential treatment to trading companies and import agents. It further argued that by favoring the importation of semi-finished products and machinery, Japan might be unable to avoid their being processed and re-exported, in which case the tax incentives for imports would become a tax system for expanding exports. However, the final report of the Japan–US SII talks cited "creation of a tax system for promoting manufactured imports" and because this was a de facto "international commitment," the Finance Ministry softened its stance. In business circles, the trading companies involved in expanding imports and the auto and electric industries with the greatest competitiveness showed an inclination to agree with the idea, but the textile, steel, and chemical industries that were then being overtaken by the newly industrialized economies (NIEs) were concerned about the negative impact of import expansion. As the specifics of the plan became clearer, however, greater consideration was given to those burdened by the obligation, and the relative interests of the more advantaged sectors were curtailed.

Even so, a tax system to promote imports of manufactured goods was initiated from April 1990 to apply for a period of three years. Items subject to import promotion were those "imported by the importers themselves (including on consignment)" and designated by "MITI Notification" as machinery, electrical equipment, and chemical industry products suitable for import promotion, in accordance with Cabinet Order. With regard mainly to items not subject to customs duties, the importer was allowed to reserve funds within 20% of the increase in imports in a system called the "reserve fund for developing a domestic market for imported products." Additionally, preferential treatment measures were adopted, such as tax deductions and bonus depreciation systems. The plan was extended by two years in 1993, and the conditions were relaxed and preferential policies expanded. A further two-year extension was made in 1995, and clothing items and automobile parts were added to the list.

In 1995, MITI evaluated the import promotion system as follows: "In FY 1990 and 1991, the value of products imported under this tax system expanded by 5% more than imports overall, and this tax system was effective." In fact, the ratio of targeted products to total imports increased from 20.4% in FY1989 to 26.6% in FY 1994, amidst an overall decrease in imports. But because tax reductions based on these measures in this period were falling, the causal relationship with import expansion was not necessarily clear. Rather, the significance of the import promotion tax system should be seen in the impact of announcing overseas that the Japanese government was aggressive about expanding imports.

3.4.2 JETRO's Import Promotion Projects

JETRO, which was founded in July 1958 to promote exports, expanded its role to import promotion from the late 1980s on and began managing exchanges on investment and technology with developed countries in Europe and with the United States, as well as economic cooperation with developing countries (Abe 2013, p. 210). Prior to that, JETRO was undertaking such projects on a small scale based on the government's budget for import promotion projects. With the approval of a large supplementary budget of 6.7 billion yen for import promotion measures in FY 1989, import promotion became a major pillar of JETRO activity. Its activities included: (1) supporting foreign exporters to Japan, (2) establishing import promotion hubs, and (3) providing information. The first of these involved dispatching specialists overseas and sponsoring exhibitions of samples. For example, in FY 1990, JETRO put together a project in which private-sector representatives with international business experience were publicly invited to go to Europe and the United States for periods of two to four years to unearth promising prospective export products. At the same time, JETRO dispatched import specialists on a short-term basis. They made purchases of samples of promising products and promoted their exhibition at conventions in various parts of Japan. The import promotion projects pursued by JETRO from around 1990 came to an end in November 2002, but in the meantime their main aim was to support the exports to Japan of products from the Western countries with which Japan was experiencing the greatest friction.

Another organization also had the mission of promoting imports: the Manufactured Imports Promotion Organization (MIPRO) was established in February 1978, and focused on exhibitions, information provision, and the sale of merchandise (Abe 2013, p. 222). Going into the 1990s, MIPRO jointed JETRO in expanding its import-promotion activities.

As MITI stated in its evaluation of the import promotion tax system, the primary significance of these measures lay in their showing the Japanese government's commitment to import expansion and in thereby allaying some of the friction on trade. For Japanese consumers, the perception of high-cost imported goods from the advanced economies of Europe and America changed with the advance of the bubble economy, as brand items and the like became familiar objects to affluent buyers. Cheaper goods imported from China were also coming into use. Imported products thus became part of daily life, and in that sense these import promotion measures had a widespread impact.

3.4.3 Action Programs for Market Opening

In the 1990s, the emphasis began to shift to import promotion policies giving direct incentives to expanding imports through JETRO and other means, as discussed above (Abe 2013, p. 283). However, because it was not easy to dispel the image that the Japanese market was closed, efforts to open up the market continued. At the Trade Conference in November 1995, (1) the further promotion of deregulation and (2)

"Guidelines for Improving Access to Japan Markets" were established to serve as a pillar in the improvement of business practices.

These steps were based on the Deregulation Action Program decided on in March, which asserted that: "The regulations on entry and on facilities, which were instituted with an eye to coordinating supply and demand in competitive industries, require a radical reassessment, even including the possibility of abolition, while taking into account the content and nature of the business in question." In place of more externally oriented market-opening policies, it was stressed that the standards and conformity assessment systems and labeling systems would "be brought into international conformity" in line with overseas demands. Furthermore, the Trade Conference proposed assessment surveys of the actual situation regarding access to the Japanese market.

With the presentation of these policies and the results of the surveys that followed, the government announced a Cabinet Decision in April 1999 on a bill titled Law on the Consolidation and Streamlining of Standards and Certification Systems Relating to the Ministry of International Trade and Industry. The law recognized the development and introduction of new technologies and improvements in quality control, and expressed the intent to review the division of roles between the public and private sectors and to build a system that would utilize private-sector capabilities and streamline regulation. In concrete terms, it permitted the entry of private sector companies into the government-designated agencies that conducted inspections and certifications. With the passage of this bill in August, the deregulation that accompanied further legal reform in various sectors continued, and the reform of public regulation in the standards and conformity system progressed as well.

3.5 Security Trade Controls and the Transformation of Policies on Exports

3.5.1 Changes in Security Trade Controls

The Coordinating Committee for Multilateral Strategic Export Controls (COCOM) was a gentlemen's agreement among nations of the free world, aimed at preventing cutting-edge technology from flowing out to the Communist sphere. Its regulations consisted mainly of objective checks of the destination countries and technical specifications of the export items, based on the so-called COCOM List of controls (Abe 2013, p. 336). The Japanese government issued export licenses under this agreement, but in 1987, when the Toshiba Machine Co. was found to have exported machine tools to the Soviet Union in violation of the rules (Toshiba–Kongsberg Scandal), the government was forced to consider measures to prevent a recurrence of such violations. MITI responded with the "Measures to prevent the recurrence of illegal exports of strategic materials (interim report)" in July and expanded and strengthened the examination and inspection systems. In addition, the Foreign Exchange and Foreign

Trade Control Law was partially revised in September to include stronger sanctions. The Bulk License System was inaugurated in April 1989 and procedures were simplified such that repeat transactions by exporters who undertook appropriate internal oversight would receive maximum two-year licenses rather than having to reapply with every transaction.

In the latter 1980s, however, due to political democratization and economic liberalization in Eastern Europe, the function of COCOM's export controls receded, and COCOM was abolished in March 1994. Nevertheless, with the emergence of regional ethnic and religious conflicts, a cautious stance was still needed for the transferal of weapons. Rather than restricting sales to certain countries, as COCOM had done, it became necessary to examine the end users and end use of the cargo. The abolition of COCOM was completed after agreement was reached to establish a new export control system to replace it.

Japan, which had based its administration of COCOM regulations on the "three fundamental rules concerning weapons exports," was familiar with the non-proliferation approach to export controls that were now being explored anew. The government therefore decided to participate actively in the new approach (Table 5).

International efforts in this area included the December 1995 Wassenaar Arrangement on Export Controls for Conventional Arms and Dual-Use Goods and Technologies (Wassenaar Arrangement, WA), agreed upon by 28 countries. In 2002,

Table 5 Wassenaar Arrangement (WA) and the former COCOM

Item	WA	Former COCOM
How the export controls work	Establishment of cooperative regulations based on detailed information exchange /Judgment regarding approval of individual projects is at the discretion of each country	Unanimous agreement
Regulated products	Both weapons and weapons-related general-purpose goods	Both weapons and related general-purpose goods (in reality only the latter)
Regulated regions	Exports to all regions (see note)	Communist countries
Participating countries	Open to new participating countries (including Russia, Eastern European countries)	Western countries only (including Japan)

In WA's operations, developed countries shared a concern about exports to four countries (Iran, Iraq, Libya, and North Korea), so Japan, too, decided to impose strict regulations on exports to these areas.

Source Abe (2013, p. 353)

33 countries were signatory to the Arrangement. It was a non-binding gentlemen's agreement among countries that were able to manufacture and supply conventional weapons and related items and that were willing to strive for their nonproliferation. The WA placed export controls on a wide range of general-purpose items that could be used for military purposes, and participating countries were asked to submit reports on any transfer of these items.

A new framework was also added regarding weapons of mass destruction, including nuclear, biological, and chemical weapons, and the missiles carrying them, using the international framework that predated the collapse of the Cold War regime. Japan, following the use of chemical weapons in the Iran–Iraq War, had already chosen on its own in 1984 to require MITI licenses for the export of substances that could be used for chemical weapons. Actual management of the materials took place through a method called a warning or "heads up," but in March 1993 the Know Regulation (catch-all regulation) in use in other countries was introduced to the Industrial Structure Council's Security Trade Controls Committee and was recommended for use in Japan. Catchall regulations target the export of all goods and technologies except wood products and food and were called "Know Regulations" ("knowing" that the exports were being used in weapons development). MITI revised the Foreign Exchange Control Order, Export Controls, and other regulations in October 1996, and was proceeding to make the shift to catchall regulations. However, the new method was also called a "catch-some regulation" due to the limited number of items covered, and these were modest measures compared with catchall regulations. Subsequently, in April 2002, almost all of the target items were shifted into a full-fledged catchall regulation system, and many companies involved in exports became subject to regulation and had to seek Security Export Control assessment of whether permission would or would not be required.

3.5.2 Changes in Export Policy

As mentioned in Chap. 1, the Export and Import Transaction Law ("Transactions Law") of 1952 was aimed at preventing unfair export transactions, but in the 1980s, its purpose expanded to countering economic friction with other countries and it thus became a powerful policy tool for carrying out voluntary export restraints. In November 1983, the government revised portions of the Transactions Law Enforcement Order, but this was because in July, the US government had imposed curbs on the import quantity of three specialty steel products. Japan decided to make these items subject to the export approval system so that they would not exceed US regulatory limits.

Simplification or abolition of the agreements based on this law was sought in the 1990s, however, from the point of view of deregulation (Abe 2013, p. 325). The number of agreements was reduced, and by January 1996, only eight such cases remained. In the latter 1990s, deregulation advanced with the March 1996 Cabinet Decision titled "On revision of the plan for promoting deregulation," and in 1998, the requirement for the MITI Minister's approval of exports based on the Transactions Law was abolished.

Meanwhile, the 1957 Export Inspection Law, which had functioned to support the reputation of export goods, was gradually brought under review. What had been more than 400 designated cargo items in 1973 was halved in 1980, and drastically reduced to 72 in 1990 and 39 in 1995.

The deregulation of export control procedures that had been progressing since the late 1970s was, in the mid-1990s, implemented through the revision or elimination of laws and regulations, or in other words, as part of a regulatory reform that itself significantly changed the policy system. In April 1994, the Export and Import Transaction Council of April decided on the early termination of the Law on the Unified Trademark for Export-Oriented Products by Small- and Medium-Sized Enterprises, which had been established in May 1970 to help exports recover. The Council also resolved to "abolish, likely in about three years," the Export Goods Design Law. In May, the Export Inspection and Design Promotion Council reported its findings that the Export Inspection Act should be abolished in about three years. MITI's March 1995 Deregulation Promotion Plan, which covered 148 items, did not make its main focus the items addressed by either of these laws, but stated clearly that these decommissioning bills should be submitted, the target timing being the regular Diet session in FY 1996. The Export Inspection Law and Export Design Law were thus brought to an end.

MITI also reviewed the Export/Import Transaction Law on the principle that its abolition was desirable now that exemptions to the Antimonopoly Act required review. In accordance with the guidelines of the Deregulation Promotion Plan, the Export/Import Council in March 1996 reported the abolition of all except a portion of its provisions. MITI, from the standpoint of actively promoting deregulation, submitted an amendment bill to the FY 1996 Diet session.

This led to the abolition of Export–Import Associations, and the only cartels that remained were those whose impact on the domestic market was neutral and those charged with implementing the WTO Agreement. In November 1995, the Council on Foreign Exchange and Other Transactions, which had been discussing changes to the Foreign Exchange Law, issued a final report in January 1997 that highlighted simplification of the system. Amendment of the Foreign Exchange Law became the front runner in the Japanese-style big bang (financial system reform) ordered by Prime Minister Hashimoto in November 1996, and the "foreign exchange" framework shifted from a "managed" system to a system based on the "principle of freedom." With the significant changes underway in the principles underlying currency trading, simplification of MITI's export control system also became inevitable, and in December 1997, MITI responded by revising portions of the Export Trade Control Order.

4 Measures for an Affluent Society

4.1 Promoting an Advanced Information and Telecommunications Society, IMS Programs, and the Home Health Care and Rehabilitation Equipment Industry

4.1.1 Toward an Advanced Information and Telecommunications Society

The Information Superhighway (National Information Infrastructure, NII) initiative announced in September 1993 by the Clinton administration acted as a stimulus for Japan's preparations for its information infrastructure. MITI and the Ministry of Posts and Telecommunications (MPT) explored policies for developing an advanced information society, not from the point of view of the suppliers, meaning networks, but with an emphasis on the user and therefore on content, or the content of information (Hasegawa 2013, p. 127, p. 755). This view was reflected in the May 1994 announcement of MITI's "Program for the shift to an advanced information society" and the MPT Telecommunications Council's "Toward reforms for a 21st-century knowledge-based society."

The Tsutomu Hata Administration in June 1994 established a High-Level Information Transmission Promotion Headquarters; the Tomiichi Murayama Administration in August that year did the same and began developing concepts for a Japanese version of the superhighway. Murayama's Information Promotion Headquarters decided in February 1995 on "Basic guidelines on the Promotion of an Advanced Information and Telecommunications Society." The ministries and agencies began advancing policies to this end, which were implemented by the Information Promotion Headquarters and councils of specialists. These basic plans understood "advanced information and telecommunications society" to mean the realization of a new socio-economic system for the free creation, distribution, and sharing of information and knowledge, and for harmonizing lifestyle and culture, industry and economy, nature and environment as a whole. They said that these goals required the prompt construction of information and telecommunications infrastructure. Furthermore, the plans also stressed that this process needed to be advanced under private sector leadership with only a limited range of government activity. Government policies were needed to (1) make the public sector information-based, (2) review the various systems for upgrading information transmission, (3) establish network infrastructures, (4) adopt measures on copyrights to respond to the shift to an information base, (5) adopt measures on security and privacy, (6) assure joint operability and joint connectivity, (7) supply the software, (8) undertake basic technological development, (9) nurture human resources, and other measures. Based on these concepts and their associated policies, 1995 was called "the first year of the internet," indicating the intent of upgrading information networks going forward.

Previously, based on the "Urgent recommendations: the new software age" issued by MITI in December 1992, policy priorities focused on "facilitating an environment for a software market" (Hasegawa 2013, p. 758). The "Urgent recommendations" included (1) establishing market mechanisms based on raising the level of software independence, (2) establishing basic conditions for the establishment of a market mechanism, (3) making an efficient supply system (through nurturing human resources and other means), (4) expanding the supply of packaged software, (5) developing user responses (such that users think of software not as an accessory to hardware, but as having value in and of itself), (6) enabling fair relationships between hardware and software vendors, and (7) developing government responses (statistical infrastructure, improvement of government procurement market, and so on).

MITI promoted this shift to an information economy in the hopes that it would act as an engine for economic recovery. Public projects for information transmission meant the construction of research facilities, the provision of computers and other information transmission equipment, and the promotion of cutting-edge technology and R&D by new industries as part of economic recovery plans. Further, from FY 1996, the government gradually expanded the areas it addressed and began promoting an "information industry policy" that would assure the interoperability of systems. It also took on the promotion of the software industry. Prior to FY 2000, MITI had thus devoted a large budget to information-related policies, and the supplementary budget related to software in particular emphasized demand through the offices of the Information-Technology Promotion Agency.

4.1.2 Promotion of e-commerce

MITI's above-mentioned "Program for the shift to an advanced information society" complemented and strengthened the role of government in private sector initiatives. Specifically, this meant promotion of an advanced information society in both the public and the private sector. The future industrial information systems as envisioned by this program were electronic commerce (EC) and computer-aided logistical support (CALS) (Hasegawa 2013, p. 780).

As part of its EC promotion projects, MITI established the Study Group for Improving the Environment for EC as a private advisory body of the Director-General for the Machinery and Information Industries Bureau and the Director-General for Commerce and Distribution Policy. In April 1995, the Study Group compiled an interim report on the legal issues surrounding e-commerce. The EC Promotion Council of Japan (ECOM) was established in January 1996 as a voluntary private sector organization for supporting experiments in e-commerce. Its activities included studies of technological development to improve the common infrastructure for EC, support and coordination of experiments in EC, and studies of institutional issues in e-commerce. Meanwhile, inter-company e-commerce was also promoted, with public offerings and expanded support for such projects by the Electronics Policy Division and the IPA (Information-technology Promotion Agency) in January 1996.

The CALS advanced in the 1990s had been devised by the US Department of Defense (DOD) in September 1985 as a measure for rationalizing DOD procurement of equipment. To promote CALS, MITI assigned approximately 400 million yen in its FY 1995 budget to R&D on integrated information systems for production, procurement, and operations support and established a technical association specifically focused on production, distribution and operations of thermal power plants.

Policies for advancing the information basis of the public sector were also promoted in the 1990s. These were in part economic stimulus projects included in the FY 1993 third supplementary budget and the FY 1994 budget in response to the weakening of the private sector due to the collapse of the bubble economy. Based on these plans, MITI formulated its own "Administrative Information Technology Promotion Plan (FY 1995–1999 Five-Year Plan)" and promoted improvements in the efficiency and sophistication of administration, including improved public access for citizens and paperless administrative services. These MITI-specific projects were regarded as pilot projects that could result in models for the government at large and led to the government's establishment in January 1997 of the "Kasumigaseki Wide Area Network (Kasumigaseki WAN)," a communication network enabling ministries and agencies to exchange e-mail.

4.1.3 Promotion of IMS Programs

In August 1989, the Factory Automation (FA) Vision Council, a private body under the Director-General of the Machinery and Information Industries Bureau, compiled a report on the outlook for factory automation. The report found that the conventional interpretation of FA as meaning the automation and integration of all business activities did not adequately convey the range of innovation in production technologies. The report called for planning for the coordination of people and machinery and for viewing the production activities of industry in their entirety as an integrated system. Intelligent Manufacturing Systems (IMS) accordingly became the first policy priority (Hasegawa 2013, p. 258).

The IMS policy was notable in its promotion of collaborative research programs internationally, an approach that flowed from separate strands of development. First was the existing industrial machinery policy, which led to policy involvement in the development of unmanned factories, the robotics industry, and mechanical systematization. Second was the ongoing trade friction with the outside world, which made forwarding systems for international cooperation a policy priority. While utilizing a range of intelligent activities in manufacturing industries and integrating intelligent machines with people, IMS could flexibly integrate and coordinate all corporate activities from order entry to design, production, and sales: it was thus defined as a system for improving productivity. In order to achieve this goal, MITI urged that Japan become an advocate for international collaborative research and development in the field of production technology.

This joint research was based on an awareness of the need to address problems shared by industrialized countries, including the hollowing out of industry and decline in manufacturing technology, changes in the working environment and the loss of manufacturing industries, the diversification of consumer needs, the emergence of "isolated islands of automation" (partial automation) at manufacturing sites, the globalization of existing technologies, the insufficient systematization of current technologies, and other issues. Joint research was expected to contribute to the effort to overcome these challenges by (1) avoiding duplicate investment in development resources, (2) developing dream technologies, and (3) unifying international understanding of production technologies. Essential to the smooth development of this joint research was the handling of intellectual property rights, and here, too, the IMS programs created international regulations and required that all participants abide by them.

With these conditions, IMS steadily added more projects year by year, and in 1999, the program's fourth year, 16 R&D projects were underway (Japan participated in 12 of these), with a total of about 400 participating enterprises, universities, and research institutes, including over 100 Japanese companies and universities. In addition, participating countries submitted proposals for over 30 new projects.

However, following the reforms of the public benefit corporation system in the 2000s, national budget allocations to public interest corporations like the IMS Center were deemed inappropriate. This made various changes necessary, such as the replacement of IMS Center leadership by the New Energy and Industrial Technology Development Organization (NEDO). It also became apparent with Phase II that the projects taking place abroad were not necessarily active. In April 2010 it was determined that IMS had sufficiently fulfilled its original aims, and the curtain was closed on its historic role.

The Council on Basic Issues in the Space Industry compiled a summary report in July 1996. Entitled "Toward the takeoff of the space industry," it proposed measures for promotion of the space industry. However, despite the hopes expressed in the report, budget allocations depend heavily on public demand in Japan, meaning that budget increases, and therefore development of the space industry, faced significant financial constraints.

4.1.4 Promotion of the Home Care and Rehabilitation Equipment ("Welfare Equipment") Industry

Among MITI's policy initiatives in the mid-1970s were subsidies and leasing systems for R&D in welfare equipment, launched in FY 1976 (Hasegawa 2013, p. 573). The subsidies began as an R&D consignment system with a budget of 300 million yen, with measures such as establishing venues for joint research by creating a Research Laboratory for the Medical and Rehabilitation Technology Research Association under the Law for Mining and Manufacturing Technology Research Associations.

The leasing systems arose from the understanding that the generally high cost of welfare equipment would act as a barrier to its spread. Methods were explored by which users would not be required to make large outlays of capital on purchasing the equipment, by making it available on a leased basis at relatively low cost. Since the leasing companies would be making bulk purchases from the producers, it was anticipated that a leasing system could increase sales as well. The leasing enterprises' purchases of the equipment were financed through the Development Bank. While this forced a large reduction in the 1980s scale of operations, the financing system continued until 1991 and thereafter as well, although the headings of the line items changed.

New developments arose in the 1990s on policies for the welfare equipment industry. One of the triggers for these developments was the June 1992 report of the Agency of Industrial Science and Technology, which took up the issue of supporting practical developments to address aging, and which also proposed that such subsidy policies be promoted to "enlarge measures complementary to the market principle." The February 1993 report by the Industrial Technology Council's Subcommittee on Policies on Welfare Equipment Technology pointed out problems in the research and development of such equipment and, significantly, urged that "it was necessary to consider appropriate legal measures." Accordingly, the Law Concerning the Promotion of Research and Development and the Diffusion of Social Welfare Equipment, jointly sponsored by MITI and the Ministry of Welfare, was passed in May 1993 and came into effect in October.

After the implementation of the Welfare Equipment Law, the Machine Information Bureau in FY 1995 began seeking data on conditions in the industry, for example with its "Survey on development trends in welfare equipment." In April 1996, a consultation group was established as a private advisory body to the Director General of the Machine Information and Commerce Bureau, and carried out surveys with the aim of better organizing the basic direction of industrial policy. It concluded that new markets could be developed through the effective use of market principles, to prompt the industry to exploit the potential for industrial development and compete to develop products oriented to consumer needs. Based on the survey results compiled by MITI's Commerce and Information Policy Bureau in March 2002, the market grew steadily from its FY 1993 level of 773.1 billion yen, but FY 2000, at 1,138.9 billion yen, was the first year to show a decrease (0.3%) from the previous year. Although expectations had been high for this new sector of industrial policy given the aging society of the twenty-first century, satisfactory results were still proving hard to come by.

4.1.5 The Promotion of Biotechnology

The Bio-industry Office of the Basic Industries Bureau believed that advances in biotechnology would contribute to the development of ecologically friendly products that use raw materials derived from renewable organisms, and from the late 1980s promoted R&D with the expectation that applications would soon be forthcoming (Yamazaki 2011, p. 370). With this aim, MITI gave its support to projects in DNA analysis, the development of biodegradable plastics, and bioremediation.

For the DNA analysis project, the Kazusa DNA Research Institute was founded in March 1991, in coordination with Chiba Prefecture plans based on the Technopolis Plan. It was intended to develop analyses of the structure of DNA, research on analytical techniques, research on DNA functions and their applications, and the collection and provision of data pertaining to DNA. It also would promote the creation of new industries, advancements in the industrial structure, and advances in chemical technologies. The research facility was completed in October 1994, and the first project was an analysis of cyanobacteria. In April 1996, the Helix Research Institute Corporation was established within the laboratory to analyze complementary DNA (cDNA) and its functions. Part of the research could not be expected to yield useful functions in the near term because of numerous international patent applications. Actively publicizing that research beginning in February 2000 played an important role by preventing further patenting. Other DNA analyses of microorganisms and related items were promoted as well, and these were boosted by policies to establish laboratories and present R&D plans that took into account the needs of people and the environment.

The October 1998 "Report of the Council on becoming a bio-industry nation in the 21st Century" recognized that, in the field of biotech research, the US dominated in human genome analysis and that Europe and the US between them dominated such intellectual property rights as gene patents, and that therefore the gap between Japan's bio-industry and that of Europe and America was only widening. The cause was understood to be the inadequacy of many systems, including R&D, human resources, technology transfer, and financing, and also the lack of organic collaboration. Thus, although the level of basic research was not inferior to that of Europe and the US, the gap was great when it came to turning that research into enterprises and industries. To reduce the disparity would require strengthening collaboration between industry, academia and government, integrating research and industry geographically, improving financing methods, and so on.

4.1.6 Efforts to Create a Biotech Industry

Efforts to make basic research commercially viable were accelerated, based on the December 1998 interim report and February 1999 final report by the Economic Strategy Council (established in August 1998 directly under the Prime Minister), which said that nurturing the biotech industry was a principal target for Japan's twenty-first-century national technological development (Yamazaki 2011, p. 391).

The "Industrial Revitalization Plan" decided by the Cabinet in January 1999 entailed the provision of support for venture businesses' technological development. In this connection, MITI strongly recommended biotechnology-related projects, and its policy was reflected in the Industrial Revitalization Plan itself. The Director-General of the Science and Technology Agency and the Ministers of MITI, Education, Welfare, and Agriculture, Forestry and Fisheries, produced the "Basic Plan for Creating a Biotechnology Industry." The "Basic Plan," although acknowledging that the biotech sector could be expected to increase high-quality employment and opportunities for new business, addressed biotech businesses that faced delays and called for (1) accelerating basic research on genome analysis, (2) strengthening support for commercializing research, (3) strengthening R&D aimed at biotechnology applications, and (4) promoting the advancement and utilization of biotechnology in universities. On this basis, the five ministries and agencies developed the "Basic strategy for creating a biotechnology industry" in July 1999. This included proposals to expand competitive financing, upgrade incentives, and facilitate the efforts of national university faculty members to engage in business, in order to strengthen research and development systems that produced creative outcomes.

Safety guidelines were reviewed in parallel with these efforts. With regard to safety in biotech industrialization, MITI announced guidelines for Recombinant DNA Technology in 1986, and the Chemical Products Council deliberated on the safety of industrialization plans formulated and planned by business operators. In September 1997, MITI established a Guidelines Examination Subcommittee reporting to the Recombinant DNA Technology Subcommittee of the Chemical Products Council to review the subject.

Its March 1998 report titled "On an ideal plan for the future industrialization of recombinant DNA" called for the following: (1) avoiding duplication in the safety assessments and examinations found in the existing guidelines and simplifying procedures, (2) alleviating the burden on businesses that were unsure how to evaluate their position because the Good Industrial Large-Scale Practices (GILSP) were designed principally to "minimize leakage," and (3) reviewing the scope of the government's certifications and simplifying those procedures as well. Deregulation of the industry was advanced based on these proposals.

4.1.7 Globalization of the Petrochemicals Industry

In the latter 1980s, the petrochemical industry faced the question of how to respond to changes in its immediate environment, including the plans for new development of large-scale petrochemical plants in the Asian NIEs, Saudi Arabia, and Central and South America, uncertainty about the future of the global economy, and fluidity in the conditions surrounding raw materials.

In January 1989, MITI consulted the Chemical Industry Committee about "the petrochemical industry of the 1990s and ideal strategies" and received the Committee's report in June 1989. Based on the three principles of internationalization, cooperation, and individuation, the report cited seven issues for policy to address: (1) raw materials, (2) demand, (3) sales and distribution, (4) security, (5) environment, (6) R&D, and (7) internationalization (Yamazaki 2011, p. 87).

Policy on raw materials included an extension of the tax exemption for naphtha that had been in effect since the 1980s and the addition of a tax exemption for heavy LNG from April 1992. Additionally, with deregulation in 1995, petrochemical businesses were permitted to import oil. Not only were raw material procurement costs rationalized through tax exemptions and deregulation, but also the foundations were laid for diversifying the raw materials in use.

Internationalization issues included the promotion of free trade through progress in tariff reductions and the issue of yen appreciation. Based on the report of the International Subcommittee of the Petrochemical Products Demand and Supply Council, the Basic Chemicals Division focused on the factors driving the domestic and international price gap in petrochemical products. These included the large number of product grades (varieties), services to customers, just-in-time delivery, and details of logistical services such as frequent, small-lot deliveries. This led to the decision to consider countermeasures for those market environments where price preferences were strengthening. As indicated in the February 1996 Report of the Council on Basic Issues in the Petrochemical Industry, "The cost competitiveness of Japanese petrochemical companies is not internationally inferior at the production stage." Based, therefore, on the recognition that "if the government improves the business environment and adopts appropriate measures, [Japanese petrochemical companies] will be able to reach a par with overseas enterprises," the decision was made to pursue efforts to establish core businesses for the global market environment.

Regarding sales and distribution, concerns were mounting in the 1990s about the commercial system, specifically such areas as logistical costs and business practices. In 1990, MITI issued guidelines for improving business practices, and in 1992, it formulated guidelines for rationalizing logistics in 21 industries, such as raw materials. These sought to assure transparency, to remove impediments to the rationalization of business operations, and to improve international harmonization. For example, when, based on the 1994 results of FY1993 survey data, improvements were sought in the commercial practices related to resins for polyolefin film, a Commercial Practices Committee was established in the Council on Basic Issues in the Petrochemical Industry in February 1995. The Committee issued a report saying that reliance on the price mechanism would be the most efficient approach to strengthening the competitiveness of resin and resin-processing manufacturers. To that end, the Committee took up the issue of correcting the commercial practice of "ex post facto pricing." Ex post facto pricing was a trading method in which the price was not finalized at the selling stage, but after the fact. The purpose of the system was to support the many medium-sized, small, and very small resin manufacturers that made up the industry. The practice was deemed to be restrictive, however, and to be hindering reasonable corporate management in that it made it hard to forecast revenue and thereby increased the cost of price negotiations. Reform therefore became desirable. By reaching out to the industry's companies through the Petrochemical Industry Association, it was possible to revise the practice, and as a result, "pre-pricing," which in 1995 was used in only 67% of low-concentration polyethylene transactions, accounted for 94.4% of transactions by 2001.

4.2 *Establishment of the Environment Law and Promotion of Recycling*

4.2.1 The UN Environment Programme and International Cooperation

A number of developments in the 1970s continued to determine the framework of response to international environmental problems (Takeda 2011, p. 475). In 1972, the International Environmental Action Plan was formulated based on the decision of the United Nations Conference on the Human Environment. In May of the same year, the OECD confirmed the Polluter-Pays Principle (PPP), and in November 1974, it adopted the "Declaration on Environmental Policy" and a 10-point action plan. Multilateral cooperative systems of this kind were also advanced on the bilateral level. For example, the Japan–US Environmental Protection Cooperation Agreement was signed in August 1975, and a joint planning coordination committee was established.

With the global economic downturn from the latter 1970s into the early 1980s, international efforts on environmental issues lagged. However, in July 1980 under US President Jimmy Carter, the Council on Environmental Quality and the State Department issued a report titled *The Earth in 2000*, triggering the call for renewed movement in this area. Japan's Environment Agency produced a report emphasizing an international approach and presented this in May 1982 at the UN Conference on the Human Environment. This led to the establishment of the World Commission on Environment and Development, which was charged with laying out an ideal vision of the global environment. The Declaration issued by the Commission in Tokyo in February 1987 pointed out the importance of sustainable development, meaning that the upgrading and improvement of the environment and resource base should take place through development, which would give rise to further progress and development.

Meanwhile, within Japan, regulatory measures were sought to address chlorofluorocarbons (CFCs), which had already become a problem in the US in the 1970s. MITI took a cautious stance towards CFC regulation by the Environment Agency. The September 1980 Basic Industries Bureau report "On Freon gas" opposed regulation on the argument that the science was not yet sufficiently clear. The Bureau's view that a clear scientific basis was needed to enact regulation was much the same as that of the Industrial Location and Environmental Protection Bureau on pollution regulations. Even so, the Montreal Protocol on Substances that Deplete the Ozone Layer was adopted in September 1987 by the United Nations Environment Programme (UNEP), a United Nations subsidiary body, and because Japan was a signatory to the Protocol, MITI and the Environment Ministry proceeded in 1988 to work on writing the necessary legislation. Thus the Law Concerning the Protection of the Ozone Layer through the Regulation of Specified Substances and Other Measures was established in May that year, and initiatives were launched to eliminate the use of CFCs.

4.2.2 Responses to Global Environmental Problems

MITI did not necessarily regard global environmental problems as a priority issue for policy until the latter 1980s, but in May 1990, the Regional Promotion and Environment Policy Subcommittee of the Industrial Structure Council's 1990s Policy Committee issued an interim report saying that the delays caused by waiting for clarification of the science would be harmful and because delay in such a matter could prove decisive, it urged both improved scientific understanding of the issues and the development of concrete measures to address them (Takeda 2011, p. 486).

MITI's position was that economic development needed to be balanced with global environmental conservation, and that industrial activities should be carefully regulated with due priority given to environmental policy. This approach, articulated in the MITI's "Earth Revitalization Plan," was adopted in the consultations on global environment conservation at the ministerial meeting one month after the above interim report.

Negotiations on the UN Framework Convention on Climate Change opened in May 1992, and along with agreeing to an international treaty on the control of emissions such as carbon dioxide, the UN Conference on Environment and Development (Earth Summit) was launched in Rio de Janeiro in June. In response to these developments, the Industrial Structure Council's Global Environment Committee prepared a report in May that cited the need for (1) efforts with a comprehensive point of view that addressed economic growth, energy, and environmental conservation as a trio of related issues, (2) acceleration of technological responses from a long-term view, and (3) promotion of international cooperation and related measures. In addition, the November Joint Meeting of the Industrial Structure Council, General Energy Research Committee, and Industrial Technology Council issued the report, "On future energy and environment measures." The report, with the subtitle, "Fourteen earth restoration proposals aimed at harmonizing environment, economics, and energy," confirmed the government's intent of treating economic growth, energy, and environmental protection together, and therefore stressed the need for technological breakthroughs; moreover, as this was by its nature uncertain, the report urged the importance of changing each individual person's lifestyle. The autonomy of business activities in environmental measures was also stressed.

Referring to the First Conference of the Parties (COP) held in 1995, Japan established the "Japan Program for Joint Implementation of the Framework Convention on Climate Change," and on the premise that the first projects based on the program would be certified by late March 1996, held repeated discussions among the ministries and agencies in the Ministry–Agency Liaison Meeting for Joint Implementation Activities. Based on the results of these meetings, it was decided that MITI would actively advance projects for joint implementation, with a special focus on the Asian region.

4.2.3 Responses to the Kyoto Conference

To formulate Japan's response to the Kyoto Protocol Climate Conference scheduled for 1997 (Takeda 2011, p. 503), the Global Environment Subcommittee of the Industrial Structure Council began in April 1996 to examine the issues involved in the Framework Convention on Climate Change. Its July "Issue Memo" pointed out the difficulty of fulfilling an international commitment to maintain per capita carbon dioxide emissions in the year 2000 at their 1990 level. According to the Memo, what was needed was (1) to strengthen the operation of the Law Concerning the Rational Use of Energy ("Energy Conservation Law"), (2) to follow up on the Vision for the Industrial Environment, and (3) to provide measures, technological development, and technical aid for developing nations directed at the years beyond the year-2000 target. The results of the examination of these issues and others were compiled in the 1997 *COP3 Kyoto Conference Guidelines*. Measures on energy conservation, new energy, and nuclear energy were strengthened, and the means most emphasized were those intended to stimulate the voluntary efforts of corporate enterprises. The Guidelines also pointed out the importance of recognizing that climate change is not just an environmental issue but an energy and economic issue as well, and that it is an issue that affects every individual.

COP3 took account of the demands of developing countries such that the agreement limited the mandatory cuts only to advanced nations. This was in part because of the severity of the conflicts of interest among the nations, but despite calls for caution from within the government, Prime Minister Hashimoto gave strong support to establishing the Kyoto Protocol, and the Prime Minister's Office took the lead in July 1997 to create a draft. Beginning in August, the government also organized the "Joint Meeting on the Relationship of Domestic Countermeasures to Global Warming Issues" to give ongoing consideration to the Protocol. At the Conference, a strong confrontation emerged between the Environment Agency and MITI on setting targets. Although MITI's proposal was deemed realistic, the proposal for standards was based on the government proposal, which prioritized the view of other participating countries. The report of the Joint Meeting pointed out that addressing global warming was a long-term task requiring efforts to reduce greenhouse gas over a period of 100 years or longer, and that the measures that were needed by 2010 included the use of new energy and nuclear power to help reduce CO_2 emissions, as well as energy conservation efforts on the demand side to meet the targets. The government attended the Kyoto Conference with these studies in hand and sought agreement on the Kyoto Protocol to the UN Framework Convention on Climate Change (Kyoto Protocol). The content of the agreement set targets for the reduction of six types of gases causing the greenhouse effect, requiring a reduction in emissions in the 2008–2012 period of at least 5% from 1990 levels—8% for the EU, 7% for the US, and 6% for Japan. The Industrial Structure Council's Global Environment Committee's views were evident in the setting of different targets for different countries, but compared with the views of the Joint Conference, and given the Committee's projections that even maintaining 1990 levels would be hard, these represented very stringent targets.

4.2.4 Efforts Toward Achieving the Kyoto Protocol

On December 12, 1997, after the conclusion of the Kyoto Conference, MITI issued "On future measures regarding global warming" in the form of a Decision of the MITI Departmental Council (Takeda 2011, p. 515). It included revisions to the Energy Conservation Law, follow-up on Keidanren's Voluntary Environmental Action Plan and supplementary measures, promoting the introduction of energy conservation technologies, and furthering the development and introduction of non-petroleum-based energy. In June 1998, the government formulated an "Outline on the promotion of measures to combat global warming," which urged a series of domestic measures.

However, criticism gradually mounted in Japan against the Kyoto Protocol's imposition of the cuts only on specific countries. The economic downturn that began in autumn 1997 strengthened business opposition to the requirements. Furthermore, the COP6 talks broke down in 2000 without producing actual results, and the US withdrew from the Kyoto Protocol in March 2001, making it hard to form consensus for its ratification even in Japan.

Keidanren had taken a cautious stance against an excessive strengthening of regulations, favoring a voluntary action plan for reducing greenhouse gas emissions. It stressed two points: first, that with the US withdrawal and the failure of diplomatic efforts to add developing countries to the framework, the treaty imposed an unfair burden, and the rush to ratify it was too hasty; and second, that measures imposed on the commercial sector were inadequate. METI (successor to MITI since 2001) accordingly reoriented its basic position to favor domestic measures with minimal impact on the economy. MITI/METI's fundamental thinking was consistent in its emphasis on balancing the needs of the environment and the economy while imposing the burden fairly on both the industrial and the commercial sectors. Agreement on an international framework for the Kyoto Protocol was reached at Marrakesh in October 2001, and the Japanese government decided to ratify it in 2002, issuing a new Decision, "Outline on Promoting Measures on Global Warming," in 2003.

Although METI adhered to its basic principles, it nevertheless shifted to the new framework in the 1990s. That is, while it hesitated to prioritize environmental conservation, which it saw as running counter to energy supply stability and sustainable economic development, it also tried to maximize voluntary action by companies and achieve the objectives where essential measures were concerned. The December 1994 Cabinet Decision on the Basic Environmental Plan (which was based on the Environmental Basic Law, to be discussed below) gave greatest stress to measures to promote consideration for the environment in corporate behavior. The envisioned measures were summarized in "Project to promote environmentally friendly corporate behavior," which was an important pillar of environmental policy in the latter 1990s.

4.2.5 Establishment of the Environmental Impact Assessment Law

The following problems were later raised in the implementation process of the Environmental Impact Assessment Act that resulted from the Cabinet Decision of August 1984: (1) the environmental assessors lacked sufficient skills, (2) businesses also lacked the technical capabilities to evaluate the survey results, and (3) the methods were not yet established. As a result of these issues, calls mounted for legal support and for institutionalizing the participation of local residents (Takeda 2011, p. 381).

Making global environmental concerns a policy issue in the 1990s necessitated a review of the existing legal framework of the Environmental Pollution Prevention Law. At the request of Prime Minister Kiichi Miyazawa, a review was launched in March 1993 to establish the legal underpinnings for an era of global environment concerns. Business organizations such as Keidanren responded by deciding that business should undertake voluntary action rather than be subject to government regulation.

The Environmental Basic Law established in November 1993 said that in order to assure a healthy and cultured life for present and future citizens and to contribute to the welfare of humanity, it was the duty of every type of business to take the environment into account and to do so in every type of business activity. The Basic Environment Plan (December 1994 Cabinet Decision) made environmental impact assessment one of the fundamental measures for environmental conservation. Further, the June 1996 report of the Comprehensive Study Group on Environmental Impact Assessment (composed of the ministries and agencies concerned) called for legislation on the environmental impact assessment law. MITI took the stance that there was little need for legislation on power generation plants; industry did not raise much objection, because factories fell outside the scope of the new law, and because there was little anticipation of the large-scale factory sites that would later become targets of the law.

The general principle of environmental impact assessment was deemed applicable to power plants, and the revision of the Electric Utility Industry Law addressed special procedures that distinguished power plants from other enterprises. With the June 1997 Environmental Impact Assessment Law and Partial Revision of the Electric Utility Industry Law, assessments of power plants, previously carried out by Ministry Decision, became subject to legal procedure.

4.2.6 Full-Scale Development of Recycling Policy

In early-1990s responses to illegal dumping, existing waste regulation emphasized the issue of disposal but lacked ways to curb waste generation itself. Once it was understood that the distinction between non-industrial and industrial waste no longer conformed to actual conditions of disposal, the need to address the problem became clear (Takeda 2011, p. 421). In August 1990, MITI created the Recycling Promotion Office and established a Committee on Waste Disposal and Resource Recycling within the Industrial Structure Council. The Committee issued a report in December 1990 titled "On future waste disposal and resource recycling measures" that laid out the direction for a number of measures for implementing waste reduction, resource recycling, and ease of processing in production, distribution, and consumption processes. Especially significant was its emphasis on the effectiveness of issuing concrete guidelines on waste products, by type, to businesses. The report envisioned a shift to an economic society that would naturally absorb resource conservation and reuse.

Based on this report, the Law for the Promotion of Utilization of Recycled Resources ("Recycling Law") was adopted in April 1991. The Law (1) stipulated that the appropriate minister was to formulate and announce basic policy for the comprehensive promotion of the use of recycled resources; (2) determined the general responsibilities of business operators, consumers, and national and local public bodies; (3) stated that recommendations would be made to businesses and dealers in industries and products specified by the government, with the aim of promoting the use of recycled resources as raw materials. In this way the bill on recycling raw materials, first conceived in the mid-1970s, was realized after more than 15 years through legal measures to encourage voluntary efforts by businesses in accordance with established guidelines.

Prior to the implementation of the Recycling Law, the Environmental Policy Division of the Industrial Location and Environmental Protection Bureau designated target industries and products and formulated and announced its basic policy on them. In September 1992, the Industrial Structure Council Waste Disposal and Recycling Subcommittee conducted a comprehensive inspection of the progress being made and urged the addition of further target areas. The Committee again studied the progress of the policy in 1993 and issued recommendations in July 1994. These investigations found that the Recycling Law and the June 1993 Law on Temporary Measures to Promote Business Activities for the Rational Use of Energy and the Utilization of Recycled Resources had achieved certain results in the use of recycled resources, but also pointed out the following issues: that waste emissions were not showing any remarkable decline, that existing disposal capacity was nearing its limit, and that the costs of disposal in general were increasing year by year. The Committee proposed a significant expansion of usage-based processing fees and of municipal sorting systems for waste, and also urged that consumers and businesses cooperate with the separation and collection of waste by municipalities and used-paper collectors. MITI added target areas and revised its guidelines in April 1996.

Through the above measures, the glass bottle and can recycling rates increased from immediately after the laws' establishment, and recycling of used paper increased from the latter 1990s on. The administrative effort to promote the municipal collection and recycling of separated items contributed greatly to these outcomes.

4.2.7 Reorganization of the Environmental Protection and Industrial Location Bureau and Promotion of Recycling

In July 1993, MITI reorganized the Industrial Location and Pollution Bureau into the Environmental Protection and Industrial Location Bureau (Takeda 2011, p. 441). This meant that industrial pollution issues came to be considered within the framework for environmental measures, and the Environmental Protection and Industrial Location Bureau thereafter advanced policies on recycling industrial waste into raw materials.

The first step was taken with the establishment of the Law for the Promotion of Sorted Collection and Recycling of Containers and Packaging in June 1995, which promoted the sorted recycling and repurposing of bottles, cans, paper, and plastic containers and packaging. The appropriate minister was to prepare and publish basic recycling policies and plans, which would take specific form in municipal and prefectural plans for sorted collection. At the same time, it became mandatory for those disposing of containers and packaging to properly sort and dispose of them and to meet set volumes for the recycling of particular types of containers. Businesses were permitted to pass the cost burden on to consumers and to use public relations efforts to seek consumers' understanding of the higher prices. The aim of this law was to change people's outlook on waste, so that waste would be curtailed and reuse maximized at each stage—product development, manufacturing, and consumption. The ultimate aim was to build economic and social systems based on recycling and on reduced environmental impact. Beginning with glass bottles and PET bottles in April 1997, items slated for recycling were added as needed. As a result of the Container Recycling Law, the volume of glass bottles in landfill was reduced by 55% as of FY 1999.

While the containers and packaging issue showed progress, recycling measures for cars, household appliances, and other such products were carried forward into the late 1990s. The disposal of cars had previously rested on buy-back payments but the cost burden was now shifted to the person disposing of the car. But new problems were emerging, such as the securing of landfill disposal sites and reducing the amount of shredder dust, which was hard to process. The Industrial Structure Council's Waste Disposal and Raw Materials Recycling Committee therefore launched studies in October 1995, and with the revision of the Recycling Law in 2000, automakers were called upon not only to reduce (reduce raw materials; increase longevity) and reuse, but also to absorb recycling into the manufacturing stage itself. The Central Environment Council's March 2002 report called for legislation, and METI and the Ministry of the Environment (successor of the Environment Agency since 2001) took up the task of creating that legislation. July saw the promulgation of the Law for the Recycling of End-of-Life Vehicles, which (1) determined the division of roles of the stakeholders, and (2) made car owners responsible for the cost of recycling. Additionally, the June 1998 Law for the Recycling of Specified Kinds of Home Appliances required manufacturers to take back and recycle their products and retailers to receive and pass them on, and for consumers to cooperate by bearing the cost burden of collecting and recycling the used products (Table 6).

While these efforts produced results for a specified period, their limits were also becoming clear. In particular, used paper, for which recycling had been instituted especially early, was designated under the Recycling Law, and its target reuse rate was raised to 55% by FY 1994, but the target was not met. At MITI's request, The Japan Papermaking Association established a new target of 56% by FY 2000, and met that goal by FY 1999, but this constituted an improvement in recycling rates of no more than 1%.

Table 6 Advances in recycling (%)

Year	Old paper		Recyclable packaging	Glass	Steel cans	Aluminium cans	PET bottles	Styrofoam	
	Recovery rate	Utilization ratio					Recovery rate	A	B
1990					44.8				
1991					50.1			12.6	
1992	52.5	51			56.8				
1993	53	51.2			61				
1994	53.3	51.7	19.9	55.6	69.8	61.1			
1995	53.4	51.5		61.3	73.8	65.7		27.3	
1996	53.6	51.3	22.7	65	77.3	70.2		28.7	
1997	54	53		67.4	79.6	72.6	9.8	30.2	
1998	54.9	55.2	25.1	73.9	82.5	74.4	16.9	31.2	51.5
1999	56.1	55.7		78.6	82.9	78.5	22.8	33.2	55
2000	57	57.7	28.8	77.8	84.2	80.6	34.5	35	58
2001	61.5	58	30.2	82	85.2	82.8	40.1	37.8	60.1
2002	65.4	59.6	31.1	83.3	86.1	83.1	45.6	39.1	64.7
2003	66.1	60.2	34.3	90.3	87.5	81.8	48.5	39.3	65.6
2004	68.5	60.4		90.7	87.1	86.1	46.4	41	69.3

Based on METI, Sangyo Gijyutsu Kankyō-kyoku 2005.
Recyclable packaging, Steel cans, and Aluminium cans: recycling rate; Glass: cullet utilization rate; Styrofoam A: material recycling rate; Styrofoam B: recycling rate including thermal recycling rate.
Source Takeda (2011, p. 441)

In January 1997, the Waste Disposal and Resource Recycling Committee issued a report titled "On future measures for industrial waste products"; because of the context of constraints on final disposal sites, the stalling of reductions and recycling, and the problem of illegal dumping, it proposed shifting to a "recycling-oriented economic system" in many major industries, involving numerical targets for the reduction and recycling of industrial waste and strengthening the waste producer's responsibility for proper disposal.

This line of thinking, and that in the July 1999 report of the Joint Subcommittee on Basic Problems (of the Waste Products and Recycling Committee in the Global Environment Committee of the Industrial Structure Council), made clear the urgency of establishing a "recycling-oriented economic system" that called for maximizing energy efficiency, and strengthening the partnership between enterprise, consumer, and administration. The result was the June 2000 Basic Law for Establishing a Recycling-Based Society as well as a Recycling Law for raw materials needed in construction and for food products. The Basic Law, aimed at forming a "recycling-oriented society," regarded all target products as "waste" products regardless of whether they had value or not, and it aimed to curb waste disposal and focus on the potential usefulness of waste products as recyclable resources.

4.2.8 Responding to Minamata Disease

In March 1973, the Kumamoto District Court ordered Chisso Corporation to pay compensation to Minamata Disease victims. This caused an immediate threat to Chisso's commercial survival. The government's response, seen in the June 1978 Cabinet Agreement titled "On Minamata Disease Countermeasures," was to maintain financial support until a fundamental review to be undertaken in 1999. Kumamoto Prefecture issued prefectural bonds in order to assist Chisso with the financing needed for the required compensation. This approach aimed to maintain the polluter pays, principle while at the same time ensuring, by maintaining and strengthening Chisso's ability to operate, that the payments themselves would not be impeded. For the same reason, the Japan Development Bank offered capital investment financing for a Chisso subsidiary beginning in 1981, while in 1994 other measures were taken to mitigate Chisso's interest burden and to establish a fund for promoting the revitalization of the Minamata–Ashikita region (Yamazaki 2011, p. 144). Despite these measures, however, Chisso's accumulated debt including the prefectural bonds exceeded 200 billion yen in 1999, and it became obvious that repayment was no longer possible. With a Cabinet Decision in February 2002, the framework decided upon in 1978 was changed to partially exempt Chisso from repayment of both the government's subsidies and its debts to financial institutions.

4.2.9 Safety Management for Chemical Substances

Safety management for chemical substances shifted toward deregulation from the 1990s forward (Yamazaki 2011, p. 485). The October 1973 Law Concerning the Examination and Regulation of Manufacture of Chemical Substances (Act on the Evaluation of Chemical Substances and Regulation of Their Manufacture) stipulated, first, that all new chemical substances, other than those publicly pronounced safe according to existing chemical rosters or examination procedures, must obtain a government determination of its safeness before being manufactured or imported; and second, that chemical substances that do not readily decompose but tend to accumulate and are toxic when absorbed over the long-term would be specifically designated by Cabinet Order and subject to regulations stipulated in the law. The former stipulation represented the first attempt to introduce the preliminary reviews that subsequently became the common approach to global chemical safety management. In May 1986, the regulation was strengthened with enhancements to the preliminary examination system and an expansion of the range of specified chemical substances. At the same time, categories were established for designated chemical substances and second-class specified chemical substances, and a post hoc management system was put in place.

With the UN in the lead, attempts were made in the 1990s to deploy on a global scale the chemical substance control efforts made in advanced economies. Agenda 21, adopted at the Rio de Janeiro Earth Summit (UN Conference on Environment and Development) in June 1992, called for adequate management of hazardous chemicals and a wide range of measures to be achieved by the year 2000. Meanwhile, the Japan Chemical Industry Association (JCIA) adopted the "Basic policy of the Japan Chemical Industry Association on environment and safety" in 1990 and began to develop projects for the voluntary management of chemical substances. Policies governing projects up to the year 2000 were compiled in March 1994, including the standards and guidelines needed for implementing "responsible care." Where the conventional approach to safety management required compliance with certain regulations, this sought the voluntary control of the impacts on the environment and on people across the entire life cycle of the substances, including their production, consumption, and disposal.

With the mounting pressure for safety management from global efforts and the exploration of voluntary action by industry, the Japanese government began to recognize the limits of administrative responses. When the Chemical Substance Control Law was first established, only about 700 new chemical substances needed annual evaluation, but by 1988, the number had grown to 5,000, and by 1989, to over 6,000. The load exceeded administrative capacity, and MITI concluded that self-management and the principle of responsibility would be an appropriate supplement to legal and regulatory measures for risk management. The February 1996 Interim Report of the Safety Measures Committee of the Chemicals Council (titled "The promotion of comprehensive safety management for chemical substances") suggested the importance of voluntary management, and the July 1999 Act on Confirmation of

Release Amounts of Specific Chemical Substances in the Environment and Promotion of Improvements to the Management Thereof also promoted not only regulation but also improved voluntary control by businesses. Specifically, it introduced the Pollutant Release and Transfer Register system and required reports on capturing the quantity of emissions and submission of an Material Safety Data Sheet (MSDS) with contents, properties, handling and other data pertaining to designated chemical substances. It was also the responsibility of business operators to follow to the chemical substance management guidelines formulated by the government, to manage the manufacture, use, and other handling of designated chemical substances, and also to work to deepen local residents' understanding of how chemical substances were managed within business operations. Based on this framework, methods were adopted to encourage businesses to undertake voluntary management.

4.3 Industrial Location Policy and Promotion of Regions

4.3.1 Reconsidering Industrial Location Policy

In May 1990, the Regional Promotion and Environment Policy Subcommittee of the Industrial Structure Council's 1990s Policy Subcommittee compiled an interim report on regional promotion and global environmental policy for the 1990s (Takeda 2011, p. 193). The report pointed out land issues, including the accelerating concentration of population and functions in Tokyo and the corollary of skyrocketing land prices, and the declining population and vitality of rural areas. These issues were the basis for the direction recommended by the report for industrial location policies in the twenty-first century, which stressed the need to (1) construct policies centered on people, (2) rebuild social frameworks, and (3) develop comprehensive, long-term, and consistent policies.

The report cited the need (1) to foster major regional centers and regional city centers and promote links among them, and (2) to strengthen administrative functions to promote regional coordination across prefectural boundaries so as to enable regional formulations with a broader perspective. But it also represented an extension of existing policy inasmuch as it once again presented the same issues in regional development.

This policy stance reflected a growing concern in the 1990s about the hollowing out of industry, when the imminent decline of factory sites forced a review of the issues. This was because, although industrial compounds had been built as planned, municipalities were left with unsold parcels of land and the heated competition to attract projects resulted in the burden of enormous subsidies.

It was in this context that the Law On Temporary Measures for Activation of Specific Regional Industrial Agglomerations was established in 1997 to address the hollowing out of industry. Its purpose was to build on the Law on Temporary Measures to Revitalize Designated Clusters of Small and Medium-Sized Enterprises ("Clusters Revitalization Act," May 1992). It also treated regional industrial clusters, which had become the foundation of *monozukuri*, as "clusters of basic technology industries," and both of them as "specially designated industrial clusters" and therefore targets for revitalization. To this end, measures were put in place to support small and medium-sized regional enterprises moving into designated fields by (1) upgrading the technology of designated businesses in the basic technology industries, and (2) enabling the revitalization of specially designated industrial clusters.

MITI had put off planning nationwide location policies to accompany the regional designations until the final 1992 Law for the Comprehensive Development of Regional Core Cities with Relocation of Office–Work Functions. In 1995, the New Industry Location Study Group, a private advisory body of the Environmental Affairs Bureau, compiled a "Report of the new Industry Location Policy Study Group: Toward enhancing attractive industrial location environments in the global economy" that laid out the direction of the new policy. The report raised the issue of changes in the form of advancing globalization, upgraded industrial structures, changing values and social environment issues in metropolitan areas, and regional urbanization. The most important point stressed here was the need to rectify the various regulations and practices that restricted potential industrial sites and to ensure greater freedom for business development.

In response to this recommendation, the interim report compiled by the Industrial Structure Council's Industrial Location Subcommittee in May 1997 emphasized the need to ease the regulations that prevented companies from locating in metropolitan areas, which led to a review of the Factory Location Law (Table 7).

Industrial location policy thus changed significantly. The prior Technopolis Law and Key Facilities Siting Law that had underpinned regional designations were replaced by the Law for Facilitating the Creation of New Business. As the new law's name suggests, these policies emphasized business creation rather than industrial location policy. Policy changes advanced even further with the 2001 abolition of the system of New Industrial Cities and Special Areas for Industrial Consolidation that had been promoted ever since the 1960s and with the lapsing of the Law on Extraordinary Measures for the Development of Coal Mining Areas. This meant the end of an industrial location policy under which the government designated certain regions and offered incentives to attract businesses to them, and a shift to regional development spearheaded by the regions themselves.

4.3.2 Advances into New Sectors for Small And Medium-Sized Enterprises and Regional Promotion

This shift in location policy was in keeping with the trajectory of change in MITI policies on small and medium-sized enterprises, which were considered key players in regional industrial development. Regarding post-bubble support for SME moves into new business sectors, the September 1993 Ministerial Conference on Economic Measures decided, as part of its emergency economic countermeasures, to "support small and medium-sized enterprises' restructuring efforts, such as entering new fields

Table 7 Progress in the new industrial relocation plan

		New Plan. 1985–2000			(cf) Old plan. 1976–1985	
		Goal	Present status	Results	Goal	Results
Item		2000	1998	2000	1985	1985
Economic frame		Medium growth driven by domestic demand			5.7%–6.3%	4.30%
(Economic growth rate)		Annual rate 4.0%	3.20%	2.70%		
Industry shipment values classified by Industrial Relocation Promotion Law in cases where the goal was met, as a share of national values	Relocation promotion region	11%	13%	11.60%	11%	18%
	Non-zoned area	54%	52%	53.30%	59%	55%
	Induction area	35%	35%	35.20%	30%	27%
	Pacific belt region	58%	61%	59.60%	60%	66%
Goal for factory relocation		Area of industrial sites in relocation promotion districts 20% lower in 2000 than in 1985	16%	21.80%	1985 area of factory sites in relocation promotion districts down 30% from 1974	15%
New expansion targets in relocation promotion		About 3/4 of cumulative new expansion nationally from 1986 to 2000 was in induction areas	Single year 62% Cumulative77%	Single year 75.60% Cumulative 77.10%	About 70% of cumulative new expansion nationally between 1976 and 1985 was in induction areas	67%
Area of factory sites where targets were met		175,000 ha	176,000 ha	168,000 ha	215,000–225,000 ha	160,000 ha

Source Takeda (2011, p. 48)
Original data from: (report) Japan Industrial Location Center (2001, p. 33); Shūgiin Chōsa Kyōku Keizai Sangyō Chōsa-shitsu (2006), *Kogyo saihaichi sokushinho wo haishi suru hoken an no yoten oyobi mondaiten*, results for the year 2000

and developing overseas markets, so that SMEs can remain vital while overcoming [the challenges of] structural changes in the Japanese economy." It was on this basis that the Temporary Law Concerning Measures for Smooth Adaptation to Structural Changes in Economy by Advancement of Specific Small and Medium-Sized Enterprises to New Fields ("New Fields Law") was established in November (Nakata 2013, p. 323). As the Ministerial Conference showed, the new law discarded the earlier feature of seeking to facilitate business conversions that were either unavoidable or urgent, and instead sought to "develop SME vitality in keeping with the new economic environment" through business conversions to meet changes in the economic structure. The new policies (1) treated expansion into new business sectors as "something that should be actively supported and advanced," (2) dramatically expanded the range of industries targeted by this policy, (3) gave support to expansion overseas, and (4) enabled SMEs that did not yet belong to the "designated industries" and individuals not yet running businesses to become eligible for support upon entry into those industries. Four industries were designated under the New Fields Law in November 1993: manufacturing, printing, software, and information management services. The number of approvals for expansion into new fields at the end of 1995 was 1,028 for manufacturing and 93 for software; 219 plans were approved for expansion overseas and 11 for opening new businesses, for a total of 1,338. However, the use of support policies in the form of loans and special tax exemptions remained at a low level.

Because the Law on Temporary Measures for Small and Medium-Sized Enterprises in Specified Areas would expire in February 1993, a Law on Temporary Measures for the Revitalization of Specified SME Clusters ("Cluster Revitalization Law") was established in May 1992. Its aim was "to strengthen the foundations of autonomous development of regional SMEs through measures to promote the revitalization of designated SME clusters, thereby contributing to the balanced development of the national economy." Its significance lay in its stress on clusters. That is, the SME Modernization Council's discussions of the Cluster Revitalization Law said that the significance of clustering SMEs lay in efficiencies in promoting joint operations, shifts to higher value-added production, and the development of new fields, and that the clusters would serve as nuclei for regional economies and society. Furthermore, the maintenance and development of these functions were themselves the concern of the entire country.

Under the framework of the law, the MITI Minister would issue revitalization guidelines according to which the prefectures were to prepare implementation plans with concrete designated areas, business goals, support project details, and other aspects for each approved SME cluster. SMEs intending to enter a specific field within an industry designated in the revitalization plan could prepare their plans for entry and submit applications to the prefectural governor. Commercial and industrial associations could also submit plans in the same way. Plans that were approved by the governor would be eligible for support measures. This meant that there were two routes of entry—by the businesses themselves and through the commercial and industrial associations.

Due to rapid globalization, however, the Cluster Revitalization Law proved to have a limited role. Although it was originally set to expire in ten years, it was abolished after just three years, in 1997. This was because a new legal framework was needed.

The New Cluster Revitalization Law was enacted in 1997 (Nakata 2013, p. 863) because of great concern about the destruction of basic technology industry clusters and production regions due to hollowing out. The new law aimed to promote vitality in regional industrial clusters by establishing new industrial infrastructure and upgrading the R&D environment. It was intended to extend the Cluster concept and also to provide support measures similar to those given designated SMEs by the Cluster Revitalization Act. The basic technology industry cluster was envisioned as a cluster district for machine industries, such as that in Tokyo's Ota Ward. The "Basic Technology Industry Cluster Revitalization Plans" were formulated in 25 regions around the country based on the new law, and by FY 2005, a total of 473 "Advanced Plans" and "Improvement Facilitation Plans" had received approval. "Specific Small Business Cluster Revitalization Plans" were also formulated in 118 areas nationwide for a cumulative total of 715 "Advancement Plans" and "Entry Facilitation Plans" approved between FY 1997 and FY 2005. MITI's December 2006 ex-post facto evaluation of the promotion of regional industrial cluster revitalization measures found that although certain results had been achieved, regional economic measures needed to apply more closely to the economic environment of the region itself. Thus the hollowing out problem had not necessarily been resolved.

The 1995 Temporary Law Concerning Measures for the Promotion of the Creative Business Activities of SMEs ("Creative SME Law") was a chance to develop new kinds of SME policies including the December 1998 Law for Facilitating the Creation of New Business ("New Business Creation Law"), which aimed to promote the development of new businesses and new products and services, as well as the Law on Supporting Business Innovation of SMEs ("Business Innovation Law"), which sought to develop policies for promoting innovation in the regions. These three laws were absorbed with the prior two into the Enterprise Innovation Law in 2005, the name of which was changed to the Law for Facilitating New Business Activities of Small and Medium-Sized Enterprises.

In order to respond to the hollowing out of some industries and the maturation of others, it was important for the Creative SME Law to work boldly on new fields based on original and superior technologies and to create new markets and develop them. The Law assumed that SMEs with a flexible and entrepreneurial spirit would play this role (Nakata 2013, p. 243). The need for policies to be implemented in a coherent manner and to be consistent with the life-stage of the SME formed the background for the enactment of the Creation Law based on the December 1994 report of the SME Modernization Council. The law was given a 10-year period.

The law aimed to "promote creative business activities of SMEs by supporting and promoting their R&D and thereby opening up new fields of business, to facilitate the transformation of Japan's industrial structure and the sound development of the people's lives" (Article 1). "Creative business activities" were understood as "aggressive efforts to develop new products and new services based on the creative ingenuity of SMEs and to develop new markets themselves." The targets for assistance were (1) SMEs, (2) incorporated associations in which two-thirds or more of the members were SMEs, and (3) individuals not yet engaged in business but expecting to found businesses in the future. Approved R&D plans would be eligible for capital investment tax cuts, as well as various specific support measures under the Small and Medium-sized Enterprise Investment Business Corporation Act and the Small and Medium-sized Enterprise Credit Insurance Act.

According to the results and evaluations compiled by the SME Agency in October 2004, the number of accredited R&D plans under the Creation Act was 10,734 at the end of July 2004, of which 36% were R&D-type SMEs. The greatest number was in Kanto (52.3%) and Kinki (17.0%), and 59.8% were in manufacturing and 25.4% in service industries. A survey commissioned in 2003 found that 40.3% of the plans that received approval had already been commercialized, 20.6% were in the process of developing the market, 16.4% were in the R&D phase, and 15.2% had been suspended or cancelled. This was considered a high rate of commercialization.

4.3.3 New Business Creation Law and Business Innovation Law

The New Business Creation Law materialized as part of the "emergency economic measures" decided by the Cabinet in November 1998 (Nakata 2013, p. 646). Its purpose was "to utilize our country's industrial resources, including human resources, and to promote the establishment of new industries and creation of new products and provision of new services, to improve business methods, and so on. In addition to giving direct support to new businesses established by individuals and companies, measures would also be taken to promote business activities using the new technologies of SMEs in addition to effectively utilizing local industrial resources, and by thus encouraging the autonomous development of regional industries, thereby establishing a vital economic society" (Article 1).

The support would take three forms: (1) support for creating new industries, (2) implementation of a Japanese version of Small Business Innovation Research (SBIR) in order to raise the technological level of SMEs, and (3) formulation of regional platforms. The targets of the support would be projects newly launched by individuals, company projects newly launched by individuals, and company projects newly launched by companies, with each version receiving support such as the designated SME Enterprise Credit Insurance. The New Business Creation Law was revised three times, of which the December 1999 revision added provisions for "New Business Development Sectors."

According to results compiled by the Small and Medium-Sized Enterprise Agency, 246 plans had been approved as of July 1, 2004, under the new designation of "new business development fields." This was regarded as a good result.

"Support for innovative SMEs" had formed part of the emergency measures that followed on the 1997 financial crisis, and the Business Innovation Law was established in that context, with SMEs as its target. The Law regarded business innovation as "the development or production of new products, the development or provision of new services, and the introduction of new methods of producing goods or selling them," and did not stipulate that the support would go only to certain industry designations, or industry associations or organizations, but instead required of individual companies that they provide numerical targets. Furthermore, it aimed not only at "business innovation" but also at "strengthening the foundations of business." If a plan was approved, financial support and special tax measures became available. According to a survey by the Small and Medium-Sized Enterprise Agency, the number of approvals reached 14,774 between July 1999 and July 2004. Kanto accounted for 38.0% of these, and Kinki for 17.5%, meaning about 50% between the two regions. Manufacturing industries accounted for almost half the approvals, at 48.5%. Although the business innovation support plan set its indicator of success at 3% or more annual increase in added value, only 35.7% of the approved companies met this target. Nevertheless, since the value-added rate achieved by the target companies was high compared with non-target companies, the outcome was considered positive.

4.3.4 Measures to Address Pit and Wastewater Mine Pollution

New systemic problems were revealed in the measures taken against mine pollution. Since no particular technology had been found to enable the complete disposal of mining waste, the cost burden of processing waste caused by earlier developers became a drag on mining operations, which also faced problems with the capital financing system (Takeda 2011 p. 647).

In March 1992, the mining industry called for an expansion and strengthening of subsidies and funds to prevent pollution from abandoned mines. In February the Mining Industry Council had pointed out the need to address the problem of permanent mine drainage treatment and the fact that the funds of those responsible were not fully secure. MITI began revising the Act on Special Measures for Pollution Caused by the Metal Mining Industry, which was passed in May and implemented in November. The main points in the amended Act were that the financial resources for permanent mine wastewater treatment could be secured by establishing a fund on the polluter-pays principle and that a system for implementing reliable and permanent mine wastewater treatment could be established through designated institutions. A mine pollution control fund was accordingly established on the following basis: (1) the MITI Minister would designate a mine pollution control organization responsible for running the fund, (2) the Metal Mining Agency of Japan (MMAJ) would pay the cost of pollution prevention from the fund's profits on investment, and (3) to the extent that the organization designated by the MITI Minister was engaged in mine pollution control, those companies with mining rights that were implementing prevention operations would be released from the pollution prevention obligation. The basic plan was revised in March 1993 based on the revised Law, and new policies were developed accordingly.

On coal mining pollution measures, the legal framework consisted of the August 1952 Extraordinary Law on Coal Mine Damage Recovery, the June 1963 Act on Temporary Measures Concerning Compensation for Coal Mine Damage, which aimed to ensure the smooth delivery of compensation in pollution cases, and the Two Basic Laws on Mining Pollution. These laws were given repeated 10-year extensions after 1972. However, with the June 1991 report of the Coal Mining Council, beginning in 1992, the aim shifted to promoting measures to counter mine pollution, in tandem with the structural adjustment of the coal industry. The aim also was for the complete elimination of accumulated damage from mining by the end of FY 2001, or in other words, within the coal mining structural adjustment period. The measures were reworked in December 1992 based on long-term plans for recovery from mining damage, and as a result, the elimination of accumulated mine pollution was announced successively in 1993 in Iwate, Aichi, and Gifu Prefectures. With the report of the Coal Mining Council in July 1999, additional measures were taken including the abolition of related laws and regulations under the expectation that the measures would be brought to completion at the end of FY 2001.

4.4 Harmonizing Energy Development and the Environment

4.4.1 Comprehensive Development of Energy Policy

From 1989 forward, the environment began to emerge as a policy issue alongside energy security and the economy. Triggering this development was the June 1989 report titled "Toward harmonization of the economy, energy, and the environment on a global level" compiled by the Roundtable on Long-term Energy Issues from a Global Perspective, a private council under the Director-General of the Agency of Natural Resources and Energy (Kikkawa 2011, p. 82).

The report held that the measures adopted by America, the Soviet Union, and China, all of which were high-CO_2 emissions nations, were inadequate and also pointed out the need to support and cooperate with the other advanced nations with respect to measures in developing countries, where energy demand was expected to increase. Proceeding with these would require (1) energy conservation, (2) fuel selection, and (3) CO_2 immobilization, which meant that a heavy emphasis needed to be placed on technological development.

In June 1990, the Coordination Subcommittee of the Advisory Committee for Energy compiled "The challenges of new trends in global energy." The report had three notable features. First, it called for developing energy policies on a global scale. Second, it gave new meaning to raising utilization rates through systematization, by making it part of energy conservation policy. This was the idea of raising efficiency rates by extending the target of policy to include the entire energy system from the supply stage through the final user stage, and even to the social system itself. The aim was a conceptual change from "energy conservation meaning savings or reduced use" to "energy conservation as compatible with affluence." Third, regarding the selection of energy sources, the report highlighted the idea of an energy mix, urged avoiding excessive dependence on any particular source of energy and for appropriate combinations of all kinds of energy, while at the same time maintained that these approaches be advanced while taking the environment into account. Looking ahead to the June Earth Summit in Rio de Janeiro, in April 1992 the Japanese government began to take on global environmental issues more systematically. In this way, the three E's became the basis of energy policy.

The economy once again took center stage in the 1990s. In December 1993, the Fundamental Policies Subcommittee of the Comprehensive Energy Research Committee produced an interim report entitled "Aiming for a strong and flexible energy supply system" (Kikkawa 2011, p. 92). The report promoted the liberalization of the electric power and gas businesses, pointing out the need for (1) measures to stabilize energy supply and demand and (2) a review of the regulations concerning the energy supply system and the importance of introducing market principles to it. Meanwhile, a more concerted emphasis was placed on the environment. Especially after about 1997, with the COP3 Kyoto Conference just ahead, the tone of policy showed increased consideration for global environmental problems. The Law Concerning Promotion of the Use of New Energy ("New Energy Law") was announced in April 1997, stipulating systematization based on the need to assure energy security and the growing need to respond to the issue of global warming. The focus was on accelerating the introduction of new energy that was ready for practical applications but that had not yet progressed due, for example, to economic limitations. The targets of this thinking were solar, wind, and waste power generation, as well as clean-energy vehicles. The Special Measures Law Concerning the Use of New Forms of Energy by the Electric Power Industry ("Renewable Portfolio Standard [PRS] Law") was passed in June 2002 and came into effect the following April. This required that a fixed ratio of the electricity bought by retailers had to be new energy. Targets of the policy included wind, solar, geothermal, small and medium hydraulic, and biomass power. In this way, Japan's policy on new energy in the early 2000s strengthened the drive to promote recyclable energy use from the points of view of both the environment and energy security (Fig. 4).

Entering the twenty-first century, further emphasis was placed on simultaneously achieving the three E's. The Energy Research Commission's Coordination Subcommittee and Energy Supply and Demand Subcommittee issued a joint report in July 2001 titled "On future energy policy," which pointed out the stringency of the goal and the need for the citizenry as a whole to take on the effort and burden required to meet that goal. The Basic Law on Energy Policy, promulgated and enforced in June 2002, carried on with this approach. Based on the provisions of Article 24, paragraph 4 of the same law, the Basic Energy Plan presented in October 2003 clarified the goals of securing a stable supply of energy, adapting to the environment, and utilizing market principles.

4.4.2 Promotion of Deregulation: Petroleum and Natural Gas Policy

The first deregulation in the energy policy field was developed from 1987 to 1993. The trigger was the report titled "On the petroleum industry and petroleum policy in the 1990s," which was compiled in June 1987 by the Committee to Review the

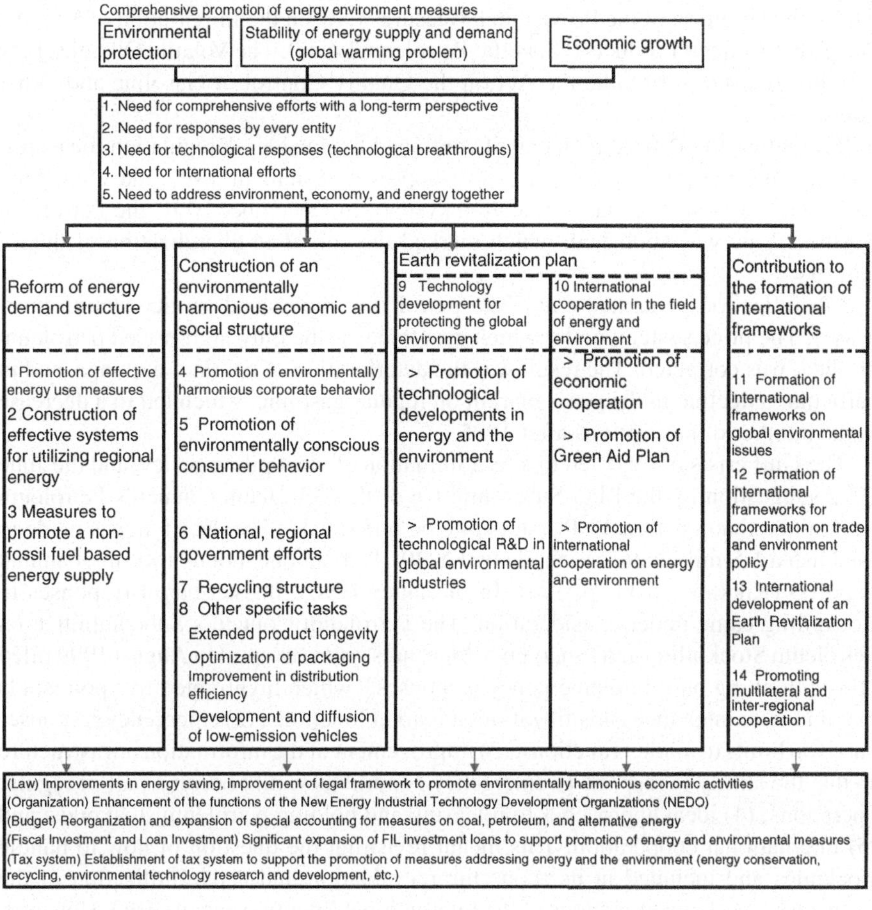

Fig. 4 Harmonizing energy development and the environment in the 1990s. *Source* Minami Ryo, "Tsusho sangyo sho no kankyo taisaku" *Jurist* 1015. 1993, p. 19. [II-5, p. 520]

Basic Issues of the Petroleum Industry that had been newly established under the Petroleum Council's Petroleum Subcommittee in November 1986 (Kikkawa 2011, p. 121). It led to revision of the restrictions on refining and sales activities that had been imposed by the Petroleum Industry and Gasoline Retail Business Laws. The move to deregulation proceeded without interruption, and with the mid-1990s call for stabilization and greater efficiency in the supply of petroleum products, the principle of competition was introduced in the import sector as well.

Further review was promoted from 1997 onwards, in what might be called a second stage of deregulation. Based on recommendations made in 1993 by the Economic Reform Study Group, which was charged with considering deregulation, the Petroleum Council in December 1994 compiled a report titled "On future ways to supply petroleum products." The Law on Establishing Related Laws to Secure a Stable and Efficient Supply of Petroleum Products was passed in April 1995, as part of the abolition of the Provisional Measures Law on the Importation of Specific Petroleum Refined Products ("Specific Petroleum Law"). The Volatile Oil Sales Law was also revised to become the Act on the Quality Control of Gasoline and Other Fuels.

Thereafter, the Petroleum Council continued to consider deregulation measures, revising the petroleum products export approval system in 1997 and abolishing the service station supplier certification system. In December 2001, the Petroleum Business Law was abolished, which marked the complete liberalization of the oil industry.

Liberalization generated entry into petroleum import and service station businesses. The price system, under which gasoline was the only high-priced petroleum product, was corrected. The result was the deterioration of operator earnings, and in particular a decline in the gross margin on regular gasoline, which led to a decrease in the number of gas stations after 1995.

The Gulf crisis of 1991 led to a reexamination of stockpiling policy, and the June 1992 suggestion by the LPG Subcommittee of the Petroleum Council's Petroleum Committee that a national LPG stockpile be introduced. The decision was made to establish a 1.5-million ton stockpile by FY 2010 (about one month's worth of annual imports) (Kikkawa 2011, p. 194). In the latter 1990s, market-based responses to stockpiling came under consideration. The Petroleum Council's Subcommittee on Petroleum Stockpiling and Emergency Measures issued a report in August 1999 titled "Basic thinking on future emergency responses," which highlighted five points: (1) maximum maintenance and utilization of market functions; (2) emergency responses based on limits to market functions; (3) improvement of the information infrastructure so that the ability to respond to emergency conditions would become part of regular operations; (4) ideal approaches to releasing and holding petroleum stockpiles; and (5) international cooperation. This meant revisiting the question of how to handle stockpiles and included in its scope the reevaluation and active utilization of the cooperative exchange functions of the International Energy Agency (IEA). However, due to the emphasis on Energy Security after the 2000s, the environment was not one in which the report's recommendations could immediately be realized.

Regarding coal policy, the Eighth Coal Policy covering 1986–1991 had concluded that an annual production of about 10 million tons was appropriate given the inevitability of the gradual reduction of domestic coal production, whereas the Post-Eighth Coal Policy (1992–2001) considered the possibility of a phased end to production. In November 1990, the Coal Mining Areas Development Council reported that the November 1981 Law On Extraordinary Measures for the Development of Coal Mining Areas would be extended for a further 10 years until November 2001.

4.4.3 Liberalization of the Electricity Market

Liberalization of the electricity market also made progress (Kikkawa 2011, p. 284). The Electric Utility Industry Law of 1965 was completely revised in 1995. The main points of the revision were: (1) to expand new entrants to the power generation sector,

(2) to create a system related to specified electricity businesses, (3) to improve and mitigate price regulation, and (4) to clarify the responsibilities of electric power companies and rationalize safety regulations. For the first, the approval system for new entrants to electricity wholesaling was in principle abolished and a bidding system introduced. This enabled the entry of independent power producers (IPP). Improving and mitigating price regulation meant the shift to a notification system from the former set price menu aimed at load leveling. It also introduced ways of assessing the fees so as to easily compare businesses in terms of their efficiency. Finally, clarifying the responsibilities of electric power companies was an effort to limit government involvement to the minimum level necessary (Fig. 5).

The "Electricity Business Act" was also revised significantly in 1999. Its main points were: (1) to partially liberalize electricity retailers and fully introduce the principle of competition in the retail sector for special high-pressure customers receiving 20,000 V (high-voltage) electric power of 2,000 kilowatts or more, (2) to establish a consignment system permitting electric power companies to open their networks to other electricity providers, (3) to shift from an approval system to a notification system with regard to reductions in electricity prices, and (4) to abolish the regulations on electricity businesses' being involved in other businesses at the same time. These revisions brought new entrants to retail electricity and encouraged the emergence of specified electric utilities called PPS, or power producers and suppliers. They also stimulated competition among the nine electric power companies. For example, Tokyo Electric Power Company (TEPCO) established My Energy Co. in March 2000, began to supply electricity in the Tohoku and Chubu Electric power districts, and participated in the bidding on electricity provision in Sendai City (in Tohoku Electric's district). The liberalization was not complete, however, and ordinary households and small and medium-sized factories were still operating in a regulated environment and supplied by their electric utilities as before.

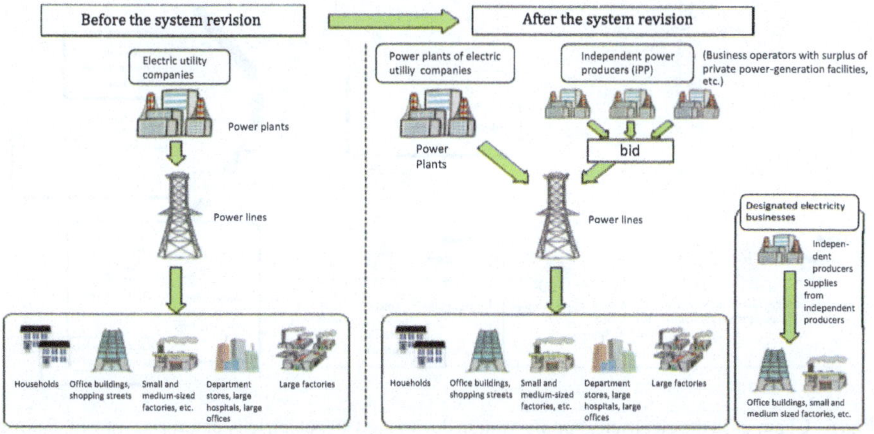

Fig. 5 Changes in the electricity supply system due to the 1990 Electricity Enterprise Reform. *Source* METI, Agency for Natural Resources and Energy (2004, p. 118); Kikkawa (2011, p. 301)

The trend toward liberalization continued. The February 2002 "Report of the Electricity Industry Committee" by the Advisory Committee for Natural Resources and Energy (established in January 2001) examined the experience of electricity liberalization thus far and took on the role of laying out new directions for deregulation. These included (1) further liberalizing the retail electricity sector, (2) reviewing the electricity retail consignment system (abolishing the transfer supply system in which charges were added for the use of transmission lines by multiple electric power companies), (3) establishing a nationwide wholesale power trading market (for PPS) and (4) reviewing the backup rules of the electric utilities (to reduce the burden on PPS by abolishing backup fees when accidents occur). These recommendations were reflected in the revised Electricity Business Law promulgated in June 2003 and implemented in April 2004 (Fig. 6).

Due to liberalization from the mid-1990s on, electricity rates declined steadily, reaching a reduction of 18% between FY 1995 and FY 2005. When liberalization of electricity retailing began in 2000, price cuts were observed not only in the sectors being liberalized but also in electricity rates for households. Despite soaring fuel costs, electricity rates declined by about 10% from FY 2000 to FY 2005. A report compiled by the Institutional Reform Evaluation Subcommittee, which was established within the Electricity Works Subcommittee in 2006, interpreted this to mean that the improvements in efficiency in the liberalized parts of the utility business were having an effect on the markets that remained regulated as well.

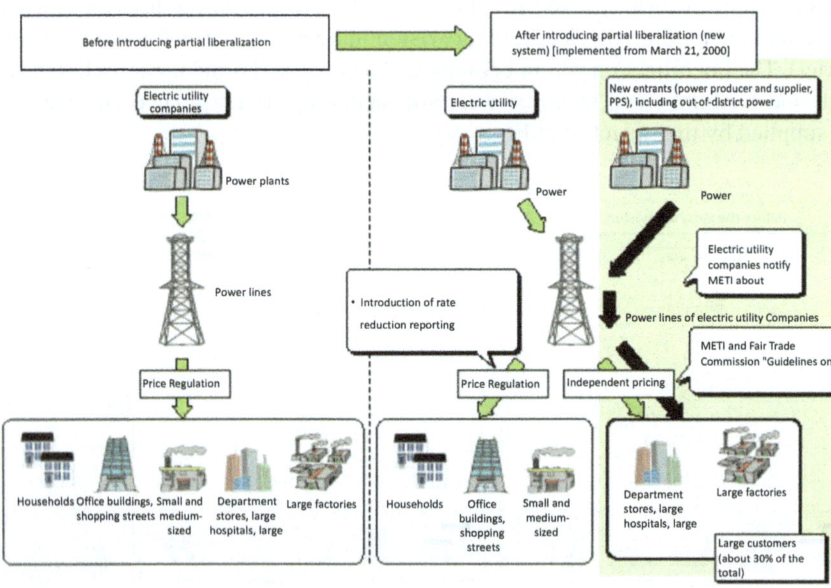

Fig. 6 Changes in the electricity supply system due to the 1999 electricity enterprise reform. *Source Enerugi hakusho 2004 nenban*, p. 118. [II-10, p. 303]

By contrast, no significant results were apparent in the realm of stimulating competition. PPS market share remained low, and almost no power company competition developed across supply districts.

4.4.4 Emphasis on Developing Nuclear Power

It was in this context that interest mounted in nuclear power as a measure to address global environmental problems, and as other new developments were not making progress, nuclear power assumed greater weight in the overall composition of energy sources for power generation. It also took on more significance as an energy security policy to alleviate the effects of higher crude-oil prices, such that nuclear power began to be regarded as effective for both environmental and energy security reasons (Kikkawa 2011, p. 317).

However, other sorts of problems arose. First, trust in the safety of nuclear power began to waver due to a number of accidents in nuclear power plants at home and abroad. Second, establishment of the nuclear fuel cycle was not progressing as had been hoped.

Regarding the first of these issues, new safety enhancements were added every time a serious accident occurred. After the damage to the steam generation heat transfer tube at Kansai Electric's Mihama Power Station #2 in February 1991, electric utilities strengthened their quality assurance activities, improved the reliability of heat transfer tubes, and strengthened their voluntary security measures, for example by improving their maintenance management measures. MITI also reviewed construction plans and revised its list of items requiring inspection, as well as strengthening its guidance on and supervision of quality assurance measures. In response to the criticality accident at the Tokaimura JCO Company uranium processing plant in September 1999, the Law on Special Measures Concerning Nuclear Emergency Preparedness was enacted in December, with the aim of strengthening and enhancing nuclear safety and disaster prevention measures by establishing a Nuclear Emergency Response Headquarters headed by the Prime Minister. At the same time, the revision of the Law on the Regulation of Nuclear Source Material, Nuclear Fuel Material, and Reactors placed Nuclear Safety Inspectors at nuclear facilities and established a system to check whether business operators were complying with safety regulations.

An organizational restructuring that contributed to a significant strengthening of safety regulations was implemented as part of the 2001 reorganization of ministries and agencies. The Nuclear and Industrial Safety Agency (NISA) was established in the Agency of Natural Resources and Energy, uniting the nuclear safety administrations variously under the jurisdiction of the Science and Technology Agency and MITI. Just after NISA was established, it was discovered in August 2002 that TEPCO had concealed a problem, and this became a significant social issue. In December 2002, the Electricity Utilities Industry Act and the Nuclear Reactor Regulation Law were revised in order to prevent the recurrence of fraud and to introduce far-reaching reform to nuclear safety regulations. The revisions were expected to enhance the activities taken by businesses to ensure security and to bolster the effectiveness of the safety regulations themselves.

4.4.5 Promotion of the Use of Natural Gas

In the 1990s, the Agency for Natural Resources and Energy brought a new approach to promoting the introduction of natural gas. The "IGF (Integrated Gas Family) 21 Plan" proposed in January 1990 called for municipal gas utilities to shift from supplying low-calorific reformed gas such as naphtha or butane, to a high-calorific natural gas (Kikkawa 2011, p. 352). This would require modifying equipment and establishing plants for receiving and supplying natural gas, which in turn would require financial support. The Hokkaido Kitami City gas leak and carbon monoxide poisoning accident in January 2007 hastened the need to shift to high-calorific gas.

The decision to increase the use of natural gas was initially due to energy security concerns, but from the latter 1990s it was also seen as necessary from an environmental point of view. The New Energy Law of April 1997 is a clear indication of this view. In the mid-2000s, natural gas also attracted notice for economic reasons, because the price of LNG was not rising much compared with the soaring price of crude oil. The shift to natural gas was therefore occurring globally at this time.

Institutional reforms to promote liberalization progressed in the gas industry in general, beginning with the revision of the Gas Utility Industry Law in June 1994. Liberalization in the retail sector was promoted for large-scale customers whose annual contract gas consumption exceeded 2 million cubic meters with a calorific value of 46 MJ. Large customers could choose gas suppliers, and charges and services were left to negotiations between the parties. The scope of liberalization continued to expand thereafter.

In November 1999, liberalization was applied to customers with annual contracts for gas consumption of 1 million cubic meters or more and a calorific value of 46 MJ, and it became possible for the gas delivery conduits of general gas providers to also be used by other gas suppliers. With the 1999 amendment, competition began to cross industry barriers—the line between gas and electric or oil companies, for example—as well as increasing among gas companies themselves. The effect of this promotion of competition became evident in the 1995–2002 period when major gas companies cut rates by about 8–12%. A Partial Revision of the Electric Utility Industry Law and the Gas Utility Industry Law was made in June 2003, as part of the Electricity Business Law and the Gas Utility Act, and institutional reform continued to advance. The policies promoting gas liberalization were characterized by an emphasis on (1) more active participation of new entrants and (2) general gas companies' actively providing large-scale supply outside their own supply districts. Gas liberalization was more successful than electric power liberalization in promoting competition. In fact, regarding point (2), general gas providers steadily increased their large-scale supply to areas outside their supply districts both in the number of such cases and in the amount supplied. General gas charges began decreasing in 2002 as well.

4.4.6 Establishment and Revision of the Act on Rationalizing Energy Use

The Act on Rationalizing Energy Use ("Energy Conservation Act") was revised several times to respond to changing conditions. The second amendment, made in March 1993, was added for the purpose of promoting energy conservation for environmental reasons (Kikkawa 2011, p. 373). The third amendment, made in June 1998, followed on the conclusion of the 1997 Kyoto Protocol and more strongly reflected the emergence of the global warming problem. Behind MITI's decision to revise the Energy Conservation Act in December 1997 was the aim of strengthening measures to secure strict energy efficiency standards in the automobile and electrical equipment sectors and to encourage rationalization in the planned use of energy in energy-consuming factories. In May 1998, the New Energy Department of the Agency for Natural Resources and Energy called for even greater energy rationalization in its Laws Concerning Rationalization of Energy Use and promoted amendment of the law in accordance with the Decision of the MITI Departmental Council.

Particularly significant in the private sector was the 1998 revision of the so-called Top-Runner System. In principle, this established the criterion that energy consumption efficiency be equal to or higher than the performance of the most energy-efficient equipment among the products on the market at that time, obliging everyone to comply with that standard.

4.5 Technology Policy: A Shift in Emphasis from Basic Technology to Practical Applications

4.5.1 *Vision of the 1990s* and Industrial Technology Policy

Industrial technology policy began to focus on basic research in the 1980s. Questions began to be raised in the 1990s about approaches to the national research institutions and change became inevitable as subsidy systems and plans for international contributions came under review. These changes took on clarity in the 1990s. That is, because of the creation of new industries and employment issues it had prioritized as policy issues, the tone of policy changed from "shifting to basics" to "shifting to practical applications" (Sawai 2011, p. 43).

The Industrial Structure Council report that laid out the industrial policy vision for the 1990s (*1990s Policy Vision*) proposed techno-globalism as the philosophy to which Japan should aspire. That is, in contrast with the growing protectionist approaches to technology (so-called techno-nationalism), Japan would now "work to cooperate with other countries to stimulate creative activities and distribution and relocation activities at the international level, with the goal of [contributing] the greatest utility that science and technology can bring to humankind." Thus the trend toward international contributions was further strengthened.

"Trends and issues in industrial science and technology: towards technological symbiosis on a global scale," a MITI publication of 1992, asserted the importance of promoting not only techno-globalism but also human- and environment-friendly technology systems. Alongside the continued promotion of basic research and international contributions, environmental concerns were added to policy thinking. The title does not refer to "industrial technology" but rather to "industrial science and technology," meaning that its contents focused on the relationship between science and technology with scientific advances encouraging the development of industrial technology and technology stimulating scientific research. The industrial technology white paper of 1988 emphasized the close relationship between science and technology, and given that the report saw industrial technology policy as referring to industrial science and technology, it is evident that policy was emphasizing the development of paths to the application of basic research. But it was in the late 1990s that the practical applications were made a clear priority.

The Innovation Study Group, established in July 1997 as a private research group of the MITI Industrial Policy Bureau's Director-General, compiled an interim report in June 1998. It suggested that technology policy should aim for a society in which innovations follow one after another. For "a new perspective on future technology policy," it highlighted the following: (1) developing of technology policy aimed at businesses and individuals; (2) restructuring the technology policy system based on implementing innovation; (3) expanding policy targets to respond to the development of information and services; and (4) improving research to support the formulation of new strategies for government and enterprises. In addition, it emphasized the importance of reflecting market needs, and "the need to move from a 'development-centric' technology policy system to a focus on aspects besides technology 'R&D' and to develop and expand policy systems that prioritize, more than before, accurate feedback of information from society." In this way, the focus of industrial technology policy shifted to applied research and practical applications.

4.5.2 The Advance of Techno-Globalism

The 1990s was marked by debate over changing the existing approaches to industrial technology policy with an emphasis in the late 1990s on the role of government in applied research. For example, the Planning Committee of the Industrial Technology Council issued a report in June 1992 titled "Techno-globalism promotion and multifaceted promotion of COE," notable for its use of the term "COE" or "Center of Excellence" (Sawai 2011, p. 72). COE refers to "a research hub that naturally draws the greatest minds from around the world, and the achievements of which are recognized globally." The aim was to promote techno-globalism by fostering COEs and international contributions in the fields of industrial science and technology. Among the concrete measures were "reforms to enable original basic research," which referred to reform of the so-called national projects. This led to a review of existing R&D projects in industrial science and technology and to bringing the FY

1993 Industrial Science and Technology Frontier Program and the New Sunshine Project to fruition.

Successive reports in the latter 1990s reflected the trend of emphasizing practical applications. For example, the July 1996 Secretariat of the General Subcommittee on Industrial Technology Council report titled "On issues for review in industrial technology policy" was based on examination of the serious problems arising from three consecutive years of decreased R&D investment. Specific industrial technology policies included (1) strategic promotion of private R&D, (2) creation of industrial "seeds" to bring together the strengths of industry, academia and government, (3) institutional reform of the national research institutions, and (4) institutional reform of the national universities. Meanwhile, another debate unfolded in the Industrial Technology Council, on the reflections or doubts that had gradually emerged about the "shift to basic research." In the 31st Coordination Subcommittee in July 1996, for example, committee members argued that "MITI had unconsciously been avoiding government involvement in applied technology over the past ten years, due to criticism from abroad, especially the US. It made its selections based on a bias toward the assumption that basic technological development was needed.... [and] given the sense of crisis in industry, which means that technological development is needed, the question should actually be whether the potential for commercial applications should be the evaluation criteria." At the 34th Coordination Subcommittee meeting in August 1997, the Secretariat went so far as to say, "The main emphasis should be the forceful promotion of R&D for the creation of new industries.... The priority, which had shifted to basic research, needs to return to industrial R&D."

Based on discussions in the Council for Industrial Competitiveness, established under Prime Minister Obuchi in March 1999, the Headquarters for Industrial Structural Reform compiled its report, "On emergency measures for employment and for strengthening industrial competition." The National Industrial Technology Strategy Review Committee followed with the "National industrial technology strategy" in April 2000. Based on the Industrial Technology Council's recommendation set forth in August 1998 in "Constructing a new industrial technology policy," the Agency of Industrial Science and Technology proceeded with its exploration of an "industrial technology strategy," the outcome of which was in turn reflected in the Industrial Technology Council's April 2000 report, "Industrial technology strategy (Future directions for industrial technology policy)." The Strategy included the following specific measures for building a system for internationally competitive "new-frontier" innovation: (1) nurturing the human resources and venture businesses that are the driving force behind technological innovation, (2) reforming the institutions that are the starting point of technological innovation, (3) strengthening true collaboration among industry, academia, and government to promote technological innovation, (4) building a flexible government system to accelerate innovation, (5) developing the foundation for support of technological innovation, and (6) forming an intellectual society capable of technological innovation. The Strategy also called for industry, academia and government to collaborate on industrial technology policy outside the framework of ministries and agencies. The proposal can be seen as a plan for establishing the necessary foundations for promoting industrial technologies linked to practical use. The "National Industrial Technology Strategy" was developed in this spirit and was reflected in the Second Science and Technology Basic Plan (FY 2001–2005).

4.5.3 Intra-Governmental Coordination with the Enactment of the Science and Technology Basic Law

In the latter 1990s, the industrial technology policy-making process was changed by the enactment of the Science and Technology Basic Law in November 1995 (Sawai 2011, p. 106). The Law charged the government with preparing a Science and Technology Basic Plan based on Council of Science and Technology deliberations in order to comprehensively and systematically advance policies on promoting science and technology. The legislative measures and the plans based on them reflected both the requests coming from university and national laboratory researchers seeking improvements in the research environment and more funds for research, and the high expectations of industry for public-sector R&D. They were concrete policies linked with the shift to practical applications and drew on views from across the government's ministries. This direction was also given support in December 1996 by the Hashimoto cabinet, which presided over a change from a bottom-up to a top-down process in policy-making. Policy developed by single ministries and agencies in response to the prolonged and severe recession had not had much effect, leading to moves to review the bureaucracy's traditional vertical divisions. MITI was already collaborating with the Ministry of Education and the Science and Technology Agency, but further intra-governmental coordination was required even from MITI to make progress in creating new industries that would maintain and expand employment.

4.5.4 Renewal of the Industrial Science and Technology Development System

The early 1990s also saw continued review of the R&D project system. National projects were examined as part of the debate on new policies for FY 1993, and the following points emerged: (1) The system needed reorganization because the differences were receding between the R&D of the Large-scale Research and Development Project system (system-oriented, LRDP) and the Next-Generation Research and Development system (elements- and materials-oriented, NGRDP); (2) active implementation of government projects was needed for technological development aimed at achieving comfort and affluence because of difficulties with the private sector actively taking the lead; and (3) comprehensive implementation of R&D in new energy (Sunshine Project), energy conservation technology (Moonlight Project), and environmental technology (especially CO_2-related technology) was needed because of the intimate relationship among these technologies. This definition of the issues meant fundamental reform of the LRDP and NGRDP programs and comprehensive promotion of technology development in energy and the environment. Domestic and international criticism formed the backdrop for these changes. In Japan, the criticism was based on the awareness that Japan was lagging in its effort to catch up with the R&D taking place in the West. Overseas, the existing approach was regarded as unfair, because it involved subsidies to specific industries.

It was in this context that the LRDP, NGRDP, and Medical-and-Welfare Technological Development systems were integrated into the Industrial Science and Technology Frontier Program ("Industrial Technology System") (Sawai 2011, p. 206). The requirements for R&D targets were (1) that they involve areas of basic or innovative research, or (2) that they were public, social, or welfare needs. These requirements were based on the idea of "shifting to basic and innovative research and to mission-oriented technological development (for public needs)." The first was aimed at "R&D that would provide basic technologies with significant spillover possibilities for industry 20 or 30 years down the line, and at organizing the foundations needed for promoting science and technology." Among the approaches adopted was a method in which R&D officers would be placed in their separate fields as defined by existing projects. This was aimed at making it easier to reduce or scrap research projects based on priority fields, thus reducing the significance given to the particular framework in which the project had been carried out.

As described above, the reorganized industrial technology system was once again reorganized in FY 1998 in line with the May 1997 "Action Plan for Economic Structural Change and Creation" Cabinet Decision. The industrial technology system referred to basic technology, and two new systems—"applied industrial technology" and "university-linked"—were added. These three projects were conceived of as "new industrial creation-oriented industrial science and technology R&D." The applied technology project was expected to support R&D at the applied research stage, where the private sector was deterred by the high risks and costs involved, even where the development of new creative technologies could be expected. University-linked R&D aimed at discoveries that could lead to a flowering of new industrialization. R&D under the new system applied to six sectors, including new materials, biotechnology, electronics–information–communications, machinery–aviation–space, people–life–society, and medical care and welfare.

Eight new projects were undertaken in the industrial technology system described above from FY 1994–1997 (until the reorganization), in the fields of new materials, biotechnology, electronics, information, communications, machinery, aerospace and space. Despite the vigorous development of these projects, it was clear from a survey of 500 companies conducted in 1999 that most companies that participated in the national projects had higher hopes of the subsidies than of the collaborative research.

4.5.5 Reform of the National Innovation System

From the late 1990s, the national innovation system underwent a major transformation due to greater industry–academia collaboration, itself the result of the sense of crisis at the decline of international industrial competitiveness (Sawai 2011, p. 226). The change was also an example of the priority placed on practical application.

The Agency of Industrial Science and Technology believed that the key to responding to the hollowing out of the industry was to create new industrial fields. It had been promoting a "regional consortium R&D system" since 1997 to foster regional enterprises that could be relevant around the world. Utilizing the existing technology "seeds"—national laboratories, universities and others—to promote R&D aimed at commercialization, these institutions and private companies together constituted a regional consortium. The recipient of government subsidies was not a specific business operator but the consortium itself, called New Energy and Industrial Technology Development Organization (NEDO), and a committee of outside judges was established to provide expert evaluation of the projects (Table 8).

The Law on Promotion of Transfer of Research Results on Technologies at Universities to Private Business Operators ("Technology Licensing Organization

Table 8 Budget for NEDO projects (million yen)

FY	New energy accounts	Account for industrial technology R&D	Investment account for industrial technology research infrastructure	Coal rationalization account	Coal mining account	Alcohol account	Total
1980	17,138			111,430			128,568
1981	38,160			220,019			258,179
1982	53,262			109,559		5,538	168,359
1983	55,152			89,859		13,046	158,057
1984	54,425			85,924		15,994	156,343
1985	60,263			79,696		12,893	152,852
1986	63,158			76,883		13,935	153,976
1987	67,322			194,311		9,212	270,845
1988	63,335	4,725	1,500	193,358		8,048	270,966
1989	67,499	15,137	2,200	161,996		9,334	256,166
1990	70,241	20,336	2,200	129,061		10,303	232,141
1991	60,884	25,536	2,400	97,432		10,843	197,095
1992	66,200	30,144	700	126,246		11,658	234,948
1993	79,808	36,421	2,400	99,034		11,635	229,298
1994	78,684	36,627	700	98,117		10,315	224,443
1995	97,506	24,877		92,850		9,544	224,777
1996	97,623	32,183		91,931	79,978	10,155	311,870
1997	95,203	41,056		92,240	81,937	11,796	322,232
1998	123,284	55,247		31,603	82,819	12,282	305,235
1999	147,007	68,908		24,760	59,209	12,602	312,486
2000	152,570	92,862		23,039	89,928	13,041	371,440

Source Sawai (2011, pp. 282–283)

(TLO) Law") was passed in May 1998 and came into effect in August. It set out government support for Technology Licensing Organizations acting as intermediaries for transferring the technology and research results of universities and other institutions to private enterprises. Support measures included: (1) utilizing the Facilitation Fund for Industrial Structural Adjustment to give debt guarantees, issue grants, and provide information for university technology-transfer projects, and (2) utilizing the special measures of investment by Small and Medium Business Investment and Consultation Co., Ltd. for venture- and small and medium-sized enterprises to make use of the results of university research. Previously, when university research was put into practical use, the private enterprise involved in a collaborative research exchange with the university applied for its own patent for the invention, and the research lab accepted the company's researchers into the lab and offered technical advice on the invention, receiving donations of scholarship funds from the companies in exchange. However, this framework invited criticism because its methods of transferring research were not systematic and SMEs could find themselves excluded. The TLO Law sought to address such concerns.

Evaluation of the National Projects also became stricter in the 1990s. A technical evaluation office was established in the General Coordination Division of the Agency of Industrial Science and Technology in October 1996 to pull together the post-project evaluations issued by the various departments. This was reorganized in July 1997 into the Evaluation Division, and added to its duties were the operation and management of the technical evaluation system covering the entire ministry. This was intended to clarify even further the distinction between the promotion and the evaluation departments. Meanwhile, in August 1997, MITI issued "Technical Evaluation Guidelines" in accordance with the "Guidelines for Implementing Evaluations Common to All National R&D" compiled by the Science and Technology Council in July. Formulated in January, the Guidelines promoted stricter evaluation. The Guidelines were based on (1) transparency, (2) neutrality, (3) continuity, (4) effectiveness, and so on. The intermediate evaluation to be conducted by August 1998 was designed to stop technically obsolete development and to establish priorities for development goals.

4.5.6 Promotion of the New Sunshine Project

In addition to the Sunshine and Moonlight Projects, each laboratory of the Agency of Industrial Science and Technology launched "Research and Development on Global Environmental Technology" beginning in 1989, to address carbon dioxide problems. Since the result was the emergence of parallel technologies, the National Institute of Advanced Industrial Science and Technology on May 25, 1992, suggested the following: "Because energy and environmental technology development (especially CO_2-related) are closely related, our new energy (Sunshine Project), energy conservation (Moonlight Project) and global environmental technology development projects should be integrated and a comprehensive R&D program promoted for basic and applied research." In December, the Industrial Technology Council's New

Energy Technology Development and Energy Conservation Technology Development subcommittees, and the Joint Planning Committee of the Global Environment Technology Committee held a "Mid-term Seminar" that compiled a report titled "Comprehensive Development of the New Sunshine Project to Support the 21st Century." This led to the establishment of the integrated "New Sunshine Project" in FY 1993 (Sawai 2011, p. 267).

The plan consisted of (1) innovative technology development: steadily accelerating promotion, in an internationally open regime, of innovative energy and environmental technology development projects aimed at realizing the "Action Plan for Preventing Global Warming," (2) large-scale international research: promotion of large-scale international collaborative research aimed at advancing the "New Earth 21" Program, and (3) collaborative research on appropriate technologies: advancing collaborative research programs on energy and environment-related technologies to support the easing of energy and environmental constraints in developing countries neighboring Japan. From FY 1993–2000, a total of 3.547 billion yen of national funds went into the projects. Among the largest research areas were coal liquefaction and gasification technology (838 million yen), solar energy (648 million yen), and geothermal energy (289 million yen). The system underwent reform in FY 1997 to stipulate: (1) an R&D period limited in principle to five years, (2) maintenance of a competitive and efficient research implementation system, and (3) the construction of a strict evaluation system (Table 9).

4.5.7 Reorganization of the New Energy Development Organization

The New Energy Development Organization (NEDO) was reorganized based on the May 1988 Law Concerning the Improvement of the System of Research and Development in the Field of Industrial Technology (effective December 1989) (Sawai 2011, p. 281). As a result, management and operations, international industrial technology-related businesses, and research infrastructure improvement projects that had been variously part of the Large Projects, Next-Generation Technology, and Welfare Equipment Technology R&D were brought into the Industrial Technology R&D Department. The Industrial Technology Department was composed of an R&D Section, an International Collaborative Research Section, and a Research Infrastructure Development Section.

Industrial technology-related tasks were added to NEDO, which was responsible for the development of new energy, and NEDO became the New Energy and Industrial Technology Development Organization (the NEDO abbreviation remained unchanged). The reorganization occurred because the management burden of the National Institute of Advanced Industrial Science and Technology was excessive given the large number of research associations. Given also that the majority of these involved joint research with the private sector, NEDO was given responsibility for coordinating among them. A further aim involved lifting the research funds for the

Table 9 Changes in the budget of the new sunshine project (million yen)

FY	Reusable energy	Advanced use of fossil fuels	Energy transport and storage	Technology for environmental measures	Systematization technology	Basic energy and environmental technology	Technology for meeting COP3 targets	Other	Total
1993	13,317	21,472	4,724	267	1,020	130		106	41,036
1994	12,411	21,015	5,186	277	2,011	107		63	41,070
1995	12,421	20,859	5,649	379	2,468	94		60	41,930
1996	12,540	20,529	5,358	385	3,100	2,020		61	43,993
1997	12,272	18,796	5,319	536	4,234	3,551		56	44,764
1998	12,092	15,612	8,514	615	4,188	3,662	2,000	58	46,741
1999	12,754	11,135	10,780	724	4,065	4,213	3,236	56	49,062
2000	11,325	7,897	9,978	4,208	3,857	4,471	4,257	151	46,123
Sub-total	99,132	137,315	55,508	7,391	24,943	18,248	9,493	611	354,752

national projects outside the "ceiling" framework. The Industrial Technology Department, having overcome the initial problem of securing human resources, added new projects in the 1990s as well as integrating existing R&D projects with one another, and promoted a range of R&D.

Among the above measures on energy, the promotion of new energy had the following results: The ratio of "new energy, etc." to the total primary energy supply did not meet the targets of 1.0% in 1980, 1.3% in 1990, or 1.1% in 2000. However, as evident in the spread of solar power, it is clear that efforts to develop new energy have seen steady progress.

4.5.8 Aligning Japanese Industrial Standards (JIS) with International Standards

The Agreement on Technical Barriers to Trade (TBT Agreement) came into effect in January 1995 as part of the WTO Agreements (Sawai 2011, p. 388). This Agreement, which inherited and built on the GATT Code of Conduct, aimed to ensure than any given country's standards and conformity assessment systems are not more trade restrictive than necessary to achieve a legitimate objective. Countries were required to adhere to the principle of non-discrimination between domestic and foreign businesses in applying systems, such as ensuring transparency when formulating standards or using international standards. Inevitably it became necessary to abide by the TBT agreement, and therefore ensuring Japanese Industrial Standards' (JIS) consistency with international standards became an urgent matter. Meanwhile, the US–European summit meeting of December 1995 triggered many proposals from US and European industries regarding standardization policy.

Against this backdrop, Japan revised its Industrial Standardization Law again in March 1997. The revision entailed a zero-based review of JIS enactment procedures and of certification systems such as the JIS mark, and so on. The first involved a comprehensive inspection of standards from FY 1997–1999 based on the Japan Industrial Standards Committee's December 1996 report titled "On reviewing the industrial standards system." For all 5,200 standards under review, a zero-based review was conducted regarding the relevant ministries, bureaus, industrial associations and users. This led to the abolition of 465 standards by FY 1999. The change was based not only on the international harmonization, but also on changes in the emphasis on standardization in the 1990s that led policy to reflect the points of view not only of efficiency and quality improvements in production but also of an aging and welfare-oriented society, consumers, the global environment, advanced technology, and so on.

4.5.9 Toward an Ideal National Examination Research Institution

In January 1990, the Agency of Industrial Science and Technology decided to review the system of test laboratories with an eye to the future (Sawai 2011, p. 408). The decision was taken because basic and original research were expected to become only more important, and "The need is growing for a review of the research system from the long-term point of view, so that the Research Institutes of the Agency of Industrial Science and Technology, which are not only a venue for promoting industry for the 21st century, but are also backed by basic and original research, can serve as a base for providing the seeds of research in our country." The Agency Decision called for (1) improvement of the system in the areas of goods and materials research and biological and ergonomic research, (2) improvement of research related to global environmental issues and to resources, security, and so on. A Review Committee was established in April and its final report, also issued in April 1992, called for a reorganization of the National Chemical Laboratory for Industry, the Fermentation Research Institute, the Research Institute for Polymers and Textiles, and the Industrial Products Research Institute. Three new institutes were proposed for establishment by January 1993: the Institute for Materials Science, the Institute for Biotechnology, and the Institute for Industrial Science and Technology.

Along with these reforms, a "Competitive R&D System" was established for industrial technology in 1997. Researchers at national research institutes were asked for research themes, and based on review by outside experts, research funds were allocated to the proposals deemed most effective for research. In 1999, the "industry–academia–government collaborative competitive R&D system" was established in recognition of the need for collaborative research by the three sectors. These represented the search for ways to utilize research resources more effectively.

Meanwhile, the December 1997 "Final Report" by the Hashimoto Cabinet's Administrative Reform Council determined that the 15 laboratories and the five labs under the Science and Technology Agency could become administratively independent. The Agency of Industrial Science and Technology responded immediately and in July 1998 established the "Industrial Technology Research Deliberation Office" to explore ideal approaches to a post-administrative-reform industrial technology system and to the establishment of a system for independent administrative corporations. In 1999, the office was reorganized into the "Industrial Technology Research Organization Development Promotion Office." The promotion office set up seven working groups, including a Basic Principles Working Group to advance these propositions. The Basic Principles Working Group issued its final report in March 2001. The report pointed out seven broad problems with the Institute of Advanced Industrial Science and Technology. The main issues were that: (1) the social role and mission of the institute was not clear, (2) the Institute's selection of appropriate research subjects, setting of goals, and intensive introduction of research resources were inadequate, (3) it did not adequately understand the needs of the citizens and industry that should be the beneficiaries of a national institute, and the cases of research with no vision of an exit was increasing, and (4) the R&D capacity of industry had improved and the role of the research institute as a core for R&D was ambiguous, and so on.

The report suggested various ways of overcoming these issues, based on the following thinking:

> To have a clear division of labor as expressed in our very terminology—*academic*, meaning basic research, *government* (National Institute), meaning applied research, and *industry*, meaning research on practical uses—is inefficient from the point of view of national investment in research. For this reason, we believe that the need will grow greater and greater for [someone] to assume the role of overseeing R&D from the entry point of technology (in former wording, "basic research") to the exit (practical use). The national laboratory, which formerly served as a bridge between academia and industry, is in the optimal position to fill this role.

The National Institute was thus expected to help bring vitality to the national innovation system by acting as a link among academia, industry, and government and keeping an eye on the entire process from basic research to practical application, or entry to exit. In concrete terms, this meant changing the framework of the National Institute. The 15 research labs under the old Institute and the 16 organizations of the Weights and Measures Training Institute together became the National Institute of Advanced Industrial Science and Technology (AIST).

As discussed above, R&D activities had either been conducted by the national government itself at national laboratories or commissioned. Collaborative research in commissioned research was conducted under the Large-scale Research and Development Project system, the Next-Generation Research and Development system, Sunshine, and Moonlight Projects, and financed by subsidies, investment and financing systems, tax credit systems, and other means.

However, these various policy tools had to change after the 1980s. Low interest rates persisted, but their significance declined as companies diversified their sources of financing; meanwhile, subsidy administration declined greatly due to serious technical conflicts. In addition, the methods governing commissioned research also came under review, and the overall restructuring of the industrial technology system, including the New Sunshine Project and others, was forwarded. The catch-up period ended in many sectors as did the era of high-speed growth, and as expressed in the Industrial Structure Council's call for "original and autonomous technological development" in its *Vision of the 1980s*, industrial technology policy as a feature of a developed country came into question.

In such an environment, it was not easy to decide on a set of "national" principles for industrial technology policy. Around 1999, the shift to "basic technology" promoted in the 1980s was recognized to have little chance of succeeding, first, because of the unavoidable inadequacy of basic research in a period of persistent trade friction and second, because the research could not immediately help in creating new products. This led to the question of what direction should be given the national projects, which had been selected through intricate information exchanges with separate industries. In other words, it revealed the difficulty of deriving a "national" point of view by bundling individual projects together.

In fact, the same problems arose even in the later stage when the emphasis had shifted to practical applications. For example, the "Public Application System for Proposals to Create New Industries" aimed to maintain and expand employment in the latter 1990s, but it proved difficult to devise concrete measures for its principles. Conversely, even programs like the Sunshine Project, which were linked with resources and energy policy and therefore had clear strategic importance, proved limited as seen in the gap between the results and the original aims. Precisely because its goals were clear, its results were subject to harsh questions and left an impression of inadequacy. In that sense, just discovering "national" tasks was not necessarily enough.

As the trend in policy continued to shift from basic research to research for practical use, various reforms were sought such as the reorganization of the national institutes, as well as subsidies for joint research and plans for research cooperatives However, the significance of collaborative research itself was not lost just because of changes in the systems of collaborative research. Rather, strategic technologies were decided on through joint research. Most private enterprises were not blessed with resources enough to pursue strategic technologies on their own. Therefore, although reviewing policy measures was important, it was also important to continue to question the role of industrial technology policy in response to the changing international environment and science and technology. Strategies were needed for finding Japanese institutions' comparative advantages for maintaining employment and creatively expanding it, and the ideal nature of the industrial technology policy was therefore a matter of debate.

4.6 New Trends in Pro-Patent Policy

4.6.1 Patent Law Revision

The intellectual property system was subject to mounting demands in the 1990s, and its role expanded as a result. Japan's position as a leading economy was only getting stronger, and if it intended to develop its competitiveness further, it would have to launch state-of-the-art technology and ideas on its own. The importance of intellectual innovation in technology was increasing dramatically, along with the importance of "information" and the advance of "globalization." This recognition was strengthened by the fact that the TRIPS Agreement came into force in 1995 and various domestic reforms thereupon came to an end (Nakayama 2013, p. 26).

The Roundtable to Consider Intellectual Property Rights in the Twenty-First Century was established as a private advisory body to the Commissioner of the Patent Office in December 1996. Its April 1997 report said that innovation in "information" systems and "globalization" were the two forces that would be key in the twenty-first century and pointed out that, in order to overcome the problems that would arise from the development of science and technology in this environment, intellectual property, beginning with technology, needed to be "created," that creation needed to be "protected" as a clear right, and that intellectual property needed to be sufficiently "used." Furthermore, the profits acquired through that use needed to be invested to create new intellectual property, in order to build an "intellectual creation cycle."

The report also noted that although the United States had emphasized "intellectual property rights" since the 1980s, Japan's recognition of the idea remained poor, and that a shift to a "pro-patent" policy, meaning a policy of active support for patents, was needed. Eight recommendations were made to define "a direction for future intellectual property rights": (1) "broad protection" for intellectual property rights, (2) "strong protection," (3) "promotion of the intellectual property rights" of universities and laboratories, (4) the establishment of a "patent market," (5) realization of "electronic patents," (6) promotion of "cooperation with developing countries," (7) establishment of a path to "a common world patent," and (8) national efforts on "intellectual property rights policy."

Based on this report, various reforms were pursued. First, the Patent Law was amended twice in the late 1990s (Nakayama 2013, p. 227) and with the amendments, the Patent Law and Utility Model Law differed greatly in character from the prior laws. This was because their purpose now was not only to ensure the prompt granting of rights and protection, but also to increase the value of the intellectual property right itself. The change reflected Japan's status as a front-runner and the emerging policy issue of how to raise the value of intellectual property rights and thereby promote innovation for the country as a whole. In April 1997, the System Committee's Subcommittee for Damages in the Industrial Property Council began deliberating on these questions and in December issued a report that led to systemic reform (Nakayama 2013, p. 283). The chief revision in the May 1998 amended law involved review of the question of civil remedies. The aim was to address those situations where infringement of patent rights was hard to prove. In the system as designed, a person who took actions that might be infringement but continued business as usual as long as the infringement was not discovered might even upon discovery only have to pay the amount equivalent to the usual royalty fee, although after the fact. Revision of the rule would make it easier to prove a loss of profits and determine an amount equivalent to the implementation costs under the specific circumstances in question, but this would also require a review of criminal penalties.

Thus even where the legal provisions on acts of infringement and on damages were eased, it was not actually easy to collect evidence from the infringing party. The need arose, therefore, for ways to enable plaintiffs to gather proof for legal proceedings. Under the revised law of March 1999, rules were established to make it harder for "infringers" to deny redress by pleading the right to maintain trade secrets. The period for requesting an appeal was also reduced from a maximum of seven years to three years. The aim was to shorten the grace period in which the patent applicant could consider whether to review the right under which the patent application was filed so as to minimize the length of time during which the rights themselves were uncertain. This was intended to pave the way for third parties to utilize the technology in question.

Revisions continued to be made to the Patent Act and Utility Model Law after 2000 as well. The "pro-patent" policy meant reforms to enable a strong, broad, and rapid means of protecting technological inventions and ideas, including a 2002 expansion of provisions for indirect infringement and 2004 rules strengthening criminal penalties for infringement.

4.6.2 Revision of the Design and Trademark Laws

Second was revision of the Design Law. In the late 1990s, "design" came to be regarded as an important element in a product's appeal and competitiveness. However, the existing laws on design had not undergone significant revision since 1984, and not only were they inadequate for addressing the diversification of design development, but skillful imitations had also become a concern as having a deleterious effect on investment in design (Nakayama 2013, p. 311). For this reason, the Design Subcommittee was added to the Industrial Property Council in April 1997. Based on the Subcommittee's report, the revised Patent Law of May 1998 included protection of partial designs. Design development had shifted increasingly to the creation of parts of products. This enabled greater added value and product differentiation. Imitations of partial designs had increased, too, creating a greater need for protection. The requirements were made more stringent to ensure that the products were not something that anyone could easily make. The revisions went further, attempting to improve protection so as to conform to the "pro-patent" policy. A revised law was announced in June 2006 that extended the duration of design rights and expanded protection to include on-screen design, among other measures.

Third was amendment of the Trademark Law (Nakayama 2013, p. 321). With the growing internationalization of economic activity in the 1990s, harmonization and simplification of the trademark system became an important issue. At the Diplomatic Conference for Adoption of the Amended Convention on Trademark Law held in Geneva in 1994, the Trademark Law Treaty (TLT) was adopted with the aim of overcoming these issues, and Japan had to respond accordingly. At the same time, the problem emerged in Japan of a narrowed range of trademark options due to the accumulation of unused trademarks. A revised Law was published in December 1996 taking these issues into account. The following revisions were made to respond to the Treaty on Trademark Law. (1) The introduction of a multi-division application system: Japanese Trademark Law prescribed the principle of a single application specifying the designated goods or services "within the classes of goods and services specified by Cabinet Order," and any number of products or services could be designated so long as they fell within that class. The Trademark Law Treaty, by contrast, required permitting the use of multi-class applications, making revision of Japanese law necessary. This simplified the procedure so that the applicant did not need to prepare a separate application for each classification. Other revisions to the Law involved (2) simplifying the items to be written in the application form, (3) eliminating the substantive examination formerly required upon renewal and of the confirmation of the use of the registered trademark, and (4) simplifying proxy procedures. The revisions of measures to address inactive trademarks included an improvement in the trial system for removing unused trademarks that aimed to strengthen procedures for checking on possession of inactive trademarks from the point of view of the public interest. Other improvements included ensuring the prompt granting of trademark rights, which was made necessary by the shortened life cycle of goods and services; improved protections for "well-known trademarks" (nationally known trademarks with high credibility); introduction of the three-dimensional trademark system; and introduction of the collective trademark system.

The Trademark Law was revised again in 1999. The aim was to promote the creation of a domestic mechanism to align with the Madrid Protocol, which established an international trademark registration system. The Protocol Relating to the Madrid Agreement Concerning the International Registration of Marks ("Madrid Protocol") was the result of a growing call for the international protection of trademarks and, adopted in June 1989, it came into effect in December 1995. Institutional measures were launched in April 1996. In response, preparations were made for the provisions accompanying the Treaty and for legislation on the trademark review period. Additionally, a system of Regional Organization Trademarks was introduced and revisions were made to protect regional branding.

Amendments to the Unfair Competition Prevention Law were also made in the latter 1990s to improve the intellectual property system, and software protection was promoted as well. Regarding protections for software, the Patent Office formulated "Operational Guidelines for Computer/Software Related Inventions" in February 1997, so that "recording Media for recording computer programs" became subject to patent. Furthermore, in December 2000, the "Criteria for Inventions Relating to Computer/Software" were revised, and it was clearly stated that those computer programs that were not recorded on recorded media would also be treated as "invented things." This judgment was given legal clarification by the 2002 revision of the Patent Law. Intellectual property rights pertaining to software were thus improved within the framework of the Patent Law.

In February 2002, Prime Minister Jun'ichiro Koizumi announced that a Strategy Council on Intellectual Property would be established and the necessary policy measures advanced, and in accordance with this policy and the Council's deliberations, an "Outline on Intellectual Property Policy" was formulated, leading to the enactment of the Basic Law on Intellectual Property in March 2003.

Chapter 5
Conclusion: The Emergence of a Twenty-First-Century Policy on the Economy and Industry

1 Establishment of the Ministry on Economy, Trade and Industry (METI)

The government carried out a major reorganization of bureaucratic administration in January 2001, and MITI's name was changed to METI: Ministry of Economy, Trade, and Industry. The reorganization was in effect a reflection of the administrative and financial reforms that accompanied the deregulation of the 1980 and 1990s and that appeared in the Administrative Reform Council's "Final Report" of 1997.

1.1 The Administrative Reform Council's "Final Report"

The December 1997 "Final Report" of the Administrative Reform Council explained the "reasons for the need to undertake administrative reform" in terms of the "principles and aims of administrative reform," which it defined first as: "to reconstruct 'how this country does things' with the aim of forming a freer and fairer society while building on Japan's achievements thus far." Specifically, it pointed out that the advances made by Japan's economy during rapid growth "had created the precious 'asset' of economic prosperity, but had also left a legacy of enormous debt, symbolized by a fiscal debt that had swelled to 400 or even 500 trillion yen; that stage is already retreating into the past." This raised the following issues: "As a result of many years of striving for an industrial society modeled on those of the West, Japan has become enveloped in an array of national regulations, conventions, and practices that have rendered society extremely uniform and rigid"; furthermore, "the steady growth of Japan's economy has come to an end, and people's values have diversified as society has matured; thus, the same systems that in the past stimulated people's will to work hard and invigorated society are today if anything promoting structures

Committee on the History of Japan's Trade and Industry Policy. RIETI,
Dynamics of Japan's Trade and Industrial Policy in the Post Rapid Growth Era (1980–2000),
Economics, Law, and Institutions in Asia Pacific, https://doi.org/10.1007/978-981-15-1987-1_5

of dependence, reinforcing the sense that Japan is a closed society, and impeding the people's creative will and spirit of challenge." In short, what was being sought was "a revision of the postwar administrative system [so as to build] autonomous individuals, and a shift to a 21st-century administrative system appropriate for forming a freer and fairer society."

These critiques of existing conditions led to the establishment of the following goals. "In order to rebuild 'the way things are done in this country,' what we need first and foremost is to reform government organizations, which have become excessively large and rigid, and to realize a streamlined, efficient, and transparent government suitable for effectively carrying out important national functions." The Report thus called for reflection, in line with these goals, as to "whether the bureaucracy was not interfering excessively in various aspects of people's lives." "The policies and regulations designed to protect the people's interest have become increasingly self-referential, with the result that they increasingly defend only the vested interests of certain people, that conflicts and contradictions between different policy objectives are handled internally without transparency, or that resolutions to problems are simply put off." The Report concluded that in order to rectify this situation, the core of administrative reform must now focus on "the rigidity of the policy planning departments that were bound by the interests and constraints of a given project; inefficient implementation [of policy] that neglected the convenience of the user; the unclear and closed policy-making process and the absence of an evaluative or feedback function; and the failure of the overall adjustment function due to an exclusive and inviolable system of jurisdictions in which ministries and agencies are divided vertically and are not permitted to speak out about areas in other administrative jurisdictions." The Report recommended that the following mechanisms and characteristics be the goal of reform to build a "21st-century administrative system appropriate for forming a free and fair society":

> First, ensuring a comprehensive and strategic approach. It is absolutely essential to be able to respond quickly to the moment-by-moment changes that sometimes occur in the internal and external environment and to the varied and sometimes contradictory policy issues that arise, to look at the entire picture of domestic and international politics and society, to make comprehensive and strategic judgments about which values to prioritize given the times and the issues at hand, and to make bold decisions on values and plan policy accordingly.
>
> Second, stressing maneuverability. The decision-making process must be speeded up dramatically, first in order to ensure that urgent and national tasks such as crisis management and security are addressed without omissions and second, to prevent, across all government administration, the folly of straying from the policy decision mechanism.
>
> Third, ensuring transparency. Fairness in policy judgments requires transparency regarding decision-making responsibilities. Also, given that this is an era of rapid change, the demand for infallibility, imposed only on government administration, can lead to breakdowns, delays, and postponements of policy decisions. Do the times not require that we change our assumptions, recognize that government administration might err, and adopt a perspective that allows for and promotes constant policy evaluation and change along with free competition on policy matters among the public and the private sectors?
>
> Fourth, pursuing efficiency and simplicity, goals that are both old and new. Psychological theorizing is insufficient to achieve this aim. We need to create a new administrative system

in which markets and society can constantly monitor the efficiency of administration and in which efficiency is considered among the most essential tasks.

The Report's specific prescriptions included the following: (1) a dramatic expansion of the functions of the Prime Minister's Official Residence and the Cabinet to ensure comprehensive and strategic policy-making, including the planning and proposal of basic policies, and to improve the capacity for comprehensive coordination on important policies; (2) separation of the policy-making and implementation functions and introduction of a reorganized system of mutual recommendations by ministries and agencies divided along functional lines; (3) ensuring transparency, beginning with administration; and (4) improving administrative efficiency—utilizing private-sector capacity through a complete public- and private-sector joint reexamination of projects and through the establishment of a system of independent administrative agencies.

1.2 METI's "Organization Plan"

A major Central Government Reform was thus implemented in January 2001, reorganizing 22 ministries and agencies into one Cabinet Office and 10 ministries (Ministry of Internal Affairs and Communications; Ministry of Justice; Ministry of Foreign Affairs; Ministry of Finance; Ministry of Education, Culture, Sports, Science and Technology; Ministry of Health, Labour and Welfare; Ministry of Agriculture, Forestry and Fisheries; Ministry of Economy, Trade and Industry (METI); Ministry of Land, Infrastructure, Transport and Tourism (MLIT); Ministry of the Environment) and two agencies (National Public Agency; Defense Agency). The Financial Reconstruction Commission and seven agencies were eliminated (Management and Coordination Agency; Hokkaido Development Agency; Economic Planning Agency; Science and Technology Agency; Environment Agency; Okinawa Development Agency; National Land Agency). Under the 1998 Basic Law on Central Government Reform, Article 21 ("Organization Plan") for the newly established METI laid out the following aims:

1. To promote economic structural reform
2. To develop industrial policy based on the following:

    a. To stop pursuing measures to promote specific industries or redistribute income among industries, or to reduce such practices and shift to policies that respect market principles.
    b. To focus on interdisciplinary policies such as the formulation and improvement of rules on economic transactions in the market, protection of industrial property rights, and policy-making across industry lines regarding technology development, and to promote the smooth transformation of the industrial structure.

3. To actively contribute to the formation of a new international economic order through regional or multilateral frameworks on industrial and trade policy, and to develop measures for international coordination regarding industry.
4. To reduce administration designed to protect SMEs or SME organizations, instead strengthening the role of regional bodies and improving the environment to encourage the creation of new industries.
5. To strengthen the role of Japan's regions and to reduce the involvement of the central government in measures to promote regional economies and industries.
6. To develop energy policy based on the following:
   a. a focus on measures for energy conservation and new energy.
   b. a significant elimination or mitigation of regulations designed to make supply-and-demand adjustments among business operators.
   c. a strengthening of policies on crisis management and the links with environmental policy.
   d. a determination of appropriate directions for future nuclear development and use.
7. To set government policy priorities regarding technological development.
8. With regard to the Economic and Fiscal Policy Advisory Council's deliberations on basic policy governing the operation of the economy as a whole, to participate as needed for those deliberations in developing plans from the perspective of industrial policy, structural reform of the economy, and the maintenance and strengthening of private sector vitality.
9. To assume the functions of the former Ministry of International Trade and Industry on information and communications without any change to the division of functions between it and the Ministry of Posts and Telecommunications.
10. The Fair Trade Commission will continue to be responsible for a policy on competition that is centered on antitrust policy, which will not be taken over by the Ministry of Economy, Trade and Industry.
11. Regarding technological development through the Large-Scale Project and other programs, the Ministry of Education, Science and Technology will be responsible chiefly for academic research and scientific research, and METI will be responsible chiefly for commercialization and practical applications.
12. The Ministry of Education, Science and Technology will be responsible for academic and scientific research on the technological development of nuclear power, and METI will be responsible for areas related to energy use.
13. METI will conduct the primary review of regulations to ensure the safety of nuclear power for energy uses, and the Nuclear Safety Commission will carry out the secondary review.
14. Reviews will be conducted of the Ministry's internal organization, such as the sections responsible for promoting specific industries, based on changes in industrial policy.

The major difference between METI and its predecessor, MITI, was found in the fact that "promotion of economic structural reform" headed the list of priorities of the organizational plan. Structural reform of the general economy and of trade and industrial policy was therefore established as a major task of policy. At the same time, in the section on industrial policy that followed, Clause 2, Item (a) called on the Ministry to "stop pursuing measures to promote specific industries or redistribute income among industries, or to reduce the practice, and to shift to policies that respect market principles," which meant, for example, as cited in Clause 4, "reducing administration designed to protect SMEs or SME organizations." In other words, industrial policy to address social gaps or terminal care for declining industries was low on the list of METI policy priorities.

Clauses 1–7 set out the main issues in economic and industrial policy, with 60 items in the Law for the Establishment of the Ministry of Economy, Trade and Industry detailing the extent of administrative authority. Clauses 9 and beyond addressed coordination with other ministries and agencies on policies concerning telecommunications, competition, technology, nuclear energy, nuclear energy safety, and so on, but these did not constitute any major change from previous policies. One of the chief concerns of the reform was for the visions and principles pertaining to the economy and society and for structural reform itself to take the information industry fully into account. Given this, the explicit statement that the jurisdictional divisions in telecommunications were to remain unchanged (meaning METI involvement was to be restricted) undeniably represented a certain lack of vision and suggests that the reform was less than comprehensive.

2 Trade and Industrial Policy at the Turn of the Century

2.1 Policy Development in Anticipation of Organizational Reform

Article 21 Paragraph 14 of the Basic Law on Reform of the Central Government Ministries and Agencies called for " reviews… of the Ministry's internal organization, such as the sections responsible for promoting specific industries." This meant seeking the dissolution of the "window guidance" that was so particular a feature of traditional industrial policy. The 1973 organizational reform had already taken this path to some extent, and industrial policy increasingly cut across specific industries with the vertical, industry-specific form of organization seen as inapt for the purpose. Under these circumstances, as repeatedly pointed out above, "market-intervention industrial policy" became less and less the preferred solution to issues from the 1980s on, as the preference became "an approach to policy that respects and promotes the market mechanism." A typical manifestation of this change was in the relationship with the Japan Fair Trade Commission. Until the high growth period, MITI often conflicted with the FTC over the operation of the Antimonopoly Law; approvals of intra-industry collaboration were regarded as valuable policy measures, and ways were therefore found to establish exemption legislation, administrative guidance, and other measures.

This thinking changed dramatically in the first half of the 1980s, however, to a new emphasis in domestic industrial policy on promoting competition and ceding coordination to the scope of voluntary action by companies. According to the 1978–1983 Industry Stabilization Law (officially the Law on Temporary Measures for Stabilization of Specified Depressed Industries), plants were supposed to be closed and companies merged under publicly authorized rules to address the post-oil crisis issue of structurally depressed industries. The 1983–1988 Structural Improvement Law (Temporary Measures Law for the Structural Adjustment of Specific Industries) that followed, however, took a different approach based on the "Six Yamanaka Principles" presented in its formulation: (1) contraction and revitalization (2) reduced influence on employment and regional economies (3) implementation of comprehensive measures, (4) respect for private-sector autonomy, (5) focus on policies for competition and adherence to open systems, (6) time-limit on policy responses. The new approach stressed due regard for the actual circumstances of the private sector (designating industries based on private-sector applications) rather than regulating imports, and undertaking preliminary negotiation with the FTC but not granting exemptions to application of the Antitrust Law. The last of these represented a major change in the relationship with the Antitrust Law, and policy shifted in the direction of supporting autonomous responses, including corporate mergers, at the company level.

Thus industrial policy came to focus less on industries than on the enterprise system and corporate organization. In the 1990s, direct engagement in advance in corporate mergers and combinations was replaced by "rule-based" policies, meaning the proposal of rules to govern policies on competition (such as reviewing the standards for examining mergers). This was evident in the June 1993 "interim compilation" (based on deliberations of the Industrial Structure Council's Fundamental Issues Subcommittee), which proposed institutional reform (for example, for pure holding companies, greater flexibility in the labor market, and so on) in its review of Japan's economic system.

These changes were moreover reinforced by overseas criticism of Japan's industrial policy, and on the fact that the Japan–US Structural Impediments Initiative (SII) talks in 1989–1990 had attributed the closed nature of Japan's economy to industrial policy. The trade problems that underlay these changes had, beginning in the late 1970s, pointed to Japan's responsibility as an "economic superpower," and Japan's large trade surplus was henceforth perceived as a problem. Japan and the United States had already seen friction over Japanese textile products, but with friction arising over one sector after another, including steel, semiconductors, and automobiles, measures for resolving the bilateral trade imbalance often took the form of voluntary restraints by Japan. At the same time, countries in Europe and America seeking to export to Japan strongly criticized the Japanese market as "closed," and demanded market opening and expansion of the import framework not only for manufactured goods but for primary products as well. Various domestic industry regulations that had been singled out as non-tariff barriers were relaxed and amended to comply with shared international rules. Overseas pressure meant that regulatory reforms were implemented first in those sectors involved with trade. Industry relied heavily on exports and therefore put a priority on preventing trade friction; market opening in the mineral and industrial products sectors therefore can be said to have proceeded quite smoothly compared with that of the primary goods sectors. The expansion of regulatory reform into areas unrelated to trade was in line with industry calls for fiscal rebuilding and demands for "small government."

However, these measures were transient and fundamentally inconsistent, given that voluntary restrictions on exports required policy involvement, on the one hand, while demands were made for minimal policy involvement regarding imports, on the other. Even in trade negotiations, therefore, industrial policy sought to address issues with rules-based approaches—that is, based on rules agreed upon by multiple countries. Regarding unilateral measures taken in the course of bilateral coordination, Japan developed clear arguments to present at the World Trade Organization (WTO) that adhered to the principle of free trade, and took the policy stance, as a principle of trade negotiation, that the scope for government intervention was limited. For example, in the Japan–U.S. Steel negotiations, MITI, in accordance with the December 1991 draft of the international rules for trade negotiations submitted to the GATT Uruguay Round, decided that "the age of voluntary [export] restraints has passed" and refused to extend its VERs on steel exports to the US. Similarly, in the negotiations on automobiles, it rejected the numerical targets requested by the Clinton Administration and finally reached agreement based on its decision to bring the matter to the WTO for a ruling if necessary.

Industrial policy thus shifted to a reliance on the market economy system, and, although later in coming, trade policy, too, began placing a greater emphasis on the market. The fact that this did not remain the ultimate target is touched on briefly at the end of the chapter.

2.2 Changing Policy Targets

The transformation of trade and industry policy not only spread the general idea of relying on market mechanisms, but also changed the nature of traditional policy tasks. An especially great change was seen in the policies on industry location and on SMEs.

Industry location policy, which had sought to correct regional disparities by dispersing factories among different localities, was until the 1980s based on the Comprehensive National Development Plan and similar plans. With industry relocation playing a leading role, the policy aimed to promote regional development through such means as the Law for Accelerating Regional Development Based Upon High-Technology Industrial Complexes (Technopolis Law, 1983), the Law to Promote the Group-Siting of Designated Types of Business Contributing to Higher Grade Local Industrial Structures (Key Facilities Siting Law, 1988), the Multi-Polar Pattern National Land Formation Promotion Law (1988), the Law for Comprehensive

Development of Regional Core Cities with Relocation of Office–Work Function (Regional Cores Law, 1992), the Office Arcadia Plan, and others. Where the main policy objectives of these measures concerned industrial location in the period of high economic growth, the 1980's saw plans to form regional cores by advancing the service sector, premised on the *1980s Vision* of a shift to a more knowledge-intensive industrial structure.

However, these policy approaches were in large part withdrawn in the latter 1990s. As explained above, Article 5 of METI's Organization Plan reduced the role of the national government, delegating more and more to regional localities; in 1998, the Technopolis Law and the Key Facilities Siting Law were abolished and the Law for Facilitating the Creation of New Business was established, with support for new venture start-ups by individual business owners and SMEs in mind. Further, in 2001, METI abolished the New Industrial City Construction Promotion Law and the Law on the Promotion of the Development of Special Regions for industrial Development.

These ideas were clarified in the 1997 New Business Creation Promotion Act that replaced the Law on Temporary Measures for Activation of Specific Regional Industrial Agglomerations; in other words, it was spurred by the shift from the concept of conventional "industrial location" to that of "business creation." The "Law on Establishing Regional Industrial Clusters and Strengthening Them by Promoting Investment and Innovation" (Regional Industrial Revitalization Law), enacted in 2007, represented a distillation of this idea in policy form.

Similarly, the social policy perspective, including that of business and distribution policy, was also reversed with regard to the kind of SMEs referred to in Clause 4 ("reducing administration designed to protect SMEs or SME organizations, strengthening the role of regional bodies, and improving the environment to encourage the creation of new industries)." Regarding the SME sector, where the economic disparity with large companies became a problem in the high growth period, efforts were made to eliminate significant gaps in productivity, corporate income, and wages, and to raise the stability and standard of living of SME owners and their workers, based on the Small and Medium-Sized Enterprise Basic Law of 1963. It was for that purpose that policies to "modernize and upgrade the corporate structure of SMEs" and to "compensate for disadvantages in business activities" were adopted.

However, entering the 1990s, the Large-Scale Retail Stores Law, which was one of the points at issue between Japan and the United States, led to a rethinking of the existing practice of protecting small-scale businesses through restrictions on store openings. Protective measures for SMEs underwent a transformation, as indicated by the Law's relaxation of restrictions on opening stores and the emphasis on promoting local areas through the concentration of commerce. The Large-Store Law was abolished in 2000, a move that was in accord with the Administrative Reform Council's recommendation that the government's "excessive intervention" be ended.

With these changing expectations surrounding SMEs and the SME role, correcting the disparities was no longer the aim of SME policy. Rather, based on hopes for growth potential in the SME sector, the nucleus of policy became to develop an environment in which SMEs would be able to fully exercise that potential. The Basic SME Law revision of 1999 demonstrated this new principle, as expressed in the statement that, “Conducting distinctive business activities in diverse business fields, providing opportunities for diverse employment, and providing opportunities for individuals to demonstrate their abilities and carry out their projects would form the foundation of our economy.” Thus the concepts underlying policy changed, and with the new policy objective of creating “diverse and vibrant SMEs,” the New Business Creation Promotion Law was enacted and the old policy measures were greatly changed.

Even in policy on the textile industry, which had numerous SMEs, the registration system began to shift toward a free-trade structure. MITI, already taking steps to rely on the market economy system and support voluntary activities by companies, abolished the Law on Extraordinary Measures for the Structural Improvement of the Textile Industries (“Textile Industries Law”), replaced it with a revised version, and ultimately abolished that as well in 1999. This constituted the end of industrial adjustment policies targeting the coal and the textile industries, meaning that at the end of the twentieth century, the curtain was falling on measures that had played such a large part in postwar industrial policy.

Industrial technology policies followed a similar trajectory in the withdrawal of central government involvement. Industrial technology policy had leaned increasingly toward basic research since the 1980s, based on the Industrial Science and Technology Agency’s “MITI National Research and Development Program” (“Large-Scale Projects”), and was promoting government-led large-scale projects as measures to secure international competitiveness through the development of original technology. Moreover, promotion of the “Sunshine” and “Moonlight” projects notwithstanding, R&D supported by the central government tended to focus more on basic research. In the late 1990s, however, the creation of new industries assumed greater importance in the face of structural recession, and technological development shifted to projects with more practical applications. The November 1995 Science and Technology Basic Plan, which derived from the Basic Law on Science and Technology (July 1996), called for the strong promotion of R&D in response to social and economic needs, also illustrating the shift to practical research, and greater stress was placed on the role of private research institutions in R&D. Following the Central Government Reform of January 2001, the National Academy of Sciences and Technology was renamed in Japanese and in April that year it changed organizationally as well, becoming the National Institute of Advanced Industrial Science and Technology (AIST).

Industrial policy on the information industry, a main focus of technology development, had originated and developed based on the 1956 Law on Temporary Measures for the Promotion of the Machine Industry (“Machine Industries Law”) and the 1957 Law on Temporary Measures for the Promotion of the Electronics Industry. Around 1990, however, the central issues shifted to the fusion of information management and telecommunications and the development of human resources as the backbone of industry. However, although the new policy issues arising with the information-oriented society often required coordination among ministries and agencies across multiple jurisdictions, the 2001 reorganization of administration did not result in consolidation. As a result, despite growing calls for the creation of an advanced information and telecommunications society, many areas requiring comprehensive policy responses were left to the Cabinet, and the twenty-first century began without the establishment of an apposite strategy.

Meanwhile, the intellectual property system emerged as a key policy issue due to negotiations on intellectual property rights in the GATT Uruguay Round. In order to further harmonize with international systems on the basis of the 1994 Agreement on Trade-Related Aspects of Intellectual Property Rights ("TRIPS Agreement"), a series of revisions were made that led to the enactment of a new Basic Law on Intellectual Property in 2002. This represented a shift to a new framework.

2.3 Policy Areas Focusing on New Issues

While some policy areas saw disengagement, others had new issues to address. The principle example was environmental issues.

Until the period of high growth, MITI had implemented regulations such as green area ratios for industrial plants, based on the Factory Location Law. This reflected the point of view of environmental conservation. Later efforts included emissions regulations to curb air pollution and regulations on the treatment of industrial waste and other issues. Environmental regulations had a considerable effect, and Japan, once described as "a leader in pollution" became "a leader in pollution control."

The movement to reduce greenhouse gas emissions bore fruit with Japan's adoption of the Kyoto Protocol including a six-percent emissions reduction in the 1997 "Third Conference of Parties to the Framework Convention on Climate Change" (Kyoto Conference on the Prevention of Global Warming, COP3). Meanwhile, the Japanese government established a "Basic Law on the Environment" in 1993 and issued a Cabinet Decision on a Basic Environment Plan in 1994. In 1997, the "Environmental Impact Assessment Law" was enacted, and the system for environmental impact assessment, long a concern, was improved and made more consistent. In the process, MITI sought to ensure maximum corporate autonomy on environmental measures, and to ensure that environmental regulation not restrict economic growth. Both these features accordingly became part of policy on the environment. MITI's policy stance recognized that environmental efforts could become a springboard for economic progress and took a flexible approach to incorporating new policy issues.

Respecting corporate autonomy and seeking to develop administrative approaches reliant on the market economy system, MITI created various legal frameworks for recycling waste products and promoted the recycling of packaging containers, scrap automobiles, and used home appliances. This approach shared features with the shift to a voluntary system concerning industrial safety and represented the basic policy response to newly emerging issues.

The core issues of energy policy had to be redefined in relation to such environmental measures. The electricity industry was liberalized and petroleum industry regulations were relaxed: both cases reflected the expectation that greater freedom in corporate activity would launch a virtuous cycle, and this point of view became a basic feature of production. Hopes were high that the basic aim that had long governed energy policy—namely, securing an abundant and low-cost supply of energy—would be served by introducing a competitive order (because competition would "lower costs") and by nuclear power generation (because it promised an "abundant" supply of energy). This was crucial because the increased supply of energy resulting from economic growth could not be made compatible with environmental demands for reduced greenhouse gas emissions without reducing fossil-fuel dependency.

METI's Basic Energy Plan of 2003 was thus based on the Basic Law on Energy Policy. Its three key issues were "ensuring stable supply," "adapting to the environment," and "utilizing the market principle." The Plan stated that METI would "continue to promote [nuclear power generation] as a main power source, premised on ensuring safety," and announced that it "planned to diversify [Japan's] energy sources," including "domestic nuclear energy." In this way, energy policies were accelerated that included the construction of new nuclear power plants, but a major shift in this policy was forced by the accident at the Fukushima Daiichi Nuclear Power Plant in March 2011.

The basic policy of emphasizing harmonization based on multilateral rules governing trade policy also fluctuated in the early twenty-first century over policies related to Asia-Pacific Economic Cooperation (APEC). This, too, represented a significant change. In particular, given that regional trade liberalization does not always proceed smoothly, participating countries' interest in free trade agreements (FTAs) signaled the need for different policy approaches than before. At the start of the twenty-first century, Japanese trade policy had to make the shift from a complete commitment to "multilateralism" to the "joint pursuit of bilateral and multilateral agreements."

3 Conclusion

Konosuke Odaka has pointed out that "from the late 20th to the early 21st century, the policy thinking explored by MITI (later METI) was the question of how to break away from 'industrialism' or the focus on industrial growth" (Odaka 2013, p. 572).[1] However, as Odaka himself cautions, it is not appropriate to narrowly interpret MITI's promotion of leading industries and new industries with growth potential as meaning that industrial "growth" was its "core" concern. The *Visions* of heavy and chemical industrialization and then of forming a knowledge-intensive industrial structure sought to create an affluent society through structural shifts to more advanced industrial structures, that is, industrial sectors with higher value-added productivity. That is why MITI dealt aggressively with the friction arising in declining industries due to structural change, and why it took social policy needs

[1]Odaka points to the following factors as triggering these changes: (1) changes in Japan's macro economy, (2) the economic globalization that began to be observed on a global scale, (3) people's declining expectations of the role of the government, and (4) the elevation of international opinion concerning maintenance and preservation of the environment.

into account in its measures for the SME sector which might well to be left behind by these changes. In that sense the move beyond "industrialism" was developing at the start of the twenty-first century.

Needless to say, however, the issues facing economic society and economic development have changed with the times, and because of the need to address these issues, the focus of policy, viewed in the near term, has also changed with the times and thus become a mirror reflecting the age. More important, however, is that the policy approaches, and the ideals supporting them, have themselves changed with the times, to a premise of reliance on the market economic system, respect for corporate autonomy, and a universally shared way of thinking that transcends national boundaries.

From the late twentieth into the twenty-first century, international economic society has undergone major structural changes due in large part to rapid growth in Asia. What is required of trade and industrial (or economic and industrial) policy is that it "play the role of effectively formulating the ideas governing macroeconomic policy" and that it "maintain constant attention to the intersections of the macro with the micro, harmonizing them through policy, and also play the important role of maintaining a balance between the domestic economy and its relations with overseas economies." Those in policy positions have striven to meet these obligations (Odaka 2013, p. 591). As MITI did before it, METI will continue to bear responsibility for responding flexibly to shifts in policy needs and for developing resolutions that address those needs effectively.

References

Tsūsho Sangyō Seisakushi, dai 2 ki, 1980–2000 (History of Japan's Trade and Industry Policy, The Second Era). Odaka, Konosuke (editor-in-chief). vols.1–12. Tokyo: Keizai Sangyō Chōsakai.

Odaka, Konosuke. 2013. vol. 1, *Souron* (General Overview).
Abe, Takeshi. (ed.). 2013. vol. 2, *Tsusho boueki seisaku* (International Trade Policy).
Okazaki, Tetsuji. (ed.). 2012. vol. 3, *Sangyo seisaku* (Industrial Policy)
Ishihara, Takemasa. (ed.). 2011. vol. 4, *Shoumu ryutsu seisaku* (Commerce and Distribution Policy)
Takeda, Haruhito. 2011. vol. 5, *Ricchi kankyo hoan seisaku* (Location, Environment and Safety Policy)
Yamazaki, Shiro. (ed.). 2011. vol. 6, *Kiso sangyo seisaku* (Basic Industry Policy)
Hasegawa, Shin. (ed.). 2013. vol. 7, *Kikai johou sangyo seisaku* (Machinery and Information Industries)
Matsushima, Shigeru. 2012. vol. 8, *Seikatsu sangyo seisaku* (Consumer Goods Industries)
Sawai, Minoru. 2011. vol. 9, *Sangyo gijutsu* (Industrial Science and Technology Policy)
Kikkawa, Takeo. 2011. vol. 10, *Shigen enerugi* (Natural Resources and Energy Policy)
Nakayama, Nobuhiro. (ed.). 2013. vol.11, *Chiteki zaisan* (Intellectual Property Policy)
Nakata, Tetsuo. (ed.). 2013. vol.12, *Chusho kigyou* (Small- and Medium-Sized Enterprise Policy)

Hashimoto, Juro. 2001. *The growth structure of the postwar japanese economy*. Tokyo: Yuhikaku.
Hosoya, Chihiro, Osamu Ishii, Tadashi Aruga, and Takuya Sasaki (eds.). 1999. *Nichibei Kankei Shiryo-shu 1945-97*. Tokyo: Tokyo Daigaku Shuppankai.
Imuta, Yoshimitsu, Ryoichi Washizawa (ed). 1993. *Tsūshō Sangyō Seisakushi, dai 1 ki* (History of Japan's Trade and Industry Policy, The First Era). vol. 14, Tokyo: Tsūsyō Sangyo Chōsakai.
Imuta, Yoshimitsu, Ryoichi Washizawa (ed). 1994. *Tsūshō Sangyō Seisakushi, dai 1 ki* (History of Japan's Trade and Industry Policy, The First Era). vol. 12, Tokyo: Tsūsyō Sangyo Chōsakai.
Institute for New Generation Computer Technology, ICOT (ed.). 1992. *Fifth generation computer systems. '92, ICOT*. In *Proceedings of the international conference on 5th generation computer systems, 1–5 June, Tokyo, Japan*. Amsterdam: IOS Press.
Japan Oil, Gas and Metals National Corporation. 2006. *Bēsumetaru Kokusai Jijō to Wagakuni Kōbutsu Shigen Seisaku no Hensen* [International Conditions and Changes in Japan's Mineral Resource Policy on Base Metals]. Kawasaki: JOGMEC.
Minami, Ryo. 1993. Tsūshō Sangyō Shō no kankyō taisaku. *Jurist* 1015: 190.
Ministry of Economy, Trade and Industry (METI), Sangyo Gijyutsu Kankyō-kyoku. 2005. *Sangyō Kōzō Shingikai Haikibutsu-syori Recycle Guideline* [Industrial Structure Council Waste Disposal and Recycling Guidelines]. Tokyo: METI, Sangyo Gijyutsu Kankyō-kyoku.

Committee on the History of Japan's Trade and Industry Policy. RIETI,
Dynamics of Japan's Trade and Industrial Policy in the Post Rapid Growth Era (1980–2000),
Economics, Law, and Institutions in Asia Pacific, https://doi.org/10.1007/978-981-15-1987-1

METI, Agency for Natural Resources and Energy (ed.). 2004. *Enerugi Hakusho 2004 nen ban.* Tokyo: Gyosei

Ministry of International Trade and Industry (MITI) Local Environmental Pollution Bureau Industrial Relocation Section (ed.). 1985. *21seiki no Sangyō Ritti Bijyon* [Industrial Location Vision for the 21st Century]. Tokyo: Tsūsan Siryō Cyōsakai.

MITI, Industrial Policy Bureau, Distribution Industry Division (ed.). 1994. *The future of the Large-Scale Retail Store Law—How to consider its revision* [Industrial Structure Council and SME Policy-Making Council Joint Conference Report]. Tokyo: Industrial Research Council Foundation.

MITI, Policy Bureau Commercial Section (ed.). 1994. *The Large-Scale Retail Law Henceforth—The Nature of the Reconsideration of the Revised Law* (Report of the Joint Meeting of the Industrial Structure Council, SME Policy-Making Council). Tokyo: Trade and Industry Survey Group.

MITI. 1997. *Denshi Kōgyō Nenkan.* Tokyo: Denpa Publications Inc.

Nakamura, Takafusa. 1995. *The postwar Japanese economy: its development and structure, 1937–1994.* Tokyo: University of Tokyo Press.

Nakato, Sachio. 2003. *Nichibei Tsusho Masatsu no Seiji Keizai-Gaku* [The Political Economics of Japan-US Trade Friction]. Tokyo: Minerva Shobo.

Nihon Denki Kōgyōkai (ed.). 1998. *Nihon Denki Kōgyōkai 50 nen no Ayumi.* Tokyo: The Japan Electrical Manufactures' Association

Shūgiin Chōsa Kyōku Keizai Sangyō Chōsa-shitsu. 2006. *Kogyo Saihaichi Sokushinho wo Haishi Suru Horitsuan no Yoten Oyobi Mondaiten.* Tokyo: Shūgiin Chōsa Kyōku Keizai Sangyō Chōsa-shitsu

Sumiya, Mikio. 1994. *Tsūshō Sangyō Seisakushi, dai 1 ki* (History of Japan's Trade and Industry Policy, The First Era). vol. 1, *Sōron* (Overview). Tokyo: Tsūsyō Sangyo Chōsakai.

Tarui, Yasuo. 2000. *Chō LSI heno Chōsen: Nichi-Bei Handōtai 50 nen to Tomoni Ayumu* (The VLSI Challenge: 50 Years of Japanese and American semiconductors). Tokyo: Kogyo Chosakai Publishing Co. Ltd.

Yamaguchi, Yoshikazu. 1980. *Genshiryoku Kiki Sangyō no Shinkō.* Tsūsanshō Kōhō (Oct. 17), p. 10.

The manufacturer's authorised representative in the EU is Springer Nature Customer Service Centre GmbH, Europaplatz 3, 69115 Heidelberg, Germany. If you have any concerns regarding our products, please contact ProductSafety@springernature.com

Printed and bound by CPI Group (UK) Ltd, Croydon, CR0 4YY
30/09/2026
02225320-0012